PRINCIPLES OF
ADMINISTRATIVE LAW

PRINCIPLES OF ADMINISTRATIVE LAW

BY

J. A. G. GRIFFITH, LL.M.

Reader in English Law in the University of London
Of the Inner Temple, Barrister-at-Law

AND

H. STREET, LL.M., Ph.D.

Professor of Public Law and Common Law
in the University of Manchester
Solicitor of the Supreme Court

SECOND EDITION

LONDON
SIR ISAAC PITMAN & SONS, LTD.

First published 1952
Second edition 1957
Reprinted 1959

SIR ISAAC PITMAN & SONS, Ltd.
PITMAN HOUSE, PARKER STREET, KINGSWAY, LONDON, W.C.2
THE PITMAN PRESS, BATH
PITMAN HOUSE, BOUVERIE STREET, CARLTON, MELBOURNE
22–25 BECKETT'S BUILDINGS, PRESIDENT STREET, JOHANNESBURG

ASSOCIATED COMPANIES
PITMAN MEDICAL PUBLISHING COMPANY, Ltd.
39 PARKER STREET, LONDON, W.C.2
PITMAN PUBLISHING CORPORATION
2 WEST 45TH STREET, NEW YORK
SIR ISAAC PITMAN & SONS (CANADA), Ltd.
(INCORPORATING THE COMMERCIAL TEXT BOOK COMPANY)
PITMAN HOUSE, 381–383 CHURCH STREET, TORONTO

MADE IN GREAT BRITAIN AT THE PITMAN PRESS, BATH
E9—(L.106)

PREFACE
TO SECOND EDITION

We have revised the text to bring it up to date and have tried to remedy some of the faults of the first edition. But we have been concerned not to alter the character or the size of the book and, despite the many changes of the last five years, this edition is very little longer than the first.

J. A. G. G.

H. S.

April, 1957

PREFACE

THE syllabus of a formal course of legal education can never be static. From time to time new topics win a place in the sun, either because of their intrinsic importance, or because they are suitable vehicles for training in mental discipline or legal methods of thought, or because they are deemed necessary for the presentation of a rounded view of contemporary society. We believe that Administrative Law is now a strong claimant for the status of a compulsory subject in legal education, both in the law degree and in the professional examinations of the Bar and of The Law Society. The fundamental issues of public welfare and individual freedom, the remarkable insights it provides into the nature of the judicial process, the outstanding illustrations of the interaction of legal, social, economic, and political forces which it furnishes, the impact of its subject-matter on everyday life: these have of course already made Administrative Law an established subject in the law schools of the United States and the civil law world of Europe and South America. We feel that the time has come in this country to attempt to draw within the covers of one book an examination and discussion of the problems of law in its relation to administration. We have another motive, less disinterested, for our attempt. We teach the subject at our respective Universities and no book has hitherto covered our syllabuses. This has caused hardship, particularly to external students. It is our hope that this book will present a compact introduction to most of the subject.

We are not, however, writing only for law students. We have tried to emphasise throughout how limited a view of law or politics or public administration is obtained if any one of these social sciences is surveyed to the exclusion of the others. It is not so much that the study of one is incomplete without reference to the others, but rather that the landscape is single and entire. There are not different views to be seen, but only different viewers with variously adjusted blinkers. We are not equipped to produce the larger synthesis. But we hope that our treatment will mean that students and practitioners of all the social sciences, not of law alone, may find something of value and interest in these pages.

No English administrative lawyer can fail to acknowledge his debt to the pioneers of the subject, in particular Sir Cecil Carr, Professor W. A. Robson, and Professor E. C. S. Wade. We have freely drawn on the fruits of their experience and research as presented in their various valuable contributions to many of the topics dealt with in this book. We are greatly indebted to many of our colleagues at the London School of Economics and Political Science and at the University of Manchester respectively, and to other friends on both sides of the Atlantic who have read portions of the manuscript and proofs and have given us invaluable advice. We acknowledge with thanks the permission given by the editors of the *Modern Law Review*, the *Michigan Law Review*, the *Political Quarterly*, and the *Law Journal* to reproduce parts of certain articles. Finally, we thank our wives who now, by enforced reading and listening, know more Administrative Law than they did and like it less.

We accept joint responsibility for the whole of the text. J. A. G. Griffith wrote the first draft of the chapters on the Legislative Powers of the Administration and on Public Corporations; H. Street wrote the first draft of the chapters on the Administrative and Judicial Powers of the Administration, and on Suits against the Administration.

J. A. G. G.

H. S.

September, 1951

CONTENTS

CONTENTS

TABLE OF CASES

TABLE OF STATUTES

TABLE OF STATUTORY RULES AND ORDERS AND STATUTORY INSTRUMENTS

BIBLIOGRAPHY

INTRODUCTORY

Sir Cecil Carr: *Concerning English Administrative Law* (1941).
Lord Campion and others: *British Government since 1918* (1950).
Report of the Committee on Ministers' Powers (1932, Cmd. 4060) and Memoranda and Evidence.

CHAPTERS II and III

Sir Carleton Allen: *Law and Orders* (2nd Edn. 1956).
Lord Campion and others: *Parliament—A Survey* (1952).
Sir Cecil Carr: *Delegated Legislation* (1921).
H. S. Morrison: *Government and Parliament* (1954).
W. M. Graham-Harrison: *Notes on Delegated Legislation* (1932).
Sir Ivor Jennings: *Parliament* (1939).
Sir Ivor Jennings: *Cabinet Government* (2nd Edn. 1951).
J. Willis: *Parliamentary Powers of English Government Departments* (1933).
Sir Cecil Carr: "Parliamentary Control of Delegated Legislation" in 1 *Public Law* (1956) 200.
Statutory Publications Office: "Subordinate Legislation" in 30 *Public Administration* (1952) 227.
Reports from the Select Committee on Statutory Instruments (from 1944).
Reports from the Select Committee on Delegated Legislation and Minutes of Evidence (H.C. 310–1 of 1952–3).

CHAPTERS IV and V

W. A. Robson: *Justice and Administrative Law* (3rd Edn., 1951).
Sir Carleton Allen: *Administrative Jurisdiction* (1956) and in 1 *Public Law* (1956) 13.
Memoranda and Evidence of the Committee on Administrative Tribunals and Enquiries (1956–57).
Inns of Court Conservative and Unionist Society: *Rule of Law* (1955).
C. J. Hamson: *Executive Discretion and Judicial Control* (1954).
R. M. Jackson: *Machinery of Justice*, Ch. VI (2nd Edn. 1953).
R. S. W. Pollard (ed.): *Administrative Tribunals at Work* (1950).
Sir David Keir and F. H. Lawson: *Cases in Constitutional Law* (4th Edn. 1954).
S. A. de Smith: "The Prerogative Writs" in 11 *Cambridge Law Journal* (1951) 40.
S. A. de Smith: "Wrongs and Remedies in Administrative Law" in 15 *Modern Law Review* (1952) 189.
S. A. de Smith: "The Right to a Hearing in English Administrative Law" in 68 *Harvard Law Review* (1955) 569.
S. A. de Smith: "The Abuse of Statutory Powers" in 1 *Public Law* (1956) 233.
H. W. R. Wade: "The Twilight of Natural Justice?" in 67 *Law Quarterly Review* (1951) 103.
H. W. R. Wade: "Quasi-judicial and its Background" in 10 *Cambridge Law Journal* (1949) 216.
D. M. Gordon: "Certiorari and the Revival of Error in Fact" in 42 *Law Quarterly Review* (1926) 521.
D. M. Gordon: "Observance of Law as a Condition of Jurisdiction" in 47 *Law Quarterly Review* (1931) 386, 557.
D. M. Gordon: "Administrative Tribunals and the Courts" in 49 *Law Quarterly Review* (1933) 94.
D. M. Gordon: "The Cab-Driver's Licence Case" in 70 *Law Quarterly Review* (1954) 203.

CHAPTER VI

G. L. Williams: *Crown Proceedings* (1948).

H. Street: *Governmental Liability* (1953).
J. D. B. Mitchell: *The Contracts of Public Authorities* (1954).

CHAPTER VII

D. N. Chester: *The Nationalised Industries—An Analysis of the Statutory Provisions* (2nd Edn. 1951).
H. S. Morrison: *Government and Parliament* (1954).
W. A. Robson (ed.): *Problems of the Nationalised Industries* (1952).
W. Friedmann: "The New Public Corporations and the Law" in 10 *Modern Law Review* (194/) 233, 377.
W. A. Robson: "The Public Corporation in Britain Today" in 63 *Harvard Law Review* (1950) 1321.
J. A. G. Griffith: "Public Corporations as Crown Servants" in 9 *University of Toronto Law Journal* (1952) 169.
Report from the Select Committee on Nationalised Industries (H.C. 235 of 1952–3).
Special Report from the Select Committee on Nationalised Industries (H.C. 120 of 1955–6).

CHAPTER I

INTRODUCTORY

THE keynote of nineteenth-century thought was individualism. Judges and politicians agreed that the maintenance of order both within and outside the country was the only "legitimate function" of government. The causes of individualism were many: it was a reaction from the earlier feudal and Stuart rule; it harmonised with the interests of the new class of manufacturers which emerged as a result of the Industrial Revolution; Locke's emphasis on the sanctity of private rights and property together with the development by Adam Smith of theories of *laissez-faire* gave it a political philosophy; it was consonant with the Puritanical view of life that man should prove his worth in God's eyes by hard work and earthly gain; Darwin's advocacy of the "survival of the fittest" was moulded by Spencer into the argument that no steps should be taken to help the incapable or the foolish to live, for that would multiply those least fitted for existence. The emphasis of the common law was on freedom of property, freedom of contract and freedom of the person; interferences with these freedoms were not to be countenanced.

The very success of *laissez-faire* was its undoing. Concentrations of large sections of the population in overcrowded cities brought problems of housing, disease, and smoke that could not be ignored. The Administration had to intervene in the interests of public safety and health, an interference necessarily inconsistent with an unlimited freedom of property and of the person. The latter portion of the century witnessed a growth in humanitarian ideas under the inspiration of Shaftesbury; if children were not to work long hours and factories were to be safe and sanitary, freedom of contract could not remain inviolate. A new and irresistible urge for social security has been born: freedom from want has become more important than freedom of property; the extension of the franchise to the working classes by the Reform Acts resulted in the formation of Administrations which introduced unemployment, sickness, and old age benefits. Increased business activity has led the State to intervene in the public interest, either, as in the United States, by the establishment of regulatory commissions, or by the British expedient of nationalisation of public utilities and basic industries. Scarcity of currencies and raw materials has compelled the Government to wield economic controls. The need to conserve and make the best use of natural resources, particularly land, has made town and country planning legislation necessary; this type of legislation has also authorised interferences with property owners in the interests of amenity—zoning laws and external advertising regulation are obvious examples.

These changes in the role of the Administration have been accompanied by changes in the methods of government: we are not considering here a Constitution under which Parliament alone has law-making powers, and the courts, like a referee at a boxing contest, merely see that fixed rules are observed; new powers and new methods have accrued to the Administration. What must be examined hereafter is the organisation of the Administration, the nature and extent of its powers, and the methods by which the functions of government are administered.

Administrative law poses that most important problem of our time which Bertrand Russell chose as the title for the first series of the Reith lectures: Authority and the Individual. We are concerned, then, not merely with the powers and processes of the Administration, but with the controls of the Administration, legal and political, without which that essential balance between individual liberty and public good is impossible.

Definition of Administrative Law

At the end of his lectures on the constitutional history of England delivered in 1887–8,[1] Maitland discussed the definitions of constitutional and of administrative law. He examined, first, the views of Austin to whom constitutional law merely determined what person or classes of persons bore the sovereign powers, while administrative law determined the ends and modes to and in which the sovereign powers were exercised.

---

[1] *The Constitutional History of England* (1908 Edn.), 526–39.

Maitland regarded this definition of constitutional law as too narrow, and certainly in the law schools to-day much more is taught under that heading. Indeed, the idea of "sovereignty" is treated as falling more within the scope of a course on jurisprudence than on constitutional law and the "rules" which determine who is sovereign must be found more in the pages of historical works and in works on political theory than in statutes and constitutional conventions. Maitland next turned to some statements by Holland whose views he summarised by saying: "I think we catch his idea if we say that, while constitutional law deals with structure, administrative law deals with function," although Holland included within his definition of constitutional law what Maitland calls "the broader rules which regulate function," such as many of the King's prerogatives and the privileges of Parliament. More recently, Sir Ivor Jennings has written: "Administrative law is the law relating to the Administration. It determines the organisation, powers and duties of administrative authorities."[1] This is the most commonly accepted definition to-day but it does not attempt to distinguish constitutional law, which in its usual meaning has a great deal to say concerning the organisation of administrative authorities. In another sense, also, this is a very wide definition, for the law which determines the powers of these authorities must include, for example, the provisions of Acts relating to public health, housing, town and country planning, the National Coal Board, and the personal health services. Indeed, almost every statute affects to some extent the powers and duties of administrative authorities. The truth is, of course, as all these writers (with the possible exception of Austin) would themselves point out, that any definitions of constitutional or administrative law and any distinctions drawn between them are arbitrary and based on the convenience of the particular writer.

There is, however, rather more to the question of the definition of administrative law than convenience. The study of administrative law in this country has not yet recovered fully from Dicey's denial of its existence. This denial arose in his comparison of English rules with those of the French over a

[1] *The Law and the Constitution* (3rd Edn.), 194.

very limited field, for Dicey dealt with *droit administratif* as though it related solely to the problem of judicial remedies. His misunderstanding of the French system was twofold. In the first place, he misunderstood and feared the idea of special courts which dealt with cases to which the Administration was a party. This misunderstanding has been revealed, the true position in France explained and the fear shown to be groundless. It does not therefore to-day have any appreciable influence. But, in the second place, Dicey, by confining his examination to that part of the *droit administratif* which deals with remedies, gave to the meaning of "administrative law" in England a similarly restricted interpretation. As a result, undue emphasis has been placed on two problems in particular. The first problem is that of subordinate or delegated legislation, by which is meant the statutory practice whereby Parliament empowers the Administration (generally a Minister or the Queen in Council) to make rules and regulations. The second problem is that of administrative adjudication by which is meant the statutory power of the Administration to decide issues arising between individuals and the Administration, or, occasionally, between two parts of the Administration itself. These are important problems, but they do not comprise the whole of the law relating to the Administration. As has been said, this law contains the rules relating to the organisation and powers of the Administration. The focusing of attention on these two problems not only tends to blur the background of organisation and powers but makes a proper appreciation of these problems very difficult. Moreover, this focusing tends to divert attention from other developments which are taking place in that more important background. Organisation and powers, as well as liabilities and duties, must, therefore, be dealt with in part. Yet no single book could cover all the powers of the Administration; and no purpose would be served by repeating the details of organisation which have already been adequately covered by others.

It is with three particular questions that this book is primarily concerned. First, what sort of powers does the Administration exercise? Secondly, what are the limits of those powers? Thirdly, what are the ways in which the Administration is kept within those limits?

This formulation excludes two matters in particular. In the first place, it excludes an examination of the content of those exercised powers. Thus, for example, the ways in which the Administration can make regulations under the Town and Country Planning Act, 1947, are relevant, but not the provisions of those regulations. To this there are, however, two exceptions. The first is that those provisions are examples of the ways in which the powers are exercised. The second is that sometimes regulations lay down procedures which the Administration proposes to follow. Similarly, although the effect of the decision of the National Insurance Commissioner that a wife who had been fifteen years in a mental home was no longer "residing with" her husband is irrelevant, the Commissioner's function cannot be understood unless it is known that this is the type of case with which he has to deal.

The second matter excluded by this formulation is the structure of the Administration. Since, however, the structure must be known for the understanding of the subject and since the meaning attached to "the Administration" must be made clear, a brief account is included in this chapter. Moreover, structure and function are so interwoven that in many cases the latter can only be explained by reference to the former. So, particularly when dealing with administrative tribunals and public corporations, details of the structure are also given.

The meaning attached to administrative law must now be more fully explained.

A. The Law

All the principal sources of law provide rules which relate to the Administration. They include statutes such as the Housing Act, 1936, the Town and Country Planning Act, 1947, the Acquisition of Land (Authorisation Procedure) Act, 1946, the Statutory Orders (Special Procedure) Act, 1945, the Statutory Instruments Act, 1946, the National Health Service Act, 1946, the New Towns Act, 1946, the Electricity Act, 1947, the Crown Proceedings Act, 1947, and very many others. It follows that case law is an important source both in the ways in which the courts have interpreted the statutes and in the exercise by the courts of their type of prerogative power. Since any valid distinction between administrative and constitutional law has already been disclaimed, conventions are a further source. Finally, there is an important group of practices some of which may develop into conventions while others by their nature will remain apart. This is one of the points at which the description of administrative law as the law relating to the Administration breaks down; or, more precisely, where the subject of administrative law moves beyond the borderline of law. Very often the control of administrative authorities and the ways in which these authorities exercise their powers are more a matter of administrative practice than of law. To take one example: many statutes require the setting up of advisory committees who are then given powers which throw corresponding duties on Ministers. These powers and duties are matters of law. But, as a matter of practice and without statutory authority, Government departments establish and consult advisory committees or refer continuously to already existing bodies on the same type of subjects and for the same sort of reasons as those provided for by the statutes. Again, the statutes which set up the National Coal Board and other public corporations empower the Minister concerned to give these corporations directions of a general character on matters which appear to the Minister to affect the national interest.[1] This is a statutory power and the corporations are fixed with a statutory duty to give effect to any such directions. In practice a large amount of the control which Ministers exercise over the corporations is indirect and not contained in formal directions. Non-statutory advisory committees and ministerial influence over public corporations are extra-legal matters. But they are actually bound up with the statutory provisions. To ignore them would be to present an incomplete picture and to fall into the fallacy of forcing a contrast between law and practice at the point where the two meet. Finally, there are the law and custom of Parliament. Parliament has powers (other than those of passing Bills into law) of investigation which it normally exercises by establishing Select Committees. One of these committees,[2] appointed each session, examines many of the subordinate laws made by the Administration, and the existence of this committee has clearly affected the

[1] See below, pp. 279–80.
[2] Select Committee on Statutory Instruments. See below, pp. 92–99.

practice of the Administration. Whether this is a matter of law depends on what definition of law is adopted; it is certain that this is a subject which must be discussed when dealing with subordinate legislation.

The law under discussion, therefore, sometimes embraces practices for which there is no strictly legal sanction. But not all this law can be dealt with; to do so would involve repeating much that has already been fully covered by books on constitutional law. Thus the established conventions of the constitution are not separately discussed; nor are the detailed rules relating to Parliament; nor public finance; nor the machinery of justice; nor, directly, the liberties of the subject; nor the armed forces; nor the Empire and Commonwealth; nor the Church. There are two other groups of legal rules which have been excluded. The first is local government law. While references to the powers and duties of local government authorities will be made, the law relating generally to the structure and liability of these authorities has been admirably dealt with elsewhere.[1] The second is town and country planning law. Here again powers and procedures will be discussed but any detailed examination of the provisions of the Town and Country Planning Act, 1947, is beyond the purposes of this book.

B. The Administration

There are three phrases which are commonly used to indicate groups of bodies with administrative powers: the Government, the Executive, and the Administration. "The Government" sometimes means the Cabinet but is often extended to mean those central departments the heads of which are directly appointed by the Prime Minister and are Ministers. More loosely the phrase is used to describe any body which has governmental power, including local authorities and other public corporations. "The Executive" covers the same ground of meaning and is often used to include all governmental authorities which put the law into effect. It normally appears in contrast to the Legislature and the Judiciary. "The Administration" sometimes serves as a modern

---

[1] For example, W. O. Hart: *Introduction to the Law of Local Government and Administration* (5th Edn.).

synonym for the Executive, and since this is the phrase in the definition under discussion its present meaning must be more fully explained.[1]

The Administration is composed of numerous bodies some of which have evolved historically while others have been established by statutes. There are three main groups.

I. THE CABINET AND THE GOVERNMENT DEPARTMENTS

The Cabinet and some of the departments are historical developments, although many of their powers have been conferred by statute. Other departments have been created by statute.

(a) The Central Organisation

The number of Ministers in the Cabinet and the number of departments in Her Majesty's Government vary. The Government formed by Mr. Macmillan in January, 1957, resulted in a Cabinet of eighteen members, Of these, the Prime Minister, the Lord President of the Council, the Chancellor of the Duchy of Lancaster, and the Lord Chancellor had no major departmental responsibilities. The remaining fourteen members were the Chancellor of the Exchequer; the Secretaries of State for Foreign Affairs; the Home Department (who was also Lord Privy Seal); the Colonies; Commonwealth Relations; and Scotland; the Ministers of Housing and Local Government[2]; Defence; Labour and National Service; Agriculture, Fisheries and Food; Education; Power[3]; and Transport and Civil Aviation; and the President of the Board of Trade. In addition, there were nineteen Ministers not in the Cabinet.

(b) Regional Organisation

During the 1939–45 war the country was for certain administrative purposes divided into a number of regions.

---

[1] For a fuller examination, see W. I. Jennings: *Cabinet Government*, Ch. IV.

[2] The Minister of Town and Country Planning was renamed Local Government and Planning with effect from 30th January, 1951, and took over many functions previously exercised by the Minister of Health (see S.I. 1951 Nos. 142, 753). The Minister of Health ceased to be a Cabinet member as a consequence of these changes. From 3rd November, 1951, the Minister of Local Government and Planning became known as the Minister of Housing and Local Government (S.I. 1951 No. 1900); in the Cabinet of January, 1957, he was also Minister for Welsh Affairs.

[3] The title of the Minister of Fuel and Power was changed to that of the Minister of Power in January, 1957 (see S.I. 1957 No. 48).

This system, in a form modified for peacetime purposes, has been continued.

At the apex of this system is a standing inter-departmental committee of officials, known as the Regional Organisation Committee, which is responsible under Ministers for keeping the regional organisation as a whole under review, dealing with any questions of general principle on organisation and machinery which may arise, keeping an oversight of the system of inter-departmental committees at regional level and for dealing with any questions affecting regional boundaries or capital towns. The Committee, which is under Treasury chairmanship, includes representatives of the Departments which have regional organisations (e.g. the Ministries of Labour and National Service, Power, Health, Supply, Agriculture, Fisheries and Food, Transport and Civil Aviation, Works, National Insurance and Pensions, Housing and Local Government, the Admiralty, and the Board of Trade).

The degree of devolution is decided by each department and obviously depends primarily on the nature of the functions performed by the department. Moreover the devolution is not to any single group in one region but to the department's own staff in that region. Co-ordination between departments at the regional level is subsequent. With the exception of the Post Office (which has eight regions) devolution is to the regional offices of the department. There are eleven regions covering England, Scotland and Wales, each with its own capital town. These towns are Newcastle-upon-Tyne, Leeds, Nottingham, Cambridge, London, Reading, Bristol, Cardiff, Birmingham, Manchester, and Edinburgh.

The co-ordination between departments at the regional level is achieved in part by ordinary informal contact and in part by the establishment of regional inter-departmental committees of which the most important are the Distribution of Industry Panel, the Physical Planning Committee, and the Building Committee. Representatives of those departments directly concerned with the work of a particular committee form its membership while other departments may receive its papers. In general these committees have parent committees at the centre of the Government machine in Whitehall, from which they obtain general guidance.

In addition there are the Regional Boards for Industry. They sit under an independent chairman and are composed of representatives from both sides of industry with certain departmental officers. Their terms of reference are very wide and include the duties of advising departments, of keeping in touch with the work of departments in the regions, of acting as a link between departments and local industry, and of dealing with questions affecting production which are referred to them. To co-ordinate the supply of information from the centre of the Government machine to the Boards and to conduct any necessary inter-departmental consultation between the headquarters of departments, there is a "parent" committee similar to those referred to above, which operates under Treasury chairmanship.[1]

2. LOCAL GOVERNMENT AUTHORITIES

These are composed of 62 county councils and 83 county boroughs; 563 urban district councils, 476 rural district councils, 318 non-county boroughs and 28 Metropolitan borough councils; and approximately 11,100 parish bodies. In addition, there is the corporation of the City of London. The county and non-county boroughs are bodies created by charter while the City of London is a corporation by prescription; they derive most of their powers from statutes. The remainder were created by statute and derive all of their powers from statutes. Local government authorities are elected bodies.

3. OTHER STATUTORY BODIES

A very large number of bodies has been created by statute to perform specific functions. They can be divided into two groups. The first group is composed of bodies established to run particular undertakings. These include commercial undertakings like the Mersey docks, the Port of London, the suppliers of coal, gas, electricity, and transport. The group

[1] For detailed examination of the whole structure see Regional Organisation of Government Departments (H.C. 233 of 1953–4) being the Sixth Report from the Select Committee on Estimates (Session 1953–4). And see the Report of the Committee (Chairman: Sir Arton Wilson) appointed to review the provincial and local organisation and procedures of the Ministry of Agriculture, Fisheries and Food (Cmd. 9732 and 557 H.C. Deb. 5s. cols. *183–5*).

also includes bodies established to provide social services like hospitals, and to build new towns. The second group is composed of tribunals established to decide issues between individuals or between individuals and the Administration.

These statutory bodies are normally appointed by a Minister but some of the older authorities are locally elected in part.

4. THE INTERRELATION OF ADMINISTRATIVE BODIES

Each body in these three groups of administrative authoritie· is invested with powers to enable it to perform its functions These functions are many and some idea of their nature and the way they are divided can be gathered from the names which are borne by Government departments, the committees of local authorities and the statutory boards, authorities, commissions, and tribunals. The departments in the Cabinet in 1957 have been enumerated. The functions of other departments include the armed forces, pensions and national insurance, supply, health, works and the Post Office. The functions vested directly by statute in local authorities include those relating to public health, housing, town and country planning, highways, the police, national assistance, and education. The most important functions performed by the other statutory bodies have been mentioned. The interrelation of these three groups must now be considered.

(a) Government Departments and Local Authorities

(i) *General Policy Control.* Most of the functions of local authorities are subject to some general control by Government departments. The amount of discretion actually enjoyed by local authorities varies considerably according to the function and the type of authority. Thus the duty of the Minister of Education as laid down in the Education Act, 1944,[1] is "to promote the education of the people of England and Wales and the progressive development of institutions devoted to that purpose, and to secure the effective execution by local authorities, under his control and direction, of the national policy for providing a varied and comprehensive educational service in

[1] Sect. 1 (1).

every area." The provision of education and the establishment and maintenance of schools are primarily the responsibility of county and county borough councils.[1] But the Minister prescribes the standards to which school premises are to conform; the general plan of the councils, which shows how they intend to carry out their statutory duties, is subject to the approval of the Minister.[2] Moreover the Minister has inspectors to examine the working of the schools. Finally, if the Minister is satisfied that an authority is failing in its statutory duties, he may give directions to enforce performance.[3] Similarly, the building and allocation of council houses are functions of urban and rural district councils, and borough councils; but the number of houses to be built in any period and the standards of building are controlled by the Ministry of Housing and Local Government. The financial dependence of local authorities makes departmental control a reality.

(ii) *Advisory*. Government departments—in particular the Ministry of Housing and Local Government—act in a general advisory capacity to local authorities. Much of this advice is issued in the form of circulars. Thus, shortly after the passing of any Act conferring new powers on local authorities or amending powers formerly enjoyed, a circular is sent to each authority concerned explaining the purpose of the enactment and the way it will affect the functions of that authority. This procedure is also followed where the Minister varies the exercise of any discretion vested in him.

Advice does not travel exclusively from the top downwards. Government departments rely on local authorities for the supply of a considerable amount of information, without which the departments would be handicapped in planning their future action.

(iii) *Delegation*. A power may be vested in a Minister with the provision that he may delegate the exercise of the power. The delegation is often made to local authorities. One example was the requisitioning of unoccupied private houses. Departmental functions in relation to trunk roads is another.

Whether the contact between a Government department and a local authority is normally made at the national or at the regional level depends on the subject-matter and the importance

---

[1] Sects. 6, 8, 9.   [2] Sects. 10, 11.   [3] Sect. 99; see also Sect. 68.

of the particular question. But local authorities are loath to give up their practice of approaching the Ministry in London.

(b) Government Departments and other Statutory Bodies

(i) *General Policy Control.* As already mentioned, Ministers have statutory power to issue general directions to many of these bodies. This is true in particular of the corporations set up since 1945. It does not apply, however, to those administrative tribunals which, within their jurisdiction, enjoy a considerable degree of independence both of Government departments and of the courts.

(ii) *Advisory.* Ministers give "informal" advice to the new corporations mentioned above. The line between an advisory opinion and an instruction is not always easy to draw even though the distinction between a statutory "direction" and any other communication is formally made. It has been objected that much of the influence of the Minister over these corporations has been exerted by the less formal, but not less effective, method of giving advice.

Like local authorities the corporations give a considerable amount of information to the Minister both informally and through official reports and returns.

(c) Local Authorities and the Statutory Bodies

There is little direct connection between these two groups. The functions of the statutory bodies were often, in the case of certain public utilities, previously performed by the local authorities. The functions do not overlap to the extent of making co-ordination necessary, however desirable it may be.

5. THE MEANING OF ADMINISTRATION

It will have been noticed that this definition of "the Administration" is a catalogue of bodies. It has not attempted to lay down some general rule by which an administrative authority can be recognised. This is because no such general rule can be discovered. Thus it is confusing and inaccurate to define an administrative authority as one which administers. The verb "to administer" means to put the law into effect. This function is indeed one which the Administration performs. But it does far more, for it also lays down rules which have the force of law and it decides disputes. The power to lay down rules, the power to decide disputes and the power to take administrative action are, in fact, widely distributed. Certain rules of law are contained in Acts of Parliament; others are promulgated by Government departments with little or no reference to Parliament, although the authority to make these rules is normally to be found in statutes; others are promulgated by the courts; others by administrative tribunals. Certain decisions which resolve disputes are made by the courts; others by Government departments; others by administrative tribunals. Most administrative action is taken by Government departments, local government authorities and public corporations. The courts have certain administrative functions; so, occasionally, have administrative tribunals.[1] Moreover, it is not possible to say that rules or decisions relating to any particular subject-matter or topic are made by one or other of the bodies named. Where any particular power lies is sometimes the result of historical development (as, for example, is the jurisdiction of the courts) and sometimes the result of statutory provision (as, for example, is the jurisdiction of administrative tribunals). No criteria have been followed and so all that can be said is that this power resides with this authority and that power with that authority.

There is a further and greater difficulty. So far it has been assumed that there is a clear distinction in kind between the power to make rules, the power to decide disputes and the power to take administrative action. But the distinction between legislative, judicial and administrative action is often difficult to draw. Obvious examples are furnished by the decisions in such cases as *Donoghue* v. *Stevenson*[2] and *Rylands* v. *Fletcher*.[3] These decisions decided disputes and can therefore be called judicial; they also established rules of law and can be called legislative. A statute may empower a Minister to requisition houses and to delegate this function to some other authority. When he delegates he may impose certain conditions (for example, that possession may not be taken of a house before the furniture is removed). Is the laying down of

[1] E.g. Agricultural Land Tribunals under Agriculture Act, 1947, Sect. 74.
[2] [1932] A.C. 562.
[3] (1868), L.R. 3 H.L. 330.

these instructions a legislative act?[1] Legislation is sometimes distinguished from administration on the ground that there is an element of *generality* about rules; they apply at least to a group of persons, whereas administration is particular in its application. But this does not result in a clear distinction, since it is not always possible to separate what is general from what is particular or specific.[2] So the judicial function merges into the legislative and the legislative into the administrative.

Yet another difficulty concerns the use of the word "judicial." The courts themselves have interpreted its meaning differently in different contexts. Thus the licensing function is sometimes regarded as judicial, and sometimes not. Finally, one single administrative process frequently involves the holding of inquiries, the making of decisions, the laying down of principles and the taking of action. The true division of the powers of the Administration into legislative, administrative and judicial is impossible for these categories are imprecise. They can, however, be broadly used as headings under which the powers may be discussed.

The Separation of Powers

This wide distribution of the powers to make rules and to decide disputes and the imprecision which attaches to the use of the words "legislative," "administrative" and "judicial" make unreal any argument which asserts that the Constitution is built on the separation of these powers in different hands. There are, it is true, three groups of authorities in this country which are called Parliament, the Executive and the Judiciary. There are other authorities which do not fall easily under one or other of these groups. The National Coal Board and the Transport Tribunal are examples. Sir Carleton Allen has suggested that the doctrine of the separation of powers as expressed by Montesquieu has been widely misunderstood. He writes that Montesquieu's first precept is "the very simple principle that the *monopoly* of power in a State, whatever its form of government, is the end of all freedom."[3] This would indeed seem to be the reverse of the usual meaning of the separation of powers; it suggests that freedom is preserved if the sum of power is

[1] See *Blackpool Corporation* v. *Locker*, [1948] 1 K.B. 349.
[2] See below, pp. 50–51.   [3] *Law and Orders*, (2nd Edn.) 9.

widely distributed and that it is more important that there should be many authorities all exercising legislative, administrative and judicial powers than that each of these three types of power should be exercised by a different authority. This standing of Montesquieu on his head does in fact indicate at least one of the ways by which political liberty is preserved in this country. Parliament has powers, the Executive has powers, the Judiciary has powers; so have administrative tribunals, public corporations and many other statutory and non-statutory bodies. It is this wide distribution of the sum of power and not the kind of power distributed which is important. This is only part of the answer. Another part is the inter-relation of these authorities. They are to a large extent dependent upon one another. Thus Ministers are politically responsible to Parliament and legally responsible to the courts. One of the functions of an Agricultural Land Tribunal is to decide whether a Minister should or should not take certain administrative action which he has proposed and the Minister must act in accordance with the decision of the Tribunal.[1] Public corporations which run nationalised industries must obey general directions given to them by the Minister who is responsible to Parliament for those directions. The courts have power to control the way in which administrative tribunals and Ministers perform judicial functions. Thus the real argument is not whether the Executive, for example, is exercising legislative or judicial powers which properly belong to Parliament or the courts (for no kind of power *belongs* to any particular authority) but whether the power is being exercised by the authority best suited to exercise it and whether the exercise is sufficiently controlled by political and legal action.

The danger to-day is not that the doctrine of the separation of powers (as popularly understood) continues to be accepted, but that it is used as a principle by which the Constitution can be explained as a series of exceptions. The Report of the Committee on Ministers' Powers states that the doctrine as advanced by Montesquieu is "a very incomplete and to some extent a misleading account" of the mechanism of the Constitution.[2] This attitude continues to prevail and is itself

[1] Agriculture Act, 1947, Sect. 74.
[2] Cmd. 4060 (1932), 8.

incomplete and misleading. The doctrine is so remote from the facts that it is better disregarded altogether.

The Limitations on the Powers of the Administration

These limitations are political and legal. The political limitation results from the doctrine of the responsibility of Ministers, the publicising of the actions of the Administration and the opportunities for criticism both inside and outside Parliament. The legal limitation results from the principle that every action of the Administration which interferes with the rights of individuals must be based on the authority either of a statute or of a prerogative. In assessing the extent to which the Administration is controlled, these two kinds of limitation must both be regarded. Frequently no appeal lies from the decision of an administrative tribunal to a Minister;[1] if he attempted to upset that decision, the courts could declare his act invalid. Another statute may provide that the decision of an administrative tribunal is advisory only, so far as the Minister is concerned. If he fails to take executive action in accordance with the decision, he may have to face considerable Parliamentary criticism.[2] Again, a Minister may make a regulation. If he had no statutory or prerogative power to do so, the courts will refuse to recognise the regulation as law; if he had the power, he may find that a Select Committee has drawn the attention of the House of Commons to that regulation on the ground that it was an "unusual or unexpected" use of the power conferred.[3] The civil servant is as anxious to avoid a Parliamentary Question as he is to avoid authorising an act which has no legal validity. The fact that the legal and political limitations are complementary does not mean that they are not to be distinguished. The traditional view of the courts has been recently restated thus—

> It is the function of a court of law to ascertain the facts and to apply to those facts as ascertained the established principles of law. I do not mean law in a narrow sense. I include also rules of equity and those rules of public policy which have become part

[1] E.g. the dismissal of a charge against a medical practitioner brought before the Tribunal under the National Health Service Act, 1946, Sect. 42.

[2] For an example on the report of an inquiry into an air accident, see 165 H.L. Deb. 5s. cols. 1125–99; 470 H.C. Deb. 5s. cols. 2099–180.

[3] Terms of reference of Select Committee on Statutory Instruments. See below, pp. 92–99.

of the substantive law. The function of Parliament is wholly different. It is to consider public interest, and on that basis to give statutory powers to individuals or authorities.[1]

There are difficulties in this formulation. The judicial function is perhaps less automatic and more creative than is here suggested. It is, for example, the courts themselves that decide how far public policy can be considered and what that policy is. Even if the limitations are difficult to separate in substance, they undoubtedly differ both in the form which seeks to ensure that they are not exceeded, and in the kind of sanction which follows if they are. A foolish but legal use of power may result in the resignation of a Minister or even of a Government. A wise but illegal use of power may result in the exercise being quashed and the award of heavy damages. This is clear enough, but the issue has been confused by the discussion which centres on the Rule of Law. The various meanings which have been given to this phrase must be examined, and an attempt made to assess its legal or political significance.

The Rule of Law

In the first place, to say that the Rule of Law operates may be simply a description of the state of a society. It means that Law rules. But this is also ambiguous for it contains two different propositions. Political philosophers used to be fond of propounding the theory of the earlier existence of a "state of nature" in which there was no organised society. The theory was used to explain the purposes of law and the reasons for its emergence but it was, even in their eyes, largely a hypothetical state. It was a state of chaos and of anarchy, in which there was no law. The individuals in this predicament then joined to establish a Rule of Law which organised their society. The other proposition assumes that there is an organised society but contrasts a society ruled by principles of law with a society ruled by the unpredictable and capricious dictates of one man or one group of men. This state of society is almost as hypothetical as the state of nature. No individual or group can govern a society without laying down certain general

[1] *Bilston Corporation* v. *Wolverhampton Corporation*, [1942] Ch. 391, at 393 (*per* Simonds, J.).

principles. These principles within that society would be binding on its members; in this sense there would therefore be a Rule of Law. If it be argued that the power of the ruler to change these principles at will excludes the notion of a Rule of Law, there are two answers. The first is that the way in which the separate rules of law can be changed does not affect the existence at any time of the Rule of Law. The second is that to say the idea of the Rule of Law is excluded in these circumstances is to attach a different meaning to the Rule of Law and to give to that Law a certainty and fixity which it does not necessarily possess. This different meaning must now be examined in its turn.

In the second place, then, the Rule of Law may mean that the society should be governed by established principles so that the actions of the Administration are foreseeable. Just as it is impossible for an all-powerful ruler to govern without laying down certain general principles, so it is impossible for a society to be ruled by general principles alone. There must remain with the Administration at least some degree of discretion, although the nature and limits of this discretion may themselves be laid down. The Rule of Law in this sense does not explain what is but argues what ought to be. Everything then turns on the amount of discretion which should be granted to the Administration. The fundamental conflict concerning the purposes of government itself at once emerges. While government concerns itself primarily with the maintenance of order within the society and the protection of the society from external aggression, general principles are sufficient to cover most of its functions. But as soon as government concerns itself with the detailed ordering of the individuals in the society, with the supply of services, with the control of industry, and with the particular circumstances of children, of the aged, of the sick and of the unemployed, then a large amount of discretionary power becomes necessary. Thus the Rule of Law, in this sense, tends to limit the scope of the action of the Administration. The first meaning which Dicey attached to the Rule of Law must be considered in this context. The Rule of Law means, he said, "the absolute supremacy or predominance of regular law as opposed to the influence of arbitrary power, and excludes the existence of arbitrariness, of prerogative, or even of wide discretionary authority on the part of the government."[1] Thus far the statement seems to have nothing to do with the arbitrary and discretionary powers which the Administration might actually enjoy under prerogative or statutory authority, but merely indicates that Dicey thought the existence of these powers to be undesirable and contrary to the meaning he gave to the Rule of Law. The next sentence, however, apparently contradicts this interpretation, for he wrote: "Englishmen are ruled by the law, and by the law alone; a man with us may be punished for a breach of law, but he can be punished for nothing else."[2] This indicates that Dicey believed that the Rule of Law in this sense actually operated in the England of his time. To-day the whole seems a confusion of a statement of what Dicey thought desirable and what he thought existed. It is still true that a man cannot be punished save where he has broken the law but if the exercise of discretionary power is authorised by law, it is immaterial, in law, how wide is that discretion. If these discretionary powers are interfered with or are impeded, this may result in a breach of the law. As Sir Ivor Jennings says, Dicey was concerned with the rights of individuals, not with the powers of the Administration.[3] He had, in short, failed to appreciate the significance of the change which the functions of government were undergoing in the second half of the nineteenth and the beginning of the twentieth centuries.

The third sense in which the Rule of Law is used is very similar to the second. The authors of a modern book on constitutional law write: "If it is contrary to the rule of law that discretionary authority should be given to government departments or public officers, then the rule of law is inapplicable to any modern constitution."[4] So far agreement is possible, but they go on to say that the rule of law "demands" the payment of compensation in certain circumstances where an individual suffers damage as the result of a change in the law or the exercise of a discretionary authority granted in the general interest.[5] Here the Rule of Law seems to be a moral

[1] *The Law of the Constitution* (9th Edn.), 202.
[2] Op. cit. 202. The whole passage is discussed and criticised by Sir Ivor Jennings in *The Law and the Constitution* (3rd Edn.), 53–61, and Appendix II.
[3] *The Law and the Constitution*, 54–55.
[4] E. C. S. Wade and G. G. Phillips: *Constitutional Law* (5th Edn.), 54.
[5] Ibid., 55.

concept, perhaps synonymous with "justice." The reason why compensation is in fact provided for is either because it is felt to be just or because it is politically expedient or, happily, both. "Discretionary power," conclude these authors, "does not mean arbitrary power."[1] That depends upon the amount of discretion. Its limits may be so wide that almost anything may be ordered; this comes close to arbitrariness.

None of these three meanings of the Rule of Law is a legal concept. The first is only descriptive and in the latter two a breach of the Rule of Law does not, on that account, involve a breach of a common or statutory law. Dicey endeavoured to show that Parliament is subject to the Rule of Law but neither he nor any other writer in modern times asserts that a statute or a principle of the common law is without legal force if it conflicts with the Rule of Law. The second meaning which Dicey gave to the phrase was "equality before the law or the equal subjection of all classes to the ordinary law of the land administered by the ordinary law courts."[2] Sir Ivor Jennings,[3] Dr. Robson[4] and others have criticised this statement. Here it is important to note that Dicey did not attempt to deny the legality of any inequality there might be in fact. He was pointing out one of the aspects of the Constitution which seemed to him a virtue. As in his first meaning, the Rule of Law seems to be at once a deduction and an *a priori* postulate.

There are two other meanings sometimes attached to the phrase. They are both accepted principles of the Constitution. The first is that all the powers of the Administration are derived from statutes or from the prerogative and that individual rights cannot be infringed without the authority of one or other of these sources of power. The Administration cannot do what it pleases; it can only do that which it has power to do. In this sense its power is not arbitrary. The second meaning is a corollary: that the Law binds the Administration. The Cabinet may, through its Parliamentary majority, give itself legal powers or remove restrictions which formerly bound it. But until the Administration changes the law, it is bound by the law. When it has changed the law, it is bound by the new law.

---

[1] Ibid.   [2] Op. cit. 202.   [3] Op. cit., Appendix II.
[4] *Justice and Administrative Law* (3rd Edn.), *passim*.

Five meanings of the Rule of Law have been suggested. There may be others, for the phrase is frequently used to support political contentions. It has a valuable emotive content so long as its use is not too closely examined. Of the five meanings only the last two have legal significance. This is not to say that the others are without influence; but their influence lies in the realm of politics. They are concerned with what is desirable and what is wise. The courts will not refuse to enforce a statute because it grants wide discretionary or even arbitrary power; or because it dispossesses a subject without compensation. But such provisions may meet with considerable opposition elsewhere; they may be attacked, not as illegal but as ill-advised. They may be condemned not as contrary to the law of the Constitution but as contrary to its spirit. They may be defended as sound reformatory measures or as showing the flexibility of the Constitution. The Rule of Law becomes a banner under which opposing armies march to combat.

Administration According to Law

In the chapters which follow the legislative, administrative and judicial powers of the Administration are considered. The legal extent of those powers is examined by the courts. They have to decide whether the alleged power does protect the Administration from contractual or tortious liability, whether the laws made by the Administration are validly made and whether the Administration in deciding a dispute is acting within its jurisdiction and in accordance with the proper procedure. In theory this should not be a difficult task. All the courts have to do is to look at the power and see if it covers the actions taken by the Administration. But the practical application of this theory is not easy. There are several reasons.

First, the power itself may be indefinite. There may be dispute whether it exists at all and, if so, what are its limits. This difficulty is particularly apparent when the power is derived from the prerogative. Secondly, the power may be imprecisely laid down in a statute. This may be due to bad draftsmanship or because the particular circumstance was not foreseen and a hidden ambiguity unnoticed. Thirdly, the power may be given in words which make the examination by the courts difficult or impossible. Often it is provided that action may be taken by a Minister if he is "satisfied" that it is "requisite," "necessary" or "expedient."[1] The limitation on the exercise of the power thus depends on the Minister's state of mind and although the courts have not always been reluctant to make inferences which determine whether or not a certain state of mind exists or could exist, they have in these cases refused to go behind the expression of the Minister's satisfaction. The attitude of the courts to the kind of provision which seems to give very wide powers is not easily predictable and they have frequently claimed the right to review conditions attached to a decision even where the power of the Administration is to make such conditions "as they think fit."[2] Fourthly, an authority may be mandatory or permissive. Statutes frequently provide that a Minister or a local government body "shall" perform some function; even more frequently the word is "may." Normally the Administration is protected from liability if it commits a tort when doing an action which it is commanded to do but is not protected if mere permission is granted unless there is no way, save one which is tortious, of doing the act.

These are all difficulties of interpretation. The courts examine the power to see if the Administration is legally justified in acting or in failing to act. But the courts go farther than this and sometimes require the action of the Administration to be a reasonable exercise of the power, or to be done in good faith or in accordance with certain principles of justice. Sometimes the courts seem to regard their power to examine the action of the Administration, on these grounds, as inherent. At other times, they prefer to regard it as a matter of interpretation, arguing that since no statute would authorise actions which were unreasonable or in bad faith or procedures which were unjust, therefore there is to be implied in the statute an injunction against such actions or procedures. The effect in both cases is the same.

Responsible Administration

The Administration is responsible and accountable for its

[1] See *Robinson* v. *Minister of Town and Country Planning*, [1947] K.B. 702; *In re an Application by Beck and Pollitzer*, [1948] 2 K.B. 339.
[2] Cf. *Roberts* v. *Hopwood and Others*, [1925] A.C. 578, and *Associated Provincial Picture Houses, Ltd.* v. *Wednesbury Corporation*, [1948] K.B. 223.

actions. Finally, its responsibility is to the people. In theory, and practice, its responsibility is to Parliament. But the Administration must listen to voices other than those of elected representatives or noble lords. It must listen to the voice of organised groups in the State and the pressure on the Administration outside Parliament is very strong. The selection of facts by the Press and the comments made on those facts; the statements of employers and of trade unions; the shrieking of prophets and the low murmur of experts of all kinds; the pronouncements of the holders of public offices; the reports of advisory committees, working parties and Royal Commissions —in fact the whole discussion, official and unofficial, of public affairs presses upon the Administration. Inside Parliament, the pressure takes the form of debate and question, of the investigation by such committees as the Select Committee on Estimates, and the Public Accounts Committee, and of the scrutiny of the legislative proposals and measures of the Government, whether they are in the form of Bills or statutory instruments. These two methods of bringing pressure on the Administration are, of course, closely linked. Outside organisations who have had no opportunity, or who have failed, to influence the Administration directly, will frequently enlist the support of Members of Parliament. The Members themselves will go to the organisations to obtain information. Debates and questions in Parliament gain prominence in the Press and thus the matter receives further publicity.

The effect of this political pressure on the Administration is imponderable. The question is often considered how far Parliament controls the Administration to-day. A great deal turns on the meaning which is attached to the word "controls." Banks control a river; a driver controls his car. The influence of a parent over a child may be greater than the power of a prison guard over a convict. The Members of the House of Commons can force a Government to resign, but a Government with a working majority is in very little danger of such defection by its own supporters. Nevertheless, the Government will not openly flout the wishes of its back-benchers and is more likely, if it cannot persuade, to drop the controversial measure. It is therefore mistaken to assume that the House of Commons and the Government are in conflict, one struggling to control the other. The Government is the Government because it has the support of a majority of the House. The conflict between the Queen and Parliament has become the conflict between the party in office and the party in opposition. The Government has the duty and the right to govern. It will be influenced in the way in which it governs by the opinions of its own back-benchers and its supporters outside Parliament; it may be ready to compromise on certain matters with its opponents. The acts of government which it performs will be criticised inside and outside Parliament by individuals and organisations of every kind. In all its actions, the Government will be ever conscious that it must, within five years, allow its whole record to be voted on. Its power while in office can be very great; its defeat at an election is complete.

All this applies primarily to the central Government. Local authorities are responsible to the local electorate. The position of the public corporation is rather different.[1] It is not directly responsible to Parliament, nor is any Minister responsible there for its actions. Ministers have certain powers in relation to a corporation for which they are responsible but these do not cover the day-to-day administration. The forms of outside influence exist but without the link with Parliamentary criticism which so strengthens them. The absence of a forum in which the public corporation can be criticised and defended is a consequence of the grant of a large measure of independence. It is possible for an organisation to have freedom of action and yet to be responsible to another body for the actions which it takes. In this country the result of the historical developments has been to place the heads of the Administration in the body to which they are responsible. This has considerable advantages. The Front Bench is the seat of power. But it is also particularly conspicuous. To be raised on a pedestal is to present a good target. If a public corporation is made largely independent of Ministers so that it is free from detailed and hampering instructions, it is to that extent made irresponsible. Responsibility to Parliament is not the only kind of responsibility to the people; but so far the other kinds have not been developed.

[1] See below, Ch. VII.

CHAPTER II

THE LEGISLATIVE POWERS OF THE ADMINISTRATION

Bills

MODERN political parties inform the electorate from time to time what is their policy and how they propose to implement it. At the time of a general election, each party produces a detailed programme, the implementation of which will require legislation; it asks the voter to put it into the position where it can legislate. It asks for a majority in the House of Commons.

A. Historical Development

The idea of a party going to the country with its legislative programme prominently displayed is quite new. Political campaigning in its modern form is usually said to have achieved its first grand expression in the series of speeches which Gladstone delivered in 1879 before the Midlothian election. As late as that year it was possible for his political opponents to write: "Official subordination is set aside when public policy is regulated, not by Parliament, but by the voice of the general population. Senators and consulars must stand aside in the presence of a dictator. Although it has long been customary for statesmen to make occasional speeches to public meetings, the extent to which the practice has lately been carried is altogether unprecedented. The result is that the Constitution is gradually weakened by the substitution of numerical majorities for the representatives of the people in Parliament. The approach of an election furnishes no sufficient justification for an innovation which accelerates the prevalence of democracy and aggravates its evil tendencies."[1]

Particular legislative reforms have always, of course, formed centres of political controversy, but the idea that a Government is responsible for the passing and administration of a specific body of legislation did not take shape until after 1832. The extension of the franchise in the middle years of the nineteenth century, which was itself the result of profound

[1] *The Saturday Review*, 29th November, 1879.

social and economic changes, brought political parties into greater reliance on the mass of the people whose desires for reform had to be met. The effect of this change was to invest the Government with more functions. Increase in functions involves increase in power, and governments in this country obtain more power by means of legislation. Although the nineteenth century saw the beginnings of this new concept of the enlarged functions of government, the process has been greatly accelerated in the course of the last fifty years. While the actual number of statutes enacted in a session has not greatly increased, Acts of Parliament have become longer and more complex. In the 1906–13 period, the average number of statutes in each session was 50; in the 1929/30–1937/8 period it rose to 57. But the number of pages for each session for the same periods increased from 335 to 995 and the average length of a statute from 7 to 17 pages; at the same time devices such as legislation by reference[1] and the elimination of much of the prolixity of the statutes of earlier periods have resulted in more actual legislative matter being contained on each page of the annual volumes of the Statute Book.[2] Nor is there any probability of a decrease in legislative output in the future; on the contrary, the indications are that the rate will continue to rise. In this critical period of social and economic history, political parties are returned to power to put into operation policies having far-reaching effects. A party of one political colour which succeeds in displacing the Government of the day will, even though it may wish ultimately to limit the number of Bills presented to Parliament, be forced to some extent to substitute its own measures first. This is, of course, particularly true at times when on certain issues the legislative intentions of the principal political parties differ fundamentally. Changes in social and economic policy cannot be effected without the power given by Acts of Parliament, and the whole process of legislation—the preparing of the Bill, the consultation with affected interests, the conferences, the drafting, the presentation to Parliament and the management of the debates—all these are governmental functions. During

---

[1] I.e. where a statute refers to and incorporates provisions of an earlier enactment.

[2] See H.C. 189–1 of 1946, para. 5719(7) and Appendix.

the periods when the Executive was relatively inactive, the prestige and status of Parliament were high and its power and influence paramount, but there is "an inherent tendency, in our system, for government, as such to reassert itself whenever the opportunity or the need might arise."[1] The demand for social and economic reform which has characterised this century has given power to the Executive with a resulting loss by Parliament of its initiating functions. The vast majority of legislative proposals now originate in the departments. In the 1936/7 session seventy General and Public Acts were passed. Of these, fifty-five were introduced by departments, eleven by private members, two by the Lord Advocate and one each by the Prime Minister and the Attorney-General. Of the eleven introduced by private members, three were backed by departments and two followed reports of departmental committees; local authority associations backed two; of the remaining four, two were supported by the R.S.P.C.A. and similar bodies, one by the Salvation Army and Church Army and the last was Sir Alan Herbert's Matrimonial Causes Act which was introduced by another private member.[2] Moreover, the Government has never hesitated to encroach on private members' time, when it considered this necessary; in three of the sessions of the inter-war period, the whole of the time was taken, while in about half of the other sessions it was more or less seriously curtailed. During the period 1906—1937/8, excluding the war years, private members' Bills averaged 11·4 days or nearly 9 per cent of the session.[3] Most importantly, the development of party discipline has consolidated the power of the Executive over Parliament during its period of office.

B. The Legislative Process

Legislation to-day is therefore a function of the Administration. The legislative process embraces the whole train of events from the conceiving of a measure to its final enactment by the Queen in Parliament. A proposal for legislation springs from some real or supposed defect in the existing statutory or

[1] L. S. Amery: *Thoughts on the Constitution*, 14–15; see also his chapter in Lord Campion (ed.): *Parliament: a Survey*, Ch. II.
[2] W. I. Jennings: *Parliament*, Appendix II.
[3] H.C. 189–1 of 1946 *Appendix to Report*, para. 15 (Sir G. Campion).

common law or in the organisation of society. While this description covers all forms of legislation, we are here concerned solely with those proposals which become public bills put forward on behalf of the Government. Sir Ivor Jennings has attempted at some length to answer his own question "Who Makes the Laws?"[1] The original suggestion may come from one of a number of sources. The idea may be a part of declared government policy; it may be departmental policy; it may be advanced by a group to which the Government is linked and on which it depends for support; it may be the result of a Commission or of an *ad hoc* committee. Whatever its source, general principles or the idea which lies behind the proposed Bill are likely to have been debated at considerable length before the first clause is drafted. If it is a matter of governmental policy, the idea has probably been thrashed out by every type of important and unimportant member of the political party for many years; it will have been the subject of articles and papers, of conferences and public meetings. The proposal may well take the form of an amending bill; if so, the practical shortcomings of its predecessor will form the basis of examination. Almost certainly some organisation will have been urging on the department concerned the desirability of the measure. A department which decides to press for legislation on a particular subject must persuade the Cabinet that it is desirable. Having done so, the department must obtain a place in the legislative programme of the Cabinet. Later, the Cabinet will examine the final draft of the Bill and further alterations may be made. For all these purposes the Cabinet normally works through committees under the chairmanship of a senior member of the Cabinet. The composition of these committees varies according to the subject-matter of the Bill, and certain departments other than the sponsoring department will attend; it also varies according to the stage which the negotiations have reached (thus the Chief Whip is always present when the legislative programme is being discussed and the draftsman is present when an actual draft is under consideration). These negotiations start many months before the beginning of the session in which, it is hoped, the Bill will be introduced. They may continue into that session, especially

[1] *Parliament*, Ch. VII.

where the Bill has a relatively low place in the order for introduction.

The drafting of the Bill commences after policy approval
and a place in the legislative programme have been obtained.
The division of the department normally gives full details to the
legal officers of the department who then instruct Parliamentary
Counsel. The next stage does not seem to have altered since
Ilbert wrote in 1901: "The first crude sketch will be gradually
elaborated. There will be daily conferences with the minister
or with the permanent head of the department, or with both.
There will be interviews and correspondence with experts in
various branches of the subject with which the measure deals.
Notes will have to be written tracing the history of previous
legislation or attempts at legislation, and explaining the reasons
for and effect of the several proposals embodied in the draft
Bill, and stating the arguments which may be advanced for
and against them, and these will soon grow into a formidable
literature of commentaries."[1] Nor will consultation and discussion be confined to those employed in an official or advisory
capacity by the department. The opinions, arguments and
view-points of those who are to be directly affected by the
measure will no doubt have already been made known to the
department. And now, while the Bill is being drafted, these
affected persons are likely to be drawn into consultation once
more. Probably the amount of detailed information on the
nature of the departmental proposal which is given to such
persons is not great; but particular points are raised and reactions
ascertained. The more matters of dispute which can be settled
outside Parliament the better for the department and the more
speedy the passage of those parts of the Bill, particularly in
Committee.

"Those who are familiar with Parliamentary procedure,"
writes Ilbert, "are well aware of the difficulties with which
the promoter of any important measure has necessarily to
contend. The measure may have gone through a long period
of gestation before its introduction to Parliament. Information
and opinions on different points will have been confidentially
obtained from various quarters; the provisions of the measure
will have assumed many varying forms; and the alternatives

[1] *Legislative Methods and Forms*, 228.

will have been carefully discussed and compared. Yet, in spite of all these precautions, as soon as the measure has been printed and circulated, swarms of amendments will begin to settle down on the notice paper, like clouds of mosquitoes."[1] The procedure in Parliament which follows is so well known that no detailed comment is called for. It is worth noting, however, that the opposition to the Bill in Parliament both in principle and on points of detail is to a large extent inspired by those sections of the community who, being directly affected, have already had some opportunity of making their opinions known. Discussion and consideration at Westminster are not confined to the recognised stages of a Bill. Often the informal meetings are more important. These are of two kinds: those which take place within each parliamentary party and those which take place between the parties. Of the first kind are the regular meetings of the leaders of the parties with their parliamentary members in the House of Commons. In these private meetings, matters of policy and detail are discussed at length and amendments to be urged (in the case of the Opposition) or made (in the case of the Government) are agreed. This is part of the planning stage for the parliamentary battle and gives an opportunity for the opinions of backbenchers to be heard once again. The second kind comprises all the negotiations on a Bill which take place "through the usual channels" or "behind the Speaker's chair." In the House of Lords in particular informal negotiations between parties may result in discussion on the merits of different parts of the Bill. Short of this, the negotiations will do much to settle the course of the battle in the Chamber and in Committee. The whole of the Bill may not be discussed in detail because of the shortage of time and the use of the kangaroo and the guillotine procedures. But eventually, on receiving the assent of Queen, Lords and Commons, the Bill becomes law.[2]

Prerogative Powers

Her Majesty in Council continues to exercise her residual powers of issuing Orders in Council, Letters Patent, and

---

[1] *Legislative Methods and Forms*, 230.

[2] For accounts of the legislative process, see H. S. Morrison: *Government and Parliament*, Ch. II, XI; Lord Campion (ed.): *Parliament: A Survey*, Ch. VI (by H. E. Dale); Sir Granville Ram: "The Improvement of the Statute Book" in 1 *Journal of the Society of Public Teachers of Law* (1951) 442.

Proclamations under the prerogative.[1] These Orders in Council must be distinguished from those issued under statutory authority.

Prerogative Orders in Council relate chiefly to the constitutions of overseas territories within the British Commonwealth, questions of colonial currency and appeals to the Judicial Committee. The first of these are the most important and there were thirty-eight such Orders and Letters Patent between 1935 and 1940; in 1946 there were fourteen and in 1947 there were fifteen. Between 1935 and 1940, there were three Orders in Council relating to currency and two relating to appeals. This power is used in wartime to govern such matters as contraband and reprisals. In 1942, an Order in Council provided that the Civil Service Commissioners should not publish in the *London Gazette* notice of appointments and promotions while the Emergency Powers (Defence) Act, 1939, was in force. While there is, therefore, great diversity in the uses to which these powers are put, they have little importance for the internal administration of the country in peacetime.

Subordinate Legislation

When Parliament passes a legislative proposal in the form of a Bill through the normal stages, and the Royal Assent is signified, the proposal becomes law in the shape of an Act of Parliament. Apart from a limited power which remains in the Queen to make prerogative Orders in Council without parliamentary assent, no person or body can transform legislative proposals into laws unless Parliament has expressly, in an Act, given its authority. The term "subordinate" or "delegated" legislation is used to describe the laws made under this authority.[2]

A. The Nature of Subordinate Legislation

These subordinate laws are known by a great diversity of names and cover an infinite variety of subjects. They may be called rules, regulations, orders, schemes, by-laws, licences, directions, warrants, instruments of approval, minutes. The majority of these laws are required to be registered, numbered

[1] For a brief account of present-day procedure see H. S. Morrison: "The Privy Council To-day" in 2 *Parliamentary Affairs* (1948), 10.

[2] For a survey prepared in the Statutory Publications Office, see "Subordinate Legislation" in 30 *Public Administration* (1952), 227.

and published.[1] But legislative instructions are sometimes issued in other ways. Thus Ministries may explain and detail the provisions of Acts of Parliament in circulars to local authorities; while most of the instructions are matters of administrative detail, the courts have on occasion held some to be legislative in character.[2] The scope of the power to make subordinate laws is, in the first place, prescribed by the Act (commonly referred to as the "parent" Act) which gives the authority. But sometimes the parent Act is phrased so widely that the laws made immediately under it are themselves too general for detailed application. So these "children" themselves authorise the making of laws which are then the "grandchildren" of the original Act. There may be as many as five "generations." Thus under the Emergency Powers (Defence) Act, 1939, Defence Regulations were made; under these Regulations, orders appeared; under these orders might come directions which in their turn authorised the issuing of licences. This practice of subdelegation is further discussed below. It is mentioned here to show that the *immediate* authority for a subordinate law is sometimes not an Act but another subordinate law.

The person or body which may exercise the power to legislate is, subject to what has just been said, indicated in the parent Act. Most commonly it is Her Majesty, a Minister of the Crown or a Government department. Apart from prerogative Orders in Council already mentioned (which are not subordinate legislation), Her Majesty is frequently authorised by statute to make Orders in Council. Such Orders often deal with the more important "national" matters, but the distinction cannot be clearly maintained; the vast majority are drafted in the departments. Ministerial heads of departments or the departments themselves (the distinction has no significance) are the most common recipients of the power to legislate. By means of this power they give effect to the parent Act which it is their duty to administer. Boards, commissions and other statutory bodies are occasionally given the power to make subordinate legislation. These bodies are, in most cases, closely connected with the work of the central Government

---

[1] See below pp. 44–61.
[2] E.g. *Blackpool Corporation* v. *Locker*, [1948] I K.B. 349, at 367–9.

and the laws which they make are normally subject to Ministerial approval.[1] However, charges schemes are prepared by the British Transport Commission and are confirmed by the Transport Tribunal which enjoys a considerable degree of independence of the Minister of Transport and Civil Aviation.[2] Other law-making authorities include the Rules Committee of the Supreme Court,[3] the National Assembly of the Church of England[4] and local government authorities.[5]

B. Special Types

There are certain types of subordinate legislation which have received special names.

Statutory Instruments: this is a generic term introduced by the Statutory Instruments Act, 1946, which is discussed below.[6] It covers many types of subordinate legislation made under Acts passed before 1948; it covers the exercise of all those delegated powers, contained in Acts passed after 1947, which are expressly made exercisable by statutory instrument or Order in Council.

Special Orders: although this phrase has been used variously in statutes, it was generally applied to orders which were subject to a procedure which involved the publicising of a draft order followed by a local inquiry, before the order was finally made. In this sense, such orders are no longer "special." Often an affirmative parliamentary resolution[7] was also necessary, but this was not universally so and cannot be regarded as having been the distinguishing feature of a special order at any time. All the Acts which granted the power to make so-called special orders have been repealed and the phrase is not likely to reappear in statutes in the future to any extent.

---

[1] E.g. National Assistance Board under National Assistance Act, 1948, Sect. 63; Public Works Loan Commissioners under Public Works Loans Act, 1875, Sect. 41.
[2] Transport Act, 1947, Pt. V as amended by Transport Act, 1953, Sects. 20–24.
[3] Supreme Court of Judicature Act, 1875, Sect. 17.
[4] Church of England (Assembly) Powers Act, 1919, Sects. 3, 4.
[5] E.g. Local Government Act, 1933, Pt. XII—power to make byelaws "for the good rule and government" of their areas and for "the prevention and suppression of nuisances therein."
[6] Pp. 44–57. What would have been known before 1948 as Statutory Rules and Orders (S.R. & O.) are now known as Statutory Instruments (S.I.). But S.I.s embrace more than S.R. & O.s.
[7] See below, pp. 87–88.

The Standing Orders of the House of Lords[1] use the phrase to mean all those orders which require affirmative resolution.

Schemes:[2] this word is often interchangeable with "regulations" and was used in Workmen's Compensation Acts, various Agriculture Acts and Pensions Acts. In another sphere, local government authorities are frequently required to submit for the approval of Ministries schemes or proposals which embody the ways in which they intend to carry out their statutory duties. These are not, however, normally regarded as examples of subordinate legislation.

Certain types of order must be specially noticed.

Compulsory Purchase Orders. Such orders relate to a particular piece of land or to a particular building and are normally[3] subject to a procedure which requires the issuing of the orders by a local authority or other body, followed by an opportunity for objection to the confirming authority (usually the Minister of Housing and Local Government), a local inquiry and the confirmation, modification or rejection of the orders. Being of a particular, limited application, they are not normally regarded as subordinate legislation.

Provisional Orders. Private Bill procedure is expensive and slow. Provisional Orders were introduced in the nineteenth century as a simplification of this procedure.[4] The promoters apply first to a Government department which holds a local inquiry at which objections can be made. If satisfied, the department then makes a Provisional Order which, sometimes with many others, is included in a Confirmation Bill and passed through Parliament. The intention is to relieve Parliament of the investigatory and semi-judicial function which it exercises in Committee on a Private Bill. But if the order is opposed while the Confirmation Bill is before Parliament, that function must still be exercised. Since the order to be effective requires parliamentary assent to a Bill, it cannot be classed as subordinate legislation.

---

[1] S.O. 216. See below, pp. 91–92.

[2] For Schemes, Special Orders and Provisional Orders see J. Willis: *Parliamentary Powers of English Government Departments*, Ch. IV.

[3] The procedure has been standardised by Acquisition of Land (Authorisation Procedure) Act, 1946.

[4] For their history, see A. S. Quekett: "Local Government and Devolution" in 34 *Law Quarterly Review* (1918), 357.

Special Procedure Orders. To overcome the delay involved in provisional order procedure and at the same time to give an opportunity for amendment by Parliament, a new procedure was introduced by the Statutory Orders (Special Procedure) Act, 1945.[1] The usual preliminaries of local inquiry and objection having been followed, the order is laid before Parliament. If, within fourteen days of this laying, a petition is presented against the order, the petition is referred for examination to the Lord Chairman of Committees in the House of Lords and the Chairman of Ways and Means in the House of Commons. The Chairmen, acting together, decide whether the petition is one for amendment of the order or of general objection to the order, and report to their respective Houses. If either House, within fourteen days after receiving this report, resolves that the order be annulled, the order becomes void.[2] On a motion for annulment, the House may, if there is a petition of general objection, refer that petition to a joint committee of both Houses. If the order is not annulled within those fourteen days and there are no petitions for amendment, the order comes into operation. If there is a petition for amendment, this goes automatically to the joint committee. Where any petition is referred to the joint committee, the committee has power to report the order either with or without amendments. Where the petition referred is one of general objection, the committee may nevertheless report with amendments or they may report that the order be not approved. If an order is reported without amendment, the order may come into operation on the date when the report is laid. If there are amendments, the order comes into operation when the Minister concerned determines, unless he considers it inexpedient that the order should take effect as amended. In this latter case, he may withdraw the order or may re-submit the order in a Confirmation Bill. Where the joint committee reports that the order be not approved, the order cannot take effect unless confirmed by Act of Parliament.

This procedure has been applied to many orders since 1945 and, in accordance with the provisions of the Act, has replaced

[1] See 414 H.C. Deb. 5s., cols. 1374–1420 and H. Molson: "The Statutory Orders (Special Procedure) Act, 1945" in 3 *Parliamentary Affairs* (1950), 458.
[2] Either House can annul although no petition is presented.

provisional order procedure for many orders contained in Acts passed before 1946.[1] The orders are statutory instruments for some of the purposes of the Act of 1946.[2]

C. Development

The entrusting by Parliament to other bodies of the power to legislate can be traced back many centuries.[3] The period before the eighteenth century is not particularly significant and it is not helpful to point out parallels before 1688. The eighteenth century itself contains few examples of any importance. This was, as Maitland says,[4] the century of private laws, a period when Parliament legislated in such detail that many of its measures would to-day be called matters of administrative instruction. The modern development is usually dated from 1834 when the Poor Law Amendment Act provided that for executing the powers given by that Act the Poor Law Commissioners "shall and are hereby authorised and required, from Time to Time as they shall see Occasion, to make and issue all such Rules, Orders and Regulations for the Management of the Poor, for the Government of Workhouses and the Education of the Children therein . . . and for carrying this Act into execution in all other respects as they think proper."[5] The growth of subordinate legislation in the nineteenth and twentieth centuries is the inevitable consequence of fundamental changes in the theory and practice of government. More and more functions have been acquired by central and local government authorities; the performance of these functions requires legislative and administrative power; and Governments have found themselves unable to submit to Parliament the full details of their administrative intentions. This inability has been due to many factors. One has been the shortage of available parliamentary time; another has been the difficulty of administering, especially in a new field, a

---

[1] For one group replacing provisional order procedure in twenty-six cases see S.I. 1949 No. 2393. For provisions in Acts passed after 1945 see Index to annual volumes of statutes under "Parliament."

[2] Statutory Instruments Act, 1946, Sect. 7 (3).

[3] For accounts of this development, see *Report of the Committee on Ministers' Powers* (Cmd. 4060) 13–15; Sir Carleton Allen: *Law and Orders* (2nd Edn.) Ch. 2. And see further below, pp. 72–73.

[4] *Constitutional History of England* (1926 Edn.), 383.

[5] Sect. 15.

scheme the details of which are largely contained in an inflexible statute. *Solvitur ambulando* is often the only answer that can be given. The opponents of subordinate legislation have been many and vociferous. But the question of its desirability is far more a matter of politics than of administrative law.

The growth of subordinate legislation can be seen from the following numbers of instruments published by the Stationery Office. The yearly average between 1894 and 1913 was 1238, the actual number varying from 950 (in 1895) to 1899 (in 1904); this latter figure was large because of the effect of the Education Act, 1902. The yearly average for the 1914–18 period was 1461. The yearly average for the period 1919–29 was 1677; for the first three years of this period the total exceeded 2000 but in the last three years averaged 1248 only.[1] In 1937 the figure was 1231; in 1938 it was 1661; in 1939 it rose to 1946. In the six years 1940–45, the average was 2049.[2] From 1948, when there were 2858 instruments, the number declined to 2144 in 1950, rose to 2335 in 1951, declined to 1761 in 1954 but again exceeded 2000 in 1955.

D. Subject-matter

Perhaps the most typical and in some ways the most important examples of subordinate legislation are those which provide the essential administrative details for the working of an Act of Parliament. Under the Town and Country Planning Act, 1947, twenty-seven sets of regulations, orders and directions were made in 1948. Twelve of the more important of these total 124 pages.[3] (The 120 sections and 11 schedules of the Act cover 209 pages of the statute book.) By the Companies Act, 1948, the Lord Chancellor is empowered to make "general rules for carrying into effect the objects of this Act so far as relates to the winding up of companies in England."[4] The rules so made total 230 and, with 112 prescribed forms, cover 131 pages.[5]

Any major reconstruction of the social and industrial

---

[1] See *Evidence given before Committee on Ministers' Powers*, p. 204 (C. T. Carr—now Sir Cecil Carr).

[2] See *Minutes of Evidence to Third Report from Select Committee on Procedure* (H. C. 189–1 of 1945–6), p. 243 (Sir Cecil Carr).

[3] See, for example, S.I. 1948 Nos. 958, 1236, 1613.

[4] Sect. 365 (1).

[5] S.I. 1949 No. 330.

services which are supplied by the Administration can only be planned by attempting to provide a general and comprehensive framework in the Act and by leaving to subordinate legislation the detailed application and explanation. This is not to say that a simple distinction can be drawn or can be found between principle and framework on the one hand and the details of both on the other. But the Education Act, 1944, the National Health Service Act, 1946, the National Insurance Act, 1946, and the Acts which between 1945 and 1950 brought under control the coal, gas, electricity, and transport undertakings, do provide the foundations and the main structure.

Although much of the subordinate legislation of recent years has been issued for the purpose of building on these particular foundations, it would be erroneous to imagine that the diversity of the subject-matter of rules, regulations, orders and all the other kinds of laws has in any way lessened. This diversity can only be revealed by examining some of the subordinate legislation made in a single year.

In 1947, the recorded legislation (other than the Defence Regulations and the subdelegated legislation made thereunder) totals 2678 pages. (The statutes for that year are contained in 2002 pages.) The subordinate legislation which occupies more space than any other subject relates to Wages Councils. By the Wages Councils Act, 1945, the Minister of Labour and National Service was empowered to establish by order Wages Councils to operate in industries and trades. Six such orders were made in 1947. Wages Councils, under the Act, may submit to the Minister detailed "wages regulations proposals" for fixing remuneration and making provisions for holidays. The Minister then makes orders embodying and giving effect to these proposals. In 1947, fifty-five such orders were made, covering thirty-one different trades. Another large group of orders was made under the Goods and Services (Price Control) Act, 1941, the title of which is self-explanatory. In 1947, sixty-six orders were made for thirty-three different commodities including alarm clocks, candles, combs, footwear, fountain pens, knitting pins, and wedding rings. Again, under the Finance Acts, arrangements may be made with the Government of any territory outside the United Kingdom to provide relief from double taxation. In 1947, twenty-two orders embodied such arrangements. Quite different provisions are contained in the subordinate legislation which was required to bring into effect part of the National Health Service Act, 1946. First, the terms of appointment of members of Executive Councils, and the procedure of these bodies were detailed in regulations.[1] Secondly, Regional Hospital Boards had to be set up. The Act did not prescribe the number of these Boards and required the Minister to appoint members, after consultation with various authorities. An Order of 1947[2] designated fourteen Regional Hospital Areas and listed the names and addresses of the members. Thirdly, superannuation regulations were made for those engaged in the scheme; these regulations occupy eighty-seven pages.[3]

A large number of regulations is made for various pension schemes. Some sixteen orders, regulations or schemes were made in 1947 under the various Pensions (Increase) Acts, and Superannuation Acts and also under the National Insurance Act, 1946, the Old Age Pensions Act, 1936, the Personal Injuries (Emergency Provisions) Act, 1939, and the Polish Resettlement Act, 1947. The nationalisation of the coal industry in 1946 produced eight sets of regulations dealing with the transfer of assets, and, including orders under the Coal Mines Acts relating to employment, lighting, support, and ventilation, the subordinate legislation for the coal industry in 1947 covers over 100 pages.

Finally may be noted the delegated powers of the Treasury to make orders exempting goods from payment of duty and requiring additional duty to be paid. In 1947, four exemption and four additional duty orders were made.

What has been said indicates the nature of some of the subordinate legislation under seven of the more important subject-heads in 1947. All the legislation under these seven heads occupies less than half of the total page-space for the year. Amongst the other subjects are agriculture, road and rail transport, education, national insurance, police, the post office, prison regulation, and town and country planning.

---

[1] S.R. & O. 1947 No. 889.
[2] S.R. & O. 1947 No. 1297.
[3] S.R. & O. 1947 No. 1755.

E. Extensive Powers

1. EMERGENCY LEGISLATION

Apart from the very large number of statutes which delegate the power to legislate within a more or less limited field, there is a series of enactments which have given a much wider power. This series starts for present purposes with the Emergency Powers (Defence) Act, 1939, which authorised the Crown to make Defence Regulations "for securing the public safety, the defence of the realm, the maintenance of public order, and the efficient prosecution of any war in which His Majesty may be engaged, and for maintaining supplies and services essential to the life of the community."[1] In 1940 a second Act of the same name extended the power to make Defence Regulations "for requiring persons to place themselves, their services and their property at the disposal of His Majesty." These Acts expired on 24th February, 1946, but many of the Defence Regulations were continued in force by the Supplies and Services (Transitional Powers) Act, 1945, as extended by the Supplies and Services (Extended Purposes) Act, 1947.[2] Under this latter Act, the Defence Regulations which were continued in force by the Act of 1945 may be extended so as to be applicable for the following additional purposes: (a) for promoting the productivity of industry, commerce and agriculture; (b) for fostering and directing exports and reducing imports; and (c) generally for ensuring that the whole resources of the community are available for use, and are used, in a manner best calculated to serve the community. These powers far exceed any previously enjoyed by the Administration in peace time.

2. OTHER LEGISLATION

There is one type of provision common in statutes which confers a wide power. This is a provision which empowers a Minister (or other authority) to make regulations "for carrying into effect the provisions of this Act."[3] In certain Acts, a

[1] Sect. 1 (1).
[2] See also Supplies and Services (Defence Purposes) Act, 1951. The Emergency Laws (Miscellaneous Provisions) Act, 1953, enacted in permanent form certain Defence Regulations.
[3] Recent examples are Local Government Act, 1948, Sects. 15 (1), 31 (1), 71 (a), 110; National Assistance Act, 1948, Sect. 15 (1); British Nationality Act, 1948, Sect. 29 (1); Legal Aid and Advice Act, 1949. Sect. 12.

power was given to make regulations, amending the parent Act, to remove difficulties which might arise in bringing the Act (or some part of it) into operation. This provision became known as the Henry VIII clause because, says the *Report of the Committee on Ministers' Powers*, "that King is regarded popularly as the impersonation of executive autocracy."[1] The Committee condemned the use of the clause which has not appeared in that form since the Report in 1932 and which is contained in only one operative statute to-day.[2] The power to make regulations, amending either the parent or some other Act, is frequently given, however, in general terms. The Army and Air Force (Women's Service) Act, 1948, is an Act of five sections. It empowers Her Majesty to raise and maintain land and air forces consisting of or including women and declares that that power is included in Her Majesty's prerogative. The Act then provides: "Her Majesty may by Order in Council make provision for adaptations and modifications of enactments appearing to her to be requisite in consequence of the preceding provisions of this Act or of things done thereunder." The Local Government Act, 1948, contains provisions empowering the Minister to make regulations "for modifying the operation of this Part of this Act in relation to any authority" if a change of boundaries occurs;[3] it also empowers the Secretary of State, in reference to a particular section, by order to "make such modifications thereof as appear to him to be proper."[4] Another section of the same Act empowers the Minister by order to vary provisions of any local Act relating to rating or valuation for rating.[5] It is impossible for a draftsman to be familiar with the very great number of local Acts, and such provisions as this are inevitable. The Gas Act, 1948, provides: "Any local enactment which is inconsistent with or rendered redundant by any regulations made under this section shall cease to have effect." The section

[1] P. 36.

[2] Local Government Act, 1894, Sect. 80 (1). Sect. 78 of National Insurance Act, 1911, was a Henry VIII clause; compare Sect. 69 (1) (*a*) of National Insurance Act, 1946.

[3] Sects. 15 (1) (*d*), 31 (1) (*d*), 110 (*d*).

[4] Sect. 99 (5); see also Sect. 109 (1). For other examples in 1948 of the power to amend the parent Act, see Companies Act, 1948, Sects. 122 (2), 454 (1) (2), Employment and Training Act, 1948, Sect. 15 (1), Agricultural Holdings Act, 1948, Sect. 78 (1).

[5] Sect. 70 (3).

gives the Minister wide powers to make safety regulations.[1] The power to amend other public general Acts is also frequently given. Sometimes the power is to amend a specific section of the other Act;[2] sometimes it is to amend a group of unnamed Acts.[3] Few go so far as the Civil Defence Act, 1948, under which, amongst other things, regulations may "(d) . . . authorise or require things to be done in contravention of, or without compliance with, any statutory provision regulating or restricting the carrying out of building, engineering, mining or other operations in, on, over or under land, or the making of any material change in the use of any buildings or other land; and (e) may authorise the employment of personnel, and the provision, construction or maintenance of premises and equipment, in excess of any limits imposed by any statutory provision."[4]

A power is often reserved to Her Majesty to make Orders in Council specifying the date on which Acts or sections shall come into operation. This device has the advantage of postponing the operation of those sections for which detailed administrative preparations have to be made.[5]

The examples of statutes giving the power to make regulations which may amend enactments have been chosen from the year 1948. The practice is common and, indeed, inevitable.

At this point it should also be noted that the Administration sometimes issues statements of the way in which it proposes to put into effect certain statutes or subordinate laws and of arrangements which it has made affecting the operation of the law between one subject and another. Thus the War Damage Commission issued "Practice Notes" and Inland Revenue authorities from time to time announce "concessions." Such statements have been dubbed "administrative quasi-

---

[1] Sect. 67.

[2] E.g. Superannuation (Miscellaneous Provisions) Act, 1948, Sect. 11 (2).

[3] E.g. Palestine Act, 1948, Sect. 3 (3); National Assistance Act, 1948, Sect. 62 (2).

[4] Sect. 2 (2) (d) (e). Para. (d) is to exclude the operation of the Town and Country Planning Act, 1947, Sect. 12. Para. (e) seems very wide. See also Sect. 6 (2). Note the special procedure required by the Church of England Assembly (Powers) Act, 1919; the parliamentary authority for a Measure is expressed by resolution. A Measure may (Sect. 3 (6)) "relate to any matter concerning the Church of England, and may extend to the amendment or repeal in whole or in part of any Act of Parliament, including this Act."

[5] See also Interpretation Act, 1889, Sect. 37.

legislation" and their effect is considerable although they are not legally enforceable.[1]

F. The Publication of Subordinate Legislation

The law relating to publication must be considered under two heads. The first head covers the law governing the publication of statutory instruments; the second head covers the law governing the publication of subordinate legislation other than statutory instruments. Before dealing with the first head, an attempt must be made to define what is meant by a statutory instrument.

1. THE DEFINITION OF STATUTORY INSTRUMENT

This definition is to be found in Sect. 1 of the Statutory Instruments Act, 1946,[2] and varies according to the date on which the parent Act was passed.

(a) Acts passed after 1947

The Act of 1946 provides—

> 1.—(1) Where by this Act or any Act passed *after* the commencement of this Act power to make, confirm or approve orders, rules, regulations or other subordinate legislation is conferred on Her Majesty in Council or on any Minister of the Crown then, if the power is expressed—
>> (a) in the case of a power conferred on Her Majesty, to be exercisable by Order in Council;
>> (b) in the case of a power conferred on a Minister of the Crown, to be exercisable by statutory instrument,
> any document by which that power is exercised shall be known as a "statutory instrument" and the provisions of this Act shall apply thereto accordingly.

The date of the commencement of this Act was 1st January, 1948.[3] The usual form of words in Acts passed after the date mentioned is "Any power to make regulations [etc.] conferred by this Act shall be exercisable by statutory instrument." The use of such words applies the provisions of the Act of 1946 to

---

[1] See R. E. Megarry: "Administrative Quasi-Legislation" in 60 *Law Quarterly Review* (1944) 125 and 218; also Sir Carleton Allen: *Law and Orders* (2nd Edn.) 221–2.

[2] This Act repealed the Rules Publication Act, 1893, and is hereafter referred to as "the Act of 1946." The words printed in italics in the following excerpts are not, of course, so printed in the Act.

[3] S.I. 1948 No. 3. For the sake of consistency "His Majesty" has been changed to "Her Majesty" throughout.

any instruments made. If such words are used, it is presumably immaterial whether the instrument is "legislative" in character or not;[1] it could, it is true, be argued that the sense of the phrase "or other subordinate legislation" indicates that the "orders, rules, regulations" must be legislative before they can be caught by this subsection. However, as will be seen, the statutory instruments made under the Act of 1946 itself do not use the word "legislation" exclusively with reference to content and speak of "subordinate legislation . . . being of a legislative and not an executive character."[2] It seems more likely that if the phrase "exercisable by statutory instrument" appears in the parent Act, the instrument is invariably caught by the Act of 1946. But it follows that if this phrase does not appear then the Act of 1946 is inapplicable however "legislative" may be the character of the subordinate legislation.[3] If the power is conferred by the parent Act on Her Majesty then the same considerations apply where the power is said to be exercisable "by Order in Council."

It should be noted that this subsection applies where Her Majesty or a Minister of the Crown confirms or approves by statutory instrument as well as where he makes subordinate legislation; some other authority may "make" the instrument in the first place but the instrument is caught by this subsection if subject to this confirmation or approval.

The Act provides[4] that where the power to legislate is con-ferred on a Government department (such as the Treasury, the Admiralty, or the Board of Trade), it shall be deemed to be conferred on the Minister of the Crown in charge of that department; and that the Treasury shall decide whether any particular body is a Government department for this purpose.[5]

(b) Acts passed before 1948

The Act of 1946 further provides in Sect. 1—

(2) Where by any Act passed *before* the commencement of this

---

[1] See below pp. 50–51 for two tests of "legislative;" the second only is relevant here.

[2] S.I. 1948 No. 1, Reg. 2 (3) (a).

[3] Whether a document containing subdelegated legislation is a statutory instrument is discussed below, pp. 55–57.

[4] Sect. 11 (1).

[5] Sect. 11 (2). See: "The Meaning of 'Government Department'" in 100 *Law Journal Newspaper* (1950) 297. And see *R. v. Baggallay*, [1913] 1 K.B. 290.

Act power to make statutory rules within the meaning of the Rules Publication Act, 1893, was conferred on any rule-making authority within the meaning of that Act, any document by which that power is exercised after the commencement of this Act shall, save as is otherwise provided by regulations made under this Act, be known as a "statutory instrument" and the provisions of this Act shall apply thereto accordingly.

Statutory rules were defined by Sect. 4 of the Rules Publication Act, 1893, to mean: "rules, regulations or by-laws made under any Act of Parliament which (a) relate to any court in the United Kingdom, or to the procedure, practice, costs, or fees therein, or to any fees or matters applying generally throughout England, Scotland or Ireland; or (b) are made by Her Majesty in Council, the Judicial Committee, the Treasury, the Lord Chancellor of Ireland, or a Secretary of State, the Admiralty, the Board of Trade, the Local Government Board for England or Ireland, the Chief Secretary for Ireland, or any other Government Department." Rule-making authorities are defined by the same section to include every authority authorised to make statutory rules. These two definitions do not assist greatly in the attempt to discover what was a statutory rule. However, Sect. 8 of the Act of 1946 provides—

(1) The Treasury may, with the concurrence of the Lord Chancellor and the Speaker of the House of Commons, by statutory instrument make regulations for the purpose of this Act, and such regulations may, in particular—

(d) determine the classes of cases in which the exercise of a statutory power by any rule-making authority constitutes or does not constitute the making of such a statutory rule as is referred to in subsection (2) of section one of this Act, and provide for the exclusion from that subsection of any such classes;

Under this power, the Statutory Instruments Regulations, 1947,[1] were made and Regulation 2 (1) provides—

Subject to the provisions of this Regulation, the following documents, namely—

(a) every document being of a legislative and not an executive character made *after* the commencement of the Principal Act by a rule-making authority as defined in the Rules Publication Act, 1893, in the

[1] S.I. 1948 No. 1.

exercise of a statutory power conferred on that authority by or under any Act of Parliament passed *before* the commencement of the Principal Act, and

(*b*) every other document which, by virtue of any enactment other than the said Act of 1893, would be subject to the provisions of Section 3 of that Act if that Section had not been repealed,

are hereby determined to constitute such a statutory rule as is referred to in subsection (2) of Section 1 of the Principal Act.

The Principal Act is the Act of 1946. This definition of what constitutes a statutory rule is wider than the definition in Sect. 4 of the Act of 1893. Paragraph (*a*) is substantially the definition adopted by Regulations[1] made under Sect. 3 of the Act of 1893. Sect. 4 of that Act referred merely to "rules, regulations and by-laws." The definition here quoted is wide enough to cover orders, schemes and other forms of subordinate legislation, and, in fact, Sect. 3 of the Act of 1893 was applied to all such legislation.

The Act of 1893 did not cover subordinate legislation which was "confirmed or approved" by a rule-making authority; it only covered legislation "made" by such an authority. It will be seen that this Regulation 2 (1) refers to "made" only, in contrast to the words in Sect. 1 (1) of the Act of 1946. Nevertheless, it was desired to bring some of the confirmations and approvals contained in Acts passed before 1948 within the provision of the Act of 1946. This was done by first re-stating the former rule in a modified form and then making exceptions. Thus Regulation 2 (2) of the same Regulations provides—

Without prejudice to any Order in Council made under subsection (1) of Section 9 of the Principal Act, the confirmation or approval by a rule-making authority of any scheme, regulations or other subordinate legislation made by a person not being a rule-making authority shall not be deemed to constitute the making of such a statutory rule as aforesaid unless it is required by the enactment under which it is made to be effected by means of an Order in Council or Order made by that authority.

The modification is the last clause, beginning with the word "unless." The meaning of this clause is not altogether clear.

[1] S.R. & O. 1894 No. 734, Reg. 1.

There are two possible readings. First, the clause can be read
to draw within the definition of statutory rule all confirmations and approvals required to be made by Order or Order
in Council whether the subordinate legislation be of a legislative or executive character. Since it seems to be largely
fortuitous whether a document made by an authority not
being a rule-making authority is required to be confirmed or
approved in this more formal way or is required merely to be
confirmed or approved without the formality, this reading
seems inadequate. Secondly, it may be that the confirmation
or approval by Order or Order in Council of a document the
content of which is executive in character is excluded from
the definition by Regulation 2 (1) (a) and is not drawn back
into the definition by this "unless" clause. This alternative
reading is more satisfactory but is difficult to reconcile with the
opening words of Regulation 2 (1), that is, "Subject to the
provisions of this Regulation." Since, however, the general
intention of the Act of 1946, and the Regulations and Order
in Council made under it, is to include, within the definition
of statutory instrument, subordinate legislation of a legislative
but not an executive character, this second reading is more
satisfactory. It is therefore adopted in the paragraphs below.
The Sect. 9 (1) referred to provides—

> If with respect to any power to confirm or approve orders,
> rules, regulations or other subordinate legislation conferred on a
> Minister of the Crown by any Act passed before the commence-
> ment of this Act, it appears to Her Majesty in Council that,
> notwithstanding that the exercise of that power did not constitute
> the making of a statutory rule within the meaning of the Rules
> Publication Act, 1893, it is expedient that the provisions of this
> Act should apply to documents by which that power is exercised,
> Her Majesty may by Order in Council direct that any document
> by which that power is exercised after such date as may be
> specified in the Order shall be known as a "statutory instrument"
> and the provisions of this Act shall apply thereto accordingly.

So far the relation between Regulation 2 (2) and this Sect. 9 (1)
is clear and we might expect to meet various Orders in Council
relating to different groups of documents made under confirmatory powers, the exercise of which was considered, in
view of their subject-matter, to justify their inclusion within

the meaning of "statutory instrument." But the Order in Council made under Sect. 9 (1) reads[1]—

> 1.—(1) Where any Minister of the Crown exercises any power conferred on him by any Act of Parliament passed before the commencement of the Statutory Instruments Act, 1946, to confirm or approve any orders or rules or regulations or other subordinate legislation made by an authority who is not a rule-making authority as defined in the Rules Publication Act, 1893, and the subordinate legislation so confirmed or approved, being of a legislative and not an executive character, is required to be laid before Parliament or the House of Commons, then, subject to the provisions of paragraph (2) of this Article, any document by which that power is exercised after the coming into operation of this Order shall be known as a statutory instrument, and the provisions of the Statutory Instruments Act, 1946, shall apply to that document accordingly.
>
> (2) This article shall not apply to any document which by virtue of subsection (2) of Section 1 of the Statutory Instruments Act, 1946, is a statutory instrument within the meaning of that Act otherwise than by virtue of this Order or would be such an instrument but for regulations made under paragraph (d) of subsection (1) of Section 8 of that Act.

It follows, therefore, that any subordinate legislation confirmed or approved by a Minister of the Crown, under a power conferred on him by any Act passed before 1948, is a statutory instrument, provided that it is legislative and not executive in character and is required to be laid before Parliament or the House of Commons. This Order in Council further provides that documents containing certain specified confirmations and approvals are to be statutory instruments, although they do not fall within the Article just quoted, as they are not required to be laid before Parliament.[2]

Finally, Regulation 2 (3) of the Statutory Instruments Regulations provides—

> Notwithstanding anything in this Regulation, subsection (2) of Section 1 of the Principal Act shall not apply to—
> (a) any document which, although of a legislative character, applies only to a named person or premises and is not required to be laid before or subject to confirmation or approval by Parliament or the House of Commons; or

---

[1] Statutory Instruments (Confirmatory Powers) Order, 1947 (S.I. 1948 No. 2).
[2] Ibid., Article 2 and Schedule.

> (*b*) any Order in Council which, being an Order for which
> the Lord President of the Council is the responsible
> authority, confirms or approves subordinate legislation
> in the nature of a local and personal or private Act; or
> (*c*) any such document as is mentioned in the Schedule to
> these Regulations.

Paragraph (*b*) covers, for example, Orders confirming the
Statutes of a University, schemes under the University and
College (Trusts) Act, 1943, and schemes under the Endowed
Schools Acts.

Paragraph (*c*) covers documents made under various
statutes relating to the armed forces, the Diseases of Animals
Act, 1894 (relating to orders admitting animals to quarantine),
and any document which by virtue of paragraph (2) of Regulation 102A of the Defence (General) Regulations, 1939,[1] is
deemed to be a statutory rule to which the Rules Publication
Act (Northern Ireland), 1925, applies.

It will be agreed that there may be doubt whether the
exercise of any power conferred by an Act passed before 1948
is or is not the exercise of a power to make a statutory rule.
The Act of 1946 provides that such a doubt may be resolved
by a Reference Committee appointed by the Lord Chancellor
and the Speaker of the House of Commons.[2]

So far the explanation of the phrase "being of a legislative
and not an executive character" has not been attempted. The
phrase does not appear in the Acts either of 1893 or of 1946.
As already noted, the Regulations made under the former Act
used it to define the meaning of "statutory rule" for the purpose
of Sect. 3 of that Act. It is reproduced in order to determine
what constitutes a statutory rule for the purpose of Sect. 1 (2)
of the Act of 1946.[3] It also appears under the Confirmatory
Powers Order, 1947, made under the Act of 1946 and set out
above. The distinction between "legislative" and "executive"
is very difficult to draw.[4] There are two tests which have been
suggested. The first is institutional: that which the Legislature

---

[1] S.R. & O. 1940 Nos. 1611, 1750.   [2] Sect. 8 (1) (*e*) (*iv*); S.I. 1948 No. 1, Reg. 11.
[3] Statutory Instruments Regulations, 1947, Reg. 2 (1) (above).
[4] A great deal has been written on this distinction. See, for example, *Report of
Committee on Ministers' Powers* (Cmd. 4060) p. 19; W. I. Jennings: *The Law and the
Constitution* (3rd Edn.), Ch. 1 and Appendix I; J. Salmond: *Jurisprudence* (10th
Edn.) 38–41; F. Green: "Separation of Governmental Powers" in 29 *Yale Law
Journal* (1920) 369; F. J. Port: *Administrative Law*, Ch. III.

enacts is legislation. Since no subordinate legislation is strictly enacted by Parliament, this is of no value. If the meaning of the word "enacts" is extended to include that which is done by Parliamentary authority, all kinds of actions are let in and solution is no nearer. Secondly, the meaning of "legislative" and "executive" may be determined by reference to the nature of the action. By this test, a power to make rules of general application is a legislative power and the rule is a legislative rule. A power to give orders in specific "cases" is, by the same test, an executive power and the order is an executive order. Similarly, a power to take specific action is an executive power and the action is an executive action. The difficulty here is that of distinguishing between what is "general" and what is "specific." These words, although they have some extreme and easily recognisable forms, do not help to solve the doubtful cases. The matter is finally one for arbitrary decision. There is no answer, save one that is arbitrary, to the old and comparable riddle: "How many sheep make a flock?" The application of the test for the present purposes is made more difficult by the provisions of the Statutory Instruments Regulations, 1947, which exclude from the definition of statutory rule in Sect. 1 (2) of the Act of 1946 "any document which, *although of a legislative character*, applies only to a named person or premises."[1]

Sir Cecil Carr has said that the application of the phrase was occasionally a matter of "doubt and discussion"[2] but he seems to have solved the difficulty in the only way it can be solved. If a document is a statutory instrument, then it is subject to the requirements for publication set out in the Act of 1946. The question whether any document is legislative or executive seems to be answered in practice by another question: "Is it desirable that this document should be published?" If the answer is "Yes," then it is called legislative.

A working definition of a statutory instrument may be summarised as follows—

1. Where by any Act passed *after* 1947, power to make, confirm or approve subordinate legislation is conferred on a rule-making authority and the power is expressed to be exercisable

---

[1] Reg. 2 (3) (a).
[2] *Evidence given before Committee on Ministers' Powers*, p. 207 and para. 2956.

by Order in Council or by statutory instrument, any document by which the power is exercised is a statutory instrument, whether it be legislative or executive in character (the Act of 1946, Sect. 1 (1)).

2. Where by any Act passed *before* 1948 either

(*a*) power to *make* subordinate legislation is conferred on a rule-making authority (Regulation 2 (1) of the Statutory Instruments Regulations, 1947); or

(*b*) power to *confirm or approve* subordinate legislation is conferred on a rule-making authority to be effected by Order in Council or Order (Regulation 2 (2) of the Statutory Instruments Regulations, 1947); or

(*c*) power to *confirm or approve* subordinate legislation is conferred on a rule-making authority and the legislation so confirmed or approved is required to be laid before Parliament or the House of Commons (Article 1 (1) of the Confirmatory Powers Order, 1947); and

(*d*) the power in (*a*), (*b*), or (*c*) above is exercised after 1947 in a document which is legislative and not executive in character;

then any such document is a statutory instrument. "Rule-making authority" means Her Majesty in Council, a Minister of the Crown or any Government department.

2. APPLICATION OF THE DEFINITION

It must now be determined what types of subordinate legislation fall within the definition of statutory instruments. Doubts can arise only in respect of subordinate legislation made after 1947 under powers conferred by statutes passed before 1948; where powers are conferred by statutes passed after 1947, the question is decided by the use of the phrases "Order in Council" or "statutory instrument."[1] What follows relates therefore only to instruments made under Acts passed before 1948.

The great majority of rules, regulations, orders, schemes and other subordinate legislation are made by Her Majesty, a Minister of the Crown or a Government department. So long as they are legislative in character, they are statutory instruments.

[1] For possible exception to this rule see pp. 55–56 (subdelegated legislation).

Special Orders: these were often, before 1948, regarded as statutory rules. Those made by the Electricity Commissioners were not ordinarily so treated, as they were not regarded as made by a rule-making authority; but, exceptionally, certain scale of depreciation orders were so treated.[1] There have been a few cases where the power to make "special orders" was exercised after 1947. They related to gas[2] and electricity[3] undertakings. The latter exemplify the change effected by the Act of 1946; they are confirmations (by the Minister of Fuel and Power) of orders made by the Electricity Commissioners but are now statutory instruments. As said above, the power to make "special orders" has now been repealed, in the case of the two undertakings mentioned, by the Electricity Act, 1947, and the Gas Act, 1948.[4]

Schemes: where schemes are made by a body not being a rule-making authority and are subject to confirmation or approval by such an authority, this confirmation or approval is sometimes required to be contained in an "order" made by the rule-making authority; in other cases, no "order" is necessary. The practice before 1948 is confusing. Confirmations and approvals were not statutory rules within the Rules Publication Act, 1893, but if made exercisable by "order" of the rule-making authority could be drawn within the definition.[5] Yet schemes made by the Herring Industry Board under the Act of 1935[6] and approved by the Minister without being contained in an "order" were treated as statutory rules.[7] On the other hand, superannuation schemes made by the Development Commissioners under the Development and Road Improvement Funds Act, 1910, were not so regarded. By an Act of 1943, the North of Scotland Hydro-Electric

---

[1] See Electricity (Supply) Act, 1926, Sects. 5, 7, 8, 12, 39 (1), Sch. 1, 2, 3; S.R. & O. 1931 Nos. 700–1, 714 and 1937 No. 1075.

[2] S.I. 1948 Nos. 312, 598–603, 804, 841–2, 1146–8, 1373–4, 1797, 2206, 2263, 2613–5; 1949 Nos. 543–4, 745, 844–6 (S. 45).

[3] S.I. 1948 Nos. 384–5.

[4] These did not come into immediate and full operation. Hence the S.I.s in the two preceding footnotes.

[5] E.g. factory rationalisation schemes made by Bacon Boards under Bacon Industry Act, 1938, Sects. 5, 6; subsidy schemes made by the Livestock Commission under Livestock Industry Act, 1937, Sects. 5, 8; schemes made by catchment boards under Land Drainage Act, 1930, Sect. 4—all these were treated as statutory rules.

[6] Herring Industry Act, 1935, Sect. 2.

[7] See S.R. & O. 1935 No. 490; 1946 No. 779.

Board was empowered to prepare development, constructional and distribution schemes, all to be confirmed by the Secretary of State, in the last two cases by "order." None was treated as a statutory rule before 1948, presumably because the Board was not regarded as a rule-making authority. From 1948, however, confirmation orders for constructional schemes appear as statutory instruments;[1] they satisfy the requirements of Regulation 2 (2), being "orders," and being legislative in character. Many schemes are made, in the first instance, by rule-making authorities, although the actual preparation may have been done by some other body. Under this head fall schemes made by the Secretary of State and (later) the Minister of National Insurance to benefit those suffering from certain industrial diseases; these were not made by "order." Thirty schemes were made between 1928 and 1947 and were treated as statutory rules.[2] Marketing schemes were effected by "order;" thirty were made between 1932 and 1939, particularly under the Agricultural Marketing Acts of 1931 and 1933 and were treated as statutory rules.[3] The position therefore seems to be that schemes similar to those which, whether made or confirmed or approved by a rule-making authority, were treated as statutory rules before 1948, will be statutory instruments; and that some schemes, which were subject to confirmation or approval and were on this ground not regarded as statutory rules, will be statutory instruments, if made after 1947, provided they are legislative in character and *either* are required to be confirmed or approved by Order or Order in Council *or* are required to be laid before Parliament or the House of Commons.

In Acts passed after 1947 the power conferred on a rule-making authority to make, confirm or approve schemes has frequently been made expressly exercisable by statutory instrument.[4] Many schemes have not been made so exercisable; the largest group comprises those made by local authorities

---

[1] E.g. S.I. 1948 Nos. 733 (S. 53), 1765 (S. 151), 2133 (S. 169).
[2] E.g. S.R. & O. 1928 No. 975; 1931 Nos. 341–6; 1939 Nos. 633–5; 1946 Nos. 591–5.
[3] E.g. S.R. & O. 1932 No. 505 (Hops); 1933 Nos. 683 (Bacon), 686 (Pigs), 789 (Milk), 1186 (Potato).
[4] E.g. crops schemes made under Agriculture (Miscellaneous Provisions) Act, 1949 (see S.I. 1949 Nos. 1370, 1454); schemes made under Superannuation (Miscellaneous Provisions) Act, 1948 (see S.I. 1949 Nos. 1015, 1106).

for carrying out statutory duties. Such schemes are subject to ministerial confirmation or approval.

Compulsory Purchase Orders: these orders are not normally treated as statutory instruments. The Minister confirms an order but does not himself issue an order. The document is not usually regarded as being legislative in character, nor has it to be laid before Parliament. Sometimes, however, a compulsory purchase order was made by "special order" which was required to be laid before Parliament and was then, if made after 1947, treated as a statutory instrument.[1]

Provisional Orders: these are not statutory instruments, being subject to confirmation by Act of Parliament.

Special Procedure Orders: these are treated as statutory instruments but are not subject to all the sections of the Statutory Instruments Act, 1946.[2]

Subdelegated Legislation. It has already been noted[3] that this legislation arises where the subordinate legislation made immediately under the parent Act confers powers to make laws in the form of grandchildren of the Act. Sometimes the authority which makes the legislation immediately subordinate to the Act confers on itself power to amend that legislation; sometimes the authority confers on another the power to beget legislation which are the grandchildren of the Act. The Emergency Powers (Defence) Act, 1939, under which were made Defence (General) Regulations expressly provided that these Regulations might empower "such authorities, persons or classes of persons as may be specified in the Regulations to make orders, rules and byelaws for any of the purposes for which such Regulations are authorised by this Act to be made."[4] But it is unusual for the parent Act so to provide and the validity of subdelegated legislation made without this express statutory authority is somewhat doubtful. The present question is whether, assuming the subdelegated legislation to be valid, the orders, directions, and other legislative documents are statutory instruments. For the exercise after 1947

---

[1] E.g. S.I. 1948 No. 384 (order made by Electricity Commissioners under the Electricity (Supply) Acts, 1882–1936, and confirmed by Minister of Fuel and Power under Electricity (Supply) Act, 1919).

[2] Sect. 7 (3).

[3] Pp. 32–33 and see below pp. 62–69.

[4] Sect. 1 (3).

of a power conferred by an Act passed before 1948, the words of Regulation 2 (1) (*a*) of the Statutory Instruments Regulations[1] appear to be sufficiently wide. On the other hand, these words are substantially the same as those which governed the publication provisions of the Rules Publication Act, 1893, and were not, before 1939, treated, for those provisions, as including subdelegated legislation. The laws made under the Defence (General) Regulations, 1939, were, however, printed as statutory rules. The governmental view in 1948 was that these laws were statutory instruments.[2] So far as subdelegated legislation under Acts passed after 1947 is concerned, the question, according to a governmental statement, "falls to be dealt with in the enabling Act itself."[3] This follows from the definition in Sect. 1 (1) of the Act of 1946. It does not, however, solve the problem. The enabling Act may provide that the power to make "regulations" shall be exercisable by statutory instrument. There may be a power, either express or implied, to make "orders" under those regulations. Are these orders also statutory instruments? Or must the enabling Act expressly declare that the power to make orders shall be exercisable by statutory instrument? In the latter case, an order made under an implied power cannot be a statutory instrument. It is to be hoped that the courts will feel able to stretch the wording of Sect. 1 (1) of the Act of 1946 to include subdelegated legislation made under a statutory instrument.

Scott, L.J., has said that the Rules Publication Act, 1893, did not and the Statutory Instruments Act, 1946, does not apply to subdelegated legislation.[4] If this is so, then the legislation made under the authority of the Defence (General) Regulations was only for administrative convenience published as Statutory Rules and Orders and Statutory Instruments. At the time of the first of these judicial *dicta*, in 1947, the Act

---

[1] S.I. 1948 No. 1. See above, pp. 46–47.

[2] 446 H.C. Deb. 5s., cols. *16–17*; 448 H.C. Deb. 5s., col. *310*. See S. A. de Smith: "Subdelegation and Circulars" in 12 *Modern Law Review* (1949) 37.

[3] 448 H.C. Deb. 5s., col. *310*.

[4] *Blackpool Corporation* v. *Locker*, [1948] 1 K.B. 349, at 369–70; *Jackson, Stansfield & Sons* v. *Butterworth*, [1948] 2 All E.R. 558, at 564. See also Denning, L.J., in *Falmouth Boat Construction Co., Ltd.* v. *Howell*, [1950] 2 K.B. 16, at 25. *Contra, Winter* v. *Simms Motor Units, Ltd., sub nom. Simms Motor Units, Ltd.* v. *Minister of Labour and National Service*, [1946] 2 All E.R. 201, at 204.

of 1946 was not in force nor were the Regulations made under that Act printed. Moreover the question whether the sub-delegated legislation in these cases ought to have been published as Statutory Rules and Orders or Statutory Instruments was not required to be decided. These expressions of judicial opinion must therefore be treated with caution.

3. THE PUBLICATION OF STATUTORY INSTRUMENTS

Sect. 2 (1) of the Act of 1946 requires that, immediately after the making of any statutory instrument, it shall be sent to the Queen's printer and numbered and, unless otherwise provided by subsequent Acts or by regulations made under the Act of 1946, copies of the instrument shall as soon as possible be printed and sold by the Queen's printer. Certain instruments are required by their parent Acts to be confirmed or approved by Parliament before they take effect.[1] Such instruments are, so far as their "making" is concerned, on the same footing as instruments which do not require confirmation or approval by Parliament, both types being regarded as "made" when the Minister or other authority signs them. Instruments received by the Queen's printer are allocated to the series of the calendar year in which they are made and numbered consecutively in the order in which they are received.[2] However, in the case of instruments subject to Parliamentary confirmation or approval or to special Parliamentary procedure, the instrument is allocated and numbered as if it had been made and received on the date on which the authority notifies the Queen's printer that the instrument has become or will become operative.[3] Certain instruments have to be laid in draft before Parliament. The "making" of these instruments follows after the laying require-ment and any conditions in the parent Act relating to Parlia-mentary resolutions have been complied with. Such instruments fall within the provisions relating to publication only after they are "made." But copies of the draft are printed and sold by the Queen's printer although they are not numbered.

For these purposes, instruments are classified as local or general according to their subject-matter and by analogy with

---

[1] See below, pp. 87–88.

[2] The three S.I.s made under the Act of 1946 were exceptions to this principle being dated 1947 and numbered 1948 Nos. 1, 2, and 3.

[3] Statutory Instruments Regulations, 1947 (S.I. 1948 No. 1) Reg. 3.

local, personal or private Acts on the one hand and public general Acts on the other. The authority which makes the instrument (the "responsible authority") classifies it; but the Reference Committee may change the classification.[1] Regulation 5 of the Statutory Instruments Regulations, 1947, provides—

> The following statutory instruments shall, unless the Reference Committee in any particular case otherwise direct under these Regulations, be exempt from the requirements of subsection (1) of Section 2 of the Principal Act with respect to the printing and sale of copies, that is to say—
> (a) any local instrument, and
> (b) any general instrument certified by the responsible authority to be of a class of documents which is or will be otherwise regularly printed as a series and made available to persons affected thereby:
> Provided that the responsible authority may, on sending to the Queen's printer of Acts of Parliament any statutory instrument certified by that authority as local, request him to comply with the requirements aforesaid.

It will be noted that this does not affect the numbering requirements. Moreover the responsible authority may certify an instrument as one which need not be printed and sold having regard to the brevity of the period during which the instrument will remain in force and to the steps taken for bringing its substance to the notice of the public. Again, the Reference Committee may overrule the responsible authority.[2] This exemption also applies under the same procedure to schedules or other documents which are identified by or referred to in a statutory instrument and where the exemption is justified having regard to their nature or bulk and to the steps taken for notifying the public.[3] The responsible authority may similarly certify that the printing and sale before the coming into operation of an instrument would be contrary to the public interest and such certificate exempts the instruments from those requirements; but the authority must notify the Queen's printer if, at any time before the operative date, he thinks that the certificate is no longer necessary.[4]

[1] Ibid., Reg. 4.
[2] Ibid., Reg. 6.
[3] Ibid., Reg. 7; see *Defiant Cycle Co., Ltd.* v. *Newell*, [1953] 1 W.L.R. 826.
[4] Ibid., Reg. 8.

Her Majesty's Stationery Office is required to publish from time to time a "Statutory Instruments Issue List" showing the number and name of each new instrument issued within the period and the date of the issue.[1] An annual edition of statutory instruments is published. It contains copies of all instruments made, printed and sold during the year and still in operation at the time of the completion of the edition, arranged according to subject-matter, a numerical list of public statutory instruments, a classified list of local instruments and tables showing the effect of the instruments contained on statutes and previous statutory rules and instruments.[2] On three occasions a complete set of volumes has been published showing the instruments and rules in force on a particular date. The volumes are arranged according to subject-matter and the latest edition contains the instruments and rules in force on 31st December, 1948.

4. THE PUBLICATION OF SUBORDINATE LEGISLATION OTHER THAN STATUTORY INSTRUMENTS

A great variety of instructions given under statutory authority emanates from Government departments and public bodies. Not all these instructions fall within the definition of statutory instrument discussed above. Where the authority is contained in an Act passed after 1947, it may be that the power is not expressed to be exercisable by Order in Council or statutory instrument. Thus the Children Act, 1948, empowers the Lord Chancellor, with the concurrence of the Lord President of the Council, to make rules prescribing the practice and procedure to be followed with respect to the constitution of appeal tribunals.[3] The Act also provides that any power to make regulations or orders conferred on a Minister shall be exercisable by statutory instrument.[4] But the rules are not statutory instruments, presumably because they are not "regulations or orders." Again, whenever the parent Act is passed, the power may be conferred on a body not being Her

---

[1] Statutory Instruments Act, 1946, Sect. 3 (1); S.I. 1948 No. 1, Reg. 9.
[2] S.I. 1948 No. 1, Reg. 10. The Statute Law Committee is responsible for the publication of the annual and the consolidated volumes and indexes; for an account of its work see 469 H.C. Deb. 5s., cols. 11–16.
[3] Sect. 80 (4).
[4] Sect. 58 (1).

Majesty, a Minister of the Crown or another rule-making authority. The Transport Tribunal confirms schemes fixing, in particular, railway fares and freight charges.[1] These are not statutory instruments. Nor are the schemes, made by local authorities and approved by the appropriate Ministers, which set out the ways in which local authorities propose to carry out their functions under various Acts; it can be argued that these schemes are administrative and not legislative in character. Again, the appropriate Ministers send circulars to local authorities explaining the functions of the authorities under Acts of Parliament; these circulars are not intended to be legislative in character and are issued, not under statutory authority, but for guidance. They may, however, contain legislative material.[2] Powers of these types abound and it is impossible to give a comprehensive list since, finally, the limits of "subordinate legislation" can only be determined by deciding arbitrarily what is and what is not "legislation."

Subordinate laws which are not statutory instruments may, in practice or by statutory requirement, be published. Thus the Children Act (Appeal Tribunal) Rules, 1949, are obtainable from Her Majesty's Stationery Office. The Transport Act, 1947, requires confirmed schemes to be "published in such manner as may be specified by the tribunal."[3] Local authority schemes are sometimes required to be made available while they are awaiting ministerial confirmation so that objections can be made; this is the procedure, for example, for development plans under the Town and Country Planning Act, 1947.[4] Sometimes the publication of the proposal is partial only—as of development plans under the Education Act, 1944, which were required to be circulated in part to managers and governors of schools.[5] Or the proposal may be circulated by county and county borough councils to district councils—as for schemes under the National Assistance Act, 1948.[6] Such schemes, proposals or plans may seem to be in a different category from a confirmation by the Transport

---

[1] Transport Act, 1947, Sects. 76–81.
[2] *Blackpool Corporation* v. *Locker*, [1948] 1 K.B. 349.
[3] Sect. 78 (5). The Railways Act, 1921, provided that confirmed schemes were "deemed to be statutory rules within the meaning of the Rules Publication Act, 1893" (Sect. 54 (1)).
[4] Sect. 10.   [5] Sect. 11 (3).   [6] Sect. 34.

Tribunal which increases a railway fare by a certain amount from a certain date. Nevertheless a local authority plan to zone areas for industrial or residential development or to build particular schools or to provide homes for the disabled may closely affect the citizen and his family and will certainly affect him financially. Wherever there is a large amount of devolution to local authorities by Acts which themselves provide only the general principles, that which is "administration" by the local authority from the viewpoint of the Government department looks more like legislation from the viewpoint of the individual. Ministry circulars to local authorities are often obtainable from Her Majesty's Stationery Office and are otherwise generally obtainable from the Ministry on request. That this is not always so is shown by the case of *Blackpool Corporation* v. *Locker*[1] which is discussed below.[2]

It is perhaps unfortunate that the Statutory Instruments Act, 1946, made the definition of a statutory instrument, where the power is contained in a parent Act passed after 1947, depend on the use by that parent Act of the phrases "statutory instrument" or "Order in Council." The effect is that there can normally be no compulsion to publish a document unless that Act has used one or other of these phrases. Where the power is contained in an Act passed before 1948, the Reference Committee has power to determine whether the exercise of the power is or is not the exercise of a power to make a statutory rule.[3] It might have been more satisfactory if the Act of 1946 had been so worded as to allow this Committee to determine similarly where the parent Act was passed after 1947. Parliament when considering the parent Bill has the opportunity to examine this point but the possibility of oversight is obviously considerable. The proposal has been made in the past that a Parliamentary committee should examine Bills which propose to delegate legislative powers.[4] It has been suggested that the Select Committee on Statutory Instruments could perform this function.[5]

---

[1] See p. 60, note 2.   [2] Pp. 64–65.   [3] Sect. 8 (1) (*e*) (iv).
[4] *Report of Committee on Ministers' Powers* (Cmd. 4060) pp. 67–68.
[5] *Minutes of Evidence for Third Report from Select Committee on Procedure* (H.C. 189–1 of 1946), paras. 4793 (9, 10), 4843–9, 4925–63, 4972–84 (Sir Carleton Allen).

G. Subdelegated Legislation

I. THE NATURE OF SUBDELEGATED LEGISLATION

When Acts of Parliament delegate to Ministers (or other authorities) the power to make laws, those laws are normally the final instructions. Sometimes, however, those laws in their turn empower the making of laws. For example, the Emergency Powers (Defence) Act, 1939,[1] authorised Her Majesty in Council to make Defence Regulations. These Regulations frequently empowered Ministers to make Orders. Under these Orders, directions were sometimes issued and licences might result from the directions. It is again necessary to be careful how the word "legislation" is used. It has been noted that a "legislative" act is often distinguished from an "executive" act by calling the former the issuing of instructions which have a general application and by calling the latter the issuing of a specific instruction to an individual. The number of "tiers" of instructions which are issued under an Act depends to a large extent on the degree of generality in the Act itself. As said above, there were sometimes four "tiers" under the Emergency Powers (Defence) Act, 1939. That Act empowered the making of such Regulations as appeared to His Majesty to be necessary or expedient for securing the public safety, the defence of the realm, the maintenance of public order, and the efficient prosecution of any war in which His Majesty might be engaged, and for maintaining supplies and services essential to the life of the community.[2] These words are very wide. Consequently, the Regulations themselves are not specific, though they are less general. One such Regulation[3] (entitled "General control of industry") provides: "(1) A competent authority . . . may by order provide—(a) for regulating or prohibiting the production, treatment, keeping, storage, movement, transport, distribution, disposal, acquisition, use or consumption of articles of any description . . . ; (b) for regulating the carrying on of any undertaking engaged in essential work . . . and an order under this Regulation may prohibit the doing of anything regulated by the order except under the authority of a licence. . . ." Under this Regulation an Order was made prohibiting ship-repairers from carrying on their business

---

[1] See above, p. 41.
[2] Sect. 1 (1).   [3] S.R. & O. 1939 No. 927, Reg. 55.

until they obtained licences permitting them to execute the specified repairs.[1] Now this Order is an instruction limited to a particular business; it is still general in that it applies to all ship-repairers but it is specific in that it applies only to ship-repairers. The licences are issued to individuals. Thus the whole process moves from the wide and general words of the Act to the specific authorisation of the licence. If the generality test is applied to determine the distinction between "legislative" and "executive," the issuing of the licence is an executive act.

2. THE RELEVANCE OF THE DOCTRINE OF "ULTRA VIRES"

An unsolved problem is the extent to which an authority empowered by statute to make subordinate laws can, in those laws, authorise the making of subdelegated legislation where the statute does not expressly empower it to do so. This difficulty did not normally arise when orders were made under Defence Regulations as the Act of 1939 provided: "Defence Regulations may provide for empowering such authorities, persons or classes of persons as may be specified in the Regulations to make orders, rules and byelaws for any of the purposes for which such Regulations are authorised by this Act to be made."[2] Subdelegated legislation made under other Acts which do not contain such provisions seems never to have been challenged on this general ground of validity.

This problem is one aspect of a larger problem, namely, the extent to which the recipient of a statutory power may delegate the exercise of the whole or any part of that power to another. The argument against such delegation is that there is a fundamental rule of law usually expressed by the maxim *delegatus non potest delegare*.[3] Most of the cases have been concerned with executive, not legislative, powers. Thus in *Allingham* v. *Minister of Agriculture and Fisheries*,[4] the Minister delegated to a county war agricultural committee his powers to give directions with respect to the cultivation, management

---

[1] Restriction of Repairs of Ships Order, 1940 (S.R. & O. 1940 No. 142).
[2] Sect. 1 (3); see above, p. 55.
[3] See J. Willis: "Delegatus non potest delegare" in 21 *Canadian Bar Review* (1943) 257, and J. F. Garner: "The Delegation of Administrative Discretion" in 27 *Public Administration* (1949) 115.
[4] [1948] 1 All E.R. 780.

or use of land for agricultural purposes. The committee left the decision to their executive officer. The court held that they could not, being delegates, delegate to another this power of deciding what fields were to be cultivated. This would normally be regarded as the delegation of a power to take executive action;[1] the committee was not required to make general regulations but to issue specific directions to individual farmers and it was this power which they purported to hand down to their officer. On the other hand, in some instances, the Minister, in delegating his executive powers, gives instructions to the delegates prescribing the manner in which they are to exercise their functions and limiting the field of their operations. Such instructions have been held to be legislative in character.[2] Before an attempt can be made to solve this problem, the leading cases must be examined. They fall into two main groups. The first deals with the requisitioning of property and the second with the issuing of licences.

Under Defence Regulation 51,[3] the Minister of Health was empowered to take possession of any land and to give such directions as appeared to him to be necessary or expedient in connection with the taking of possession of that land; he was also empowered to delegate these functions, to such extent and subject to such restrictions as he thought proper. In *Blackpool Corporation* v. *Locker*,[4] the delegation was effected by circulars addressed to certain local authorities, including Blackpool Corporation. These circulars contained certain conditions. One of these conditions was that furniture should not be requisitioned; another was that if the owner within fourteen days of the notice of requisition notified to the local authority his intention of occupying the house as a residence for himself, the local authority must not proceed further in the matter. Blackpool Corporation requisitioned a house with furniture in it and did not desist from attempting to requisition the house after the owner had given the necessary notification. The Court of Appeal held that the requisitioning of the furniture made the whole requisitioning inoperative. Two of the Lords Justices also held that the continued action of the local authority

---

[1] See above, pp. 50–51.
[2] E.g. *Blackpool Corporation* v. *Locker*, [1948] 1 K.B. 349 (see below).
[3] S.R. & O. 1939 No. 927 as amended by Supplies and Services (Transitional Powers) Act, 1945.   [4] See note 2.

after the owner's notification rendered the requisitioning inoperative. Scott, L.J., said—

> The Minister's "circulars" were not mere executive directions but delegated legislation with statutory force, conferring powers on the corporation which they would not otherwise have possessed and imposing on them duties for the reasonable protection of the individual house-owner.[1]

Evershed, L.J., said—

> Were the "conditions" expressed in those circulars, as applicable to the exercise by the plaintiff corporation or its clerk of their powers of requisition, limitations or restrictions on the delegated powers or merely conditions which the Minister imposed, as between himself and his delegates, and by way of instructions to them by him, without limitation upon the delegated powers themselves? The learned county court judge concluded in favour of the former alternative and, in my judgment, he was right so to do.[2]

Undoubtedly, the vast majority of the circulars which are issued from the Ministries to local authorities contain only administrative instructions and advice on Acts and statutory instruments, but, according to this view, some may go further and have legislative force. Evershed, L.J., indicated that he thought the provision relating to the duties of the local authority, on being notified of the owner's intention to occupy the house as his personal residence, to proceed no further in the matter, might be "more akin to a direction or instruction than to a limitation of powers."[3] In *Patchett* v. *Leathem*,[4] however, Streatfeild, J., did not accept this distinction although it does not appear that the point was argued before him. In these cases there was no doubt that the Minister had power to give instructions having legislative effect which limited the powers of the local authorities. Where, however, no such power exists, the result of holding part of a circular to be "legislative" would be to invalidate that part.

The most important of the licensing cases is *Jackson, Stansfield & Sons* v. *Butterworth*.[5] Defence Regulation 56A required a

---

[1] At 367.   [2] At 385.   [3] At 388–9.
[4] (1949), 65 T.L.R. 69. See also *Carltona, Ltd.* v. *Commissioners of Works and Others*, [1943] 2 All E.R. 560; *Carlish* v. *East Ham Corporation, and Edwards*, [1948] 2 K.B. 380; *Lewisham Borough Council* v. *Roberts*, [1949] 2 K.B. 608. And see S. A. de Smith: "Subdelegation and Circulars" in 12 *Modern Law Review* (1949) 37.
[5] [1948] 2 All E.R. 558. Followed in *J. Dennis and Co., Ltd.* v. *Munn*, [1949] 2 K.B. 327.

licence, granted by the Minister of Works, for the carrying out of certain building operations.[1] The power to grant licences for certain work was delegated by the Minister of Works to clerks or other duly appointed officers of local authorities in circulars issued by the Ministry of Health. These circulars, and others issued by the Ministry of Works, contained instructions, which, amongst other things, clearly indicated that the licences should be written and not oral. The question in this case was whether an oral licence satisfied the Defence Regulation. The Court of Appeal (Jenkins, L.J., dissenting) held that it did not. Scott, L.J., was of opinion that the circulars, though in character mainly administrative, were legislative in two respects—(i) in the elaboration of the instructions about licences and (ii) in the effective delegation of power and discretion to the local authorities to perform the function of licensing which the regulation had entrusted to the Minister of Works, and to no other authority. He was further of opinion that neither the Minister of Health nor the Minister of Works had power to legislate as they had purported to do under this Defence Regulation, but he examined both the administrative and the legislative parts of the circulars "to establish the real nature of the process and requirements of licensing, and thereby to demonstrate the mischief to which the regulation by His Majesty in Council was addressed."[2] Jenkins, L.J., was of opinion that the Defence Regulation did not necessarily require a written licence.

An example was given above of subdelegation under the Defence Regulations resulting in the making of the Restriction of Repair of Ships Order, 1940, which required licences to be obtained by ship-repairers. The Admiralty appointed licensing officers and in *Falmouth Boat Construction Co., Ltd.* v. *Howell*,[3] the question arose whether these licences had to be in writing. To avoid delay, the Admiralty in a circular authorised their officers to give oral permission for repairs to be started "pending the actual issue of a licence." Denning, L.J., said that the Order

[1] S.R. & O. 1942 No. 1596. Work done in excess of the licence is illegal. See *Bostel Bros. Ltd.* v. *Hurlock*, [1949] 1 K.B. 74.
[2] Asquith, L.J., expressly excluded from consideration anything outside the four corners of the Defence Regulation but arrived at the same interpretation (at 566).
[3] [1950] 2 K.B. 16.

was not an Act of Parliament and should not be treated as such. Nor was it even a Defence Regulation. . . . It was merely an order made by the Admiralty under the authority of the regulation. . . . It could be made without any formality or publicity and—this is the point—it could be revoked or varied likewise.[1]

The Lord Justice therefore held that, assuming the original Order required a written licence, the Admiralty circular was evidence that that Order had been varied so as to enable oral permission to be given and that the court should assume that this variation had taken place.[2] He was also, on another ground, prepared to hold that the ship repairers had not acted illegally in carrying out the repairs without a written licence assuming that that were required. The Defence Regulation empowered the making of Orders. The other members of the court decided the case in the same way by holding that the Order did not necessitate a written, as distinct from an oral, licence. The *Jackson, Stansfield* case was distinguished by the court principally on the ground that the two operations—building and ship repairing—were dissimilar.

Certain propositions may be deduced from these cases. In the first place, an instruction may be held to be legislative in character although it is not formally issued but is given in a circular or letter or some other way. As Scott, L.J., said in *Blackpool Corporation* v. *Locker*: "it is the substance and not the form, or the name that matters."[3] Secondly, Scott, L.J., in *Jackson, Stansfield & Sons* v. *Butterworth* was of opinion that the legislative instructions issued in that case by the Ministers of Health and of Works were invalid because the Defence Regulation did not authorise the kind of instructions which were made—in particular, because the Regulation did not authorise the Minister of Works to transfer his own functions either to the Minister of Health or to local authorities. Thirdly, where a Minister (or other authority) is given power in a statute or an instrument to exercise executive, as opposed to legislative,

[1] At 542. *Winter* v. *Simms Motor Units, Ltd. sub nom., Simms Motor Units, Ltd.* v. *Minister of Labour and National Service*, [1946] 2 All E.R. 201, conflicts with this dictum. There it was held that where a Defence Regulation empowers a Minister to deal with a matter "by Order" he cannot issue less formal instructions which vary his previous Order; and that an Order means a properly published Order.
[2] The House of Lords in affirming the decision refused to make this assumption, [1951] A.C. 837 at 844, 848–9. Their Lordships held that a written licence was required but that it could be retrospective.
[3] At 368.

powers—as, for example, to requisition property or to issue a licence—and delegates those powers generally, then any instructions which he gives to his delegates *may* be legislative.

Suppose, however, that a Minister is given legislative powers. Is he prevented, in the absence of express authority, from delegating those powers? If he is given judicial powers, must he personally exercise them?[1] It seems clear that if a Minister may delegate his powers, be they legislative, executive or judicial, then he may also give instructions to his delegates and these instructions may be in the nature of legislation.

A Minister is not expected personally to execute all the powers given to him by statute.[2] His departmental officials make most of the decisions. This is as true of judicial and legislative as of executive decisions. Nor is it necessary for a Minister specifically to delegate particular functions to particular officials.[3] Questions concerning the authority given by Ministers to their officials to sign statutory instruments have been asked in the House of Commons[4] where it was observed that, in 1946, 282 officials in eight Ministries were so authorised. The Financial Secretary to the Treasury in his reply pointed out: "The fact that a particular official signs an Order does not, of course, mean that he makes it. The Order is made by the responsible Minister and the signature is merely to authenticate."[5] Nevertheless it does not seem to follow that the Minister may authorise *any* individual to sign documents or take action on his behalf, and it remains difficult to discover any general rules which govern the extent to which a Minister may delegate the exercise of his statutory powers to those who are not in his department.[6] It is the statute which must be

---

[1] In *Barnard* v. *National Dock Labour Board*, [1953] 2 Q.B. 18 at 40, Denning, L.J., said: "While an administrative function can often be delegated, a judicial function rarely can be. No judicial tribunal can delegate its functions unless it is enabled to do so expressly or by necessary implication." See also *Vine* v. *National Dock Labour Board*, [1957] 2 W.L.R. 106.

[2] See Lord Greene, M.R., in *Carltona, Ltd.* v. *Commissioners of Works and Others* (above), at 563; *Woollett* v. *Minister of Agriculture and Fisheries*, [1955] 1 Q.B. 103.

[3] See *Lewisham Borough Council* v. *Roberts* (above).

[4] 423 H.C. Deb. 5s., cols. 993, 1323, 1358, *13–14, 122, 151–2, 162–3, 173, 184, 188, 217, 272, 385;* 424 col. *279;* 458 col. *196.*

[5] 425 H.C. Deb. 5s., cols. 1874–6.

[6] In *Point of Ayr Collieries* v. *Lloyd George*, [1943] 2 All E.R. 546, at 548 Lord Greene, M.R., made clear that the fact that the Minister did not himself sign an Order had no effect on its validity. At the same time, he hinted that certain subordinate laws might require the Minister's own signature. He mentioned Defence Regulation 18B; he seems to have meant detention orders under that Regulation.

looked at. If the Minister is empowered to take a multitude of actions over the whole area of the country, then it is possible that an authority to delegate this power to local officials, whether of the Ministry or of the local government authority, will be implied.[1] If it were otherwise, the exercise of the power might be administratively impossible. It seems to follow that the Minister may issue instructions to such delegates and the courts may hold these instructions to be legislative. If the Minister is empowered to make subordinate legislation, it is suggested that his power to authorise himself or others by such subordinate legislation to make subdelegated legislation depends on the generality of the statute and the extent to which the powers to legislate are there defined. If the statute is so widely phrased that two or more "tiers" of subordinate legislation are necessary to reduce it to specialised rules on which action can be based, then it may be that the courts will imply the power to make the necessary subdelegated legislation. In the absence of authority, it is not possible to be more dogmatic.

H. Duration of Subordinate Legislation

The power to make subordinate laws may be exercised "from time to time as occasion requires."[2] Moreover, where an Act passed after 1889 confers a power to make rules, regulations or byelaws, the power is, unless the contrary intention appears, to be construed as including a power, exercisable in the like manner and subject to the like consent and conditions, if any, to rescind, revoke, amend, or vary the rules, regulations or byelaws.[3] The specific use of these last four words appears to exclude other forms of subordinate legislation but the power to revoke or vary is commonly

---

[1] In the *Jackson, Stansfield* case Scott, L.J., said of the employment by the Minister of clerks of local authorities as his agents: "I concede without hesitation or qualification that it is on the whole the most convenient and the most practical system for the government and the public alike" but he proceeded to question its validity on the ground that the Minister was not entitled to transfer his functions to local authorities. It is submitted, with respect, that, as a matter of statutory interpretation, Parliament should be deemed to have intended "the most convenient and the most practical system for the government and the public alike" to be used.

[2] Interpretation Act, 1889, Sect. 32 (1).

[3] Ibid., Sect. 32 (3).

inserted in statutes.[1] Occasionally, however, subordinate laws are made unalterable.[2]

The period for which subordinate laws are to remain in force is not normally limited and the laws remain valid until revoked. When the enactment under which subordinate laws are made is repealed, the laws, being regarded as provisions of the statute, are repealed also, unless the repealing Act expressly saves them.[3] Occasionally, subordinate laws are limited by the empowering Act in the period of their duration.[4] Subdelegated legislation is presumably revoked by the revocation of its parent provision.

Statutes sometimes require the amendment of subordinate laws which in the opinion of the Minister or some other specified authority have failed to secure specified results.[5] This amendment may be required because of a High Court decision. The Police Pensions Act, 1948, provides that the amending regulations "shall have effect as from the date of the coming into force of the regulations which they amend,"[6] thus not merely reversing but nullifying any decision of the court.

The operation of an Act is frequently postponed until a commencement order is made under the Act. The Interpretation Act, 1889, provides that such an order may be made although, inevitably, there is no operative Act under which it can be made.[7]

I. Constitutional Significance

The *Report of the Committee on Ministers' Powers* summarised the principal arguments of those who criticise the delegation of the power to legislate.[8] The first criticism was that

---

[1] E.g. Town and Country Planning Act, 1947, Sect. 111 (4). Explanatory Memorandum to this Act states that the Interpretation Act makes this subsection necessary.

[2] E.g. War Damage (Public Utility Undertakings, etc.) Act, 1949, Sect. 3 (8).

[3] E.g. Merchant Shipping (Safety Convention) Act, 1949, Sch. 1, para. 1. The express saving may be so worded as to defeat a challenge that the subordinate laws (or their identical predecessors) are *ultra vires;* see *Re Fletcher,* [1956] Ch. 28.

[4] E.g. Agricultural Marketing Act, 1949, Sect. 4 (3); National Insurance Act, 1946, Sect. 77 (4) proviso.

[5] E.g. Commonwealth Telegraphs Act, 1949, Sect. 6 (4).

[6] Sect. 2 (2).

[7] Sect. 37. See *R.* v. *Minister of Town and Country Planning, ex parte Montague Burton, Ltd. and Others,* [1951] 1 K.B. 1.

[8] Cmd. 4060, pp. 53–54.

Acts of Parliament might be passed in skeleton form, containing only the barest general principles and omitting certain matters of great importance. This practice was suggested by some "to have assumed the character of a serious invasion of the sphere of Parliament by the Executive"[1] and to endanger our civic and personal liberties. The second criticism was that there was inadequate scrutiny by Parliament of the rules and regulations made. "There is a danger that the servant may be transformed into the master."[2] The third criticism was that the powers might be so wide as to deprive the citizen of the protection of the courts from harsh or unreasonable action by the Administration. The fourth criticism was that some powers were too loosely defined. The fifth was that full publicity and consultation with those affected was not always practicable and the sixth was that the privileged position of the Crown made the obtaining of redress difficult.

As a complement to these criticisms may be set the safeguards urged by Sir Cecil Carr.[3] His first safeguard was that the power should be given to a trustworthy authority which commanded the national confidence. The second, and this relates to the third and fourth criticisms, was that the limits within which the power is to be exercised ought to be definitely laid down. The third and fourth safeguards, relating to the fifth criticism, required the consultation of affected interests and full publicity of the instruments when made. The fifth safeguard was designed to improve parliamentary scrutiny of the instruments and relates to the second criticism.

Recent developments have to some extent met these criticisms by instituting or improving these safeguards. The House of Commons Select Committee on Statutory Instruments, the provisions of the Statutory Instruments Act, the development of consultation, the absence in recent statutes of the Henry VIII and "conclusive evidence" clauses, and the passing of the Crown Proceedings Act, 1947, have together had a considerable effect. But Acts are still frequently passed in what can be

---

[1] Ibid., 53.   [2] Ibid.
[3] *Delegated Legislation* Ch. IV and *Concerning English Administrative Law* 49–64. See also Sir Carleton Allen: *Law and Orders* (2nd Edn.) especially Chs. I, II; J. A. G. Griffith: "The Constitutional Significance of Delegated Legislation in England" in 48 *Michigan Law Review* (1950) 1079 and "The Place of Parliament in the Legislative Process" in 14 *Modern Law Review* (1951) 279.

regarded as skeleton form and the Administration continues to be invested with wide discretionary powers. These are the two most important criticisms and they continue to be made to-day, twenty-five years after the Committee on Ministers' Powers reported and over thirty years after Sir Cecil Carr first wrote on the necessary safeguards.[1]

When the delegation of the power to legislate is criticised as representing "an invasion of the sphere of Parliament by the Executive" and when the fear is expressed that "the servant may be transformed into the master," it is clear that the question is one which straddles the fields of constitutional theory and political persuasion. It is possible to make much the same speech in the one direction as in the other. Slightly different words may be used but the meaning will be the same. Delegated legislation is a power in the hands of the Administration. Those who think the Administration should use more power are likely to support it as a practice and buttress it with theoretic contentions on the nature of the State, the function of Parliament and the meaning of freedom. Those who think the Administration should use less power are likely to restrict it as much as possible and speak of the evils of centralisation, the sovereignty of Parliament and the meaning of freedom.

Until the end of the seventeenth century the constitutional battle was fought between Parliament and the King as part of a larger campaign. The powers of Parliament were gradually accumulated at the expense of the royal power and this was particularly so in the case of the prerogative powers which the King claimed in the legislative sphere. In the eighteenth and nineteenth centuries the field in which the personal influence of the King could operate became smaller and the power of decision in matters of government passed to the modern form of the Cabinet. The Cabinet becomes a group of the most important Ministers of the Crown, most of whom are members of the House of Commons, and all of whom are, with the other

---

[1] In 1952, a Select Committee of the House of Commons was appointed "to consider in what respects the existing procedures, by which the control of this House over Delegated Legislation is exercised, need to be improved or supplemented and by what means this can best be achieved." The Chairman was Mr. Clement Davies. The Report of the Committee made a few minor recommendations but accepted none of the more drastic reforms suggested to it (H.C. 310 of 1952–3). The Government accepted some of these recommendations (526 H.C. Deb. 5s., cols. *119–20*).

Ministers outside the Cabinet, responsible to Parliament. The Revolution of 1688 did not end the conflict between the King and Parliament, although it gave a substantial victory to Parliament. The ending of the conflict came in two stages. The first stage was when it became established, early in the eighteenth century, that Ministers should be drawn from that party (or combination of parties) which commanded a majority in the House of Commons.[1] The second stage was marked by the withdrawing of the King from party disputes and by his consequent identification with the Government of the day, while retaining his supra-governmental and constitutional functions.

The passing of the power to govern from the King to the King's Ministers and the establishment of the doctrine that the Ministers should not only sit in Parliament but should be Ministers because they collectively command a majority in the House of Commons have resulted in an increase in governmental power which is not offset by the doctrine of ministerial responsibility. At the same time that responsibility is very real. It is easy to deny that Parliament controls the Administration, but to say that the Administration controls Parliament tends to overlook the great influence which Members of Parliament have on the actions of the Administration. The Administration leads its political parliamentary party but must pay close attention to the feelings and opinions of the members of that party. The fact that a back-bencher answers to the Whip does not mean that he is a driven mule. There is a form of majority rule within the party and if a back-bencher records his vote for the Administration feeling very dubious of the wisdom of the decision, it is probably because he has, outside the Chamber, given expression to his opinion, perhaps at a meeting of the parliamentary party, but has found himself in a minority. Further, the criticisms of the Opposition must be faced and an answer found. Modifications may have to be made on matters of detail if not of principle. The Administration is involved in a political struggle in Parliament,

---

[1] The practice originated in the period 1693-6, when William III dismissed his Tory ministers and "confided all the great offices of state to the Whigs, who had a majority in the Commons. The result was that the House which had been turbulent became docile; and the ministers by winning its confidence were able to guide it and to obtain the appropriations that were required." A. L. Lowell: *Governments and Parties in Continental Europe* Vol. 1, p. 3.

though not, in the older sense, in a political struggle with Parliament.

The proper relationship between Parliament and the Administration lies at the back of all debate on the constitutional position of delegated legislation. The doctrines of the separation of powers and of checks and balances and the contention that the ship of State needs to preserve its "stability curve"[1] are used to test the nature and present condition of this relationship. It is argued that delegated legislation gives the Administration too much power by authorising the making of laws without, in many cases, the opportunity for parliamentary scrutiny before they are made. Sometimes the argument is cast in a stronger, if perhaps an extreme, form and the contention is advanced that Parliament is the Legislature and should therefore be the only legislative body. But, to-day, most critics of delegated legislation admit its inevitability and concern themselves with keeping it within the closest practicable bounds.

In a perpetually changing constitution, the question is not: Is this development unconstitutional? It is rather: Is this a development which should be controlled and restricted or is this a development which should be fostered and improved? The answer to that question depends, as has been said, very largely on the social and political outlook of each individual. If an Administration wishes to change part of the structure of society, it must use the device of delegated legislation. Parliament has not the time to examine the full details of every proposal nor can the details of extensive changes be so accurately foreseen that they can be provided for in the principal statutes. Statutory provisions must be adaptable; discretionary powers must be entrusted to the Administration. One answer which is sometimes made is that there should be no more legislation than Parliament can properly consider. To this the reply is made that procedural defects must not be permitted to delay the passing of legislation which the electorate has voted for. This argument can clearly be continued indefinitely.

If it is admitted that some amount of delegated legislation is inevitable, two consequences seem to be particularly desirable. The first is that care should be taken to ensure that Bills contain

[1] Sir Carleton Allen: *Law and Orders* (2nd Edn.) 17.

those matters involving principles of policy and execution which Parliament is particularly fitted to examine, and that matters of detail only should be reserved for subordinate legislation. This distinction is undoubtedly imprecise but it is easy to find examples of Bills loaded with details, often of a technical nature, and of subordinate laws which enunciate principles. The principal difficulty seems to be that Bills are framed by Government departments as blue-prints for future administration and are not primarily designed to facilitate parliamentary examination. It has been argued above that legislation is a function of the Administration and it seems most satisfactory to regard parliamentary examination as a part only, although a most important part, of the whole process of legislation. If this view is accepted then both the contents of a Bill and the way in which it is framed become matters of the utmost importance to Parliament.

The second consequence complements the first. If certain laws are not to be dependent on full parliamentary examination and approval mainly because they contain the details of administration, it is all the more important that they should be considered by those who are likely to be affected by them and who will be able to grasp their significance and assess their practicability and likely effect. It is this which makes the consultation of interests, which is discussed below,[1] an integral part of the legislative process and which makes its wider adoption seem to be desirable. If the democratic method of parliamentary examination is necessarily inadequate to-day, the best solution is to extend the application of that method to the other parts of the legislative process. Whether or not it be true that delegated legislation has "assumed the character of a serious invasion of the sphere of Parliament by the Executive," the answer may be found not in restricting the legislative powers of the Executive, but in applying the principle which lies behind the parliamentary function itself—that the Executive must submit its proposals to the public for examination and criticism—to subordinate laws. In this way it may be possible to make the control of policy primarily a matter of political responsibility and the control of details and techniques primarily the responsibility of the specialist.

[1] Pp. 126–41.

CHAPTER III

THE CONTROL OF THE LEGISLATIVE POWERS OF THE ADMINISTRATION

Parliamentary Control

A. Bills

The procedure by which Parliament deals with Bills is well known. The stages of first and second reading, committee, report, and third reading, and the rules governing the relationship between the two Houses result in two kinds of parliamentary examination. The debate on the second reading gives an opportunity for general criticism and defence of the policy on which the Bill is based, while detailed examination and proposals for amendment take place primarily in committee.

The principal right and duty of Parliament in relation to legislation is to examine, criticise and approve with or without amendment the proposals of the Administration. The rejection of a Government Bill, of course, like the defeat of the Government on a policy motion or the refusal in the last resort to grant supply,[1] entails the conclusion of the Parliament then sitting and a general election. The functions of Parliament in relation to the legislative proposals of the Government do not differ in kind from its functions in relation to the policy proposed by the Government. But the examination of legislative proposals is more detailed. In so far as a Government Bill expresses in concrete form a part of Government policy, this is natural and proper, although it may be noted that a statement of Government policy on, for example, foreign affairs may have as far-reaching effects as any Bill. The average number of days spent in each session on public Bills during the period 1906–13 was 72·6; during the period 1919–29, it was 59·7 and during the period 1929–38 it was 73·9. These figures represent, roughly, 50, 45 and 46 per cent of the total session.[2]

The Government is always short of time and reforms in the

---

[1] As did the Upper House of the Parliament of Victoria in October, 1947.
[2] H.C. 189–1 of 1946 *Appendix to Report*, para. 13.

procedure of the House of Commons are frequently initiated by the Government of the day which, in the words of a Government memorandum of 1946 "must be constantly mindful of their legislative requirements, and proceed with the main object of facilitating the passage through Parliament of legislation which the Government regard as necessary for the well-being of the nation."[1] In 1945 a Select Committee was appointed to report what alterations, if any, in the procedure of the House were desirable for the more efficient dispatch of public business; the Committee was further instructed to report as soon as possible upon any scheme for the acceleration of proceedings on public Bills submitted to them by His Majesty's Government.[2] The scheme submitted was originally drafted by a committee of Ministers of the Coalition Government to meet the special circumstances of the period of transition from war to peace.[3] It dealt in the main with the Committee stage of Bills and proposed first, that substantially all Bills should be referred to standing committees; secondly, that the number of standing committees should be increased, their size if necessary being reduced; thirdly, that the number of hours for the sitting of these committees should be substantially increased. The Select Committee approved these three proposals[4] and Standing Orders have been amended accordingly.[5]

Sir Gilbert Campion[6] suggested to the Select Committee in 1946 a scheme for the reorganisation of the committee and report stages of Bills. This was, briefly, to appoint two large standing committees of seventy-five to a hundred members. The committee stage would be delegated to sub-committees of twenty-five members each, to whom fifteen would be added in respect of each Bill. Each sub-committee would report its Bill not to the House but to its parent committee which would consider the Bill as the House does at the report stage. The standing committee would then report it to the House which could recommit but not amend. The two standing committees might be designated "The Central Government Standing

---

[1] Ibid., para. 3180 (1).
[2] H.C. 9–1 of 1945, Terms of Reference.
[3] Ibid., *Appendix to Report*, paras. 3, 4.
[4] Ibid., Report, paras. 6–15.
[5] 443 H.C. Deb. 5s., cols. 1765–72. See S.O.s 57, 58, 63.
[6] Now Lord Campion (then Clerk of the House of Commons).

Committee" to deal with Bills relating to defence, national finance, law and justice, etc., and "The Trade and Social Services Standing Committee" to deal with Bills falling under the heads suggested by its name.[1] The Select Committee rejected this scheme, the principal ground being that it interfered drastically with the rights of private Members to move amendments to the Bill at the report stage.[2] The Government agreed with the rejection.[3]

Two other well-known proposals for parliamentary reform must be mentioned here. The first is that Members of the House should be allocated to committees which would deal with the work carried out by a department or group of departments. Such a scheme was proposed to a Select Committee in 1931 on behalf of the Independent Labour Party. Each committee would consider all matters appropriate to its department, including supply votes and the committee stages of all Bills falling within the province of the department. It would have the right to question both civil servants and the Minister.[4] If the functions of such committees are not limited to the acquiring of information and, perhaps, to the examination of relevant Bills on the committee stage, but are extended to include the examination and questioning of Ministers and civil servants on current departmental work, they begin to control policy; to do this they require to be able to initiate expenditure and "if they are given control of policy and the initiative in expenditure, they cannot fail to duplicate the functions of ministerial departments and thus produce an undesirable division of government responsibility."[5] The second proposal is that suggested by Sir Winston Churchill before the same Committee that an economic sub-Parliament should be set up of 120 members; forty would be Members of Parliament experienced in economic matters and eighty would be business men, trade union representatives or authorities on economic matters. All Bills relating to trade or

[1] H.C. 189-1 of 1946, *Appendix to Report*, para. 26.
[2] Ibid., *Report*, para. 11 and paras. 3124-55.
[3] 443 H.C. Deb. 5s., col. 1551.
[4] H.C. 161 of 1931, pp. 153-5; similarly, evidence (Appendix No. 6) of Sir Horace Dawkins, then Clerk of the House. Also W. I. Jennings: *Parliamentary Reform* (1934), Chaps. IV, IX.
[5] Sir Gilbert Campion: *Introduction to the Procedure of the House of Commons* (2nd Edn.) 50-51.

industry would normally go to this sub-Parliament after the second reading and other Bills or clauses could be referred to it by resolution of either House. The sub-Parliament itself could initiate inquiries or discussions and report to Parliament.[1] Both these proposals are designed to keep Parliament closely in touch with the actions of the Government and at the same time to delegate some of the functions of the House itself to subordinate bodies so relieving the House of part of its great volume of work.

The Government is often influenced by the speeches of Members during debate and changes its policy in some detail accordingly. Here the influence results indirectly in the altera- tion of the proposal. Where amendments are made to a Bill altering the effect of a particular clause and this amendment is accepted by the Government although not originally sponsored by it, the influence of the House on the proposal is clearly more direct. As with policy, if the criticism of part of the Bill in the House is severe and appears to be representa- tive of the feeling in the country generally and not merely of the views of the Opposition, the Bill may be considerably modified and even withdrawn. The Incitement to Disaffection Bill, 1934, and the Population (Statistics) Bill, 1937, were withdrawn.[2] The Government, in order to facilitate the passage of a Bill, often makes concessions, especially in the committee stage, and Members with particular knowledge are able to make constructive suggestions which the Government is wise to adopt.

Criticism of the Bill in the House of Commons is in effect controlled in its amount by the use of the closure, the kangaroo and the guillotine. The first may, of course, be used on all kinds of motions; if moved (normally by a Government Whip), accepted by the Speaker or Chairman and supported by not less than 100 Members in the majority, discussion on the question is ended. It is not uncommon for the Speaker or Chairman to refuse to accept the motion in order to protect the rights of the minority. He is often consulted before the Government proposes to put the motion and often indicates at this stage that he will not accept it if it is put.[3] Under the

---

[1] H.C. 161 of 1931, p. 351 f.   [2] W. I. Jennings: *Parliament* 230.
[3] H.C. 161 of 1931, para. 997. See S.O.s 29, 30.

kangaroo power, the Speaker on the report stage, the Chairman of Ways and Means in committee of the whole House, and the Chairman of a standing committee have power to select the new clauses or amendments to be proposed. Since this power is provided for by Standing Orders[1] and does not require a motion, it cannot accurately be called a governmental power; its effect, however, is to speed the passage of Bills. Guillotine resolutions, under which discussion on stages of Bills or parts of stages terminates at fixed times, are moved by the Government, although agreed timetables for proceedings on a Bill are often the result of consultation with the Opposition. In 1945, the Speaker, giving evidence before the Select Committee on Procedure, agreed that the effect of all timetables was to put the minority more and more in the hands of the Chairman, but he continued: "At the same time, if you have no sort of timetable, you get the Opposition talking, and nobody else talks in order to get the matter through, while, if you have a guillotine, the Opposition may have an amendment and they can discuss it and it may be answered from the other side, and the debate is more instructive in consequence. I think there is that to be said for a guillotine procedure; it gives a reasonable amount of time."[2] However, guillotines are not popular and their use is condemned by the Opposition of the day, which, being concerned to criticise and delay most of the Government's legislative proposals, is quick to argue that guillotines prevent full discussion and so are contrary to the spirit of the Constitution. In 1945 the Government submitted to the Select Committee on Procedure a plan to make the regular use of the guillotine more acceptable to the House and, in particular, to the Opposition. The details of this plan were that a special guillotine resolution, to be approved by the House, would specify the time to be allowed for each of the stages of a Bill and that a new Emergency Business Committee would subdivide the stages.[3] The Select Committee rejected this proposal and suggested instead that, where the Government wished to prescribe a timetable for a Standing Committee, the guillotine motion should name the date by which the Bill was to be reported and that the detailed allocations of sittings

[1] S.O. 31.   [2] H.C. 9–1 of 1945, para. 23.
[3] Ibid., *Appendix to Report*, paras. 8, 9, 12.

should be the work of a sub-committee of the Standing Committee.[1] The Government accepted this suggestion as an improvement on their own proposal so far as that proposal applied to Standing Committees; the suggestion was approved by the House and is in operation under Standing Orders.[2] This, however, did not apply where the committee stage was taken on the floor of the House, nor did it apply to the report stage of any Bill. For those two purposes the Government asked the Select Committee to reconsider the proposal for a Business Committee ("Emergency" being dropped) and to enable it to function both under guillotine resolution and where the length of time to be devoted to a particular stage had been fixed by voluntary agreement.[3] The Select Committee, however, declined to reopen the question.[4] The Government thereupon moved, successfully, in the House that the Business Committee be set up for these purposes; it consists of the members of the Chairmen's panel and five other Members nominated by the Speaker and thus totals seventeen. Its recommendations have, of course, to be approved by the House.[5]

It is difficult to assess the importance of parliamentary examination of Government Bills. The text of a Bill when first introduced often does not appear superficially to differ greatly from the text of the Act which it becomes. The general appearance, the main proposals and most of the details of the one are much the same as the other. But small changes may be significant and greatly affect administration. It has already been shown that parliamentary examination is only a part of the legislative process. The form of words which Parliament first sees is the result of considerable research, experience and discussion. There is a considerable pressure behind the Bill, pushing it through Parliament where time for its examination is short. The Government is deeply implicated in its provisions and largely committed to the course of action which it proposes. It is not surprising, therefore, that parliamentary amendments are, when viewed against the whole scope of the Bill, generally small. It is not perhaps inaccurate to regard the proceedings in Parliament as the last opportunity

[1] Ibid., *Report*, paras. 16–18.   [2] S.O. 64.
[3] H.C. 189–1 of 1946, para. 3180 (19).   [4] Ibid., *Report*, para. 60.
[5] S.O. 41.

for the opponents of a Bill to extract from the Government
some concessions and for the supporters of the Government
in Parliament to suggest some improvements. The battle for
and against important Government Bills has been joined long
since and decided principally at the preceding general election.
From the Opposition benches, the debates in Parliament are
a rear-guard action during which damage can be inflicted on
the enemy, the line of his advance partially diverted and its
speed somewhat diminished. The Bill in its essentials will go
through because the Government and a majority in the House
of Commons wish it to go through.

B. Prerogative Powers

Any matter of constitutional importance is likely to be raised
by question or discussed in the course of debate in Parliament.
This is no less true when the remedy sought is a new or amended
prerogative Order in Council. The Government, of course,
needs no parliamentary authority to make such an Order in
Council, which is, moreover, not subject to any proceeding
in Parliament for its validity. Parliamentary control is therefore always indirect.

One of the most important prerogative Orders in Council of
recent years was that prescribing a new constitution for Ceylon.
In 1945, after much investigation, including that carried out
by a special Commission,[1] the Government issued a White
Paper[2] containing a statement of policy, which outlined the
provisions of a proposed new constitution. A debate on this
statement was asked for but the request does not seem to have
been very strongly urged.[3] Some six months after the statement an Order in Council was made and its provisions were
explained to the House of Commons by the Secretary of State
for the Colonies in a written answer.[4] Subsequently the Secretary of State was asked if he would amend a clause in the Order
in Council; he refused.[5] This particular chapter in the story
of the movement of Ceylon towards Dominion status closed
with a statement in the King's Speech on the prorogation of

[1] For report see Cmd. 6677.
[2] Cmd. 6690.
[3] 415 H.C. Deb. 5s., cols. 431–3; 417 col. 635.
[4] 422 H.C. Deb. 5s., cols. 281–3.
[5] 425 H.C. Deb. 5s., col. 229; 428 cols. 1379–80.

Parliament recalling that the Order in Council had been made.[1]

The nature of parliamentary control here is clearly similar to that exercised over the administrative powers of the Government. Those powers are likely to be based on statute, whereas the powers we are discussing are based on the prerogative. In neither case is express parliamentary approval required for the exercise of the power but Parliament may indirectly and to some extent control the actions of the Government by question or, where opportunity arises, by general debate.

C. Subordinate Legislation[2]

Parliamentary control over subordinate legislation is exercised in three ways. First, Parliament has an opportunity of examining the power to make such legislation either when it appears in a Bill or on general Motions. Secondly, many subordinate laws are required by parent Acts to be laid before Parliament and, in most cases, made subject to parliamentary procedure. Thirdly, subordinate laws may in other ways be questioned or debated by Parliament.

I. DEBATES ON BILLS AND GENERAL MOTIONS

These occasions provide Members with the opportunity to attack the granting of particular power and to criticise generally the practice of delegating legislative power. The Parliaments of the nineteenth century were not particularly vocal on the question although some debates did take place.[3] During the first thirty years of the present century opposition to the whole practice of delegation grew and culminated in the appointment of the Committee on Ministers' Powers which reported in 1932.[4] Clauses delegating powers were criticised on several occasions, notably those contained in the Local Government Bill which was passed in 1929. Most of the criticisms, although based on particular clauses, developed into general condemnations of the practice. Debates on general Motions have occasionally dealt with delegated legislation—notably in

[1] 428 H.C. Deb. 5s., col. 1403.
[2] See Sir Cecil Carr, Q.C.: "Parliamentary Control of Delegated Legislation" in 1 *Public Law* (1956) 200.
[3] For an account of the attitude of Parliament to delegated legislation from 1832 to 1930 see Chih-Mai Chen: *Parliamentary Opinion of Delegated Legislation* (Columbia University Press, 1933).
[4] Cmd. 4060.

1917,[1] 1929,[2] 1937,[3] and 1943.[4] In the last twenty years, parliamentary attention has shifted from the power to its exercise. Subordinate legislation has been recognised as inevitable and the constitutional question of the general desirability of delegation is less frequently debated. Instead, Parliament has paid more attention to the instruments themselves.

It cannot be said that the immediate effect of debates on Bills and general Motions has been great. But there can be no doubt that the increased interest of Members in the question, especially since 1939, has resulted in greater control being exercised by Parliament.

2. LAYING BEFORE PARLIAMENT

(a) Proceedings in Parliament

Where an Act delegates the power to legislate it usually, but not invariably, requires the subordinate legislation so made to be laid before Parliament.[5] Further, the Act usually subjects that legislation to one of several parliamentary procedures. These statutory provisions may be summarised under the following heads.

(i) *Laid with no Further Directions.* An important example of such a provision is to be found in the Foreign Jurisdiction Act, 1890, which empowers the making of various Orders in Council. The Act provides: "Every Order in Council made in pursuance of this Act shall be laid before both Houses of Parliament forthwith after it is made, if Parliament be then in session, and if not, forthwith after the commencement of the then next session of Parliament."[6] Similarly, Orders in Council made under the Merchant Shipping Act, 1894, are required to be laid before Parliament within one month after they are made.[7] A more recent example is to be found in the Agriculture Act, 1947, which empowers the Minister to make

---

[1] 92 H.C. Deb. 5s., cols. 1363–98.   [2] 226 H.C. Deb. 5s., cols. 2505–17.
[3] 319 H.C. Deb. 5s., cols. 1026–36, where Mr. Dingle Foot, M.P., moved in the words of Dunning's resolution of 1780 "That in the opinion of this House the power of the Executive has grown, is growing and ought to be diminished."
[4] 389 H.C. Deb. 5s., cols. 1593–694.
[5] Not until after the early years of this century did the provision become common: W. M. Graham-Harrison: *Notes on Delegated Legislation* 91.
[6] Sect. 11.   [7] Sect. 738.

schemes for providing goods and services to persons managing or farming agricultural land and which provides: "Any scheme under this section shall be embodied in an order which shall be laid before Parliament forthwith after being made."[1]

In such cases, the subordinate legislation is valid when it is made. Members are not empowered to move its annulment, nor is the Government required to obtain a resolution before it becomes operative.

(ii) *Laid and Made Subject to Annulment within Forty Days*. This is by far the most common provision. The usual form of words in Acts passed before 1948 is: "Any regulations [etc.] made under this Act shall be laid before Parliament immediately after they are made, and if either House, within the period of forty days after the regulations are so laid before it, resolves that the regulations be annulled, the regulations shall thereupon cease to have effect, but without prejudice to the validity of anything previously done thereunder or to the making of new regulations." The period for laying varied considerably in different statutes. The Statutory Instruments Act, 1946, fixed the uniform period of forty days.[2]

Where any Act passed after 1947 provides that any statutory instrument made thereunder shall be subject to annulment by resolution of either House of Parliament, the instrument must be laid before Parliament for forty days, and within that period either House may resolve that an Address be presented to Her Majesty praying that the instrument be annulled. Her Majesty may then by Order in Council revoke the instrument. This revocation, as above, does not affect the validity of anything previously done nor prevent the making of new instruments.[3] As a result of these provisions the usual form of words in Acts passed after 1947 is: "Any power conferred by this Act to make regulations [etc.] shall be exercisable by statutory instrument which shall be subject to annulment in pursuance of a resolution of either House of Parliament."

In reckoning the period of forty days, no account is taken of any time during which Parliament is dissolved or prorogued or during which both Houses are adjourned for more than

[1] Sect. 103 (1).   [2] Sect. 5 (2).
[3] Sect. 5 (1). The revocation of instruments made under Acts passed before 1948 is now also effected by Order in Council pursuant to the resolution of annulment. For discussion see 486 H.C. Deb. 5s., cols. 1037–43.

four days. This procedure is often called the "procedure by negative prayer" or the "negative procedure." Any Member may within the period of forty days move the annulment of any subordinate law which is subject to the procedure. This motion, since it is made in pursuance of a statute, is exempt from the operation of the eleven o'clock rule in the House of Commons and may therefore be taken after the normal close of business for the day.[1] Until recently, this procedure was not often used and seems to have been regarded as of little value. It is true that the chances of the motion succeeding are small since the Government will not hesitate to put on the Whips, while the mover may find difficulty in persuading enough members to stay with him at that late hour.[2] But as an opportunity for drawing attention to probable injustice or for criticising the Government on the way in which it is using its powers, it has considerable value. In the last few years several important debates have taken place on motions for annulment.[3] Moreover, it is not uncommon for Ministers, as a result of views expressed during debate, to agree to withdraw subordinate legislation which is then resubmitted in another form.[4] Finally, these motions complement the work of the Select Committee on Statutory Instruments which is discussed below.

It is very rare for an Act, when requiring subordinate legislation to be laid before Parliament and made subject to this or any other procedure, to provide for the amendment of that legislation by Parliament.[5] The power is usually to accept or reject. One of the purposes of the Statutory Orders (Special Procedure) Act, 1945, was to meet this difficulty.[6]

[1] Under Sessional Orders, such a motion cannot be entered upon after half-past eleven and the Speaker has power to terminate or adjourn debate on such a motion at that time (525 H.C. Deb. 5s, cols. 2168–89).
[2] On one occasion the motion was successful because the Government failed to appoint tellers for the Noes (478 H.C. Deb. 5s., col. 420–25).
[3] See for example, those discussed by C. J. Hughes: "Prayers to Annul Delegated Legislation—House of Commons 1947–8" in 27 *Public Administration* (1949) 111 and Sir Carleton Allen: *Law and Orders* (2nd Edn.) 146–8.
[4] See Memorandum submitted by Ministry of Health to Committee on Ministers' Powers paras. 11–12 and, for modern examples, 449 H.C. Deb. 5s., cols. 2134–46; 551 H.C. Deb. 5s., col. 154.
[5] For examples of amending power see Nurses Registration Act, 1919, Sect. 3 (4); Electricity (Supply) Act, 1919, Sect. 26; Gas Regulation Act, 1920, Sect. 10.
[6] See above, pp. 36–37.

Subordinate legislation subjected to the negative procedure is valid when it is made, and so has effect at the time when it is laid before Parliament. The effect of a failure to lay is discussed below.[1]

(iii) *Laid and Made Subject to Affirmative Resolution.* There are two kinds of provision to be examined under this heading. The first kind[2] provides that the subordinate legislation "shall be of no effect unless it is approved by resolution of each House of Parliament." The second kind provides that the subordinate legislation "shall cease to have effect on the expiration" of a stated period "unless at some time before the expiration of that period it has been approved by resolution of each House of Parliament."

The former is the more common while the latter is used particularly for certain financial orders made by the Treasury (in which case resolution by the House of Commons alone is required). Theoretically, this affirmative procedure is used for more important subordinate legislation but it is impossible to find or, perhaps, to make, any clear distinction. The Select Committee on Statutory Instruments has drawn attention to the need for some distinguishing criterion.[3] We shall see that some subordinate legislation is required to be laid in draft and approved. Taking this provision also into account, seventy of the statutes in force at the end of 1944 required the affirmative resolution for some of the subordinate legislation made under their provisions as did a further fifty-six of those passed between December, 1944, and December, 1950.

The principal differences in practice between the negative and the affirmative procedures are that in the case of the latter the Government must find the time for the resolution and any debate that may ensue; and that a subordinate law made under the first kind of affirmative provision is not operative until approved.[4] The affirmative procedure is also exempt from the operation of the eleven o'clock rule.

(iv) *Laid in Draft and Made Subject to Affirmative Resolution.*

[1] See below, pp. 110–11.
[2] The first example is probably to be found in Military Manoeuvres Act, 1897: W. M. Graham-Harrison: *Notes on Delegated Legislation* 97.
[3] See below, p. 97 and see memorandum by Sir Alan Ellis (First Parliamentary Counsel) submitted to Select Committee on Delegated Legislation (H.C. 310–1 of 1952–3, pp. 31–33).
[4] See *Metcalfe* v. *Cox*, [1895] A.C. 328.

Under the three procedures discussed above, the subordinate legislation is "made" before it is laid. Legally, it exists although it may cease to exist or not come into effect for a period, or at all, according to the provisions of those procedures. Where, however, the legislation is required to be laid in draft it has no legal existence; it has not been "made."

The provision under consideration is framed to make this clear and is generally in these terms: "Before any order [etc.] is made under this section, a draft thereof shall be laid before each House of Parliament, and the order shall not be made until the draft has been approved by resolution of each House." If the subordinate legislation is in the form of an Order in Council, the wording is: "A draft of any Order in Council under this section shall be laid before Parliament, and the draft shall not be submitted to Her Majesty unless each House of Parliament presents an Address to Her Majesty praying that the Order be made."

(v) *Laid in Draft and Made Subject to Annulment within Forty Days.* Provisions to this effect are less common than the last three procedures discussed. By the Statutory Instruments Act, 1946, where such provisions are contained in Acts passed before 1948 but the period is other than forty days, then the Act of 1946 operates to amend the period to one of forty days.[1] By the Act of 1946, where a provision is contained in an Act passed after 1947 requiring the laying of a draft before Parliament and not prohibiting the making of the instrument without the approval of Parliament, then the draft must lie before Parliament for forty days and is subject to annulment within that period.[2] In this latter case, therefore, the words "A draft of any instrument made under this section shall be laid before Parliament" are sufficient to subject the instrument to the negative procedure, without any express provision.[3]

(vi) *Laid before Operative.* The Statutory Instruments Act, 1946, makes an important change in procedure for instruments required to be laid before Parliament after being made. It provides that such instruments are to be laid before Parliament before they come into operation.[4] In exceptional cases where

---

[1] Sect. 6 (2).   [2] Sect. 6 (1).
[3] E.g. Criminal Justice Act, 1948, Sect. 76 (2).
[4] Sect. 4 (1). Sect. 7 (3) of the Act provides: "The provisions of sections four and five of this Act shall not apply to any statutory instrument being an order

it is essential that instruments should come into operation before being laid, notification must be sent forthwith to the Lord Chancellor and the Speaker of the House of Commons explaining the reason.[1] Standing Orders of both Houses require this notification to be communicated to Parliament,[2] and the Select Committee on Statutory Instruments is empowered to draw the attention of the House of Commons to cases where there has been unjustifiable delay in notifying the Speaker.[3] This requirement to notify is to be treated as having been complied with, in a case in which notification forthwith is impossible by reason of a vacancy for the time being in the office of Lord Chancellor or of the Speaker, whether occurring by death, resignation, dissolution of Parliament, or otherwise, if the notification is sent immediately after the vacancy is filled.[4]

One result of this provision was that the notification procedure had to be followed when it was desired to make and operate an instrument at a time when Parliament was not sitting. In order to avoid this consequence, the House of Commons made a Standing Order which provided that an instrument, other than one required by its parent Act to be laid before Parliament for a period before it came into operation (requiring affirmative resolution or required to be laid in draft), delivered to the Votes and Proceedings Office on any day during the existence of a Parliament was deemed to be laid before Parliament.[5] When a similar Standing Order was moved in the House of Lords, objections were made that it was *ultra vires* in that it attempted to modify the meaning of "laid

which is subject to special Parliamentary procedure, or to any other instrument which is required to be laid before Parliament, or before the House of Commons, for any period before it comes into operation." At first sight it would seem that the effect of Sect. 4 (1) is normally to make every instrument one which is required to be laid before Parliament for a period before it comes into operation. This interpretation would mean that Sect. 7 (3), being the later section, would nullify the provisions of Sect. 4 (1). It is clear that Sect. 7 (3) refers to instruments which are subject to special parliamentary procedure or which require an affirmative resolution for their validity or which are required to be laid in draft. Sect. 4 (1) thus applies to instruments subject to the procedures numbered (i) and (ii) in the text and to those instruments under (iii) which cease to have effect if not affirmed.

[1] Sect. 4 (1) proviso.
[2] S.O. 111 (Commons) (formerly S.O. 95); S.O. CVI (Lords).
[3] See 445 H.C. Deb. 5s., col. 1825.
[4] Laying of Documents before Parliament (Interpretation) Act, 1948, Sect. 2.
[5] S.O. 110 (when first made, it was numbered 94). See 443 H.C. Deb. 5s., cols. 1783–4; 445 H.C. Deb. 5s., col. 1825.

before Parliament" in the statutes.[1] As a result, the Laying of Documents before Parliament (Interpretation) Act, 1948, was passed.[2] This Act provides that a reference in an Act or subordinate legislation to the laying of a document before Parliament is to be construed as a reference to the taking, during the existence of a Parliament, of such action as is directed by virtue of any Standing or Sessional Order or other direction or practice of that House to constitute the laying of that document before that House, notwithstanding that the action consists in part or wholly of action capable of being taken otherwise than at a time when that House is sitting.[3] The Houses of Parliament are therefore empowered to lay down what they mean by "laid before Parliament" and any doubt on the validity of the Standing Orders is removed.

The Statutory Instruments Act, 1946, also requires each instrument to bear on its face a statement showing the date on which it came or will come into operation, and a statement either showing the date on which copies were laid before Parliament or indicating that copies are to be laid before Parliament.[4]

(vii) *No Laying Requirement.* The practice of requiring subordinate legislation to be laid before Parliament was occasionally adopted during the nineteenth century.[5] The absence of the requirement is now exceptional but cases continue to occur without, generally, any apparent reason.

Sometimes orders which are particular rather than general in application are not required to be laid—an example can be found in the Exchange Control Act, 1947.[6] On the other hand, under the Furnished Houses (Rent Control) Act, 1946, regulations may be made "generally for carrying into effect the provisions of this Act" and there is no laying requirement.[7]

---

[1] S.O. CV. See 153 H.L. Deb. 5s., cols. 331–52.
[2] For debates, see 454 H.C. Deb., cols. 796–828, and 157 H.L. Deb. 5s., cols. 897–9.
[3] Sect. 1. (The House of Lords approved S.O.s CV and CVI and ruled that they should take effect from date of royal assent to this Act; see 157 H.L. Deb. 5s., cols. 1277–81.)
[4] Sect. 4 (2).
[5] An early example occurs in the Act for the Prevention of Cholera, 1832, Sect. 10. See *Minutes of Evidence given before Committee on Ministers' Powers*, pp. 34–5 (Sir W. Graham-Harrison). And see above, p. 84 note 5.
[6] See Sch. 6 which is headed "Orders not required to be laid before Parliament." Such an express provision is unusual. The absence of a requirement for laying has the same result.   [7] Sect. 8 (*d*).

Wide powers to make Orders in Council, regulations and rules are conferred by the British Nationality Act, 1948, and although they are required to be exercisable by statutory instrument, there is no laying requirement.

Finally, the Civil Aviation Act, 1946, provides an excellent illustration of the various laying provisions. Orders concerning the functions of the three new airways corporations and regulations to deal with consecrated land and burial grounds are subject to parliamentary annulment.[1] The Order in Council constituting the Air Transport Advisory Council must be laid in draft and is subject to annulment.[2] Regulations relating to the compensation of officers must be approved by parliamentary resolution.[3] Orders to stop up or divert highways are subject to the Statutory Orders (Special Procedure) Act, 1945.[4] If the Minister wishes to provide for the creation of easements and other rights in his favour, his order must be preceded by public notice and local inquiry and is subject to challenge in the High Court.[5] Regulations governing the issue, transfer, etc., of corporation stocks, for the establishment and maintenance of pension schemes for employees, for keeping a register of births and deaths and governing the safe-custody and redelivery of property found are not required to be laid before Parliament at all.[6]

(b) Proceedings in Parliamentary Committees

(i) *Special Orders Committee of the House of Lords.* Under a Standing Order of the House of Lords,[7] there is a special provision for subordinate legislation presented to or laid, or laid in draft, before the House where an affirmative resolution is required before the legislation, or any part thereof, becomes effective or before it is made or for its continuance. Such legislation is, with certain exceptions, referred to the Special Orders Committee. If the provisions of the legislation are

---

[1] Sect. 2. This Act has now been repealed and its provisions replaced by Civil Aviation Act, 1949, and Air Corporations Act, 1949.
[2] Sect. 36.   [3] Sect. 42.   [4] Sect. 28.   [5] Sect. 27.
[6] Sects. 8 (3), 20, 43, 45.
[7] S.O. of House of Lords relative to Private Bills, etc. No. 216 (H.L. 31, 133 of 1945–6). For Reports of Select Committees of the House of Lords appointed to examine this question see H.L. 9 of 1924, 119 of 1925, 13 and 117 of 1934. The original S.O. (No. 212) was first made in 1925. For further discussion see W. I. Jennings: *Parliament* 486–90. For a debate relating to the Committee, see 179 H.L. Deb. 5s, cols. 1057–74 (17th December, 1952).

similar to those of a public Bill, the Committee reports whether the House should examine it more fully. If the provisions are similar to those in a private or hybrid Bill, petitions may be presented against it and are referred to the Committee. If petitions are presented, the Committee reports whether there ought to be a further inquiry by a Select Committee.

This Committee was set up in the first place to deal with those Special Orders made under the provisions of the Electricity (Supply) Act, 1919, and the Gas Regulation Act, 1920, which required an affirmative resolution for certain orders and which shortened the provisional order procedure. Under these two Acts, Parliament had power to modify the orders before approving them—a power which has already been noted as unusual. It would seem that where this power is not granted by the parent Act the proceedings of the Committee can only serve to guide the House in its decision whether or not to pass the necessary resolution in its original form or to persuade the Minister to withdraw the subordinate law and replace it by an amended version.

(ii) *The Select Committee on Statutory Instruments.* Statutory instruments can be regarded from two standpoints. First, their likely effect may be looked at, and examination is then directed to their merits to see if their provisions are desirable. Secondly, they may be considered as the formal results of the delegated power, in which case the question is whether they are the type of instrument which the Legislature intended or expected to emerge.

The Select Committee regards the formal or constitutional aspects. The Committee was first appointed in 1944,[1] after a debate in that year,[2] to consider every statutory instrument laid or laid in draft before the House of Commons, upon which proceedings might be taken in either House in pursuance of any Act of Parliament, with a view to determining whether the special attention of the House should be drawn to it on any of the following grounds: that it imposes charges, is not open to challenge in the courts, appears to make unusual or unexpected use of the powers conferred, purports to have retrospective effect where the parent statute confers no such

[1] 401 H.C. Deb. 5s., cols. 310–11. It is a Sessional Committee.
[2] 400 H.C. Deb. 5s., cols. 202–99.

express authority,[1] there appears to have been unjustified delay in publication or in laying before Parliament or in notifying the Speaker in accordance with Sect. 4 (1) of the Statutory Instruments Act, 1946,[2] or that for any special reason its form or purport calls for elucidation. The powers of the Committee include the requiring of written or oral explanation from Government departments and the reporting to the House of this explanation; before drawing the attention of the House to any instrument, the Committee must give departments an opportunity for such explanation. This order of reference gives the Committee no power to inquire into the merits of an instrument. The function of the Committee has been thus described by its Chairman: "If Members of Parliament were all perfect and able to do an inestimable amount of work, they would read all [the statutory instruments] through themselves and, if they desired, they could put down a prayer against any particular one but to save them doing that, this Committee is set up. Our function is to go through them and report to the House for their action if we think there is anything unexpected or any unjustifiable delay or something that calls for elucidation."[3] The Committee as such never makes an official "prayer" in the House, although members of the Committee are free to do so.

The distinction made by the Committee between examination of the merits and policy of an instrument and the decision that an unusual or unexpected use has been made of the power to legislate has been exemplified by Sir Cecil Carr: "The line taken from the beginning has been: if you have a price-fixing order for potatoes . . . and the price goes up 2d. or down 2d., that is policy and merits, but, if you found it went up suddenly by 10s., that was something you might regard as an unusual or unexpected use of the power."[4] This formulation has its difficulties. The decision to increase the price by 10s. clearly indicates a change of policy whereas the variation of a few pence may, for example, be seasonal only. It seems simpler to disregard the question of "policy and merits" and

[1] Added in 1946.
[2] Added in 1948.
[3] *Minutes and Proceedings for Third Report of Select Committee on Procedure* (H.C. 189–1 of 1946) para. 4704 (Sir Charles MacAndrew).
[4] Ibid., para. 4669.

to say that the Committee draws the attention of the House
to the exercise of discretion which seems to pass beyond the
limits within which Parliament intended the power to be
exercised.

From its first sitting until the end of the 1954–5 session the
Committee examined some 8350 instruments, and submitted
to the House an average of fifteen reports each session. It drew
the attention of the House to thirty-five instruments which
appeared to make an unusual or unexpected use of the powers
conferred. Four examples may be given. The first was
one of the type suggested by Sir Cecil Carr in the example
quoted above. Under the Raw Cocoa (Control and Maximum
Prices) (Amendment) Order, 1947,[1] the price of raw cocoa to
manufacturers in this country was raised from 51s. to 119s. per
hundredweight, and the Ministry of Food sent a senior official
to the Committee to explain the reason for the increase. The
second example concerns the Seizure of Food Order, 1948.[2]
This Order provided for the seizure and sale of any article of
food in respect of which an offence against Regulations 55 and
55AB of the Defence (General) Regulations[3] had been or was
believed to have been committed. In addition it authorised
the deduction of expenses incurred by or on behalf of the
Minister whether conviction or acquittal of the accused ensued.
The proceeds of sale, less these expenses and subject to certain
directions which might be made by the courts, were to be
returned to the owner. The Committee particularly requested
to be informed of the statutory provision which authorised the
deduction of expenses. The Ministry of Food sent a memorandum to the Committee.[4] Thirdly, the Knacker's Yard Order,
1948,[5] required the occupier of a knacker's yard to obtain a
licence from the Minister of Food, to keep records and to make
returns. This Order was made, after consultation with local
authorities, under the Defence Regulations and the Supplies

---

[1] S.R. & O. 1947 No. 552.   [2] S.I. 1948 No. 724.
[3] S.R. & O. 1939 No. 927; 1945 No. 1611.
[4] The Parliamentary Secretary to the Ministry of Food gave an undertaking in
the House of Commons that the Order would be amended to provide that no
expenses would be deducted where a conviction was not obtained (449 H.C.
Deb. 5s., col. 2141). The amending Order (S.I. 1948 No. 953) in fact deleted all
reference to expenses. See also 449 H.C. Deb. 5s., cols. 53, 2134–46. Compare
H.C. 170 of 1952–3 (Seventh Report).
[5] S.I. 1948 No. 2353.

and Services (Transitional Powers) Act, 1945, and, since the purpose was to prevent meat being sold as animal food above controlled price or being disposed of illegally for human consumption, the Ministry submitted that it fell clearly within the words of that Act: "to secure a sufficiency of supplies and services essential to the well-being of the community or their equitable distribution or their availability at fair prices."[1] Fourthly, under the Public Health Act, 1936, local authorities may make an annual charge not exceeding 2s. 6d. for each dustbin provided and maintained by them. Local Acts provide similarly. An Order of 1949[2] raised the maximum to 5s. This Order also was made under Defence Regulations. On these last two examples, the Committee said that their purpose in drawing attention to the Orders was that "a possibly permanent amendment of permanent statute law might have been expected to be made by Act of Parliament and not by an order deriving its authority from temporary regulations."[3]

From 1944 to the end of the 1954-5 session the Committee drew the attention of the House to twenty-nine instruments the form or purport of which called for elucidation and to thirty-eight instruments where the publication or laying before Parliament appeared to have been unjustifiably delayed. In 1946 the Committee expressed strongly their disapproval of instruments which purported to have retrospective effect although there was no express statutory authority for this:[4] as a result, the power of drawing the attention of the House to such instruments was added to the terms of reference, and this has been exercised on two occasions. The Committee had discovered one instrument which imposed a charge within the meaning of the first head of reference[5] and none which was made in pursuance of an enactment containing specific provisions excluding it from challenge in the courts (the second head). The total number of instruments, therefore, to which the attention of the House had been drawn by the Committee up to the end of the 1954-5 session was one hundred and five. The total number of instruments registered is, of course, far greater than the number examined. A scrutiny of the instruments registered under the

[1] Sect. 1 (1) (a).   [2] S.I. 1949 No. 120.
[3] H.C. 324 of 1948-9 (Special Report, para. 7).
[4] H.C. 187 of 1945-6 (Second Special Report, para. 3).
[5] H.C. 96 (Third Report) and 105 (Fourth Report) of 1952-3.

numbers 1–200 for 1948 shows that only seventy-one of these were examined by the Committee. Of the remainder, seventy-two were not published by the Stationery Office for sale to the general public; there are broadly four categories in this group: first, local instruments; second, any general instrument certified by the Minister concerned to be a class of documents which is or will be otherwise printed as a series and made available to the persons affected; third, temporary instruments; fourth, instruments the printing and sale of which would be "contrary to the public interest" in the opinion of the Minister concerned. Again, forty-seven of the 200 were not required by the parent Act to be laid before Parliament; these include orders under the Wages Councils Act, 1945, the Requisitioned Land and War Works Act, 1945, the Trading with the Enemy Act, 1939, and eighteen other statutes. A further seven were laid but were not examined because no provision had been made rendering them subject to parliamentary proceedings.

Indirectly and through Special Reports, the Committee has had considerable influence. The Seventh Report of the 1945–6 session Committee drew attention to thirteen instruments the publication or laying before Parliament of which appeared to have been unjustifiably delayed; its Ninth Report listed seven more; the Tenth to Fourteenth totalled another seven; none appeared in the Fifteenth to Twenty-first Reports.[1] In the whole of the 1946–7 session, the attention of the House was drawn to two such instruments;[2] in the 1947–8 session, to one;[3] in the 1948–9 session, to none;[4] in the 1950 session, to one;[5] in the 1950–1 session, to five;[6] and in the four subsequent sessions, to none. The need for consolidation of over-amended instruments has been urged;[7] so has the desirability of descriptive short titles.[8] The issue of explanatory notes was welcomed

---

[1] H.C. 187 of 1945–6.
[2] H.C. 141 of 1946–7 (Second and Sixth Reports).
[3] H.C. 201 of 1947–8 (Eighth Report).
[4] H.C. 324 of 1948–9 (Special Report, para. 2 (i)).
[5] H.C. 178 of 1950 (Third Report).
[6] H.C. 239 of 1950–1 (Special Report, para. 2).
[7] H.C. 187 of 1945–6 (Second Special Report, para. 4); H.C. 141 of 1946–7 (Special Report, para. 4); H.C. 201 of 1947–8 (Special Report, para. 10); H.C. 324 of 1948–9 (Special Report, para. 2 (ii)); H.C. 178 of 1950 (Special Report, para. 2).
[8] H.C. 187 of 1945–6 (Second Special Report, para. 5, and Third Special Report, paras. 11–15); H.C. 201 of 1947–8 (Special Report, para. 9); H.C. 324 of 1948–9 (Special Report, para. 2 (iii)).

by the Committee. It cited the following instrument: "The Laundry (Control) Order, 1942, as amended by the Laundry (Control) (No. 2) Order, 1942, shall have effect as if sub-paragraph (3) of paragraph 2 were omitted and the Laundry (Control) (No. 2) Order, 1942 is hereby revoked." The Committee commented: "To that unilluminating provision the following explanatory note is added: 'The effect of this Order is that a launderer is no longer required to give notice to the Board of Trade if he intends to close down his business either temporarily or permanently.'" The Committee suggested that the explanatory note might have been placed, with advantage, in the forefront of the Order itself.[1] Subdelegation has also been the object of the Committee's attentions,[2] and concern is expressed "over the difficulty of knowing in each case whether the directions, requirements or other details will or will not take the form of statutory instruments and whether they will or will not escape any provision in the parent statute which would cause them to be laid before the House and be subject to annulment on motion,"[3] In 1944 the Committee referred to "the apparent absence of any principle determining the choice between the procedure by affirmative resolution and the procedure for annulment of rules and orders by adverse prayer."[4] In 1947 the Committee again drew attention to the need for "some considered formula,"[5] but the Lord President of the Council answering a question in the House refused to lay down any rules.[6] One additional power must be noted. Under the Statutory Instruments Act, 1946, instruments may, exceptionally, be laid *after* becoming operative. To avoid criticisms similar to those directed against provisional rules under the Rules Publication Act, 1893, the Speaker of the House of Commons must be notified of any such instruments.[7] The Select Committee has been empowered to consider any of these notifications, and, as noted above, to draw the attention of the House to cases of unjustifiable delay in notifying the Speaker.[8]

[1] H.C. 187 of 1945–6 (Third Special Report, paras. 7–10).
[2] Ibid. para. 16.
[3] H.C. 201 of 1947–8 (Special Report, para. 3).
[4] H.C. 113 of 1943–4 (Special Report, para. 4).
[5] H.C. 141 of 1946–7 (Special Report, paras. 5–6).
[6] 443 H.C. Deb. 5s., cols. 1830–1.
[7] Sect. 4 (1).
[8] E.g. see H.C. 324 of 1948–9 (First Report).

The idea of a Select Committee operating in this way was generally opposed as impracticable before it was tried. Sir Arthur Robinson, Secretary to the Ministry of Health in 1931, failed to see how the Committee could avoid going into the question of merits.[1] Sir Ivor Jennings considered that the task would be impossible and that Members could not be found to undertake it.[2] On the other hand, the Donoughmore Committee recommended that a Standing Committee be established in each House with the duty of scrutinising not only the regulations but also every Bill containing proposals for conferring legislative powers on Ministers.[3] Sir Carleton Allen has more recently supported this latter recommendation.[4]

It has sometimes been suggested that there should be a special check on the way in which certain subordinate laws operate. This has to some extent been effected by the requirement that annual reports must be made to Parliament by marketing boards.[5] Sir Gilbert Campion proposed to a Select Committee of the House of Commons that the Statutory Instruments Committee should inquire into the operation of instruments which had been the subject of reasonable complaints. He was not supported. It was not clear how the proposal could be made effective at all, but there was agreement that the Committee was not the proper organ.[6]

To sum up: the amount of work, most of it drudgery, which is done by the Committee with the assistance of the Counsel to the Speaker is considerable. The value and importance of this work are undeniable. The very existence of the Committee must prevent more shortcomings than the Committee detects; unjustifiable delay in publication and laying before Parliament has almost ceased; statutory instruments have become somewhat more intelligible. There was a fear that the Select Committee would be swamped and forced to be less thorough. In the 1946–7 session, 795 instruments were

---

[1] *Evidence given before Committee on Ministers' Powers*, paras. 1935–47.
[2] *Parliament* 491. The idea was, however, welcomed by Dr. W. A. Robson in 3 *Political Quarterly* (1932) 354–5.
[3] Cmd. 4060, pp. 62–4, 67–70.
[4] H.C. 189–1 of 1946, para. 4793 (8)—(20). (*Evidence given before Select Committee on Procedure.*)
[5] Agricultural Marketing Act, 1931, Sect. 10.
[6] H.C. 189–1 of 1946 *Appendix to Report*, para. 30 (2); para. 5719 (42) and (46); paras. 4621 (p. 244), 4676–7, 4681.

examined. In the 1947-8 session the figure was 1189. In the 1948-9 session, it was 1300. As a result of the Statutory Instruments Act, 1946, the effect of which is now beginning to be felt, not only those instruments made but also those confirmed or approved by a Minister and required to be laid before Parliament, come before the Committee. Yet in the three full sessions of 1951-2, 1952-3 and 1953-4 the Committee examined only 930, 680 and 595 instruments respectively. There seems to be no reason to believe that the work of this Committee will prove too onerous.

3. PARLIAMENTARY QUESTION AND DEBATE

In addition to all that has been said above, any Member may put down a motion or ask a question relating to a particular subordinate law and to administrative action based on it. Motions of this kind are not frequent in the House of Commons, because of the difficulty of finding time. Questions are often asked. They vary from requests for information on the numbers of instruments made and revoked and on the authority for the making of instruments to requests for the revoking or replacing of particular instruments and explanations of parts of particular instruments. The Member who asked the question sometimes returns to the matter on the motion for the adjournment. In the House of Lords, a peer can "move for papers" and force a division; or he can ask a question.

Judicial Control

A. Bills

The courts can only control the legislative powers of the Administration after the proposals have been duly promulgated as Acts of Parliament or subordinate legislation. While it is possible for the courts to inquire whether any statutory procedure required for the making of subordinate legislation has been complied with and to declare the legislation invalid on proof of non-compliance, failure to follow the customary procedure in either House during the passage of a Bill does not render the Bill invalid.[1] All that is necessary is that the assent

---

[1] *Anon.* (1488), Jenk. 177; *The Prince's* case (1606), 8 Co. Rep. 13b. It is not clear why changes in parliamentary procedure on Bills need ever be provided for by Act of Parliament. See debates in 1949 on Consolidation of Enactments (Procedure) Bill (especially 464 H.C. Deb. 5s., cols. 1371, 1372, 1378).

of the two Houses and the royal assent should be given. Where, however, there is an informality in the agreement of the two Houses, the position is more doubtful. It has happened that amendments made by one House have, through an oversight, not been agreed to by the other. No such statute has been questioned in the courts, but Parliament has itself rectified the errors by further legislation. Similarly, Parliament has regarded as invalid Acts which have not properly received the royal assent.[1]

Whatever may have been the attitude of the courts in the past, it is clear that to-day no statute can be set aside by the courts on the ground that it is contrary to natural law or is absurd or unreasonable or for any other reason relating to its content, except its express or implied repeal by a later statute.[2] The power of the courts to alter the provisions of an Act, and, it may be, to frustrate the intention of those who made and approved it only exists where, because of some doubt about the meaning of words in an Act, the courts are called on to give their interpretation.

The rules of interpretation cannot be set out here but it has been stated that the duty of the court is to endeavour to ascertain the intention of Parliament. In this endeavour the courts are, however, handicapped by a rule which forbids them to consult relevant authorities such as Government statements, explanatory memoranda, parliamentary debates, and the reports of commissions and similar bodies. However, there is another approach which the courts sometimes adopt which permits judges to remove their blinkers and cast their eyes beyond the written words of the statute they are interpreting. It has been recently restated by Denning, L.J., in these words—

> The English language is not an instrument of mathematical precision. Our literature would be much poorer if it were. This is where the draftsmen of Acts of Parliament have often been unfairly criticised. A judge, believing himself to be fettered by the supposed rule that he must look to the language and nothing else, laments that the draftsmen have not provided for this or that, or have been guilty of some or other ambiguity. It would certainly save the judges trouble if Acts of Parliament were

[1] Sir T. Erskine May: *Parliamentary Practice* (15th Edn.), 575–8.
[2] T. F. T. Plucknett: *Concise History of the Common Law* (4th Edn.), 318–20. For a modern example of this principle, see *Attorney-General* v. *Prince Ernest Augustus of Hanover*, [1957] 2 W.L.R. 1.

drafted with divine prescience and perfect clarity. In the absence of it, when a defect appears a judge cannot simply fold his hands and blame the draftsman. He must set to work on the constructive task of finding the intention of Parliament, and he must do this not only from the language of the statute, but also from a consideration of the social conditions which gave rise to it and of the mischief which it was passed to remedy, and then he must supplement the written word so as to give "force and life"[1] to the intention of the legislature . . . A judge should ask himself the question, how, if the makers of the Act had themselves come across this ruck in the texture of it, they would have straightened it out? He must then do as they would have done. A judge must not alter the material of which the Act is woven, but he can and should iron out the creases.[2]

How better can the mischief be discovered than by referring to the parliamentary and other history of the Act? In an earlier case, Lord Halsbury referred to the Report of a Commission which had sat to inquire into the working of an Act which had been superseded by the Act he was interpreting.[3] This was explained by Lord Wright in these words—

Lord Halsbury refers to the Report, not directly to ascertain the intention of the words used in the Act but because, as he says, "no more accurate source of information as to what was the evil or defect which the Act of Parliament now under construction was intended to remedy could be imagined than the report of that commission."[4]

Professor Willis has observed that "the intent of the Legislature" is "at most only a harmless, if bombastic way of referring to the social policy behind the Act."[5] The following contradictory propositions seem to follow. First, the courts, in ascertaining the intention of Parliament, must not look at the

---

[1] This phrase is taken from *Heydon's* case (1584), 3 Co. Rep. 7a, 7b, where the principle here enunciated was authoritatively advanced.
[2] *Seaford Court Estates, Ltd.* v. *Asher*, [1949] 2 K.B. 481, at 499.
[3] *Eastman Photographic Materials Co.* v. *Comptroller-General of Patents, Designs and Trademarks*, [1898] A.C. 571, at 575.
[4] *Assam Railways and Trading Co., Ltd.* v. *Commissioners of Inland Revenue*, [1935] A.C. 445, at 458–9.
[5] "Statute Interpretation in a Nutshell" in 16 *Canadian Bar Review* (1938) 1, 3. See also on the whole question W. F. Craies: *Statute Law* (4th Edn.), 121 ff.; P. B. Maxwell: *The Interpretation of Statutes* (9th Edn.) 27–30; D. J. Ll. Davies: "The Interpretation of Statutes in the Light of their Policy by the English Courts" in 35 *Columbia Law Review* (1935) 519; J. A. Corry: "Administrative Law and the Interpretation of Statutes" in 1 *University of Toronto Law Journal* (1936) 286; W. Friedmann: "Statute Law and its Interpretation in the Modern State" in 26 *Canadian Bar Review* (1948) 1277.

parliamentary and other history of the Act, but may have regard to the mischief which the Act was designed to remedy. Second, the courts, in ascertaining the nature of this mischief, may look at the parliamentary and other history of the Act. It rather appears as if the Judiciary, having argued itself into a position, is now engaged in arguing itself out of it. The practical result seems to be that counsel will be stopped if they cite parliamentary debates and other similar guides to intention but that judges will often refer to them although their provisions will not be incorporated in the decisions.

It is rare for an enactment to be so drafted that no literal meaning can be extracted from it. But it is frequently said that a judge can only seek the intention of Parliament where there is an ambiguity in the words or in the meaning. It must be remembered, however, that it is the judge who decides whether the ambiguity exists. If he decides there is no ambiguity and that there is a plain literal meaning which he must follow even if the result is absurd or unjust, he is in effect refusing to perform his "constructive task." Judges are frequently reluctant to adopt an approach other than the literal.

An example of this reluctance is to be found in the opinion of Lord Simonds in *Magor and St. Mellons Rural District Council* v. *Newport Corporation*, where he expressly disapproved the view expressed by Denning, L.J., in *Seaford Court Estates Ltd.* v. *Asher*, quoted above. Lord Simonds said—

> "The general proposition that it is the duty of the court to find out the intention of Parliament—and not only of Parliament but of Ministers also—cannot by any means be supported. The duty of the court is to interpret the words that the legislature has used; those words may be ambiguous, but, even if they are, the power and duty of the court to travel outside them on a voyage of discovery are strictly limited."

Lord Simonds said further that the proposition that the court, having discovered the intention of Parliament and of Ministers, must proceed to fill in the gaps could not be supported: "It appears to me," he said, "to be a naked usurpation of the legislative function under the thin guise of interpretation. . . . If a gap is disclosed, the remedy lies in an amending Act."[1]

[1] [1952] A.C. 189 at 191.

A literal interpretation occasionally results in a decision which fails to remedy the defect or evil aimed at by the Administration with parliamentary approval. When the courts by interpretation, in a doubtful case, decide that the provisions of an Act do or do not cover the facts before them, their decision has the force of law within the terms of the doctrine of precedent. They are, inevitably, performing a legislative function. An Act which is a deliberate statement of social policy will normally be vigorously opposed both in Parliament and elsewhere on that ground. Judges who are called on to interpret the Act may find it difficult to exclude altogether from their minds their personal feelings on the social policy involved. There are, moreover, certain presumptions which have been handed down by previous generations which may conflict with this policy. These include presumptions against the taking away of common law rights and the confiscation of property, against barring the subject from the ordinary courts and interfering with his personal liberty.[1] Moreover it has been often asserted that certain types of statute have been viewed with disfavour by the judges; for example, those dealing with workmen's compensation, trade unions, housing, married women, limitations on the powers of the courts to order flogging, and "administrative law" generally. Sir Ivor Jennings has written—

> There is certainly no evidence in England of a deliberate misuse by the courts of their control powers. Indeed, the English judicial tradition of independence and "impartiality" is so strong that such a misuse would not be tolerated. What does appear is that the common law itself is biased against administrative law, and that on occasions judges have, without in any way offending against the law, used that bias in such a way as to impede the administrative machine.[2]

It cannot be said that this bias has been particularly noticeable in recent years, when judges have been faced with an increased amount of "administrative" legislation.

---

[1] See the judgment of the Judicial Committee of the Privy Council (delivered by Lord Radcliffe) in *A.-G. for Canada* v. *Hallett & Carey Ltd.*, [1952] A.C. 427 at 450–1.

[2] "Courts and Administrative Law—The Experience of English Housing Legislation" in 49 *Harvard Law Review* (1936), 426, 434–5. See also *Report of Committee on Ministers' Powers* (Cmd. 4060) Annex V (H. J. Laski); and the articles referred to above, p. 101, note 5.

B. Prerogative Powers

It may be assumed, by analogy with parliamentary legislation, that the procedure in Council which precedes the making
of orders, proclamations and letters patent cannot be disputed
in the courts. By the same analogy, it may be that a defect in
the formality which gives a document the force of law—such
as the signing or the affixing of the Great Seal or the Privy
Council Seal—invalidates that document.

The limits of this prerogative power are not capable of
precise definition but, in the first place, it is clear that Orders
in Council cannot alter statutory provisions or the established
rules of the common law.[1] Secondly, the decision of the House
of Lords in *Attorney-General* v. *De Keyser's Royal Hotel Ltd.*[2]
(which decided that the Crown cannot rely on a prerogative
power to take administrative action when the power has been
impliedly superseded by a regulation made under statutory
authority), seems capable of extension into the legislative
field. This would mean that where a statute, or subordinate
legislation made under statutory authority, empowers the
Administration to legislate specifically on a certain subject,
Her Majesty in Council cannot exercise her prerogative power
to legislate on that subject. Thirdly, once the overseas territory
has been granted a representative Legislature, the prerogative
power disappears while the Legislature exists unless it has been
preserved by the letters patent or other document establishing
the Legislature.[3] In these three cases it would seem that the
courts would be prepared to hold invalid Orders in Council,
proclamations or letters patent.

C. Subordinate Legislation

There are two principal forms of judicial control over
delegated legislation. The first relates to the procedure which
the Administration is required to follow in making subordinate
laws and includes the laying before Parliament of these laws.
The second relates to the subordinate laws themselves. It is,
in the absence of statutory words to the contrary, always possible
to challenge these laws on the ground that the Act under which

---

[1] *Case of Proclamations* (1611), 12 Co. Rep. 74; *The Zamora*, [1916] 2 A.C. 77.
[2] [1920] A.C. 508.
[3] *Campbell* v. *Hall* (1774), Lofft. 655; *Sammut* v. *Strickland*, [1938] A.C. 678.
See E. C. S. Wade and G. G. Phillips: *Constitutional Law* (5th Edn.), 434–5.

they are made does not in fact give the necessary authority. These two forms of control are sometimes referred to as the doctrines of procedural and substantive *ultra vires*, or as defects of procedure and substance.

(a) *Procedural* Ultra Vires

In the first place, as already noted, the Administration may be required by statute to consult with particular bodies, before making subordinate legislation. It may also be required to publish draft proposals and to hear representations or objections. It is probable that a failure to consult, publish or hear[1] will invalidate any document subsequently made.[2] Under the London Traffic Act, 1924,[3] the Minister of Transport was empowered to declare that any street was one in which omnibus traffic might be restricted and to make regulations. Before doing either he was required to refer the matter to an advisory committee, set up under the Act, for their advice and report. In *May* v. *Beattie*[4] it was contended that the advisory committee was improperly constituted. The contention was not accepted but it was not disputed that its acceptance would have been fatal to any order or regulation. In *Thorneloe and Clarkson Ltd.* v. *Board of Trade*[5] a declaration was sought that an order establishing a development council for the clothing industry was *ultra vires* and void. The Act provided that an order should not be made "unless the Board or Minister concerned is satisfied that the establishment of a development council is desired by a substantial number of persons engaged in the industry."[6] The Board or Minister was also required to consult representative organisations; this was done and a draft Order was submitted for consideration to the industry. The plaintiffs contended that the establishment of the council was not desired by the required "substantial number." The Attorney-General for the Board of

---

[1] The "hearing" requirement may give rise to questions of natural justice and subordinate laws, no less than statutes, may acquire a gloss in the process of interpretation. See *R.* v. *Housing Appeal Tribunal*, [1920] 3 K.B. 334.

[2] But any particular provision may be held to be directory only. See below pp. 107–8.

[3] Sects. 1, 7.

[4] [1927] 2 K.B. 353. See also *R.* v. *Minister of Transport, ex parte Skylark Motor Coach Co.* (1931), 47 T.L.R. 325.

[5] [1950] 2 All E.R. 245.

[6] Industrial Organisation and Development Act, 1947, Sect. 1.

Trade argued that it was not open to the court to consider this which, he said, was for the Board of Trade to decide. Sellers, J., held that, in the view which he took of the facts, the court did not have to decide this issue. But he expressly stated that the position might have been different "if it had been established that there was no support whatsoever from the industry for this development council Order."[1]

The legal position of the Minister in relation to the National Insurance Advisory Committee[2] is no doubt similar. If he neglected to submit to that body the preliminary draft of the regulations he proposed to make, those regulations would be invalid. On the other hand where, as is often the case, an Act requires a Minister to consult "such bodies as appear to him to be representative of the interests concerned," proof of failure to consult becomes difficult; when the requirement is to consult "such bodies (if any)"[3] it becomes impossible. Nor is the meaning of "consultation" without difficulty. The courts have considered this meaning in the context of the New Towns Act, 1946, by which the Minister is required to consult local authorities before designating an area as the site of a new town. In *Rollo* v. *Minister of Town and Country Planning*,[4] Bucknill, L.J., said that consultation meant: "on the one side the Minister must supply sufficient information to the local authority to enable them to tender advice, and on the other hand, a sufficient opportunity must be given to the local authority to tender advice."[5]

The difficulty of clearly distinguishing legislative and executive acts has already been remarked.[6] This is particularly so when the powers of local authorities to make schemes and orders are considered. A demolition or compulsory purchase order on a single house may, if generality be the test of legislation, be regarded as executive in character. But a scheme which involves the clearance of a whole area covering, it may

---

[1] At 247. It may be, however, that Sellers, J., meant that, if there was no support whatsoever, the Minister in making an Order would not be acting in good faith.

[2] See below, pp. 133–8.

[3] E.g. Sea Fish Industry Act, 1938, Sect. 2 (5); Cinematograph Films Act, 1938, Sect. 41 (2).

[4] [1947] 2 All E.R. 488; [1948] 1 All E.R. 13.

[5] [1948] 1 All E.R. at 17. See also *Fletcher* v. *Minister of Town and Country Planning*, [1947] 2 All E.R. 496.

[6] See above, pp. 50–51.

be, hundreds of houses and giving, on confirmation, considerable powers to a local authority has many similarities to
an Act of Parliament. So also has an order under the New
Towns Act, 1946, and a development plan under the Town
and Country Planning Act, 1947. In such cases, statutes
normally prescribe a procedure involving publication of the
proposal, followed by an opportunity for objections and the
holding of a public local inquiry. This procedure has given
rise to a considerable amount of litigation, but, although its
relevance here should be noted, it is better treated later.[1]

Failure to follow the procedures outlined above has generally
been regarded as fatal to any exercise of the delegated power
to legislate. The position with regard to those now to be mentioned is not, however, so clear. A distinction has long been
drawn, as a matter of statutory interpretation, between those
provisions which are imperative (or mandatory) and those
which are merely directory. In the case of the latter, failure
to take the prescribed procedure does not invalidate the action.
Difficulties arise where the statute is silent on the effect of
non-compliance. In many cases, it is impossible to foresee
whether the courts will regard a provision as imperative or
directory. If non-compliance defeats the intention of the
statute, then the provision will be regarded as imperative.
Beyond this, it is impossible to generalise. In 1877, Lord
Penzance said—

> I believe, as far as any rule is concerned, you cannot safely go
> farther than that in each case you must look to the subject-
> matter; consider the importance of the provision that has been
> disregarded, and the relation of that provision to the general
> object intended to be secured by the Act; and upon a review of
> the case in that aspect decide whether the matter is what is called
> imperative or only directory.[2]

After a subordinate law has been made, it is often required
to be published and to be laid before Parliament. Are these
requirements imperative so that non-compliance will invalidate
the law?

---

[1] See below, pp. 169–83.
[2] *Howard* v. *Bodington* (1877), 2 P.D. 203, at 211. Also P. B. Maxwell: *Interpretation of Statutes* (10th Edn.) 374 *et seq.* See also *Montreal Street Railway Coy.*
v. *Normandin*, [1917] A.C. 170, at 175.

The rules relating to the day on which subordinate legislation comes into effect are linked to the question of publication.
A statute takes effect from the first moment of the day on which
it is passed, if no other day is expressly named.[1] If a day is
expressly named, it takes effect immediately on the expiration
of the previous day.[2] Some subordinate laws, including nearly
all statutory instruments,[3] indicate the day on which they are
to take effect. Subject to what is said below, they take effect
from the first moment of that day[4] or, if no day is named, they
presumably take effect, by analogy with the rule relating to
statutes, on the expiration of the day preceding that on which
they are made.

Most subordinate laws, including the great majority of
statutory instruments,[5] are required to be published. It has
been stated that the similar provision in the Rules Publication
Act, 1893, was directory.[6] It has been held that an Order
made under the Defence of the Realm Regulations did not
come into effect until it was published; its operation was
therefore suspended and, had the order never been published,
it would presumably never have come into force.[7] Such an
Order, however, was not regarded as caught by the Act of
1893 so that there was, on this view, no statutory provision,
imperative or directory, requiring publication. In another
case, a Secretary of State was empowered to make Orders "of
which notice shall be given in such manner as he may direct."[8]
It was not proved to the satisfaction of the court that he had
given such notice or had directed how the notice should be
published. The order had been published in accordance with
the Act of 1893 some ten months before its contravention.
The court was not, however, prepared to accept this as the
required "notice"; but it decided that the requirement was
"directory only" and that the order came into effect when it
was made.[9] On the other hand, in *Winter* v. *Simms Motor Units*

---

[1] *Tomlinson* v. *Bullock* (1879), 4 Q.B.D. 230.
[2] Interpretation Act, 1889, Sect. 36 (2).
[3] Required by Statutory Instruments Act, 1946, Sect. 4 (2) (a).
[4] Interpretation Act, 1889, Sect. 36 (2).
[5] Statutory Instruments Act, 1946, Sect. 2 (1).
[6] W. M. Graham-Harrison: *Notes on Delegated Legislation* 85.
[7] *Johnson* v. *Sargant and Sons*, [1918] 1 K.B. 101. Bailhache, J., wavered between
"not published" and "not known" as the basis of his decision.
[8] *Jones* v. *Robson*, [1901] 1 K.B. 673.
[9] At 680. See also C. T. Carr: *Concerning English Administrative Law* 129–32. In

Ltd.[1] the power of the Minister to make an Order was said to mean "a Statutory Rule and Order which must be published in the proper way for the information of the public and those who are bound to comply with the Regulations" under which the Order was to be made. The failure of the Minister to follow the procedure for publicity rendered his "instructions" invalid.

It is arguable, however, that, since the proceedings which lead to the making of a subordinate law are not publicised as are those which lead to the making of an Act, a subordinate law is not to be treated as analogous to a statute, and that it only comes into force on its publication.

The Statutory Instruments Act, 1946, provides[2]—

> In any proceedings against any person for an offence consisting of a contravention of any such statutory instrument, it shall be a defence to prove that the instrument had not been issued by His Majesty's Stationery Office at the date of the alleged contravention unless it is proved that at that date reasonable steps had been taken for the purpose of bringing the purport of the instrument to the notice of the public, or of persons likely to be affected by it, or of the person charged.

Presumably an announcement in the national press or, it may be, through the B.B.C. would be sufficient notice. This provision would not, however, protect a person who had entered into a contract between the making and publishing of an instrument which avoided the contract; nor does it cover those subordinate laws which are not statutory instruments.

If the statutory instrument has been issued at the date of the offence, can the person charged with its contravention plead that, through no fault of his own, he was not aware of its provisions? It has been noted that the decision in *Johnson* v. *Sargant and Sons* can be read to suggest that publication does not, in every case, lead to an imputation of knowledge.[3] Moreover the subsection of the Act of 1946 following that just set out reads—

---

a recent Canadian case it was held that an unpublished order has no effect. See *R.* v. *Ross* (1945), 1 W.W.R. 590 and the comment in 24 *Canadian Bar Review* (1946) 149.

[1] [1946] 2 All E.R. 201 *sub. nom. Simms Motor Units, Ltd.* v. *Minister of Labour and National Service.*

[2] Sect. 3 (2). See *Defiant Cycle Co., Ltd.* v. *Newell,* [1953] 1 W.L.R. 826.

[3] See p. 108, note 7.

Save as therein expressly provided, nothing in this section shall affect any enactment or rule of law relating to the time at which any statutory instrument comes into operation.

Whether or not that reading of *Johnson* v. *Sargant and Sons* is preserved by this provision must await judicial decision.

It has been noted that bulky schedules to statutory instruments need not be printed if the Minister or other responsible authority certifies accordingly.[1] In *Reg.* v. *Sheer Metalcraft, Ltd.*[2] those charged with infringement of the Iron and Steel Prices Order, 1951,[3] pleaded that the schedules to the Order had not been printed, that no certificate had been issued and that therefore the instrument was invalid. The Crown submitted that the failure to certify merely put the Crown to proof that the purport of the instrument had been brought to the notice of the public or of those likely to be affected by it or of the person charged, in accordance with Sect. 3(2) of the Act of 1946, just quoted. Streatfeild, J., considered that the "making" and "issue" of an instrument were different actions and that the printing (or, alternatively, the giving of a certificate), the inclusion in a list published by Her Majesty's Stationery Office and the issue were procedural requirements the failure to follow which did not invalidate an instrument.

The effect of non-compliance with the requirement that a subordinate law be laid before Parliament is also uncertain. In *Bailey* v. *Williamson*[4] it was held that rules, which were required to be laid before Parliament and made subject to annulment, were valid before they had been laid. In a later case[5] Channell, J., doubted whether the laying requirement was more than directory.[6]

In the *Sheer Metalcraft* case (above) Streatfeild, J., said—

"In my judgment the making of an instrument is complete when it is first of all made by the Minister concerned *and after it has been laid before Parliament.*"[7]

[1] P. 58.
[2] [1954] 1 Q.B. 586.
[3] S.I. 1951 No. 252.
[4] (1873) L.R. 8 Q.B. 118; the operation of part of the authorising statute was postponed for one month and this may have influenced the court.
[5] *Starey* v. *Graham*, [1899] 1 Q.B. 406, at 412.
[6] In a West Indian case (*Springer* v. *Doorly*) also, the requirement was held to be directory (see 28 *Canadian Bar Review* (1950) 791). In an Australian case it has been held to be imperative (*Bain* v. *Thorne* (1916), 12 Tas. L.R. 57).
[7] [1954] 1 Q.B. 586 at 590 (our italics).

Even if this is correct, the statement does not indicate what would be the effect of a failure to lay. In 1944 it was discovered that a series of regulations made under the Fire Services (Emergency Provisions) Act, 1941, had not been laid before Parliament. An Act was passed indemnifying the Secretary of State who had made the regulations "from and against all consequences whatsoever, if any," incurred by the failure to lay, and providing that the regulations should be deemed to have been duly laid.[1] Doubts were expressed in the course of the debate in the House of Commons,[2] whether the regulations had been invalidated by the failure to lay, for if not there seemed little reason for the Bill. Neither the Home Secretary nor the Attorney-General was prepared to commit himself to an opinion on the legal position in the absence of judicial authority.

It has been mentioned that the Act of 1946 provides that an instrument which is required by its parent Act to be laid before Parliament after being made "shall be so laid before the instrument comes into operation" or, if it is essential that the instrument should come into operation earlier, that the Speaker and the Lord Chancellor must be notified.[3] If the laying requirement in the parent Act is properly considered as directory only, it would seem to follow that the "laying before operative" provision in the Act of 1946 is also directory. This would seem to be equally true of the notification requirement, but, if so, the provision in Sect. 2 of the Laying of Documents before Parliament (Interpretation) Act, 1948, referred to above,[4] is not necessary to preserve the validity of an instrument.

The view that the laying requirement is directory only is less easy to accept when a draft is to be laid. Here the laying precedes the making and even where no affirmative resolution is required, it seems likely that the courts would consider the requirement as imperative. Where the parent Act requires an affirmative resolution, the statutory provision is clearly a condition precedent to the validity or continued validity of any subordinate law.

---

[1] National Fire Service Regulations (Indemnity) Act, 1944, Sect. 1. See also Price Control and other Orders (Indemnity) Act, 1951.
[2] 402 H.C. Deb. 5s., cols. 1207–51.
[3] Sect. 4 (1); see above, pp. 88–89.
[4] P. 89.

(b) *Substantive* Ultra Vires

The doctrine of *ultra vires* depends for the extent of its application on two separate factors. It depends on the generality or otherwise of the empowering provisions and it depends on the attitude which the courts adopt.

It has already been noted that the power to legislate is sometimes very widely phrased. In wartime or times of economic crisis the Administration is given very great powers. The wording of the Emergency Powers (Defence) Act, 1939, is so wide that it is difficult to see how any Defence Regulation could be beyond its scope. Sect. 1 (1) of the Act has been set out above.[1] Subsect. (2) gives certain powers which are, however, "without prejudice to the generality of the powers conferred by the preceding subsection." A judge of the Chancery Division did hold that part of a Defence Regulation was invalid under subsect. (2)[2] but the Court of Appeal in another case[3] disagreed with him and were of opinion that if a Defence Regulation fell within the terms of subsect. (1) then it was valid. The later statutes[4] which extend the validity of Defence Regulations and give other powers are equally widely phrased. In such cases, the doctrine of *ultra vires* scarcely operates at all.

The second factor mentioned also needs further explanation. It is exemplified by the attitude which the courts adopt to byelaws of local authorities on the one hand and to departmental rules, regulations and orders on the other. Dealing with a byelaw made by a county council, Lord Russell, C.J., said in *Kruse* v. *Johnson* that there might be cases when it would be the duty of the court to condemn byelaws as "invalid because unreasonable." He gave examples of the meaning of "unreasonable" in this context—

If, for instance, they were found to be partial and unequal in

---

[1] P. 41.

[2] Bennett, J., in *E. H. Jones (Machine Tools), Ltd.* v. *Farrell and Muirsmith*, [1940] 3 All E.R. 608.

[3] *R.* v. *Comptroller-General of Patents, ex parte Bayer Products, Ltd.*, [1941] 2 K.B. 306; followed in *Progressive Supply Coy, Ltd.* v. *Dalton*, [1943] Ch. 54. See also *T. P. Gilbert and Son, Ltd.* v. *Birkin*, [1941] 2 All E.R. 489; *Toxford and Darsham Farmers Association, Ltd.* v. *Llewellin*, [1946] 2 All E.R. 38.

[4] Supplies and Services (Transitional Powers) Act, 1945; Supplies and Services (Extended Purposes) Act, 1947; Supplies and Services (Defence Purposes) Act, 1951.

their operation as between different classes; if they were manifestly unjust; if they disclosed bad faith; if they involved such oppressive or gratuitous interference with the rights of those subject to them as could find no justification in the minds of reasonable men, the court might well say "Parliament never intended to give authority to make such rules; they are unreasonable and *ultra vires*."[1]

In this case, Lord Russell was concerned to restrain the courts from interfering with byelaws made by local councillors for, as he said, "such representatives may be trusted to understand their own requirements better than judges." On the other hand, in the case of departmental legislation, the courts have been prepared to upset such legislation only when it fails to follow a procedure which the courts regard as imperative or where it is unsupported by express statutory authority.

Attempts have been made to set aside departmental legislation on the ground of repugnancy to fundamental concepts of law. In *Berney* v. *A.-G.*[2] the plaintiff asked for a declaration that, *inter alia*, an Order made under a Defence Regulation was "repugnant to natural justice and to the common law of England." The declaration was not made and Lord Goddard, C.J., said that if the action of the department "has to do with the purposes of the order, then I think that the only thing that a court can do is to say whether what they have done is within the words of the order itself."[3] In an earlier case[4] it was claimed that an Englishman could not, by regulation, be deprived of his right to call himself by any name he pleased. The court replied—

> When the Defence of the Realm Act delegated during war time the power of altering the law to His Majesty in Council, any alteration so made was equivalent to an alteration made by Act of Parliament, and the regulations might therefore take away a person's status and privileges or subject him to statutory obligation.[5]

---

[1] [1898] 2 Q.B. 91, at pp. 99–100. The reference to parliamentary intention and to *ultra vires* makes it appear that the courts are merely interpreting the statute. But in effect the courts decide how far, if at all, they will check for unreasonableness and what is the standard to be applied.
[2] [1947] L.J.R. 983.   [3] At 989.
[4] *Ernest* v. *Commissioner of Metropolitan Police* (1919), 35 T.L.R. 512.
[5] At 513.

On the other hand, as *Chester* v. *Bateson*[1] shows, the courts are reluctant to spell out of an Act a power to make subordinate laws which infringe fundamental rights—in this case the right of access to the courts. It is in this connection, particularly, that the views of the majority of the House of Lords in *Liversidge* v. *Anderson*[2] are remarkable and surprising. In *Institute of Patent Agents* v. *Lockwood*[3] where rules required an annual fee to be paid by those who wished to be placed on a register, it was argued that the department had no express statutory power to "tax" and that therefore the rules were *ultra vires*. The words of the statute were very wide and general but the House of Lords held that the annual fee was authorised by those words.[4]

The attempt to subject departmental legislation to the test of "reasonableness" has been no more successful. In *Sparks* v. *Edward Ash Ltd.*[5] the Court of Appeal had to consider the effect of the Pedestrian Crossing Places (Traffic) Regulations, 1941,[6] made by the Minister of Transport under the Road Traffic Acts, 1930 and 1934. It was contended that the Regulations were invalid in the requirements exacted by them from the drivers of motor vehicles and because they involved the slowing down of all motor traffic to an extent injurious to the commercial community of the country. Scott, L.J., after quoting from Lord Russell's judgment in *Kruse* v. *Johnson*, including the extract set out above, said—

> If it is the duty of the courts to recognise and trust the discretion of local authorities, much more must it be so in the case of a Minister directly responsible to Parliament and entrusted by the constitution with the function of administering the department to which the relevant field of national activity is remitted. Over and above these grounds for trusting to that Minister's constitutional discretion is the further consideration

---

[1] [1920] 1 K.B. 829. In *R.* v. *Local Government Board, ex parte Arlidge*, [1914] 1 K.B. 160 at 175–6 Vaughan Williams, L.J., seems to go farther than this. He said "An Act of Parliament may be so worded as expressly to authorise a procedure inconsistent with the principles of justice recognised by the common law of England. Parliament is omnipotent. Rules, however, made under statutory authority, although express, may, in my opinion, be inoperative because they are *ultra vires*, or inconsistent with the principles on which English law is based." The decision was reversed on appeal; see [1915] A.C. 120.

[2] [1942] A.C. 206.   [3] [1894] A.C. 347.

[4] But see *A.-G.* v. *Wilts United Dairies, Ltd.* (1922), 91 L.J. K.B. 897.

[5] [1943] K.B. 223.

[6] S.R. & O. 1941 No. 397.

that these regulations have to be laid on the table of both Houses . . . and can be annulled in the usual way. For the above reasons, this court has, in my opinion, no power to declare these two regulations invalid for unreasonableness, certainly not on any ground submitted in argument before us.[1]

Finally, in *Taylor* v. *Brighton Borough Council*,[2] the Court of Appeal was asked to declare unreasonable a provision in a town planning scheme requiring the consent of a local authority for the holding of a fun fair on a particular piece of land. In argument, Lord Greene, M.R., asked whether *Kruse* v. *Johnson* had ever been held applicable to departmental regulations. On being answered that there was no such thing as an absolute discretion exercised without regard to the common law, Lord Greene further asked: "The common law does not control Parliament, and if Parliament confers on a Minister a power to make regulations how can the court inquire into those regulations beyond ascertaining whether they are within the power?"[3] In his judgment, he added—

It was said that some restriction ought to be read into the language of the Act prohibiting this particular provision on some principle of what is called reasonableness and that a delegated power such as this must be used reasonably rather on the same principle as the power to make a byelaw. In my judgment, the analogy of the byelaw, even if it could carry the appellant as far as suggested, is quite out of place in the present circumstances. We are dealing with a totally different class of subject-matter and one in which the ultimate arbiter is the Minister himself.[4]

The test of good faith is similar to that of reasonableness. The courts have long exercised the right to declare invalid administrative actions which, while prima facie authorised by statute, are proved to have been taken for ulterior motives.[5]

---

[1] At 229–30. The last phrase suggests that there might be other grounds. If a court held that regulations were "so unreasonable that no reasonable Minister could have made them" the regulations might be invalidated as not being within the powers conferred by the Act—a change of substance masquerading as a change of form only, cf. *Associated Provincial Picture Theatres, Ltd.* v. *Wednesbury Corporation*, [1948] 1 K.B. 223.

[2] [1947] K.B. 736.

[3] At 739.

[4] At 748–9. The Australian courts seem to have reached the same conclusion. See *Jones* v. *Metropolitan Meat Industry Board* (1925), 37 C.L.R. 252 and *Victorian Chamber of Manufacturers* v. *The Commonwealth* (1943), 67 C.L.R. 413.

[5] E.g. *Sydney Municipal Council* v. *Campbell*, [1925] A.C. 338. But see statement by du Parcq, L.J., in *Re a Decision of Walker*, [1944] K.B. 644, at p. 650.

This is not the place to examine this method of control in detail and we know of no cases where regulations or rules have been rejected on this ground. The courts seem, however, to regard this control as extending to the exercise of the delegated power to legislate.[1] In *Point of Ayr Collieries Ltd*. v. *Lloyd-George*[2] the appellant sought to have set aside an Order made under the Defence Regulations whereby the Minister of Fuel and Power took control of their undertaking. The Minister relied on words of the Regulation which gave him authority to make such Orders if it appeared to him necessary. Lord Greene, M.R. (with whom the other members of the Court of Appeal agreed), said that the court could not decide whether the action was necessary; that was for the Minister to decide. Nor need the Minister produce any evidence to show the necessity. At the same time Lord Greene stressed that in this case there was no suggestion of bad faith.

The courts will upset subordinate legislation where it contains provisions not authorised by the Act. Thus in *R*. v. *Minister of Health, ex parte Davis*,[3] an improvement scheme empowered a local authority to sell, lease or otherwise dispose of, as they thought fit, the area which was to be cleared. The Court of Appeal held that the Housing Act, 1925, did not authorise this provision. In another case[4] a byelaw made by the Wheat Commission which purported to exclude the Arbitration Act, 1889, was held *ultra vires*. Equally invalid are instructions, legislative in character and issued in the course of administration of an Act, where the Act gives no authority to legislate on their subject-matter. In this case, as already mentioned, much depends on the classification—legislative or administrative—which the court attaches to the "instructions" which are given.[5]

This refusal of the courts to declare subordinate legislation invalid because it infringes fundamental rights or is unreasonable is the same approach as that adopted when considering an Act of Parliament. In 1848 it was not disputed that

[1] The point was apparently argued and rejected in *Underhill* v. *Ministry of Food*, [1950] 1 All E.R. 591, at 594.

[2] [1943] 2 All E.R. 546.   [3] [1929] 1 K.B. 619.

[4] *R. & W. Paul, Ltd.* v. *The Wheat Commission*, [1937] A.C. 139; although called a byelaw, this legislation is more similar to a departmental regulation than to a byelaw of a local authority.

[5] *Jackson, Stansfield and Sons* v. *Butterworth*, [1948] 2 All E.R. 558.

rules made by Commissioners under statutory authority and approved by the King in Council had the force of an Act of Parliament.[1] In 1875, Lush, J., said that an order made under a power given in a statute was "the same thing" as if the statute enacted what the order directed or forbade.[2] The courts have treated subordinate legislation as part of the empowering Act and have construed the two together. As Lord Alverstone, C.J., said: "Where a statute enables an authority to make regulations, a regulation made under the Act becomes for the purpose of obedience or disobedience a provision of the Act."[3] The status of a *validly made* subordinate law is that of an Act of Parliament.[4] This proposition clearly does not protect a law not made in accordance with prescribed procedures or not within the purposes of the parent Act. Such a law is not "validly made."

The basis of this logical and workable proposition was threatened when in *Institute of Patent Agents* v. *Lockwood*[5] in 1894 the House of Lords first considered the effect of a statutory provision that rules when made were to be "of the same effect as if they were contained in this Act." Lord Herschell, L.C., accepted the proposition stated above and expressed the opinion, which was not necessary to his decision, that the effect of this provision could only be to protect from judicial examination subordinate legislation not validly made. He was supported by Lords Watson and Russell but not by Lord Morris. Lord Herschell was not prepared, it appeared, to regard the words as meaningless or merely declaratory of the proposition stated because he believed that they were "found in legislation only in comparatively recent years."[6] It has been shown[7] that the words (in one form or another) are in fact to be found in the earliest examples of statutes delegating legislative power and continued to be inserted in the statutes of the nineteenth century mainly because draftsmen were over-cautious

---

[1] *Richards* v. *A.-G. of Jamaica* (1848), 6 Moo.P.C. 381 at 398.
[2] *R.* v. *Walker* (1875), L.R. 10 Q.B. 355, at 358.
[3] *Willingale* v. *Norris*, [1909] 1 K.B. 57 at 64.
[4] In *Falmouth Boat Construction Co., Ltd.* v. *Howell*, [1950] 2 K.B. 16 at 24–6, Denning, L.J., expressly treated an Order, made under subdelegated powers and not published, as having a lower status than an Act. See above, p. 66.
[5] [1894] A.C. 347.
[6] At 360–1.
[7] W. M. Graham-Harrison: *Notes on Delegated Legislation* 63–68.

in their desire to protect orders validly made. Much discussion[1] has followed *Lockwood's* case and the Committee on Ministers' Powers[2] thought that *Minister of Health* v. *The King (on the prosecution of Yaffé)*[3] had made clear that Lord Herschell's *dicta* were not to be followed. The words are no longer used by draftsmen but still remain in force in certain statutes. It seems probable that if the point arises before the House of Lords again and forms the central part of the case (which it was not in either *Lockwood's* or *Yaffé's* cases), that court would find itself able to evade the full force of Lord Herschell's interpretation.[4]

Another phrase which has been used in the past provides that confirmation by a Minister of schemes or other subordinate legislation "shall be conclusive evidence that the requirements of this Act have been complied with and that the order has been duly made and is within the powers of this Act." In *Ex parte Ringer*[5] it was held that such a provision made impossible the examination by the courts of the validity of a compulsory purchase order. The modern form of this conclusive evidence clause is a modification. Schemes and orders of different kinds are often only challengeable for a limited period (normally six weeks) after they are made. The High Court may quash the subordinate legislation or any part of it if satisfied that it is not within the powers of the Act or that the interests of the applicant have been substantially prejudiced by a failure to comply with a requirement of the Act. Apart from this procedure, the legislation "shall not be questioned in any legal proceedings whatsoever." It has been suggested[6] that the "substantial prejudice" provision also applies where the legislation is alleged to be "not within the powers of the Act" but it is possible that this view would not be supported. This procedure is applied commonly to schemes, compulsory purchase orders, and development plans,[7] initiated often by

---

[1] See particularly J. Willis: *Parliamentary Powers of English Government Departments*, 62–101; C. K. Allen: *Law and Orders* (2nd Edn.) 295–300; W. M. Graham-Harrison op. cit.   [2] Cmd. 4060, p. 40.   [3] [1931] A.C. 494.

[4] For a discussion of a recent group of cases see C. K. Allen op. cit., Appendix 3, based on *Miller* v. *William Boothman & Sons, Ltd.*, [1944] K.B. 337.

[5] (1909), 25 T.L.R. 718.

[6] Branson, J., in *Re Manchester (Ringway Airport) Compulsory Purchase Order* (1935), 153 L.T. 219.

[7] E.g. Housing Act, 1936, Sch. 2; Acquisition of Land (Authorisation Procedure) Act, 1946, Sch. 1 Pt. IV; New Towns Act, 1946, Sect. 1; Town and Country Planning Act, 1947, Sect. 11.

local authorities and confirmed by a Minister, but not to the more clearly legislative regulations and rules made by Government departments.

In *Smith* v. *East Elloe Rural District Council*,[1] a compulsory purchase order was made on the appellant's land and, after the six weeks' period had elapsed, she brought an action against the local authority which had made the order, its clerk, and the Government Department which had confirmed the order, claiming damages, an injunction and a declaration that the order was made and confirmed wrongfully and in bad faith. The House of Lords unanimously held that the action might proceed against the clerk for damages but, by a majority of three to two, held that the statutory provision that after six weeks' period "a compulsory purchase order shall not be questioned in any legal proceedings whatsoever" ousted the jurisdiction of the Court even where bad faith was alleged. Two of their Lordships were of the surprising opinion that bad faith could not upset an order although the action was properly brought within the six weeks.

It has been suggested at different times that subordinate legislation gains some additional validity by being laid before Parliament. We have already seen that the laying requirement coupled with the annulment procedure was one of the considerations which led Scott, L.J., in *Sparks* v. *Edward Ash Ltd.*[2] to reject the contention that a regulation could be *ultra vires* because unreasonable. In *Ex parte Foreman*[3] the court reserved its opinion whether a rule once laid before Parliament and issued could be impeached on the ground that it was *ultra vires;* in this case the statute provided for laying without further parliamentary proceedings. In *Lockwood's* case Lord Herschell, when dealing with the question whether Parliament could have intended to delegate a power to fix fees, said that the power was—

> committed to a public department, and a public department largely under the control of Parliament itself; and not only so . . . the result is to leave the matter completely in the control of Parliament, because any of the rules made by the Board of Trade may be annulled by either House of Parliament

[1] [1956] A.C. 736.
[2] [1943] K.B. 223 at 230 (see above, p. 114).
[3] (1887), 18 Q.B.D. 393.

within forty days after they are laid on the table, and the laying of them on the table is made compulsory.[1]

The rules were therefore not *ultra vires* because of the nature of the power entrusted to the Board of Trade. In *Yaffé's* case, Viscount Dunedin pointed to the laying requirement in *Lockwood's* case as a distinguishing feature.[2] While the requirement may be of assistance in rejecting the contention of unreasonableness or in showing that Parliament may well have intended extensive powers to be used, the main question is different. If a subordinate law is alleged to be invalid, will the fact that it has been laid before Parliament preclude the courts from passing on its validity? In *Lockwood's* case Lord Morris said of the rules—

> As regards the question of their receiving any further sanction from the fact of their being laid before both Houses of Parliament. That is a matter of precaution; they do not receive any *imprimatur* from having been laid before both Houses of Parliament; it is only that an opportunity is given to somebody or other, if he chooses to take advantage of it, of moving that they be annulled.[3]

The answer to the question seems to be that the courts are not precluded.[4] Even if the strongest example on the other side is taken, the answer is the same. For even an affirmative resolution passed by both Houses of Parliament cannot make valid that which was invalid[5] and a subordinate law otherwise *ultra vires* is not, it is suggested, made valid by such a resolution.[6] It would seem that the same applies to an order made subject to special parliamentary procedure.

---

[1] [1894] A.C. 347, at 357.

[2] [1931] A.C. 494, at 502–3.

[3] [1894] A.C. 347, at 366.

[4] In *Merricks* v. *Heathcoat-Amory and the Minister of Agriculture, Fisheries and Food,* [1955] Ch. 567, the Attorney-General submitted that for the court to interfere was "clearly a breach of the privilege of Parliament and punishable as a contempt" (at 569–70). Upjohn, J., saw "much force in the arguments put forward by the Attorney-General" that the court was precluded but preferred not to express an opinion (at 576). And see *Re Fletcher,* [1956] Ch. 28.

[5] Compare *Bowles* v. *Bank of England,* [1913] 1 Ch. 57; *Stockdale* v. *Hansard* (1839), 9 A. & E. 1.

[6] Under Air Corporations Act, 1949, Sect. 3 (3), the Minister may by order "define" the powers of the airways corporations. This order is subject to annulment. It is suggested that the courts are *at any time* free to hold that the words of the order are wider than the statutory powers of the corporations, that the order does not "define" and is *ultra vires.*

Other Control
A. Types of Control

There are many ways, apart from the parliamentary and the judicial, in which the Administration is influenced and controlled in the exercise of its legislative powers. Public discussion of all kinds in the Press, on the wireless and from public platforms has its effect. The opinions of trade unions, employers' federations and individual persons of particular eminence or power are constantly being brought to bear on those who command the legislative machine. The importance of the pressure exercised by these and many other groups is very great; it influences policy which is crystallised in legislation. But the examination of these influences lies beyond the purposes of this book. One administrative practice has, in some cases, become law by being incorporated in statutes. This practice is the consultation of interests.

B. Consultation of Interests

I. BILLS

Government by consent has always, no doubt, depended to some extent on direct consultation as well as on the more usual indirect consultation through parliamentary representatives. Proposed Bills have long been discussed outside Parliament before introduction.[1] This follows inevitably from the fact that legislative proposals have usually been the subject of discussion amongst the interested groups for a considerable period before the Government is persuaded that reform is necessary or that the cause is one which they ought to adopt as part of their fundamental policy. Further, the Government is not a group of isolated individuals objectively considering the merits and demerits of proposals urged on them by the interested groups. They are members of one political party (save in a coalition) and have themselves actively examined the proposals throughout most of their political careers. Ideas which have reached the stage of being adopted in a Bill are generally well-worn. Varying reforms in the fields of local government, public health, housing, national insurance, town and country planning, and education, for example, have long been advocated and the arguments have moved backwards

[1] Above p. 30.

and forwards between the political parties and the groups who have advocated them. The merits and demerits of the nationalisation of industry have been discussed throughout most of this century, and the first examples of public corporations as a method of government are to be found in the mid-nineteenth century and earlier. When, therefore, a Government department considers the drafting of a Bill, its difficulty is likely to be one of giving proper consideration to the multitude of statements which have been made by the opposing interests, and of putting its policy into practical effect.

An example of this type of evolution is to be found in the history of the discussions which culminated in the National Health Service Act, 1946.[1] After the coming into effect of the National Health Insurance Scheme in 1913, it was felt that the general practitioner service should be supplemented by a consultant service. Discussions were started and, after a break, resumed towards the end of the war of 1914–18, between the National Health Insurance Commissioners and leading members of the medical profession on the general subject of the extension of the services. Shortly after the establishment of the Ministry of Health in 1919,[2] a Consultative Council in Medical and Allied Services was appointed. This Council and a similar body for Scotland made comprehensive Reports in 1920.[3] In the next year came a Report from the Voluntary Hospitals Committee which had been set up by the Minister to examine the financial position of those hospitals.[4] In 1936 the Committee on Scottish Health Services reported[5] and in 1937 the Voluntary Hospitals Commission,[6] set up by the British Hospitals Association, made certain recommendations. Other bodies which contributed included King Edward's Hospital Fund for London, the Contributory Schemes Association and the Nuffield Provincial Hospitals Trust. The British Medical Association published in 1930 and 1938 comprehensive proposals for a general medical service[7] and in 1942

---

[1] For much of what follows see *A National Health Service* (1944) (Cmd. 6502, Appendix B).
[2] Ministry of Health Act, 1919.
[3] Cmd. 693 and 1039.
[4] Cmd. 1206 and 1335.
[5] Cmd. 5204.
[6] Under the chairmanship of Lord Sankey.
[7] *A General Medical Service for the Nation.*

the Medical Planning Commission, organised by the Association, offered further suggestions.[1] A younger professional group known as Medical Planning Research, the Society of Medical Officers of Health, and Political and Economic Planning also made reports. There was also considerable discussion in the national and professional Press. In 1944 the Government published a White Paper[2] which explained that three stages in the evolution of the Government's proposals had been envisaged. It was arranged that the medical profession, the voluntary hospitals and the major local government authorities should, for the first stage, appoint small groups of representatives of their own choice to take part in general preliminary discussions which would enable the Ministers concerned "to get a general impression of the feeling of these representatives on some of the main issues involved and to help them to clear the ground." The second stage was one of "public discussion in Parliament and elsewhere." The White Paper was issued to focus the discussion. The third stage was the one in which the Government settled what exact proposals they would submit in legislative form for the decision of Parliament. On the first stage, the White Paper states—

> Discussions took place with each group on those aspects of a comprehensive service which most affected them. For the purpose of discussion the Ministers offered to each group—in memoranda and orally—a series of suggestions and ideas for them to consider. They made it clear throughout that they welcomed criticism and alternative suggestions and were not at any stage confronting any of the groups with a predetermined scheme. They received suggestions from the groups on many of the subjects involved, and discussion from the outset was on the frankest basis. Inevitably there was divergence of opinion on some of the issues involved, which each group approached from a different background of experience and opinion, but the discussions were useful as a preliminary sounding of the expert view.[3]

The Government at this time was the wartime coalition Government. In 1945 it was succeeded by the Labour Government which brought forward the National Health Service Bill. On the second reading an amendment was put down on the order paper in which the movers said they were

---

[1] Draft Interim Report.
[2] Cmd. 6502.
[3] Ibid., Appendix B.

"unable to agree to a measure containing such far-reaching proposals involving the entire population without any consultation having taken place between the Minister and the organisations and bodies representing those who will be responsible for carrying out its provisions." The Minister of Health, in defending himself against this charge, replied—

> I have met the medical profession, the dental profession, the pharmacists, nurses and mid-wives, voluntary hospitals, local authorities, eye services, medical aid services, herbalists, insurance committees, and various other organisations. I have had twenty conferences. The consultations have been very wide. In addition, my officials have had thirteen conferences, so that altogether there have been thirty-three conferences with the different branches of the profession about the proposals. Can anyone argue that that is not adequate consultation? Of course, the real criticism is that I have not conducted negotiations. . . . If there is one thing that will spell the death of the House of Commons it is for a Minister to negotiate Bills before they are presented to the House. I had no negotiations, because once you negotiate with outside bodies two things happen. They are made aware of the nature of the proposals before the House of Commons itself; and furthermore, the Minister puts himself into an impossible position, because, if he has agreed things with somebody outside he is bound to resist amendments from Members in the House. Otherwise he does not play fair with them. . . . So there has not been negotiation, and there will not be negotiation, in this matter. The House of Commons is supreme, and the House of Commons must assert its supremacy and not allow itself to be dictated to by anybody, no matter how powerful or how strong he may be.[1]

The procedure indicated in the White Paper and the speech just quoted show the lengths to which previous consultation can go and its limits. Governments generally refuse to circulate details of proposed Bills before their introduction in Parliament. But it is clear that the borderline between "discussions" and "negotiations" is difficult to draw. The arguments continued after the Bill became an Act, and, before the scheme of the Act came into effect, the Minister undertook to introduce an amending Bill.[2] In the interchanges preceding this Bill, he seems to have departed to some extent from the speech

---

[1] 422 H.C. Deb. 5s., cols. 60–61 (Mr. Aneurin Bevan).
[2] This became the National Health Service (Amendment) Act 1949.

just quoted. In a letter to the British Medical Association, the Minister agreed to include in the amending Bill, which had not then been put before Parliament or finally drafted: (1) whatever clarification of the position of partnerships might be found necessary in the light of the report of the legal committee then examining the question; (2) a provision to make clear that a whole-time salaried general medical service could not be introduced without an Act of Parliament; (3) a provision for executive councils to have the right to select their own chairmen in the future; (4) a provision to enable the professional member of the tribunal to be one of a panel of available members and not a fixed individual; (5) a provision empowering executive councils, where the local practitioners agreed, to cover the costs of the local medical committee.[1]

The National Health Service Act, 1946, despite a fundamental agreement on the necessity for a comprehensive scheme, was a controversial measure. It involved a professional body which was both strong and proud of its service. A great amount of detailed consultation was, therefore, necessary if the words of the Act were to become a reality in practice. But consultation is not confined to such important matters. One of the characteristics of the twentieth century is the multiplicity of organisations which have sprung up to bind together in single groups those whose interests are one. It is only when those who are affected form a large part of the whole community that there is difficulty in fully consulting them. It cannot be said, for example, that those who might be patients under the health scheme were consulted in the same way as those who might be physicians and surgeons. It is the duty of a popularly elected Government to represent the electorate and its children. For this reason, amongst others, it is desirable that a political party should indicate in broad intelligible outline at the time of the general election what major changes in social policy it proposes to make if it is returned to power. Where, however, a group is organised in its own interest, it will in most cases have the opportunity of making known to the Government its opinion on a proposed Bill; normally, its opinions will be sought; and the group will itself very often be continually

[1] See *The Lancet* (5th June, 1948, p. 880).

pressing successive Governments to bring about the reforms which it considers necessary.[1]

2. PREROGATIVE POWERS

Legislation from Whitehall for overseas territories clearly involves a continuous interchange of opinions between the Government department and those concerned with administration in the territories. This book deals with the powers of the Administration in the United Kingdom and the examination of this practice does not therefore fall within its scope.[2]

3. SUBORDINATE LEGISLATION

Much of what has just been described relates also to subordinate legislation. But the importance of this practice when applied to delegated legislation is obviously much greater, as parliamentary consideration will not automatically follow. When consultation works well and fully, it solves much of the constitutional problem involved in the delegation of legislative power. For to Parliament, a general body, are left those general matters for the examination of which it is both fit and has opportunity, while to the interests affected or their representatives is left the examination of particular, specialised and technical details. The parliamentary function is therefore doubly important, for it is not only to debate principle and policy but also to ensure that no sectional interest is able to exert a disproportionate influence in any particular sphere of legislation. Since, however, the function is performed when the Bill containing the power to legislate is being considered and therefore precedes the exercise of the power, it becomes clear that the central and recurrent problem of delegated legislation is how to determine what is general and therefore should be in the Bill for parliamentary consideration, and what is particular and therefore should be left for governmental regulation.

[1] For a protest that industrial interests had not been fully consulted before the Second Reading debate (on Inventions and Designs (Crown Use) Bill) and the consequent adjournment of the debate, see 184 H.L. Deb. 5s., cols. 788, 798 (1st December, 1953).

[2] For an illuminating article see Sir Ivor Jennings: "The Making of a Dominion Constitution" in 65 *Law Quarterly Review* (1949) 456.

(a) Departmental Practice

The desire of Government departments to issue efficient and workable statutory instruments clearly makes the practice of consultation necessary. As Sir Cecil Carr has said, "It is unthinkable that any important rules would be made about solicitors in England without consulting The Law Society or about doctors without consulting the British Medical Association or about local government without consulting the County Councils Association and the Association of Municipal Corporations."[1] The Ministers of Health and of Transport, the Board of Trade, the Procurator-General and Treasury-Solicitor, the First Parliamentary Counsel and others all gave evidence before the Donoughmore Committee on Ministers' Powers that the practice was widespread, desirable, and inevitable. "No Minister in his senses," said Sir W. Graham-Harrison, "with the fear of Parliament before his eyes would ever think of making regulations without (where practicable) giving the persons who will be affected thereby (or their representatives) an opportunity of saying what they think about the proposal."[2] The memorandum submitted by the Ministry of Health to the Committee was particularly informative. According to that memorandum, some of the bodies consulted in connection with local government regulations were the County Councils Association, the Association of Municipal Corporations, the Urban and Rural District Councils Associations, the National Association of Local Government Officers, and the Association of Poor Law Officers; those consulted in connection with Public Health, Housing, and Town Planning include the Royal Sanitary Institute, the Royal Institution of Chartered Surveyors, the Royal Institute of British Architects, the Town and Country Planning Association, and the Town Planning Institute.[3] When regulations were proposed changing the law concerning the use of preservatives in food, notice of the publication of the draft was sent to over sixty associations and individuals including the Food Manufacturers Federation, the London Chamber of Commerce, the Royal

---

[1] *Concerning English Administrative Law* 54. Consultation between Government departments is normal practice; occasionally statutes require a department to consult the Treasury.

[2] *Minutes of Evidence given before Committee on Ministers' Powers*, pp. 35-36 (4).

[3] Ibid., 120 (3).

Sanitary Institute, the Society of Medical Officers of Health, the British Medical Association, the Association of Municipal Corporations, the County Councils Association, and the Manufacturing Confectioners Alliance; many deputations were sent from these and other bodies and their proposals resulted in a large number of alterations being made.[1] This and many other examples that might be cited show quite conclusively that, in the words of Earl Russell, "Government departments do not sit down in a closed room and evolve these regulations out of their own heads . . . they do their best to adapt them to the circumstances for which they are intended."[2]

A recent example concerns the development charge regulations under the Town and Country Planning Act, 1947. On the motion to approve these regulations, the Minister told the House of Commons that he had consulted forty-two organisations including local authorities, the Town Planning Institute, the Royal Institute of British Architects, the Chartered Auctioneers and Estate Agents Institute, the Land Agents Society, the Incorporated Association of Architects and Surveyors, the Valuers Institution, The Law Society, the Association of British Chambers of Commerce, and the Royal Institution of Chartered Surveyors. These bodies were not shown the regulations but were asked to comment on the principle of a 100 per cent charge.[3]

In addition, the great increase in the number of advisory bodies to Ministers brings affected interests into close touch with the departments. There are certain advisory bodies whose purposes are expressed by the originating statute to be the consideration of draft regulations. But, apart from these, a very large number of bodies have a general advisory function, and their influence on policy and administration does, in practice, affect the type and content of subordinate legislation. Between 1919 and 1939 the Minister of Health appointed twenty advisory committees, two joint committees, five consultative councils, and forty-nine departmental committees. During the same period, the Minister of Labour, for unemployment problems and conditions of work, appointed

[1] Ibid., 122 (7).   [2] Ibid., para. 3309.
[3] 451 H.C. Deb. 5s., cols. 297–8.

twenty-seven temporary or *ad hoc* committees and fifteen permanent or standing committees.[1] These bodies create problems of their own; when they are strong and united on a particular matter, they naturally expect their advice to be accepted, whereas the Minister may decide otherwise. Also, the fact that an advisory committee must be a fairly small body often means that its members are representatives of representative bodies so that consultation with those affected is only obtained at one or two removes. Again, to be of value, the committee must reflect all the major bodies of opinion on the subject and these tend to cancel out one another and discussions are "influenced," as it has been gently put, "by what may be called economic considerations rather than pure considerations of merit."[2]

This departmental practice has become more and more common during the course of this century. To-day, if a Minister makes a regulation which affects some interested group which has not been consulted, that group will often protest vigorously.[3]

(b) Statutory Requirement

It has been argued that the departmental practice should be made obligatory by statute in all cases. The Rules Publication Act, 1893, required the publication of proposed rules at least forty days before they were made and required the rule-making authority to consider any representations made by any public body.[4] Certain departments were excluded by the Act from its operation and a great number of subsequent statutes excluded their regulations. The Statutory Instruments Act, 1946, in repealing the Rules Publication Act, 1893, did not make any provision for this type of ante-natal publicity. This omission was defended by the Lord Chancellor on the ground that the development of the departmental practice

---

[1] See R. V. Vernon and N. Mansergh (ed.): *Advisory Bodies* 462–71, 474–5.

[2] *Minutes of Evidence given before Committee on Ministers' Powers*, para. 3444 (Sir Charles Hipwood).

[3] In March, 1951, when motions to annul S.I.s were keeping the House of Commons in session throughout several nights, the President of the Board of Trade suspended price talks with trade organisations. The Leader of the Opposition spoke of this as a threat "to subject to great hardships large and important sections of manufacturers and others in the country, by denying them their rights and treating them severely" (485 H.C. Deb. 5s., col. 2330).

[4] Sect. 1.

made the provision both inadequate and superfluous. He said, "We no longer promulgate the regulations or rules in the *Gazette* and wait for representations to be made. We go to the trade or interest concerned and deal with it by getting them round the table, hearing what they have to say, and then drafting the rules after obtaining their views."[1] At the same time, the general requirement of the Rules Publication Act, 1893, has for a long time been paralleled by specific requirements in particular Acts. These requirements have been most fully developed in the National Insurance Act, 1946, under which the Minister has to submit his regulations to a statutory advisory committee for their consideration, and in such Acts as the Dock Workers (Regulation of Employment) Act, 1946, where the legislation may be proposed by those individuals whom it will affect. An account of the ordinary types of statutory requirement must, however, precede the extraordinary. The ordinary types are two. The first requires that individuals affected by the proposed instrument shall have an opportunity of stating their case to the rule-making authority. The second requires the Minister to consult specified interests including statutory advisory bodies.

(i) *Individual Objection.* This type of statutory requirement is well exemplified by the Factory Acts. The Act of 1833 to regulate the Labour of Children and Young Persons in the Mills and Factories of the United Kingdom, empowered inspectors to make "all such Rules, Regulations and Orders as may be necessary for the due Execution of this Act. . . . Provided, nevertheless, that any such Orders may be altered and disallowed by one of His Majesty's Principal Secretaries of State, on complaint made to him by memorial from any party interested."[2] Again, under the Factory and Workshop Act, 1891, the Chief Inspector was authorised, after the Secretary of State had certified the necessity, to propose special rules in particular cases to the factory occupier, who could object within twenty-one days. If the occupier objected and the Secretary of State did not meet his objection, "the matter in difference between the Secretary of State and the

---

[1] 139 H.L. Deb. 5s., col. 330. The American Administrative Procedure Act, 1946, on the other hand, favours formal procedures and requirements.
[2] Sects. 18–19.

occupier" was referred to arbitration. The two arbitrators and the umpire were empowered to examine witnesses on oath and to consult counsel and any engineer or scientific person.[1] The Act of 1895 provided that in such cases the arbitrators or umpire could on the application of workmen employed in the factory, appoint a person to represent the workmen on the same footing as the other parties.[2] The constitutional interest of this procedure needs no stressing. Had it been developed, this idea of requiring a Minister, represented by an official, to submit to arbitration on an equal footing with an individual having an interest might well have altered the whole aspect of delegated legislation. Whether it would have remained possible to conduct administration on these lines may be doubted. At all events, the procedure did not survive. The consolidating Act of 1901 empowered the Secretary of State to make regulations for dangerous trades. If objections were made to his proposals a public inquiry was held.[3] The Factories Act, 1937, has similar provisions for the making of "special regulations."[4] A modern example of this type of statutory requirement can be found in the Radioactive Substances Act, 1948, which provides for publication of the proposal to make regulations, and opportunity for objections followed by either public inquiry or a personal hearing.[5] This type of procedure is of course common for provisional orders, special orders and special procedure orders.

(ii) *Consultation with Specified Interests.* The Minister is here required to consult certain specified interests before he makes the instrument. These interests are, normally, either statutory advisory bodies or representatives of those likely to be affected or local authorities. The London and Home Counties Traffic Advisory Committee set up by the London Passenger Transport Act, 1933,[6] following an earlier model, and the Merchant Shipping Advisory Committee set up under the Act of 1906[7] are well-known examples.[8]

---

[1] Sects. 8–12, Sched. 1.   [2] Factory and Workshop Act, 1895, Sect. 12.
[3] Factory and Workshop Act, 1901, Sects. 80–86.   [4] Sect. 129, Sched. 2.
[5] Sect. 9.   [6] Sects. 57–66, Sched. 12.
[7] Merchant Shipping Act, 1906, Sect. 79.
[8] Other Acts requiring consultation with similar bodies for this purpose include Importation of Plumage (Prohibition) Act, 1921; Therapeutic Substances Act, 1925; Fertilisers and Feeding Stuffs Act, 1926; Agricultural Development Act,

Before making a development council order under the Industrial Organisation and Development Act, 1947, the department concerned is required to consult any organisation appearing to be representative of substantial numbers of employers and workers in the industry. The Agriculture Act, 1947, requires the Minister to consult bodies representative of the interests of landlords and tenants before making certain regulations and orders. Ministers are frequently required to consult local authorities before making statutory instruments.[1]

The following may be called the extraordinary types of consultation.

(iii) *Preparation by Affected Interests.* Here the power to draft the instrument is delegated to the individual or group and the Minister becomes a confirming or approving authority. Local authorities, of course, have long exercised this power, but in this case the relationship of the local to the central authority is special and not to be compared with that of the individual to the Administration.

Marketing schemes under the Agricultural Marketing Acts, 1931 to 1949, are made by persons substantially representing the producers of a product in an area with elaborate procedures for public inquiries and polls. Redundancy and price schemes under the Cotton Industry (Reorganisation) Act, 1939, followed a similar procedure. In these two cases an advisory committee examined the scheme and its report was laid before Parliament. Under the Hill Farming Act, 1946, a land improvement scheme may be submitted to the Minister by any person having an interest in the land or desiring to acquire an interest or by two or more such persons, and the Minister may approve the scheme and make grants.

The Dock Workers (Regulation of Employment) Act, 1946,

1939; Goods and Services (Price Control) Act, 1941; Licensing Planning (Temporary Provisions) Act, 1945; Coal Industry Nationalisation Act, 1946; National Insurance (Industrial Injuries) Act, 1946; Fire Services Act, 1947; Agriculture Act, 1947; Radioactive Substances Act, 1948; Cinematograph Films Act, 1948; Police Pensions Act, 1948; White Fish and Herring Industries Act, 1948; Gas Act, 1948; Agricultural Holdings Act, 1948; Forestry Act, 1951; and note the procedure in Monopolies and Restrictive Practices (Inquiry and Control) Act, 1948, as amended by the Monopolies and Restrictive Practices Commission Act, 1953.

[1] E.g. Distribution of Industry Act, 1945; Housing (Financial and Miscellaneous Provisions) Act, 1946; Fire Services Act, 1947; Probation Officers (Superannuation) Act, 1947.

provides that schemes "for ensuring greater regularity of employment for dockworkers and for securing that an adequate number of dockworkers is available for the efficient performance of their work" may be prepared jointly by bodies representative of dockworkers and employers. If the Minister is satisfied with the scheme, he prepares a draft order embodying the scheme and publishes it. Instead, he may remit the scheme with his comments for re-consideration. If no objections are made to the published draft, the Minister may approve the scheme with minor modifications. If objections are made, the Minister "shall cause inquiries to be made" and may, after considering "the result of the inquiries," make the order with modifications. If no scheme is so prepared by the representative bodies, and it appears to the Minister unlikely that it will be prepared within a reasonable time, he is empowered to prepare a scheme.[1]

(iv) *Approval by Statutory Body*. Under a few recent statutes regulations have to be submitted to a statutory body by the Minister and the report of that body has to be laid before Parliament. The effect is that the Minister must either accept the report with its proposed amendments or be prepared to defend his refusal to do so in Parliament. It is right that the last word should rest with the Minister; but he will be a very foolish Minister who repeatedly insists on having it by refusing to accept the advice of a statutory body specially charged with advising him. Three examples of this type of consultation are to be found in the Control of Employment Act, 1939,[2] the Requisitioned Land and War Works Act, 1945, and the National Insurance Act, 1946.[3] This last Act merits further consideration.

The affected interest under the National Insurance Act is the whole nation. The number of categories is too large for representation on any committee. At random, one can think of housewives, charwomen, students, orphans, lawyers, doctors, fishermen, airmen, public officers, schoolteachers, nurses, professional sportsmen, and commercial travellers, all of whom

---

[1] E.g. S.R. & O. 1947 No. 1189.

[2] For example of Report of the Committee under this Act see H.C. 107 of 1939–40.

[3] Sect. 77, Sched. 5. The National Insurance Act, 1911 (Sects. 103, 113, Sched. 9), provided for individual objection to certain orders, adopting the procedure in Factory and Workshop Act, 1901 (see above). And see *R. v. Hudson*, [1915] 1 K.B. 838.

clearly present different problems of administration. The Act establishes the National Insurance Advisory Committee. Apart from the chairman, the authorised number of the Committee is not less than four nor more than eight, including at least one woman; one of the members is to be appointed after consultation with organisations representative of employers, another after consulting workers' organisations, a third after consulting friendly societies, and a fourth after consulting the appropriate Northern Ireland authority. The four other members are: a vice-chairman of an Executive Council (under the National Health Service Acts) in Scotland; a professor of social administration; a woman J.P. with Welsh connections; and the Warden of a University Hall of Residence for Women. The chairman is Sir Will Spens. Members are appointed by the Minister, normally for five years. No member of the House of Commons may sit and the Minister has power to dismiss any member for unfitness or incapacity.

The functions of the Committee are to give advice and assistance to the Minister in connection with his duties under the Act, and in particular to consider and advise him on any special matters which he refers to them.[1] Before making any regulation under the Act, the Minister must submit a preliminary draft to the Committee, save in certain cases. The Committee must publish notice of the fact that a draft has been received, state where copies may be obtained and explain how and when objections may be made. The objections must be written and specify the particular alterations asked for. The Committee also hears oral evidence at its discretion. The Committee examines the draft and the objections, and reports to the Minister who, having considered the report, makes the regulation or draft regulation; this is laid before Parliament together with the Committee's report and a statement by the Minister showing amendments made by him since the Committee's report, the effect of the Committee's recommendations and the reasons for not adopting any particular recommendation. In cases of urgency or for any other special reason, the Minister may make the regulations before receiving the Committee's report but such provisional regulations are only valid for three months after he has received the report.

[1] Sect. 41.

During the first six parliamentary sessions of its existence (1947–8 to 1954–5), the Committee examined seventy-eight sets of regulations and reported on eleven special questions submitted to them by the Minister. The first of these questions was whether share fishermen should be treated as employed or self-employed persons for the purposes of the Act.[1] The Committee received written representations and also heard oral evidence. The manner in which the Committee dealt with this matter indicates the thoroughness of their general approach. They made certain recommendations based purely on the policy that, because of the presence in a very unusual degree of "a sense of solidarity, of social equality, and of identity of interest between members of the crew concerned, irrespective of ownership of the boat in whole or part," it would be most unwise to drive a wedge between an owner or part-owner and the rest of the crew. That this method of approach is desirable can hardly be doubted, but it is worth noting that the Committee could easily have taken a much more restricted view of their functions or even have merely argued the question whether share fishermen who owned or partly owned a boat fell within the dictionary meaning of "employed," or within that of "self-employed"; the attitude of the Committee that they are, within the intention of the Act, a policy-recommending body makes their reports of the greatest interest and value.

The Committee recommended amendments of varying importance in forty-three of the seventy-eight sets of regulations. In only one case did the Minister not accept their recommendations in full;[2] in only one case were their recommendations not unanimous.[3] In addition, on several occasions, undertakings were obtained from the Ministry on the strength of which amendments were not recommended. The liaison between the Committee and the Ministry obviously has to be close if the system is to work satisfactorily; it certainly appears from the reports that this is so. On more than one occasion

---

[1] H.C. 137 of 1947–8. Also H.C. 37 of 1948–9 where the Committee had second thoughts on this problem. For the other special questions, see H.C. 165 of 1947–8; H.C. 262 of 1948–9; Cmd. 8446, 8483, 8549, 8558, 8600, 8894, 8860, 9432.

[2] H.C. 228 of 1948–9.

[3] H.C 172 of 1947–8.

he Committee has asked the Ministry to redraft and resubmit
parts of regulations which appeared to be unnecessarily obscure
and this has been done;[1] there seems every reason to expect
that the intelligibility of National Insurance regulations will
as a result become a model for other departments. The number
of important recommendations made and accepted as amendments is very large. Only a few can be indicated here. A
maternity benefit regulation was amended to ensure that
officers of the Ministry could not make inquiries about the
advice given to a woman by her doctor or midwife.[2] The
question of supplementation by employers of unemployment
benefit was considered.[3] It was recommended that doctors
employed whole-time in all hospitals should be insured as
employed persons; so also whole-time coroners employed
under public or local authorities; so also registrars of births,
deaths or marriages who are not salaried officers;[4] the cases
of many other groups were considered and recommendations
made or not made. A contributions regulation exempts from
liability to pay all those who are receiving full-time education
up to the age of 18, and those who are receiving full-time
training at a course provided by or on behalf of a Government
department; representations were made to the Committee
that this exemption should be extended to cover all students
continuing whole-time education beyond the age of 18;
certain amendments were recommended.[5] The procedure
for the determination of claims and questions was closely
examined and recommendations made relating, amongst
other things, to legal representation, reasoned decisions,
notification of rights of appeal, and the exclusion of Press and
public.[6]

It is most important to remember that the Committee is
far more than a hearing body which merely weighs evidence
and evaluates objections; it frequently makes recommendations based simply on its own knowledge and all its recommendations are finally its own, however impressed it may in

---

[1] H.C. 140 of 1947–8, para. 12; H.C. 56 of 1947–8, para. 16; H.C. 36 of
1948–9, para. 42.
[2] H.C. 147 of 1947–8, paras. 14, 17.
[3] H.C. 161 of 1947–8, paras. 37–39.
[4] H.C. 172 of 1947–8, paras. 12, 14, 17.
[5] H.C. 177 of 1947–8, paras. 27–39.
[6] H.C. 144 of 1947–8, paras. 12, 17, 36, 40–48.

fact have been by a particular representation. It is, to repeat, a policy-recommending body. It is not always possible to rely on objections being made to a proposed regulation either by individuals or bodies. As already indicated, some groups affected are too large or too scattered for organisation to be possible; individuals come together into an organisation for a large number of reasons, but generally in addition to common interest there must be a special reason. Before considering the regulations relating to married women and those relating to widows and guardians the Committee gave special notice, as is their custom, to organisations which they considered might be specially interested. In the former case, three representations only were made;[1] in the latter, none at all.[2] No doubt the reason why so few representations were made in these two cases is the absence of any bodies specifically concerned with the welfare of married women, widows or guardians; on the other hand, one would have thought that there were many organisations (no doubt those to whom the Committee gave notice) sufficiently connected with these groups to be interested.

The essential differences between this Advisory Committee and those others which by statute must be consulted by a Minister before regulations are made, are first, that the detailed procedure of the Committee for its purpose of eliciting objections and representations from those affected is laid down in the Act, and second, that its report must be laid before Parliament with the Minister's explanations.

The statutory obligation imposed on a Minister to consult such bodies as appear to him likely to be affected or to consult a specific advisory committee may mean much or little in practice. The requirement to consult, moreover, may be regarded on the one hand as a safeguard to ensure that the Minister has all the relevant information on which to base his decision; this is the normal purpose where committees are appointed to advise the Minister generally on a special subject, often of technical difficulty. On the other hand, where the committee is specifically appointed for the purpose of examining subordinate legislation, a different consideration is relevant. For here the committee, although it will give the Minister

[1] H.C. 150 of 1947–8, para. 3.   [2] H.C. 156 of 1947–8, para. 6.

much valuable information, is in fact examining a legislative proposal the substance of which Parliament has not examined and probably will not examine. This type of committee represents a constitutional development which has become necessary and desirable because of the inevitable growth of delegated legislation. Its purpose is not therefore primarily to provide further information for the Minister but to act as a body (appointed by the Minister who retains the ultimate control) in a more or less representative capacity. It is not representative as the House of Commons is representative, but it is normally composed of members who can put the point of view of the persons affected by the proposal. Where the subject-matter of the proposal is special and the number of persons affected therefore comparatively small, these points of view will be accurately presented. But even where the subject-matter is general and the number of persons affected very large, the example of the National Insurance Advisory Committee shows how valuable can be examination by a small, well-chosen body.

(c) Conclusions

Where the Administration is empowered to make subordinate laws, there is entrusted to the Administration a discretion to lay down rules of general applicability. Subject to what has been said about parliamentary control, the exercise of that discretion, provided it is within the power granted, is final until revoked. The Act empowers the Administration to supplement the statutory provisions and the Administration decides what shall be the content of the supplements. Parliament rarely investigates this content. The courts only investigate to see if it is *intra vires*. It becomes, therefore, most important to ensure that the Administration, when exercising this discretion, is in full possession of the facts and viewpoints which bear on the particular matter. The procedures designed for this end derive, as shown above, partly from statute and partly from departmental practice. But the purpose of these procedures is not merely the better information of the Administration. It is also to enable those affected, from powerful groups to ordinary individuals, to state their case against the proposed action and to urge that it be modified or dropped.

There is a third purpose also: the explanation of the reasons for the proposed actions so that, when the whole is seen, the smallest parts become (it is hoped) less apparently irrational.

For these purposes, there are three principal methods of procedure. There is the method of the advisory committee appointed by the Administration; there is the method of direct consultation with affected organisations; and there is the method of the public inquiry.

Where the Administration is seeking expert technical advice, the advisory committee has obvious advantages. The only alternative is to circulate the questions separately to those institutions or individuals who have the necessary specialised knowledge. The appointment of an advisory committee draws together the same persons in one body and thus both prevents duplication of work and enables one solution to be put forward which is the product of several minds. Where opinions of organised groups, likely to be directly affected by the proposal, are sought then the direct consultation method is indicated. At the same time, when the proposals are many and relate to a few organisations in particular, or it is desired to bring together "both sides of industry," an advisory committee may save time and effort. Sometimes, as noted above, those affected are so numerous that they cannot properly organise themselves. In the case of national insurance the method of an advisory committee has worked well within certain limits. When the National Insurance Advisory Committee has to deal with questions relating to particular groups in the community, it resorts as far as possible to the direct consultative method and hears representatives from organisations. Where the group or the individual affected is drawn from one locality, the public inquiry is the method most commonly employed. Where the proposed action will interfere with private property rights, this method gives to the owner an opportunity of stating his case in a formal proceeding. Where the proposed action affects a whole neighbourhood (as under the New Towns Act, 1946) the method is less effective; but this is mainly because the objections at the inquiry are thought to play a relatively small part in the ultimate decision.

How far is it desirable that these procedures should be "adversary" in character? A procedure is adversary when

two or more parties with conflicting views put forward
arguments and attempt to demolish the arguments of their
opponents. If the procedure in a technical advisory committee
becomes adversary, it is so by chance and not by design. Those
who serve on such committees are not normally chosen in two
groups to represent orthodox and heretical views. Disagree-
ments are indeed likely but they are incidental. This is also
true of those advisory committees which are set up because
there is no representative body which can be directly consulted.
On the other hand, most of the bodies acting as advisory
committees on industry are deliberately composed of equal
numbers of employers and trade unionists. Yet in many cases
the Administration is striving to obtain the greatest amount
of co-operation between these two groups and the procedure
by which, it is hoped, the best conclusion will be found is not
designed to be adversary.

The method of direct consultation is not necessarily adversary
as between the Administration and the organisation consulted.
But there may be conflict between two or more of these organisations and this conflict may be voiced at any conference
which the organisations are invited to attend. The Transport
Tribunal is in a peculiar position. It hears the arguments
for and against any increase in rates. Then it takes a decision
or, in certain circumstances, advises the Administration. The
Transport Commission is a party to the dispute. The procedure
is as "adversary" as that of the High Court.

A local inquiry, on an order proposed by a local authority
and objected to by an individual, is an adversary procedure.
This is less clearly so where the order is proposed by the
department whose official presides at the inquiry (as under
the New Towns Act, 1946). It would be more clearly so if the
Administration explained in greater detail the reasons for its
proposal. This is a matter of very great importance.

Government departments seem to be extremely reluctant
to explain in detail the reasons which have led them to make
their proposals, and are often reluctant to impart the details
of their proposals. Sometimes drafts of subordinate legislation are circulated to those concerned. Sometimes merely
the "principle" or a specific point is communicated. There
may be good reasons for this. It may be necessary that the

provisions shall take effect without warning; there may be national security reasons. In these cases, however, there is unlikely to be any consultation at all. There is a fear of criticism in Parliament if information is given to individuals or groups before it is given to M.P.s; this criticism has little merit in the case of subordinate legislation if the consultative procedures are regarded as necessary supplements to Parliamentary examination. It is suggested that Government departments should give as much information in a summarised form as possible. This is important for each of the types of procedure but it is vital where there is a local inquiry on a matter affecting the whole locality. Criticism of the draft order for a New Town cannot be informed if the reasons leading the Minister to his tentative conclusion are not known. There seems no reason why the opinions of the Minister's expert advisers should not be made known.[1]

Finally, wherever possible, the opinions of the advisory committees, the organised groups and the individual objectors should be published and laid before Parliament, accompanied by a statement from the Minister. In cases where the number of objections is very considerable and varied, the Minister's statement should be wide enough to cover all without answering each in detail. This laying procedure should be followed even where the ministerial order of confirmation itself is not required to be laid.

By these methods, it is suggested, the procedures can be made more effective and more confidence will be placed in the discretionary decisions of the Administration.[2] Thus can be performed that function of examination, criticism and defence which Parliament is unable by its nature and in the time at its disposal to exercise.

---

[1] For the Departmental attitude to some of these problems, see the evidence of Dame Evelyn Sharp before the Committee on Administrative Tribunals and Enquiries (Third Day, paras. 613–725).
[2] For a general analysis of safeguards in respect of delegated legislation, see R. Fuchs, "Administrative Rule-making" in 52 *Harvard Law Review*, (1938) 259.

CHAPTER IV

THE ADMINISTRATIVE AND JUDICIAL POWERS OF THE ADMINISTRATION

Classification

It is commonly asserted that the actions of the Administration (other than those which are legislative) may be divided into three clearly distinguishable types, judicial, quasi-judicial, and administrative (or executive). Once he has classified the act, the draftsman of a statute conferring new powers is said to have a straightforward task.

A. Conceptual

The high-water mark of this theory is reached in the *Report of the Committee on Ministers' Powers*, which states[1]—

A true judicial decision presupposes an existing dispute between two or more parties, and then involves four requisites—(1) the presentation (not necessarily orally) of their case by the parties to the dispute; (2) if the dispute between them is a question of fact, the ascertainment of the fact by means of evidence adduced by the parties to the dispute and often with the assistance of argument by or on behalf of the parties on the evidence; (3) if the dispute between them is a question of law, the submission of legal argument by the parties; and (4) a decision which disposes of the whole matter by a finding upon the facts in dispute and an application of the law of the land to the facts so found, including where required a ruling upon any disputed question of law.

A quasi-judicial decision equally presupposes an existing dispute between two or more parties and involves (1) and (2), but does not necessarily involve (3), and never involves (4). The place of (4) is in fact taken by administrative action, the character of which is determined by the Minister's free choice. . . . Decisions which are purely administrative stand on a wholly different footing from quasi-judicial as well as from judicial decisions and must be distinguished accordingly. . . . In the case of the administrative decision, there is no legal obligation upon the person charged with the duty of reaching the decision to consider and weigh submissions and arguments, or to collate any evidence, or to solve any issue. The grounds upon which he acts, and the means which he takes to inform himself before acting, are left entirely to his discretion.

[1] Cmd. 4060 (1932), 73–74, 81.

Judicial decisions should, according to the *Report*, be made by the courts in the absence of "exceptional reasons," while quasi-judicial and, *a fortiori*, administrative decisions should be made by Ministers of the Crown.[1]

In the opinion of the Committee, the essential distinction between a judicial and a quasi-judicial function is that in the former there is never an element of discretion, whereas there is invariably statutory permission to exercise discretion in the performance of a quasi-judicial function. Both these are to be distinguished from an administrative decision in that the exercise of judicial and quasi-judicial functions "presupposes the existence of a dispute and parties to the dispute."[2]

The Committee assumes that the function of the courts is mechanical, uncreative and never discretionary. Yet courts do exercise discretions, for instance, in fixing criminal sentences, or in deciding whether to grant a divorce to a petitioner who has committed adultery. They exercise wide discretions in the field of public law: for instance, if a person aggrieved by the order of a borough council for a payment out of the rate fund should appeal to the High Court, that court "may give such directions in the matter as they think proper."[3] Nor can it be seriously maintained that the doctrine of judicial precedent prevents the courts from law-making in the marginal case.

It is agreed that courts usually have a lesser degree of discretion, and that they do not exercise it in the same open manner as administrative bodies. Advocates of the conceptual approach suggested by the Committee try to save their position by arguing that the discretion vested in administrative bodies is different in kind from that which courts exercise because "the discretion is merely the administrator's own idea of expediency, incapable of being declared wrong in *law* by any higher authority."[4] To this may be added the similar view of D. M. Gordon[5]—

Judicial tribunals must treat legal rights and liabilities as

---

[1] Op. cit., 115 *et seq.*
[2] Op. cit., 75.
[3] Local Government Act, 1933, Sect. 187 (3); cf. Housing Act, 1936, Sect. 15 (2) (a).
[4] H. W. R. Wade: "Quasi-Judicial and its Background," in 10 *Cambridge Law Journal* (1949) 216, at 224.
[5] "Administrative Tribunals and the Courts" in 49 *Law Quarterly Review* (1933) 94, at 107-8.

pre-existing, because such tribunals declare themselves bound by a fixed objective standard; they profess not to confer rights or impose liabilities themselves, but only to do what is dictated by law. But administrative tribunals, which act upon policy and expediency, themselves dictate what is politic and expedient; they are not concerned with pre-existing rights and liabilities, but themselves create the rights and liabilities that they enforce. A judicial tribunal looks for some law to guide it; an administrative tribunal, within its province, is a law unto itself.

For these conceptualists, "judicial" has a constant meaning, to be ascertained by the above test. How then can one explain why the House of Lords has declared illegal the payment by a local authority, empowered to pay such wages "as it thinks fit," of a minimum wage of four pounds a week to its employees even though the act was held not to be judicial?[1] Plainly, the courts may review acts which are administrative in the sense in which the conceptualists use the term. The difference in discretions is one of degree only: the courts decide whether in the instant case the bounds of discretion beyond which the body must not stray have been exceeded. That is fatal to the argument of the conceptualists.

There is a further serious weakness in the case of those who aver that there is a simple dichotomy between judicial and administrative acts. The courts are required to determine the meaning of "judicial" in many varying contexts: certiorari lies to judicial bodies;[2] judicial bodies must observe the rules of natural justice;[3] there is a tortious immunity for acts performed in the exercise of judicial tasks; newspaper reports of judicial proceedings are absolutely privileged in the law of libel; an organ of government may not violate a written constitution which prohibits the delegation of judicial power to the executive;[4] the Crown is not liable in tort for anything done by any person while discharging "any responsibilities of a judicial nature."[5] There is no one definition of *judicial* for these several purposes. For example, certiorari lay to the courts of referees set up by the employment insurance legislation[6] but the members of those courts did not enjoy judicial

---

[1] *Roberts* v. *Hopwood*, [1925] A.C. 578.
[2] See below, pp. 230 *et seq*.   [3] See below, p. 155.
[4] E.g. British North America Act, 1867, Sect. 96.
[5] Crown Proceedings Act, 1947, Sect. 2 (5).
[6] Now replaced by the tribunals set up under the National Insurance Act, 1946; see below p. 160.

immunity for their acts.[1] This weakness clearly stems from the denial of the creative role of judges. The attitude of the courts towards bodies such as the courts of referees is explained by a desire to supervise administrative bodies and to curtail their privileges as much as possible.

It remains to consider the validity of the suggestion that administrative acts are characterised by the absence of a dispute. The *Report* gave two examples of this:[2] the placing by the Admiralty of a departmental contract for stores, and the grant of naturalisation to an alien. When it is remembered that the definitions of the *Report* are intended to be guides to legislative action the defect in this characterisation is clear. The only reason why there is no dispute between the alien and the Executive is that Parliament has denied the alien any redress in court.[3] This is a mere distinction in procedure not in the nature of the act. The placing of a Government contract is in a different category: this is not justiciable because it is regarded as a matter of internal regulation, just as, for example, would be a decision of the Postmaster-General that the form of application for a radio receiving licence should contain ten questions instead of nine.

A variant of the insistence of the Committee on a dispute is the contention that judicial but not administrative bodies deal with *lites inter partes*. An examination of the statement of D. M. Gordon[4] that this test was laid down by Lord Herschell in the House of Lords[5] both underlines the uselessness of this test and the fundamental error of the conceptual approach. There is a *lis inter partes* where a court tries an issue between two parties the result being reached after hearing the evidence of the parties. Lord Herschell pointed out that an application for a liquor licence was not a *lis inter partes* because, although there was a hearing before the justices, the issues raised between the applicant and the objectors need not cover the whole area of controversy—the function of the justices was to consider this evidence in deciding whether in the public interest to grant

---

[1] *Collins* v. *Henry Whiteway & Co.*, [1927] 2 K.B. 378.   [2] At 81.

[3] Cf. F. F. Blachly and M. E. Oatman: *Administrative Legislation and Adjudication*, 98: "Although the action may appear quasi-judicial or even judicial in nature, it is prevented from being so by the fact that the government does not allow itself to be sued."

[4] Op. cit., 111.

[5] *Boulter* v. *Kent Justices*, [1897] A.C. 556, at 569.

the licence. But the House of Lords, although saying that the
justices were acting administratively in the sense that the courts
could not review the manner in which the discretion was
exercised, did not say that certiorari would not lie to licensing
bodies: on the contrary, the courts have since that time
regularly granted the order against liquor licensing bodies.[1]

B. Functional

The only valuable approach to administrative law is the
functional one. Of course, with the abandonment of *laissez-
faire* the Administration has more and more tasks to perform
and impinges more and more on the citizen. Its main tasks
are no longer police and political; it is performing vast regulatory and managerial tasks, assuming benefactory and protective
relationships to the individual and may increasingly in the future
act as an intermediary between powerful rival economic forces.
The problem is always what is the best organisation to achieve
the particular administrative end, paying due regard to democratic safeguards and standards of fair play. The action called
for might be to guide conduct to prevent a dispute from arising,
rather than the normal judicial task of adjusting relations after
action has been taken. Sometimes this directing function
involves incidental adjudication; sometimes the adjudication
is more than incidental and the act begins to resemble the
work usually assigned to the judiciary. These, and many
other factors subject to more detailed consideration later,
ought to be taken into account by legislatures authorising
administrative action and should determine the organisation
of the responsible body, and the manner in which it is to perform
the act. Parliament should also consider whether any body is
fitted to review the act, and, if so, should identify that reviewing
body best qualified to do so and specify the extent of review
allowed. Responsibility and accountability should always be
interdependent in public administration.

The British Parliament has conspicuously failed to evaluate
the determining criteria, and has on the whole evaded the
issues by imprecise provisions. There is no "ginger" group

---

[1] E.g. *R.* v. *Woodhouse*, [1906] 2 K.B. 501 overruled on other grounds *sub nom.
Leeds Corporation* v. *Ryder*, [1907] A.C. 420; cf. *Sharp* v. *Wakefield*, [1891] A.C. 173,
and see below p. 231.

of Members of Parliament on administrative procedures comparable with the diligent and persistent Active Back Benchers' group on statutory instruments. The lack of statutory precision has left the courts much freedom of action to decide for themselves how closely they shall supervise administrative action. They have not, it is submitted, first characterised the act and then applied the appropriate review; rather have they looked at the consequences of the various possible characterisations, decided to what extent they wished to interfere, and then as far as possible categorised the act so as to attain the desired end. Of course, this process is inarticulate, and the judgments are cast in a mould of formal logic which conceals the skill and discretion with which the choice of premises has been made. As has been pointed out in Chapter III no functional consideration of administrative action can ignore statutory interpretation.

In the light of the preceding considerations a more detailed analysis of administrative acts must now be attempted.

1. INTERNAL MANAGEMENT

With matters of internal management not affecting legal rights, the courts have no concern. The dustman is not to ask for tips, the post office is to close at six o'clock, Z R.A.F. station is to buy newspapers for its recreation room from X not Y: like any private business the Administration is allowed to keep its own house in order, subject only to the ubiquitous parliamentary question.

2. MINISTERIAL ACTS

Another class of act that can be classified is the ministerial act. This is to be distinguished from other official acts in that the law prescribes the duty to be performed with such certainty as to leave nothing to the exercise of the discretion or judgment. The execution of warrants is perhaps the most common illustration. It is a consequence of the complexity of modern administration that the proportion of ministerial acts is rapidly declining. If the problem is intricate, investigation of facts or exercise of discretion must precede action. Perhaps in part because of the declining importance of ministerial acts present remedies for them are believed to be adequate. These include

an action in tort if some invasion of the rights of the plaintiff outside the scope of the duty of the official takes place,[1] or sometimes an order of mandamus to enforce the performance of the
duty.[2]

3. ADJUDICATIONS ON MATTERS OF LAW AND FACT

In the large remaining segment of the administrative process
private rights are affected, and decisions on facts and sometimes on law are called for. Why, it may be asked, should the
making of decisions on law and fact not be invariably entrusted
to the Judiciary, whose normal function this is? This can best
be answered by reference to an important example of this type
of administrative adjudication: national insurance. The State
administers a vast system of comprehensive insurance against
death, sickness, industrial injury, and unemployment. Claims
are too numerous to be handled by the courts; many of them
are claims for small sums made by persons of small means;
a cheap procedure is therefore needed; the cases are largely
repetitive; continuity and uniformity of decision are desirable;
a Government department is in existence to frame rules and to
dispose of that great majority of claims which is settled informally, and there is much to be gained by the closest integra-
tion of that organisation and the adjudicatory body; sometimes
the sympathetic treatment of a particular type of claim might
be prevented by the rigid adherence of the courts to *stare
decisis*. Workmen's compensation claims may be cited as an
illustration to show how compelling these reasons are. In
the period between 1897 and 1946, when these claims were
decided by the ordinary courts, one textbook on the subject ran into thirty-seven editions, and a series of law reports
devoted exclusively to these claims had forty-seven volumes. It
occasioned little surprise, therefore, when the National
Insurance (Industrial Injuries) Act, 1946, transferred this
jurisdiction to administrative tribunals.

4. ADJUDICATIONS ON MATTERS OF LAW AND FACT
AND THE APPLICATION OF STANDARDS

In cases of the type discussed in the preceding section the facts
governing the decision are specific and susceptible of proof

[1] See below, p. 241.   [2] See below, p. 233.

or disproof. One of the features of a developed legal system is a recognition of the difficulty, if not impossibility, of framing exhaustive bodies of norms applicable to defined fact-situations. Although the courts with their yearning for certainty protest at this tendency towards standards rather than fixed rules, they, too, are affected by it. One cannot lay down the precise circumstances when careless driving will be tortious; one can only ask: "Has the driver shown 'reasonable' care?" Administrative bodies, not sharing this aversion to standards, are frequently entrusted with their application. It is characteristic of the standard that it gives the expert freedom of action. One may expect, therefore, to find non-legal specialist personnel on tribunals of this class. What is a "fair" rent, "adequate" compensation for a dispossessed landowner; are premises "educationally suitable;" is a building of "special architectural interest," is work "available;" will national service cause "exceptional hardship"? These are typical examples of legal standards the working out of which has been entrusted to administrative bodies.

5. DOMESTIC BODIES, TRADE AND VOCATIONAL TRIBUNALS SUBJECT TO A MEASURE OF GOVERNMENTAL CONTROL

Separate from administrative tribunals are domestic tribunals. These are organs set up by associations of individuals to control members of the association, whether the association be the Jockey Club, a trade association or The Law Society. With these as such administrative law is not concerned, but recently some types of these tribunals have been subject to governmental interference, either because of a public interest in the maintenance of standards of justice within an association having close relations with the public, or because the particular segment of national life represented by the association has come under some measure of governmental control. The main characteristic of these tribunals is that, besides determining questions of law and fact, they may be empowered to impose fines or other punishments.

6. REGULATORY FUNCTIONS

One comes next to the most controversial field of administrative action—the exercise of regulatory functions by the

State. Here the Administration subjects citizens to control, discipline or other interference in furtherance of legislative policy. In England the most common example has been of interference with the landowner, either to ensure the adequate housing of the population or to carry out effective town and country planning. The United States has made even more extensive use of the device: it has been the means by which private enterprise has been harnessed to the public interest without being nationalised. One important regulatory instrument used in both England and the United States is the licence, whereby the right to carry on particular businesses or occupations in particular localities may rest on State permission. The characteristic of regulatory functions is that although they may include fact-finding, and sometimes determination of legal points, there is usually a freedom of choice greater even than in the application of standards. This has led the Legislature and the courts to see two stages in the process—a fact-finding one followed by the making of a choice or what is usually called a policy decision. In general, according to this line of reasoning, some form of judicial control of the first stage is requisite, but the second stage is a matter for political responsibility, for responsibility to Parliament and not elsewhere.

This word "policy" must be looked at circumspectly: it has an emotive force which conjures up a vision of some matter which should be settled at Cabinet level. A consideration of typical cases of regulatory action reveals that they do not involve policy in this sense at all. Consider for instance Sect. 25 of the Housing Act, 1936, which aims at the clearance of slum areas. If a local authority is satisfied that houses are unfit for human habitation, that all the buildings in the area should be demolished, that there is other accommodation for the displaced residents, and that it can afford the expense of the project, it may make a clearance order which is effective only when confirmed by the Minister of Housing and Local Government. The latter causes a public local inquiry into the facts to be held before deciding whether to confirm the order. It is an exaggeration to say that this decision is one of policy. Properly understood, policy should be limited to the ultimate value judgments. There is a graduated scale of decisions at one end of which the ethical judgment is all important, and at the other end of which is a factual proposition, and all issues between are a blending of the two. Only where the normative or ethical element is relatively big in relation to the factual should there be merely political responsibility to Parliament. In short, these are cases of discretions, as the courts themselves have acknowledged, since they will review for abuse of discretion.[1] A further source of confusion is that the factual investigatory procedures do not cover all the factual elements of the case; the important distinction between evidence of facts and expert opinion on facts is not recognised; this in practice gives undue weight to the discretionary element. In the housing cases, for instance, there are many matters, engineering reports, reports of surveyors, financial data, contained in Government files, and motivating decisions but not divulged to interested parties, which are factual, yet shelter under the cloak of policy. The Executive dislikes the publication of its files, and it has used its influence over the Legislature to prevent their publication here in the same way as it has, at great injustice to the citizen, secured in the Crown Proceedings Act, 1947, a provision forbidding him access in litigation to Government documents.[2] The courts have supported this artificial extension of the area of discretion. Lord Shaw said in the *Arlidge* case,[3] without, unfortunately, elaborating the point, that for the Administration to disclose its files would be inconsistent with "efficiency, with practice, and with the true theory of complete parliamentary responsibility for departmental action." Lord Greene, too, held that the Minister "may have, and is entitled to have, present to his mind his own views as to general policy as well as material acquired in a purely executive capacity, such as reports and opinions obtained from sources within or outside the Ministry."[4]

The limits of the discretion in regulatory action are even more obvious in licensing, whether of liquor, or of cinemas or of occupations, as the cases dealing with review of discretions fully prove.[5] It may be said then, that these regulatory

---

[1] See below, p. 219.   [2] Sect. 28.
[3] *Local Government Board* v. *Arlidge*, [1915] A.C. 120, at 137.
[4] *Robinson* v. *Minister of Town and Country Planning*, [1947] K.B. 702, at 713.
[5] See below, pp. 219 *et seq.*

functions of the Administration are made up of two parts, a fact-finding process and the making of a choice circumscribed within limits which Parliament has or should have defined with some certainty.

This is not to deny that there may be cases where Parliament thinks the discretionary element so dominant that it will lay down no principles, making the Minister empowered politically responsible, and only authorising a factual inquiry as a means of informing the mind of the Minister or of acquainting him with public opinion. This, one might think, ought to be the exceptional case. Such a one is contained in the New Towns Act, 1946, whereby the Minister of Housing and Local Government may designate a particular area as a new town area to accommodate the overspill from some overcrowded city. Although a statutory obligation to conduct a local inquiry is imposed, here is a true policy decision, not a mere finding of administrative ways and means, as the House of Lords has recognised.[1]

7. DECISIONS OF "PURE POLICY"

Higher still in the scale is what has been called the "pure policy" decision. Usually it is a prerogative power, and its characteristic is, or should be, its uniqueness, which prevents the laying down by Parliament of any guiding principle. Unlike the last-mentioned category, there is not even any prescribed factual inquiry. In this category are such acts as recognition of a foreign Government and the declaration of war. Unfortunately, this category has been extended beyond its reasonable limits. The Home Secretary decides in his uncontrolled discretion whether to deport an alien, who may not ask the courts to quash the act on the ground that no factual investigation took place. There seems no good reason why the preponderance of legal and factual matters involved in deportation cases should not result in the alien in England having that right to a fair hearing which he has in the United States.

8. SUMMARY POWERS

There is another class of discretionary administrative action which affects private persons who are none the less denied a

---

[1] See below, p. 178.

hearing. The control of scarce materials and currency is effected in this way. So, too, the applicant for a driving licence is not entitled to a hearing before the Administration. The justification for this must be that the official has on the application form all the materials requisite for his decision. In contrast to the application for a liquor licence there is no question of considering local opinion or other oral evidence. Nor where a driving test is prescribed would there be any purpose in giving the examinee a right to argue his case before some tribunal, because that body would almost inevitably accept the expert opinion of the examiner. The practical test is the proper one where the issue of the licence depends on matters of skill or technical knowledge which can readily be checked in such a test. There is no injustice in these summary procedures, particularly when it is remembered that a person who is refused a licence may nevertheless have a judicial review of the exercise of this summary power on the ground of abuse of power or other illegality. Quantitatively these summary powers are very important.

9. INQUIRIES AND INVESTIGATIONS[1]

In pursuance of its general interest in accident prevention the Administration has been empowered to conduct formal investigations into accidents, railway, factory, aviation, and the like. These inquiries resemble the inquests of coroners in that without subsequent adjudication by a court they cannot affect individual rights. Nevertheless, their findings may result in criminal prosecutions or be the basis of civil actions. There are, therefore, as in coroners' inquests, good reasons for affording interested parties the right to be heard. The need for a fair hearing has recently become much more compelling with the nationalisation of many industries. For instance, should the Minister of Transport and Civil Aviation be closely identified with tribunals investigating accidents in which aircraft of a nationalised airline under his jurisdiction are involved? In 1950 the Government, differing from the committee which it set up to report on this problem,[2] thought that ministerial

[1] For a survey, see Robson, "Public Inquiries as an Instrument of Government" in 1 *British Journal of Administrative Law* (1954), 71.
[2] *Report of the Committee of Nationalised Civil Aviation Consultative Council on Accident Investigation Procedure* Cmd. 7564 (1948).

responsibility to Parliament was in itself an adequate safe-guard against bias on the part of the Minister.[1]

Inquiries are, of course, held for widely different purposes. Sometimes, as in the inquiry just described, the object is the ascertainment of facts. In others, the Minister desires to be informed of public opinion before formulating policy: in these cases, at least, he obviously has an interest in allowing an unrestricted right to a hearing to all interested parties.

The Constitutions, Powers and Procedures of Administrative Tribunals

It was the need for greater efficiency in government which gave rise to the development of administrative powers. So, too, the Administration must be assessed by the efficiency with which it performs its tasks. One must acknowledge the great variety of these acts; administrative law cannot be evaluated by discovering whether the Administration is acting judicially or administratively and then applying rigid criteria to the act. The extent of the power in relation to its economic and sociological purpose and the political philosophy behind it, the constitution of the body exercising it, its procedures, the degree of accountability of those responsible—all these aspects of the working of the administrative process must be considered as a whole to determine whether a proper balance is struck between competing public and private interests. It is proposed first to describe the various types of tribunal and then to suggest some general considerations which ought to be weighed by Parliament when setting up these tribunals.

A. Ministerial Acts

No consideration of the purely internal administrative acts is required because they do not impinge on private rights. Nor do ministerial functions present many difficulties. Many of them, the execution of a warrant on the goods of a judgment debtor for instance, have been preceded by a judicial investiga-tion into the facts. In such a case, there can be no objection to vesting these functions even in inferior officers and also afford-ing the officers immunity so long as they are acting within their powers. It is reasonable that the constable should be

[1] See now Civil Aviation (Investigation of Accidents) Regulations, 1951, S.I. 1951 No. 1653.

protected when executing a warrant for arrest even though the justice issuing it acted outside his jurisdiction.[1] Where there has been no prior judicial inquiry the officer acts at his peril,[2] and the need for responsible officials in such cases is obvious. Ministerial acts are never invalidated by bias, because they are not "judicial" for the purpose of the rule that bias in the exercise of judicial functions is contrary to law.

B. Tribunals Determining Issues of Law and Fact, or Applying Standards

These tribunals are entirely statutory creations, and it is mainly to their creating statutes that one must look for information. When Parliament first established these administrative tribunals on a large scale at the beginning of this century it did not detail their procedures. It fell to the courts to determine whether they were to conform to normal judicial methods. The matter was decided by the House of Lords in *Board of Education* v. *Rice*[3] and *Local Government Board* v. *Arlidge*,[4] although neither of these cases concerned administrative tribunals of the type now being discussed.

I. THE RULES OF NATURAL JUSTICE

The principle behind these decisions is that administrative tribunals should not be required to observe court procedures but should be free to work out their own rules subject to the provision of certain minimum safeguards.

> . . . they must act in good faith and fairly listen to both sides. . . . But I do not think they are bound to treat such a question as though it were a trial. . . . They can obtain information in any way they think best, always giving a fair opportunity to those who are parties in the controversy for correcting or contradicting any relevant statement prejudicial to their view.[5]

This theme was developed in the *Arlidge* case. Lord Haldane said that "they must deal with the question referred to them without bias, and they must give to each of the parties the opportunity of adequately presenting the case made."[6] These

---

[1] Constables Protection Act, 1750, Sect. 6.
[2] *Eshugbayi Eleko* v. *Government of Nigeria*, [1931] A.C. 662. He may of course sometimes be indemnified by statute.
[3] [1911] A.C. 179.   [4] [1915] A.C. 120.
[5] *Board of Education* v. *Rice*, [1911] A.C. 179, at 182 *per* Lord Loreburn, L.C.
[6] At 132.

two principles have been commonly called the "rules of natural justice," a phrase used extensively in the nineteenth century by the courts in their control of courts of summary jurisdiction. It seems to have been assumed that these two principles, that a man must not be judge in his own cause, and that both sides must be heard, are the minimum and the only requirements for administrative tribunals. Yet it must not be forgotten that the House of Lords laid down that whether a body was to observe them was a matter of statutory interpretation.[1] It would seem, therefore, that the rules of natural justice might be of variable content—that perhaps tribunals of the type now under discussion might have more rigorous standards than the regulatory bodies considered in the *Arlidge* case. In line with this is the view of Lord Parmoor in the same case that in determining the principles of substantial justice to which a tribunal must conform "regard must necessarily be had to the nature of the issue to be determined and the constitution of the tribunal."[2] It is submitted, therefore, that it is still open to the House of Lords to exact higher minimum procedural standards than those laid down in the *Arlidge* case from other categories of tribunal.

It is only when bodies are performing "judicial" functions that they must observe the principles of natural justice. The meaning of "judicial" need not be examined here[3]: it is enough to say that all the tribunals of the type now under examination are "judicial" and subject to the rules of natural justice.

(a) Bias

The prohibition of bias strikes against factors which may improperly influence a judge in deciding in favour of one party. The first of the three disabling types of bias is bias on the subject-matter. Only rarely will this bias invalidate proceedings. "A mere general interest in the general object to be pursued would not disqualify," said Field, J., holding

[1] At 130 (*per* Viscount Haldane).
[2] At 140. Many other dicta suggest that these minimum implied standards are not constant for all types of tribunal, e.g. *R. v. L.C.C., Re The Empire Theatre* (1895), 71 L.T. 638, at 640 (*per* Wright, J.); *General Medical Council v. Spackman*, [1943] A.C. 627, at 638 (*per* Lord Atkin); *Russell v. Duke of Norfolk*, [1949] 1 All E.R. 109, at 120 (*per* Tucker, L.J.).
[3] See above p. 144 and below p. 230.

that a magistrate who subscribed to the Royal Society for the Prevention of Cruelty to Animals was not thereby disabled from trying a charge brought by that body of cruelty to a horse.[1] There must be some direct connection with the litigation.[2] If there is such prejudice on the subject-matter that the court has reached fixed and unalterable conclusions not founded on reason or understanding so that there is not a fair hearing, that is bias of which the courts will take account, as where a justice announced his intention of convicting anyone coming before him on a charge of supplying liquor after the permitted hours.[3] The Committee on Ministers' Powers went much farther and held that opinions about policy are a basis for disqualification.[4] It can be stated with confidence that this, which so obviously rests on that assumption of the Committee previously referred to,[5] that policy issues are never relevant to judicial determinations, is not the law. The effective answer to it has been made by Frank, J., in the United States[6]—

> If, however, "bias" and "partiality" be defined to mean the total absence of preconceptions in the mind of the judge, then no one has ever had a fair trial, and no one ever will. The human mind, even at infancy, is no blank piece of paper. We are born with predispositions; and the processes of education, formal and informal, create attitudes which precede reasoning in particular instances and which, therefore, by definition, are prejudices . . .

Secondly, a pecuniary interest, however slight, will disqualify, even though it is not proved that the decision is in any way affected.[7]

The third type of bias is personal bias. A judge may be a relative of a party, or he may be personally hostile as a result of events happening either before or during the course of a trial. The courts have not been consistent in laying down

---

[1] R. v. Deal Justices, ex parte Curling (1881), 45 L.T. 439, at 441.
[2] R. v. L.C.C., Re The Empire Theatre (1895), 71 L.T. 638; in Franklin v. Minister of Town and Country Planning, [1947] 1 All E.R. 612, the Court of Appeal for the same reason rejected the claim that the Minister was biased on the matter of water supply.
[3] R. v. Rand (1913), 22 C.C.C. 147.
[4] Op. cit., 78.
[5] See above, p. 142.
[6] In re Linahan (1943), 138 F. 2d 650, at 652.
[7] Dimes v. Grand Junction Canal (1852), 3 H.L.C. 759; R. v. Sunderland Justices, [1901] 2 K.B. 357.

when bias of this type will invalidate a hearing. The House of Lords in *Frome United Dairies* v. *Bath Justices*[1] approved an earlier test of whether "there is a real likelihood of bias." The House of Lords has since approved[2] a dictum of Lord Hewart[3] that "justice should not only be done, but should manifestly and undoubtedly be seen to be done" although it did not mention another test suggested by him in the same judgment:[4] "Nothing is to be done which creates even a suspicion that there has been an improper interference with the course of justice."

If a statute sanctions a breach of these rules, then *pro tanto* they do not apply.[5] It seems also that in cases of necessity, that is, where every qualified judge is biased, there is no irregularity.

(b) Audi Alteram Partem[6]

"Both sides should be heard" is the second implied rule. The corollaries to the rule, rather than the rule itself, are important. There is no inherent right to an oral hearing.[7] Ordinarily, no evidence must be given behind the back of the other party, so that if written evidence is given it must be made available to the other party.[8] A party is entitled to notice of the hearing;[9] since the reason of the rule is that the party shall have an adequate opportunity of rebutting the case against him it might be that this notice ought to inform the party of the case which he has to meet.

Besides being entitled to be informed of all evidence, a party is entitled to rebut that evidence. If, however, his counsel is

---

[1] [1926] A.C. 586.

[2] *Franklin* v. *Minister of Town and Country Planning*, [1948] A.C. 87.

[3] *R.* v. *Sussex Justices, ex parte McCarthy*, [1924] 1 K.B. 256, at 259.

[4] Ibid. The current trend of Divisional Court decisions, especially with regard to justices, is towards a narrow interpretation of bias and a preference for the "real likelihood" test; e.g. *Reg.* v. *Camborne Justices*, [1955] 1 Q.B. 41.

[5] *Wilkinson* v. *Barking Corporation*, [1948] 1 K.B. 721; *R.* v. *Salford Assessment Committee, ex parte Ogden*, [1937] 2 K.B. 1 at 17–8 (*per* Slesser, L.J.).

[6] See de Smith, "The Right to a Hearing in English Administrative Law" in 68 *Harvard L.R.* (1955), 569.

[7] *Local Government Board* v. *Arlidge*, [1915] A.C. 120, at 134 (*per* Viscount Haldane); *R.* v. *Amphlett*, [1915] 2 K.B. 223; *West Riding C.C.* v. *Wilson*, [1941] 2 All E.R. 827.

[8] *Stafford* v. *Minister of Health*, [1946] K.B. 621; *R.* v. *Architects Registration Tribunal*, [1945] 2 All E.R. 131.

[9] *Spackman* v. *Plumstead Board of Works* (1885), 10 App. Cas. 229, at 240.

stopped from making a speech about matters of which he is not going to call evidence, this gives him no cause of complaint.[1] Logically, there should also be a right to cross-examination, an argument supported by the following dicta of Swift, J.[2]

> . . . there must be some impropriety which goes to the root of the matter. If one party is heard without the other having an opportunity of knowing what he has said or of testing what he has said by cross-examination, or of making answer to what has been said, then clearly there has been an infringement of the rules of natural justice.

In the absence of further English authorities, the matter must remain in doubt. It is also doubtful whether there is any inherent right to legal representation.[3]

The rule that evidence must not be taken behind the back of a party extends to real evidence. *R. v. Paddington & St. Marylebone Rent Tribunal, ex parte Bell London & Provincial Properties, Ltd.*[4] might even go further than this. Before a hearing the rent tribunal inspected the premises and in the presence of servants of the landlords measured the height of the ceilings. The landlords were taken by surprise when the tribunal gave as one of its reasons for lowering the rent the fact that the ceilings were of less height than that required by modern standards. Although it was not suggested that the tribunal's observation was inaccurate, it was held that to take into account this matter without intimation to the landlords at the hearing was a breach of natural justice. If this case decided that a tribunal must limit its reasons to those factors which a party thought material and argued before it, it would seem wrongly decided: no more can a court be confined to the points of law argued before it. It should be accepted only for the proposition that a tribunal, subject to any statutory provisions,[5] must not base its decision on evidential facts, as

---

[1] *Re London (Hammersmith) Housing Order—Application of Land Development, Ltd. and Another*, [1936] 2 All E.R. 1063.

[2] *Marriott* v. *Minister of Health* (1935), 154 L.T. 47, at 50; cf. *In re Macqueen and Nottingham Caledonian Society* (1861), 9 C.B. (N.S.) 793.

[3] *Reg.* v. *Assessment Committee of St. Mary Abbotts*, [1891] 1 Q.B. 378. See *Current Law Year Book* (1953) para. 4 for a list of Tribunals before which legal representation is forbidden, and of Tribunals before which it is only allowed by consent; and see 179 H.L. Deb. 5s., cols. 1075–8.

[4] [1949] 1 K.B. 666.

[5] Sect. 2 (2) of the Furnished Houses (Rent Control) Act, 1946, authorises tribunals to make "such inquiry as they think fit." Is that expression wide enough

distinct from matters of professional experience, unless the parties have been informed of the facts so found by the tribunal.[1]

2. AN EXAMINATION OF SOME OF THESE TRIBUNALS

(a) *National Insurance and National Assistance*

For forty years tribunals have handled disputes arising out of claims for social benefits administered by various departments. With the unification and vast increase of social insurance effected by the National Insurance Acts, 1946–1953,[2] the National Insurance (Industrial Injuries) Acts, 1946–1953,[3] and the National Assistance Act, 1948,[4] this work has become even more important.

Under the control of the Ministry of Pensions and National Insurance is the administration of claims for unemployment benefit, family allowances, sickness and death benefits, old age and widows' pensions, and industrial injury benefits. The Ministry has local offices throughout the country to handle the millions of claims which are made annually. Most claims are settled by staff of the department, "insurance officers" appointed by the Minister. Claims for national assistance are first handled by the officials of the National Assistance Board.

Where these decisions do not satisfy claimants, or where the official elects not to decide himself, there is provision for further adjudication. The National Insurance Act authorises the Minister to determine the following: whether the contribution conditions for any benefit are satisfied, the class of insured person in which a claimant is to be placed, and the priority of rival claimants for a death grant.[5] Why these, and no other

to make it unnecessary for tribunals to disclose the results of their own factual observations? Cf. *R.* v. *Brighton and Area Rent Tribunal, ex parte Marine Parade Estates* (1936), *Ltd.*, [1950] 2 K.B. 410; see below, p. 165.

[1] *R.* v. *Howard*, [1902] 2 K.B. 363; *Errington* v. *Minister of Health*, [1935] 1 K.B. 249; *R.* v. *Westminster Assessment Committee*, [1941] 1 K.B. 53; *Moxon* v. *Minister of Pensions*, [1945] K.B. 490; *Reynolds* v. *Llanelly Associated Tin Plate Co.*, [1948] 1 All E.R. 140; *Goold* v. *Evans*, [1951] 2 T.L.R. 1189.

[2] And see the National Insurance (Determination of Claims and Questions) Regulations, 1948, S.I. 1948 No. 1144; amended by S.I. 1951 No. 1208; 1952 No. 1310; 1955 No. 1788.

[3] And see the National Insurance (Industrial Injuries) (Determination of Claims and Questions) Regulations, 1948, S.I. 1948 No. 1299, S.I. 1954 No. 352.

[4] And see the National Assistance (Appeal Tribunals) Rules Confirmation Instrument, 1948, S.I. 1948 No. 1454.

[5] He has similar powers under the National Insurance (Industrial Injuries) Act, but not under the National Assistance Act. Unfortunately these are not the only instances of Ministers of the Crown determining questions solely of law and

questions (which are questions of law and fact) should be left to the political head is not obvious. Typical determinations are that a nurse supplied to a hospital by a nursing association, and whose fees were paid by the hospital to the association, which then in turn paid them to her after deducting commission, was employed by the hospital; and that a chemist, given a grant by a firm of manufacturing chemists to carry out university research work in which they were interested, on the understanding that the benefits of the research should accrue to the firm, was not engaged in insurable employment.

The Minister may decide all issues within his jurisdiction without any hearing.[1] If he thinks fit, he may, before deciding, appoint a person to hold an inquiry and to report to him. No qualifications are laid down for this delegate; his appointment is in the unfettered discretion of the Minister. He is empowered to take evidence on oath and to summon persons to give evidence or to produce documents. He must give notice of the inquiry to interested persons, who may attend and be legally represented. The procedure is such as the person conducting the inquiry shall determine. No express right to cross-examine or to call witnesses is given. It is therefore, as in all cases where the statute prescribes some of the procedural details, a problem of statutory interpretation to be decided by the courts whether the rules of natural justice not expressly mentioned in the statute need be complied with. The Minister is not required to give reasons for his decision or to publish the report. He may refer a question of law to the High Court, and an applicant may himself appeal on a question of law to the High Court and demand such a statement of the grounds of the decision as will enable him to determine whether any question of law has arisen upon which he may wish to appeal. This provision will be difficult to apply, since most issues will be determinations of statutory terms on the borderland of law and fact.[2]

---

fact, e.g. a dispute about superannuation between a local authority and employee (Minister of Housing and Local Government); a parent dissatisfied with a school attendance order made in respect of his child by the local education authority (Minister of Education).

[1] He may review his decision if he is satisfied that it was given in ignorance of, or was based on a mistake as to, some material fact: National Insurance (Industrial Injuries) Act, 1953, Sect. 4.

[2] Interpretation of the terms of a contract is a question of law for this purpose; Gould v. Minister of National Insurance, [1951] 1 K.B. 731.

All other disputes are adjudicated by local tribunals.[1] The enormous number of cases includes such issues as whether a claimant for industrial injuries benefit was injured in the course of his employment, or whether an applicant for unemployment insurance benefit was capable of and available for work, or the amount of national assistance needed by a claimant.[2] Clearly, these tribunals should be manned by persons with experience of the common-place happenings in the lives of ordinary people. The National Insurance Local Tribunals, the National Assistance Appeal Tribunals and the Industrial Injuries Local Tribunals are similarly organised. They have jurisdiction over a limited area, and have three members, only one of whom, the chairman, is paid. He often is, but need not be, a lawyer, and is appointed and can be dismissed by the Minister who also draws up his conditions of service. The Minister creates a panel of persons representing employers and insured non-employed persons, and a panel representing employed persons; one member of each panel sits on each tribunal.[3] All members hold office for the period determined by the Minister and have no security of tenure. They are always part-time appointments. There is no published information on the method of drawing up the panels.

Neither the Press nor the public is admitted to hearings.[4] Interested parties must be given notice of them, and are entitled to be present and to be represented by any other person not being a lawyer. The insurance officer "and any other person nominated by the Minister" not being a lawyer, may be present. They may determine their own procedures, and are not required to keep a record.[5] The National Assistance Tribunals excepted, they must state their reasons for

[1] But questions of disablement are decided by a Medical Board and a Medical Appeal Tribunal.
[2] See also Family Allowances Acts, 1945–52, and the Family Allowances (References) Regulations, 1946, S.R. & O. 1946, No. 139, for the organisation and procedure of tribunals deciding claims for family allowances.
[3] The third member of the National Assistance Tribunal is not an employer's representative, and the Minister is unrestricted in his choice here: he could even appoint an official of the National Assistance Board. Non-employed persons are not, of course, on the employers' panel for the Industrial Injuries Local Tribunals.
[4] Except to the Industrial Injuries Tribunals, unless the tribunals for special reasons otherwise direct, Reg. 18.
[5] Except that the National Insurance (Industrial Injuries) Act, 1946, Sect. 46 (2), requires the tribunals to make "a statement of their findings on questions of fact material to the decision."

decisions. Their clerk, but no one else, is present when they reach their decision. None of them has power to take evidence on oath[1] or to call evidence.

There is no right of appeal from the National Assistance Appeal Tribunal, but there are appeals from the others, with leave, or where the decision is not unanimous, or at the instance of the insurance officer, or if any of certain associations of which the applicant is a member so requests. This appeal lies to the Commissioner,[2] a barrister appointed by the Crown to hold office during good behaviour. At his discretion he may allow an oral hearing. Legal representation at these appellate hearings is allowed. Those decisions which the Commissioner selects are published.

(b) Pensions Appeal Tribunal

An interesting comparison with the last-mentioned arrangements is provided by those relating to service pensions.[3] A person aggrieved by the decision of the Minister of Pensions and National Insurance can appeal to a Pensions Appeal Tribunal, and from it on a point of law to a nominated judge of the High Court with his or the tribunal's leave. Legal representation is allowed before the tribunal, and the rules of evidence are expressly waived. Cross-examination is expressly permitted, and hearings must be in public, unless that would be prejudicial to the appellant. Reasons for decisions are given, and a special series of pensions reports is published.[4]

(c) The Lands Tribunal and the Rent Tribunals

Two recently instituted tribunals applying standards laid down by Parliament as well as deciding matters of law and fact deserve particular attention. The Lands Tribunal set up under the Lands Tribunal Act, 1949, is thought to be admirably devised, whereas the Rent Tribunals functioning under the

---

[1] Unless they are caught by the Evidence Act, 1851, Sect. 16; see *General Medical Council* v. *Spackman*, [1943] A.C. 627 at 638 (*per* Lord Atkin).

[2] Styled the Industrial Injuries Commissioner in the case of industrial injuries, but in fact the same person at present. There are also several Deputy Commissioners.

[3] Pensions Appeals Tribunals Acts, 1943–9.

[4] Another administrative tribunal of the law/fact type the procedures of which are generally satisfactory and from the decisions of which an appeal on points of law lies to the High Court is the General Commissioners of Income Tax.

Furnished Houses (Rent Control) Act, 1946, have been severely criticised in Parliament, in the courts, and in the daily Press.

The Lands Tribunal has jurisdiction over various valuations of property.[1] These include, firstly, any question directed to be determined by a member of the panel of official arbitrators under the Acquisition of Land (Assessment of Compensation) Act, 1919, or of the panel of referees under Part 1 of the Finance (1909-1910) Act, 1910, secondly, claims for injurious affection under the Lands Clauses Acts; thirdly, apportionments of rentcharge on acquisition of land under the Lands Clauses Consolidation Act, 1845; fourthly, various disputes about payments under the Town and Country Planning Acts, 1947-54; fifthly, appeals from the local valuation courts on the valuation of property for rating; sixthly, valuations arising from the discharge or modification of restrictive covenants under Sect. 84 of the Law of Property Act, 1925, and seventhly, compensation for the acquisition of property under the Lands Clauses Consolidation Act, 1845, where the local authority is unable to treat.

It consists of the president and such members as the Lord Chancellor determines and appoints. Its president must have held judicial office or have been in practice as a barrister for seven years. The others may be barristers or solicitors or "persons who have had experience in the valuation of land appointed after consultation with the president of the Royal Institution of Chartered Surveyors." The composition of the tribunal can be adjusted to meet the requirements of the particular case, so that, for example, where the problem is primarily legal, more lawyers will sit at that hearing. The tribunal ordinarily sits in public and travels round the country. There is a right of audience and of legal representation. Affidavit evidence is allowed by consent of the parties or on presidential order. One expert witness on each side is permitted. Its procedures have been settled in detail and published.[2] When it views the land, it gives notice to interested parties who are entitled to be present. It is empowered to take

---

[1] Its jurisdiction over any questions of land valuation can be extended by Order in Council.

[2] The Lands Tribunal Rules, 1949, S.I. 1949 No. 2263; amended by S.I. 1951 No. 2004; 1955 No. 54.

evidence on oath and can summon evidence. Its decisions are written and reasoned. Any party can insist on the tribunal's stating a case to the Court of Appeal on a point of law.

The Rent Tribunals are set up under the Furnished Houses (Rent Control) Act, 1946. They are empowered to determine the reasonable rent of furnished premises, and of other houses first let after 1st September, 1939.[1] In the course of applying this standard they may be called upon to decide many mixed questions of law and fact, such as whether a standard rent had previously been fixed or whether the first "letting" was after the specified date.

The tribunals, which function locally, consist of a chairman and two others, all appointed by the Minister of Housing and Local Government.[2] The qualifications of the personnel vary greatly—it is to be regretted that there is no information about the mode of selection. There is no lawyer on many Tribunals. They are paid, and hold office during the pleasure of the Minister.

Their procedures afford an excellent example of how statutes can eat into the principles of natural justice. The tribunal is to give notice to each party of his right to insist on being heard by the tribunal or to send written representations. If one party asks for a hearing, the other party must be given notice of it.

Regulation 7 provides that "at any hearing before a Tribunal a party . . . may appear in person or by counsel or a solicitor or by any other representative or may be accompanied by any person whom he may wish to assist him thereat."[3] Regulation 8 adds that "subject to the provisions of these regulations the procedure at a hearing shall be such as the Tribunal may determine, and the Tribunal may if they think fit, and at the request of either party shall unless for some special reason they consider it undesirable, allow the hearing to be held in public."[4] In *R.* v. *Brighton and Area Rent Tribunal, ex parte Marine Parade Estates* (1936) *Ltd.*[5] the tenant had submitted

---

[1] These were added by the Landlord and Tenant (Rent Control) Act, 1949; and see the Housing Repairs and Rents Act, 1954, Part II.

[2] For procedural details, see the Furnished Houses (Rent Control) Regulations, 1946, S.R. & O. 1946 No. 781, and the Landlord and Tenant (Rent Control) Regulations, 1949, S.I. 1949 No. 1096, amended by S.I. 1950 No. 1763; S.I. 1954 No. 1046.

[3] See preceding note (1946).

[4] Ibid.   [5] [1950] 2 K.B. 410.

written evidence and was legally represented at the hearing requested by the landlords. Counsel made a statement on behalf of the tenant but there was no opportunity to cross-examine him on his written evidence. It was held by the High Court that these proceedings could not be quashed for breach of the rules of natural justice. The rules quoted established that ordinarily the tribunal could decide without hearing any evidence, i.e. it could act on its own knowledge, and that if there was a hearing a party could elect to give written evidence.[1] It may be that Regulation 7 allows a party to call witnesses.

There is no power to administer oaths[2] or to summon evidence. No record has to be kept; no reasons need be given for decisions, which are not published. There is no appeal from decisions. A perusal of the cases where decisions of these tribunals have been quashed for *ultra vires* confirms the general view that these tribunals are not sufficiently tried and trusted to merit the lax organisation and procedures which they possess.[3] The need for an appellate tribunal is also obvious.[4]

C. Trade and Vocational Tribunals Subject to a Measure of Government Control

Voluntary organisations such as clubs may regulate their own affairs except that the courts will interfere if disciplinary measures have been taken against members in violation of the standards of natural justice or the rules of the club. Some internal trade organisations have, however, progressed beyond the status of a mere voluntary domestic body.

I. MARKETING BOARDS

These marketing boards are corporate bodies set up under statute and representing the producers or distributors of particular commodities and controlling the production and sale

---

[1] This decision casts doubt on the dicta in *R.* v. *Paddington & St. Marylebone Rent Tribunal, ex parte Bell London & Provincial Properties, Ltd.,* [1949] 1 K.B. 666, that the Tribunal acted illegally in taking note of the ceiling height of the premises without informing the parties to the hearing. A decision will be quashed if the tribunal does not give the landlord an opportunity of giving evidence: *R.* v. *Kingston-upon-Hull Rent Tribunal, ex parte Black,* [1949] 1 All E.R. 260.

[2] But see Evidence Act, 1851, Sect. 16, and above p. 163 n. 1.

[3] See also *R.* v. *Paddington & St. Marylebone Rent Tribunal, ex parte Bedrock Investments, Ltd.,* [1948] 2 K.B. 413; *R.* v. *Croydon & District Rent Tribunal, ex parte Langford Property Co., Ltd.,* [1948] 1 K.B. 60.

[4] Cf. Sir Alfred Denning: *Freedom under the Law,* Lecture 3.

of those commodities.[1] They are empowered to buy and sell all the commodity at prices fixed by them. Their effectiveness depends on their being able to punish members by fines or exclusion. The very extensiveness of their powers, and their impact on the consumer (unfortunately a secondary consideration) has made them a matter of governmental concern. Not only must the Minister of Agriculture approve the scheme, but, following on much public criticism supported by Government reports, statutory instruments laying down the composition of the tribunals which will hear complaints of breaches of the schemes by members have also been made. The Agricultural Marketing Act, 1949, provides that each Board shall consist of four to eight members of whom at least two but not otherwise more than one fifth shall be appointed by the Minister. The Disciplinary Committee consists of four to six members of the Board with an outside chairman who is a lawyer of at least seven years standing. Parties are entitled to an oral hearing in public, and the Committee has power to summon evidence, and to take evidence on oath.[2]

2. VOCATIONAL TRIBUNALS—THE NATIONAL HEALTH SERVICE ACT

There is usually no objection to allowing vocational organisations to maintain their professional standards by their own arrangements. Architects, barristers, patent agents, and solicitors all have their domestic tribunals.[3]

When, however, the State assumes responsibility for the administration of the service which members of that profession help to perform, it can no longer regard the matter as purely domestic. Its desire to maintain standards and its duty to the public require it to set up adjudicative procedures under its direction. The arrangements made under the National Health Service Act, 1946, will now be examined.[4]

[1] Pigs, herrings, hops, bacon, and milk have all been thus regulated. Many schemes were suspended in 1949, but among those at present operative are those for potatoes, cucumbers, hops, wool, and tomatoes.

[2] For a current scheme incorporating the requirements of the Act, see the Hops Marketing Scheme, 1932 (S.R. & O. 1932 No. 505), as amended; Halsbury's *Statutory Instruments*, vol. 1, p. 173.

[3] There is an increasing tendency for Parliament to give a right of appeal to the ordinary courts: e.g. the Medical Act, 1950, Sect. 20 (3).

[4] And see the National Health Service (Services Committees and Tribunal) Regulations, 1956 (S.I. 1956 No. 1077).

Executive Councils appoint medical service, pharmaceutical service, dental service, and joint services committees to investigate alleged breaches of service. These committees are to consist of three lay members appointed by the lay members of the executive council and three appointed by the appropriate local committee of practitioners. Non-legal assistance is allowed at the hearings, which are in private and are followed by a report to the Executive Council whose decision is communicated to interested parties. The Council can recommend to the Minister that he makes a deduction from the remuneration of the practitioner. Any person aggrieved by a decision also has a right of appeal from the council to the Minister, who may hold a local inquiry. This must be conducted, where failure to use reasonable care and skill is alleged, by not more than three persons of whom one must be a practitioner in the same service as the party whose conduct is being investigated. Legal representation is allowed at the inquiry, which is followed by a report to the Minister. His decision is final, but before directing that money be withheld he must refer the case to a Medical Advisory Committee and consider its report. The Press is never given the names of practitioners found guilty of these breaches of service, although other details are supplied.

The local medical or other appropriate committee may recommend to the Minister action to be taken in respect of charges of over-prescribing, negligent certification or bad record-keeping which the Minister asks it to investigate.

Representations that the continued inclusion of a practitioner in the service is prejudicial to its efficiency are considered by a tribunal appointed by the Lord Chancellor. This sits *in camera* unless the respondent otherwise requests, and allows legal representation. Copies of its report are made available to interested parties. The practitioner has a right of appeal to the Minister, who appoints a person, assisted by a practitioner, to hold an inquiry and to hear the appellant.

D. Regulatory Tribunals

Two types of regulatory administrative action will be examined. The first is the process whereby the planning of land may be effected and if necessary the appropriate authority may be empowered to acquire it compulsorily.[1]

I. THE HOUSING ACTS

Under the Housing Acts the local authority makes a draft clearance or compulsory purchase order which becomes operative only if the Minister confirms it. If there are objections to the order, the Minister must cause a local inquiry to be held. He is not required to conduct this himself, but after considering the report of it and the objections he may confirm the order. Because of the frequent use of this process and the large sums involved, there has been a spate of litigation arising out of it. What has to be considered is the procedure to which the Minister and his inspector conducting the inquiry must conform.

The only relevant statutory provision is[2]—

> . . . if no objection is duly made by any of the persons upon whom notices are required to be served, or if all objections so made are withdrawn, . . . the Minister may, if he thinks fit, confirm the order with or without modification, but in any other case he shall, before confirming the order, cause a public local inquiry to be held, and shall consider any objection not withdrawn and the report of the person who held the inquiry, and may then confirm the order either with or without modification.

What follows is in essence a history of the attempts made by landowners to establish that all stages of this process were judicial and had to be conducted in accordance with the principles of natural justice.

If they succeeded so far as the Minister was concerned, then he would be unable to discuss the proposed action in the absence of the landowner. A great fillip to these efforts was given by the decision of the Court of Appeal in *Errington* v. *Minister of Health*.[3] After the Minister had caused a local inquiry to be held into a proposed clearance order in Jarrow, his officials had a discussion with the town clerk and medical officer of health of Jarrow. Later, Ministry representatives, accompanied by councillors and municipal officers, visited the site. The order was afterwards confirmed by the Minister, and the landowners alleged that he had acted improperly by

---

[1] See 185 H.L. Deb. 5s. col. 9167 *et seq.* for a discussion of the problems.
[2] Housing Act, 1936, Sch. 1, para. 4.
[3] [1935] 1 K.B. 249.

discussing the matter behind their backs, an allegation which the Court of Appeal upheld.[1]

In a series of cases brought by the landowners, encouraged by this decision, attempts were made to impose the same standards of conduct on the Minister before objections were made. The courts held that the Minister could before objections were made discuss the terms of a proposed clearance order,[2] look at the site,[3] advise the local authority of the schemes of other local authorities,[4] and obtain information from other Government departments[5] and public authorities.[6] Any other holding would have imposed an unjustifiable clog on the administrative process. The cases then firmly establish that before the objections are made the Minister is under no duty to observe any rules of procedure.

Is the Minister under any procedural restrictions after the inquiry is held? It is commonly stated that he is not, but nevertheless there is no decision to that effect. The case usually relied on is *Horn* v. *Minister of Health*.[7] Between the holding of the inquiry and the Ministerial decision an official of the Ministry received a deputation from the local authority, when there followed a general discussion about the proposed action of the local authority under the Housing Acts. The Court of Appeal found nothing illegal in this, not because it occurred after the inquiry, but because the particular compulsory purchase order was not even mentioned in the discussion. The view of those who contend that the Minister's duty to observe procedural restrictions ends after the inquiry is summarised in the following *obiter dictum* of Lord Greene[8]—

But his functions are administrative functions, subject only to the qualification that, at a particular stage and for a particular

---

[1] Although the Housing (Temporary Provisions) Act, 1944, authorised the Minister, at his discretion, not to hold a local inquiry he still could not take evidence behind the back of a party: *Stafford* v. *Minister of Health*, [1946] K.B. 621.

[2] *Frost* v. *Minister of Health*, [1935] 1 K.B. 286.

[3] *Re Manchester (Ringway Airport) Compulsory Purchase Order* (1935), 153 L.T. 219.

[4] *Offer and Another* v. *Minister of Health*, [1936] 1 K.B. 40.

[5] *Miller* v. *Minister of Health*, [1946] K.B. 626; *Summers* v. *Minister of Health*, [1947] 1 All E.R. 184.

[6] *Price* v. *Minister of Health*, [1947] 1 All E.R. 47.

[7] [1937] 1 K.B. 164.

[8] *B. Johnson & Co. (Builders), Ltd.* v. *Minister of Health*, [1947] 2 All E.R. 395, at 399–401. His *dictum* is *obiter* because the point at issue was the duty of the Minister before objections were made.

and limited purpose, there is superimposed on his administrative character a character which is loosely described as "quasi-judicial." The language which has always been construed as giving rise to the obligations, whatever they may be, implied in the words "quasi-judicial" is to be found in the duty to consider the objections, which, as I have said, is superimposed on a process of ministerial action which is essentially administrative. That process may begin in all sorts of manners—the collection of information, the ascertainment of facts, and the consideration of representations made from all sorts of quarters, and so forth, long before any question of objections can arise under the procedure laid down by the Act. While acting at that stage, to carry the Act into effect or for purposes relevant to it and bearing on it, the Minister is an executive officer of government, and nothing else. The administrative character in which he acts reappears at a later stage because, after considering the objections, which may be regarded as the culminating point of his quasi-judicial functions, there follows something which again, in my view, is purely administrative, viz., the decision whether or not to confirm the order. That decision must be an administrative decision because it is not to be based purely on the view that he forms of the objections, *vis-à-vis* the desires of the local authority, but is to be guided by his view as to the policy which in the circumstances he ought to pursue . . . the Minister, in coming to his decision whether to confirm a compulsory purchase order, is entitled to have his mind informed in a number of ways. In other words, he is not limited to material contained in the objections.

The much discredited and misunderstood *Errington* case must now be examined more carefully. The contention of the Attorney-General was that the matters discussed were financial and other issues of policy outside the range of the inquiry, in respect of which the Minister had no judicial or quasi-judicial duty. The Court of Appeal found that, in addition, a matter the subject of the inquiry, viz. whether the premises could be repaired, was discussed. This was the basis of the judgments of both Lord Maugham and Lord Roche which are inconsistent with the view of Lord Greene. Lord Maugham said[1]—

That is not to say that there may not be matters which were not in dispute at all at the inquiry, . . . with regard to which he might, if he thought fit, inform himself. I am dealing with a case where something which is the subject of an objection definitely put and urged before the gentleman who holds a public

[1] [1935] 1 K.B. 249, at 272–3.

inquiry is before the Minister after the report has been made, and with regard to which he subsequently obtains *ex parte* information from one side or the other. My conclusion is that although the act of affirming a clearance order is an administrative act, the consideration which must precede the doing of that act is of the nature of a quasi-judicial consideration, and the Minister is bound to the extent mentioned by the House of Lords in the *Board of Education* v. *Rice*.

Whether Greer, L.J., would have found for Errington had only financial matters been discussed is uncertain, but his statement[1] that "in deciding whether a closing order should be made in spite of the objections which have been raised by the owners the Minister should be regarded as exercising quasi-judicial functions" suggests that he might have differed from his colleagues. Greer, L.J., must be sympathised with in his difficulty, for Parliament certainly failed to indicate whether the Minister was free to avail himself of any evidence he chose outside the range of the inquiry. There are two separate questions: whether the Minister has a discretion which enables him in the public interest to overrule an objection, and whether all evidence of fact must be produced at the inquiry. The judicial attitude has been so consistent since the *Errington* case that one must probably accept that not only does the Minister have that discretion but also he can peruse files and reports and consult departments after the inquiry behind the back of parties. It has been said above that the judges have sometimes not perceived that these are to some extent evidential facts.[2] It is thought that the observations of Lord Greene on this topic are open to challenge[3]—

. . . the idea that a Minister can be compelled to disclose to anybody information of that kind [government files] which he has obtained as a purely administrative person, is alien to our whole conception of government in this country.

Even if the Minister may after the inquiry take evidence behind the back of objectors, what limits are there to this right? Both Lord Maugham and Lord Roche held in the *Errington* case that a Minister cannot ignore the rules of natural justice on anything which is the subject-matter of the inquiry.[4]

---

[1] At 259.   [2] See above, p. 151.   [3] *Johnson's* case, at 401.
[4] Nor can the inspector view the site in the absence of one party and in the presence of the other; cf. "Ryder v. Minister of Housing and Local Government," *Journal of Planning Law* (1954) 508.

Somervell, L.J. (the Attorney-General in the *Errington* case), in his concurring judgment in the *Robinson* case summarised the *Errington* decision as follows[1]—

. . . the Minister could not, after the public inquiry had been held, receive *ex parte* statements from the local authority which were not communicated to the objectors, dealing with the subject-matter of the objections as investigated at the inquiry.[2]

Provided always that the matter was raised at the inquiry, is the Minister precluded from getting evidence behind the back of a party, even if it is contained in Government files?[3] If the answer is "Yes," then does it follow that objectors can take advantage of the failure of the Act to define "objections" by raising financial and other matters of public and not merely private interest, and thus make the action of the Minister in subsequently taking factual evidence from files and reports illegal?[4]

The inspector holding the inquiry must obey the rules of natural justice.[5] Swift, J., after denying that the inspector was a mere collector of information, added[6]—

. . . he comes more nearly to the position of a judicial functionary, or as nearly to that position as the Minister himself does. It seems to me obvious that he, in discharging his duties, must be bound by the dictates of natural justice. His inquiry must be an inquiry which is fair to all parties interested. He must hear everything which any of them desire to say and should not hear anything without giving an opportunity to the other parties

---

[1] [1947] K.B. 702 at 723.

[2] Cf. the statement of Lord Loreburn in *Board of Education* v. *Rice*, [1911] A.C. 179, at 182, that a party must be given a fair opportunity to contradict prejudicial evidence in proceedings to which the rules of natural justice apply, and Cohen, L.J., in the *Johnson* case at 405: ". . . once the *quasi-lis* has started, if he receives from some third party a document relevant to the subject of the *quasi-lis*, he should give both parties an opportunity of commenting on it."

[3] The distinction between taking fresh factual evidence and, before decision, consulting experts on the materials already put in evidence is not clearly drawn.

[4] Cf. Denning, L.J., in *Steele* v. *Minister of Housing and Local Government* (1956), 6 P. & C.R. 386, C.A. at 392 (on the Housing Acts): "The Minister . . . must only consider the report and the material properly before him. He must not act on extrinsic information which the houseowner has had no opportunity of contradicting. . . ." On the Acquisition of Land (Authorisation Procedure) Act, 1946, however, see *Darlassis* v. *Minister of Education* (1954), 52 L.G.R. 304, p. 175 below.

[5] The Local Government Act, 1933, Sect. 290 lays down a code for the conduct of most of the local inquiries (dealing with such points as the power to take evidence on oath and to summons witnesses) discussed in this section.

[6] *William Denby & Sons, Ltd.* v. *Minister of Health*, [1936] 1 K.B. 337, at 342.

interested to answer that which is said; he should not receive anything from one behind the back of the other, and although he is not bound in any sense by the rules of evidence or procedure which apply to an ordinary court of law, he must, before making his report, comply with the ordinary dictates of natural justice as to the obtaining and consideration of the matters which go to form the opinions or conclusions which he expresses in his report.

The conduct of inspectors has rarely been questioned, and one must conclude that they maintain a high standard of fairness. They are not usually lawyers and are given by the Minister certain rules of evidence to guide them in the conduct of inquiries.[1]

It has been decided that an inspector may stop counsel of an objector from detailing the future intentions of his client when that client is not giving evidence himself.[2] Swift, J., has suggested that the inspector must allow witnesses to be cross-examined.[3] An important point was raised in *In re Sir J.W.B. Simeon Bt.*[4] At an inquiry under the Public Works Facilities Act, 1930, the request of an applicant to argue a legal point was refused by the inspector on the ground that such a legal point should be determined by the Minister. The Minister did not appoint a time for his representative to hear the legal argument. The application to set aside the compulsory purchase order failed, but the legal issue was not determined because it was not proved that any request to have the legal argument heard was made to the Minister.[5] It is submitted that the question is solely whether the hearing of legal argument is within the jurisdiction of the inspector.[6] Nor is the landowner entitled to see the report of the inspector to the Minister.[7] In *Fredman* v. *Minister of Health*[8] it was held that the

---

[1] For these rules, see the *Committee on Ministers' Powers, Minutes of Evidence,* Vol. 2, 168. Although Sir Arthur Robinson, on behalf of the Ministry of Health, did not deny that these rules were drafted in 1850, and although he admitted that they required "overhauling" (Q. 2858, p. 201) they have not yet been changed, and are issued to the inspectors of the Ministry of Housing and Local Government.

[2] *Re London (Hammersmith) Housing Order—Application of Land Development, Ltd.,* [1936] 2 All E.R. 1063.

[3] *Marriott* v. *Minister of Health* (1935), 154 L.T. 47, at 50.

[4] [1935] 2 K.B. 183.

[5] But *contra,* W. O. Hart: *Introduction to the Law of Local Government and Administration* (5th Edn.) 484.

[6] Cf. *R.* v. *Hudson,* [1915] 1 K.B. 838; *In re An Application by Beck and Pollitzer,* [1948] 2 K.B. 339.

[7] *William Denby & Sons, Ltd.* v. *Minister of Health,* [1936] 1 K.B. 337: *Steele* v. *Minister of Housing and Local Government* (1956), 6 P. & C.R. 386.

[8] (1936), 154 L.T. 240.

landowner could not insist on being heard by the local authority before it resolved that an area be declared a clearance area under the Housing Act, 1930.

2. THE ACQUISITION OF LAND (AUTHORISATION PROCEDURE) ACT, 1946

This Act, which provides a uniform procedure for authorising the compulsory purchase of land by local authorities, where power to authorise the purchase is conferred by existing legislation other than Part III of the Housing Act, 1936, may be compared with the last-mentioned Act.

The local authority makes the compulsory purchase order and submits it to the appropriate Minister for confirmation, having given the usual notice in the Press about the inspection of the order and the making of objections. Except that the Minister may, instead of causing a local inquiry to be held, afford to any objector "an opportunity of appearing before and being heard by a person appointed . . . for the purpose"[1] the provisions regarding the confirmation of the order are very similar to those of the Housing Acts. In *Darlassis* v. *Minister of Education* it was held that the Minister could, after an inquiry into a suitable school site, consult another Ministry on a matter of policy, viz., whether houses were to be erected on an alternative site suggested by an objector, but it was stated (*obiter*) that it would be unlawful not to disclose to an objector information which had been obtained from the other Ministry behind the objector's back and "which concerned the relevant merits of the two sites."[2]

3. DESIGNATION ORDERS UNDER THE TOWN AND COUNTRY PLANNING ACTS

By the Town and Country Planning Act, 1944, the Minister was empowered, on the application of a local planning authority, to make a draft order designating areas of extensive war damage or of bad layout and obsolete development as subject to compulsory purchase. Before the Minister made his draft order into law he had, on request, to hold a local inquiry. This procedure differed materially from the procedure of the Housing

---

[1] Sch. 1 Pt. I, para. 4 (2).
[2] (1954), 52 L.G.R. 304.

Act in that the Minister had only to confirm his own order: in no sense could he be said to be adjudicating on a dispute between two other parties. It is not surprising, therefore, that Lord Greene has said that the purpose of this inquiry could only be to inform the mind of the Minister who, in making his decision whether to designate an area, was not limited to the evidence presented at the inquiry.[1] Nevertheless, he conceded (*obiter*) that the Minister acted in a quasi-judicial capacity on matters connected with the inquiry.[2] Somervell, L.J., was prepared to assume, without deciding, that the *Errington* case would apply to this procedure.[3]

Lord Greene said that the local public inquiry "must be conducted on proper principles as being what is loosely called a 'quasi-judicial' proceeding."[4] Cases on procedure at local inquiries where the Minister eventually confirms his own draft order are few. It has, however, been held that an inquiry into a draft compulsory purchase order of the Minister of Transport was not invalidated because the inspector refused to let an objector cross-examine a Ministry official on the necessity of the proposals or on alternative schemes, although this official gave evidence at the inquiry.[5] It is suggested that this decision is not applicable to Housing Act inquiries.[6]

The power to designate land for compulsory purchase has been extended by the Town and Country Planning Act, 1947, which replaces the Town and Country Planning Act, 1944. In addition to the circumstances mentioned in the Act of 1944, land may be designated where it is allocated by the development plan for any of the functions of any Minister, local authority or statutory undertaker. Two important differences of procedure must be mentioned. The Minister need not hold a local inquiry on objections; instead he may merely afford an opportunity of appearing before and being heard by a person appointed by a Minister for the purpose.[7] How far this hearing must comply with the rules of natural justice is a difficult problem of statutory interpretation which awaits

---

[1] *Robinson v. Minister of Town and Country Planning*, [1947] K.B. 702.
[2] At 715.   [3] At 723.   [4] At 715.
[5] *London-Portsmouth Trunk Road (Surrey) Compulsory Purchase Order (No. 2) 1938*, [1939] 2 All E.R. 464.
[6] Cf. *Magistrates of Ayr v. Lord Advocate*, [1950] S.C. 102.
[7] Sect. 37 (4), Acquisition of Land (Authorisation Procedure) Act, 1946, Sch. 1, Pt. I, para. 4 (2).

judicial decision. Secondly, Sect. 10 (3) makes the *audi alteram partem* rule inapplicable to the Minister by providing that, if, after objections have been lodged to a plan, the Minister is of opinion that the local planning authority or any other authority or person ought to be consulted before he comes to his decision "he shall consult that authority or person, but shall not be under any obligation to consult any other authority or person, or to afford any opportunity for further objections or representations or to cause any further local inquiry or other hearing to be held."

4. THE NEW TOWNS ACT, 1946

Similar to this town-planning legislation is the New Towns Act, 1946, the purpose of which is the creation of new towns for overspill from cities. Under the provisions of Sect. 1 of that Act—

> . . . if the Minister is satisfied, after consultation with any local authorities who appear to him to be concerned, that it is expedient in the national interest that any area of land should be developed as a new town by a corporation established under this Act, he may make an order designating that area as the site of the proposed new town.

He must first publish a draft order and give an opportunity for objections to be made.

> If any objection is duly made to the proposed order and is not withdrawn, the Minister shall, before making the order, cause a public local inquiry to be held with respect thereto, and shall consider the report of the person by whom the inquiry was held.[1]

Like the town-planning legislation, this differs from the Housing Acts in that the Minister is a party throughout. Further, the Minister is not statutorily required to consider the objections. It is obvious, as the statute itself states, that the creation of new towns is of national interest.

The courts had to interpret this Act in connection with the ministerial order designating an area at Stevenage.[2] An applicant sought to quash this order for three reasons. Before the Act was passed, the Minister had announced in a public

---

[1] Sch. 1, para. 3.

[2] *Franklin* v. *Minister of Town and Country Planning*, [1947] 1 All E.R. 396; [1947] 1 All E.R. 612 (C.A.); [1948] A.C. 87.

speech his intention to create the new town, and had used the
following words[1]—

> The project will go forward because it must go forward. . . .
> While I will consult as far as possible all the local authorities, at
> the end, if people become fractious and unreasonable, I shall
> have to carry out my duty.

It was contended that he had a closed mind before the
inquiry; secondly, that the inquiry was improper in that no
evidence in favour of the order was given; thirdly, that the
Minister had admitted after the inquiry unsolved difficulties
of water supply raised at the inquiry, and could not have
weighed these objections with an open mind. The House of
Lords unanimously confirmed the decision of the Court of
Appeal not to quash the order. They found that the Minister
had considered the objections based on water supply. They
further rejected the view of the court of first instance that the
Minister acted in a judicial capacity in relation to the inquiry.
Lord Thankerton said[2]—

> The respondent's duties under Section 1 of the Act and
> Schedule 1 thereto are, in my opinion, purely administrative,
> but the Act prescribes certain methods of or steps in discharge
> of that duty. . . . It seems clear also, that the purpose of
> inviting objections, and, where they are not withdrawn, of having
> a public inquiry, to be held by someone other than the respondent,
> to whom that person reports, was for the further information of
> the respondent, in order to the [sic] final consideration of the
> soundness of the scheme of the designation. . . . I am of opinion
> that no judicial duty is laid on the respondent in discharge of
> these statutory duties, and that the only question is whether he
> has complied with the statutory directions to appoint a person to
> hold the public inquiry, and to consider that person's report.

The remaining second contention of the appellant was
disposed of by the House of Lords deciding[3] that "the object
of the inquiry is further to inform the mind of the Minister,
and not to consider any issue between the Minister and the
objectors" and that therefore no evidence need be given for
the Minister. The *London-Portsmouth Trunk Road*[4] case was
approved.

Lord Thankerton did not analyse the meanings of "judicial"
and "administrative" nor did he specify the particular factors

[1] [1948] A.C. at 104–5.
[2] At 102.   [3] At 106.   [4] [1939] 2 All E.R. 464.

which motivated his classification. It is permissible to conclude
that he looked at the Act as a whole, applying a theory of
interpretation similar to the rule in *Heydon's* case.[1] Presumably
he took account of the national importance of providing overspill areas for London, and thought that Parliament had here
vested in the Minister a degree of discretion so wide and subjective[2] that at all stages in its exercise he should be responsible
not judicially to the courts but politically to Parliament. To
what extent it is important that the Minister both initiates and
makes the order is uncertain.

The effects of this important decision must be measured.
Lord Justice Denning has referred to the widely-held view
that it overrules the *Errington* case, and that neither the Minister
nor inspector need "observe the elementary rules applicable
to judicial functions . . . so long as the statutory procedure
is complied with."[3] There seems, however, no justification for
attributing to the *Franklin* case a holding that the inspector need
not observe the rules of natural justice. Indeed, Lord Thankerton said[4]—

> . . . no suggestion is made that the public inquiry was not
> properly conducted. . . . In such a case the only ground of
> challenge must be . . .

which suggests that there are standards to which the inquiry
must conform. It is submitted that it is erroneous to assume
that only express statutory requirements must be complied
with; on the contrary, it is thought that the courts will read
into a statutory requirement that an inquiry be held the
implication that it "must be properly conducted," that is, the
no bias and *audi alteram partem* rules must be observed. *A
fortiori*, the cases laying down the duties of inspectors under the
Housing Acts seem unaffected.

It is interesting to note how little difference there is between
the duty, as laid down in the *Franklin* case, of the Minister
carrying out his duties under the New Towns Act and that of

---

[1] (1584), 3 Co. Rep. 7a, 7b.
[2] The statute reads: "If the Minister is satisfied . . ."— a purely subjective
discretion, not "If he has reasonable grounds for satisfaction" or any other words
which would enable the courts to decide whether he had acted reasonably. But
see *Liversidge* v. *Anderson*, [1942] A.C. 206; and cf. *Nakkuda Ali* v. *M. F. de S.
Jayaratne*, [1951] A.C. 66.
[3] *Freedom under the Law*, 121–2.   [4] At 102.

180   PRINCIPLES OF ADMINISTRATIVE LAW

the Minister who, according to the *Errington* case, has to observe the rules of natural justice in relation to a Housing Act inquiry. The House of Lords held that it would be a ground for challenging a New Towns order that the Minister "did not in fact consider the report and the objections . . . or that his mind was so foreclosed that he gave no genuine consideration to them. . . ."[1] Even under the Housing Act, the plea of necessity would prevent any complaint of pecuniary or personal bias on the part of the Minister. In short, the only difference is that the Minister under the New Towns Act may take evidence behind the back of objectors even though it concerns matters objected to at the inquiry.

Some critics impatiently dismiss attempts to distinguish between the effect of the various statutes as "barren."[2] It is submitted, however, that the thoroughness with which the courts have analysed the statutes in the *Errington, Robinson, Johnson,* and *Franklin* cases and the emphasis which they have placed on the fact that their decisions have been based solely on the statute under consideration make such an approach inevitable. Whether the *Franklin* case applies to the designation orders of the Town and Country Planning Act, 1947, can matter hardly at all in view of Sect. 10 (3) of the Act. The Act of 1944 did not contain a similar provision, and Lord Greene, it will be remembered,[3] expressed the opinion that the Minister had quasi-judicial duties in relation to the inquiry. The question is, whether the duties of the Minister under a particular statute are administrative throughout. The Act of 1944 is similar in wording to the New Towns Act; the Minister is a party; perhaps the development of extensive blitzed and blighted areas was in 1944 as much a matter of policy as the overspill from cities was in 1946. The Housing Act is worded differently—the Minister is expressly required to consider objections; he is acting in a matter to which the original parties are the local authority and the objectors; the schemes foreshadowed by the Housing Acts are much more local in scope and it may be that Parliament thought that a lesser degree of policy was involved. Even if the *Franklin* case overrules the dicta of Lord Greene in the *Robinson* case on the

[1] At 103.
[2] H. W. R. Wade: "Quasi-Judicial and its Background" in 10 *Cambridge Law Journal* (1949), 216 at 240.   [3] See above, p. 171.

Town and Country Planning Act, 1944,[1] the *Errington* case on the Housing Acts is not necessarily affected.[2]

5. OTHER PROVISIONS OF THE TOWN AND COUNTRY PLANNING ACT, 1947

(a) *Permission for Development*

Sect. 12 (1) of the Act provides that subject to many exceptions[3] permission must be obtained from the local planning authority, i.e. the county council or county borough, for any development or change of use of land which is carried out after 1st July, 1948. The authority, in dealing with the application, "shall have regard to the provisions of the development plan, so far as material thereto, and to any other material considerations."[4] Any person interested may also apply in writing to the local planning authority in order to have it determined whether proposed operations are development within the meaning of the Act.[5] Moreover, the Minister has exercised the power given to him by Sect. 14 (3) (c) of requiring the local planning authority, before deciding applications, to consult with such authorities as he shall prescribe.[6] The Act makes no other provision for notifying interested parties or giving them a hearing. It has been held that where a firm obtained planning permission without the owner being notified or given a hearing and then sought a compulsory purchase order, the Act did not require notice or opportunity to be heard to be given.[7]

The Minister also exercises jurisdiction in connection with these applications. Sect. 15 (1) authorises him to direct planning authorities to refer all or any planning applications to him for determination. An applicant aggrieved by the

---

[1] In *Darlassis* v. *Minister of Education* (1954), 52 L.G.R. 304, Barry, J., treated Lord Greene's dicta as still operative. and indeed applied them to the case, one on the acquisition of Land (Authorisation Procedure) Act, 1946; see p. 175 above.

[2] In *Steele* v. *Minister of Housing and Local Government* (1956), 6 P. & C.R. 386, Denning, L.J., treated the *Errington* case as still applying to the functions of the Minister under the Housing Act, 1936.

[3] See the Town and Country Planning (Use Classes) Order, 1950, S.I. 1950 No. 1131; the Town and Country Planning General Development Order and Development Charge Applications Regulations, 1950, S.I. 1950 No. 728.

[4] Sect. 14 (1).

[5] Sect. 17 and Reg. 5 of S.I. 1950 No. 728; see above note 3.

[6] S.I. 1950 No 728, Regs. 7 and 9. The planning authority is under no duty to inform the applicant of this consultation.

[7] *Hanily v. Minister of Local Government and Planning*, [1952] 2 Q.B. 444.

decision of a local planning authority under Sects. 12 or 17 may appeal to the Minister. In either case the Minister shall at the request of either the applicant or the planning authority "afford to each of them an opportunity of appearing before and being heard by a person appointed by the Minister for the purpose."[1] Again, there is no statement whether the rules of natural justice are to apply. The fact that on appeal the Minister may seem to be deciding a *lis* between the planning authority and the applicant has led some writers to state that he must observe the rules of natural justice.[2] The right of the Minister to deal with the appeal as if the application "had been made to him in the first instance"[3] suggests that, the Minister, like the local planning authority, is not bound by the rules of natural justice.

(b) *The Preservation of Trees and Historic Places*

The local planning authority can make orders preserving woodlands or restricting the demolition or alteration of buildings of special architectural or historic interest. These orders are effective only when confirmed by the Minister, who must afford an opportunity for the making of objections and consider any objections before he confirms the order. Contraventions of the orders are punishable by fines on summary conviction. If alterations to buildings are made without permission the local planning authority can serve notice on the owner or occupier of the building requiring him to restore the building to its former state. On appeal a court of summary jurisdiction may not only quash the notice if it finds that no works have been carried out but also may vary it if it is satisfied that the requirements of the notice exceed what is necessary for restoring the building to its former state.[4]

(c) *Advertisements*

The Act regulates the display of advertisements in the interests of amenity or public safety. Although the Act envisaged

[1] Sects. 15 (2), 16 (2), 17 (2); by Sect. 104 the Minister "may cause a local inquiry to be held for the purpose of the exercise of any of his functions under this Act. . . ."
[2] J. Charlesworth: *Principles of Planning Law*, 31; de Smith, in R. S. W. Pollard (ed.): *Administrative Tribunals at Work*, 107.   [3] Sect. 16 (2).
[4] Sects. 29 (2) (b), 23 (4); Town and Country Planning (General) Regulations, 1948, S.I. 1948 No. 1380, Reg. 6.

that an independent tribunal might hear appeals from the decision of the planning authority, the Minister has made a regulation that appeals shall lie to him.[1] This provides as follows—

> . . . if after considering the grounds of the appeal . . . the Minister is satisfied that he is sufficiently informed for the purpose of reaching a decision as to the matters to which the appeal relates, he may decide the appeal without further investigation: but otherwise the Minister shall, if either party so desire, afford to each of them an opportunity of appearing before and being heard by a person appointed by the Minister for the purpose.

Contraventions are punishable summarily by fine.

6. LICENSING TRIBUNALS AND PARTICULARLY
TRANSPORT LICENSING

That other main type of regulatory process, the licence, must now be examined. The licence is used for revenue purposes, for example, radio-receiving licences, but these are not material here. Licensing is used to control admission to professions or the right to carry on particular trades,[2] to maintain standards of public health[3] and morality[4] and of order and safety,[5] to regulate the conduct of industry,[6] to conserve natural resources,[7] and to control scarce materials and currency.[8]

Two of the most important spheres of licensing are transport and intoxicating liquor. Because the need for controlling the retail sale of intoxicants was realised at a time when the justices of the peace were exercising both judicial and administrative functions, this system of licensing was entrusted to and has remained in the hands of the justices of the peace. Since transport licensing is of comparatively recent origin, it is

---

[1] Sect. 31 (2) and Town and Country Planning (Control of Advertisements) Regulations, 1948, S.I. 1948 No. 1613, Reg. 20.

[2] For a recent example, see the Food and Drugs Act, 1955, Part II, under which a licence is necessary before milk may be sold by retail.

[3] E.g. the Milk (Special Designation) (Raw Milk) Regulations, 1949, S.I. 1949 No. 1590, as amended by S.I. 1950 No. 410; S.I. 1954 No. 1267.

[4] E.g. Theatres Act, 1843 (licensing of stage plays).

[5] E.g. Cinematograph Acts, 1909–52 (licensing of premises for cinematograph exhibition).

[6] E.g. Sea Fish Industry Act, 1951 (by the White Fish Authority).

[7] E.g. Town and Country Planning Act, 1947.

[8] E.g. Exchange Control Act, 1947.

effected by administrative tribunals, which will, by way of illustration of licensing procedures, now be examined.

In order to protect railways from crippling competition from road transport, to avoid excessive highway congestion, and to satisfy the public interest in the fitness of vehicles and in the hours and conditions of work of drivers, a special licence is required before a person may carry goods in vehicles, and a heavy goods vehicle driver's licence may also be required by those driving such vehicles. Three types of carrier's licence are issued, the "A" which allows the road haulier to carry the goods of any person, the "B" which permits the "ancillary user," who owns vehicles as an ancillary to his commercial undertaking, sometimes to use them as a road haulier, and the "C" licence, which allows the ancillary user to carry goods in connection with his own commercial undertaking.[1]

Public safety demands that the operators of road passenger transport[2] hold a licence as proof of their personal suitability for the trade, and a licence in respect of the fitness of each of their passenger vehicles, and that the drivers and conductors be licensed only on proof of their competence. Public convenience and the need to co-ordinate transport insist that no one be allowed to run a particular service without a road-service licence which will also control stopping places and fares.

For the purpose of carrying out this licensing of goods and passenger transport the country is divided into ten traffic areas.[3] Three officers, formerly known as the Traffic Commissioners, are appointed for each area. The office of chairman is a full-time appointment made by the Minister of Transport and Civil Aviation. No qualifications are laid down for this officer who is dismissible at Her Majesty's pleasure.[4] The other two members are part-timers appointed by the Minister for three years, one from each of the two panels nominated by the county councils and the other local authorities (county and non-county boroughs and urban district councils) respectively. Carrier's licences are granted by the chairman of the area (then known as the Licensing Authority for Goods Vehicles)[5] from

[1] See the Road and Rail Traffic Act, 1933.
[2] See the Road Traffic Act, 1930.
[3] Ibid., Sect. 62.
[4] Chairmen of Traffic Commissioners, etc. (Tenure of Office) Act, 1937.
[5] Transport Act, 1947, Sect. 117.

whom an appeal lies to the Transport Tribunal.[1] This consists of three permanent members, a presiding lawyer, a person of commercial experience, and a person with transport experience. Appeals lie from it on points of law to the Court of Appeal.[2] Licences relating to public service vehicles are granted by the Traffic Commissioners, then known as the Licensing Authority for Public Service Vehicles, with an appeal, surprisingly, not to the Transport Tribunal, but to the Minister.[3] The Licensing Authority for Public Service Vehicles grants drivers' and conductors' licences. The appeal here lies to the courts of summary jurisdiction.[4]

Transport licensing furnishes interesting examples of the vesting of discretion in administrative bodies. Drivers and conductors may be refused licences only if they fail to comply with specific statutory conditions, or for misconduct or physical incapacity.[5] Even narrower is the discretion to grant public service vehicle licences. If there is no personal objection to the applicant and the public service vehicle examiner certifies the fitness of the vehicles, the licence is unconditionally granted.[6] With this may be contrasted the application for a road-service licence. The authority is enjoined to consider various criteria including the public demand for the service and the co-ordination of all forms of passenger transport.[7] It may, however, attach conditions to the licence, some of which, for example, that fares are not to be unreasonable, are contained in the Act. Similarly, the legislature directs the tribunal to consider certain economic and technical matters before granting carrier's "A" and "B" licences and imposes statutory conditions in licences.[8]

The traffic commissioners in their several capacities must allow parties to be heard orally and to be legally represented. Adequate notice of hearings must be given. They may (and when dealing with road-service licences, must) sit in public.

---

[1] Sect. 73, and Road and Rail Traffic Act, 1933 (Transfer of Jurisdiction of Appeal Tribunal) (Appointed Day) Order, 1951, S.I. 1951 No. 1467; S.I. 1955 No. 1521. This tribunal also has jurisdiction over transport charges, schemes, services, and facilities.

[2] Railways Act, 1921, Sect. 26; Road and Rail Traffic Act, 1933, Sect. 37 (13). Transport Act, 1947, Sch. 10, para. 5; Transport Tribunal Rules, 1949, S.I. 1949 No. 989, Reg. 60; Transport Act, 1953, Sect. 31 (3).

[3] Road Traffic Act, 1930, Sect. 81.   [4] Ibid., Sect. 82.
[5] Ibid., Sect. 77.   [6] Ibid., Sect. 68.
[7] Ibid., Sect. 72.   [8] Road and Rail Traffic Act, 1933, Sect. 6.

Cross-examination and rebuttal evidence are permitted; reasoned decisions are announced, and reports of traffic cases are published. All their decisions are subject to an unlimited right of appeal. Even more like ordinary judicial procedure is that of the Transport Tribunal.[1] This embodies much of the pre-trial procedures of ordinary courts: summons for directions before a Registrar, formal applications and answers, for example. It sits in public, has the powers of a court of record, may summon witnesses, demand the production of documents, take evidence on oath, and commit for contempt. It hears cases on appeal completely afresh, and ignores the record in the tribunal of first instance. It may sit in any part of Great Britain convenient for dealing with the particular business. Reasoned decisions are given, and the important ones are published in the traffic cases series.

Transport-licensing procedures are so well defined that it will seldom be necessary to imply the *audi alteram partem* rule. It is doubtful how far licensing tribunals are bound by the rules of natural justice.[2] Are licensing procedures to be presumed to be divided into two separate stages, a factual "judicial" stage and an "administrative," when the body draws on its accumulated experience in making its discretionary decision, just as it has been suggested that there is a split between the local inquiry and the ministerial decision in the regulatory procedures discussed above? To put a specific case: a local authority may allow premises to be used for the sale of ice-cream;[3] if it thinks the premises "unsuitable" it must hear interested parties and their witnesses. After it has heard the parties, may it, in deciding how to exercise its discretion consult officers who have argued before it at the hearing? Is the body intended to base its decision only on the materials adduced in evidence? Or may it even take factual evidence from its officers? It is purely a matter of statutory

[1] Transport Act, 1947, Sect. 72; Transport Tribunal Rules, 1949, S.I. 1949 No. 989; Transport Tribunal Rules, 1954, S.I. 1954 No. 103.

[2] Whereas in *R. v. Caernarvon Licensing Justices*, [1948] W.N. 505; *R. v. L.C.C., Re The Empire Theatre* (1895), 71 L.T. 638; *R. v. Hendon R.D.C., ex parte Chorley* [1933] 2 K.B. 696; and *R. v. Prestwich Corporation* (1945), 109 J.P. 157, the rules of natural justice were held to apply, in *Hanily* v. *Minister of Local Government and Planning*, [1952] 2 Q.B. 444, *Nakkuda Ali* v. *M. F. de S. Jayaratne*, [1951] A.C. 66, and *Reg.* v. *Metropolitan Police Commissioner*, [1953] 1 W.L.R. 1150, they were held inapplicable. Reconciliation of these conflicting lines of decision seems impossible.

[3] Food and Drugs Act, 1955, Sects. 16 and 19.

interpretation. It would hardly be straining the Act to hold
that a council may take advice from its staff experts before
deciding, just as the courts have recognised that powers given
to a Minister can be exercised in his name by an officer in his
department:[1] no one has yet held that a judge who talks over
a problem of law with a fellow bencher at the Inn dining table
before recording his decision on a present case is breaking the
rules of natural justice.

E. Pure Policy

Of the procedure relating to the prerogative acts of pure
policy, such as the recognition of foreign governments, there
is nothing to be said, because it is accepted that the State may
perform such acts as it thinks fit. Placed in the same category,
though not necessarily with the same justification, are the
naturalisation and deportation of aliens. An alien may not
be naturalised unless he fulfils certain statutory conditions,
but even if he should fulfil them, he has no right to the certificate
should the Home Secretary decline to grant it. Similarly, the
Home Secretary may deport him; there is an advisory committee which the Home Secretary may consult before acting.
If he does not consult it the alien is without remedy.[2] It
is difficult to explain why the United States, with far more
aliens to handle, can give them the right to a fair hearing and
due process of law, and yet England should treat these administrative acts as lying in the realms of pure uncontrolled policy.

F. Summary Powers

So numerous and varied are administrative tasks that if a
hearing were always to precede their execution the administrative function would come to a standstill. The imposition of a
quarantine, the consideration of an application for a foreign
currency allowance, the laying of pipes in a highway: all
these are effected without a hearing. The citizen can
challenge the legality of the act in the courts; the matter
can be raised in Parliament, and he knows that the civil

---

[1] *Carltona, Ltd.* v. *Commissioners of Works,* [1943] 2 All E.R. 560; *Lewisham
B.C.* v. *Roberts,* [1949] 2 K.B. 608.

[2] *R.* v. *Secretary of State for Home Affairs, ex parte Venicoff,* [1920] 3 K.B. 72. But a
naturalised person can insist on being heard by a committee of inquiry before he
is deprived of his citizenship; Deprivation of Citizenship Rules, S.I. 1950, No. 593.

servant will bring professional competence and integrity
to his task. Sometimes he has a further protection in that
adjudication must follow the act. So, the food inspector may
seize the bad food exposed for sale, but the retailer cannot be
punished until the inspector has brought the food before a
justice of the peace who must give the retailer a hearing.[1]

Which matters should be settled summarily is controversial.
Ought the employees of the State or public bodies to be equated
with employees in private industry or should their official
position result in their claims against their employers being the
subject of an administrative adjudication? If the latter, should
that adjudication be official or domestic? The practice varies:
a teacher can be dismissed without a hearing; a civil servant
has a tribunal which has no legal status; there are compensation tribunals for nationalised industries whose existence (but
not procedures) is authorised by statutory instruments.[2]
What factors should determine whether an applicant for a
licence is to be granted a hearing? The effect on his property,
his person, or his livelihood? Should it be conclusive that the
relevant evidence can be given in documentary form?

Just as it is difficult to decide which powers ought to be
exercised summarily, so also must the courts occasionally find
difficulty in deciding whether a statutory power may be
exercised without notice and hearing. Two cases, one on each
side of the line, illustrate this. The Metropolis Management
Amendment Act, 1862, empowered local authorities to
demolish insanitary dwellings, and imposed no procedural preliminaries. The court decided that it was illegal to demolish
without notice to the landowner.[3] In *Hutton* v. *Attorney-General*[4]
the courts had to consider the claim of a landowner that he
had been expropriated without a hearing. The Defence Act,
1842, authorised lords-lieutenant of the county to issue certifi-
cates that the taking of land for military purposes was necessary
and expedient. It was held that the landowner was not entitled
to a hearing before the issue of the certificate. Although the
courts conceal their reasons behind the words "judicial" and

---

[1] Food and Drugs Act, 1955, Sects. 8 and 9; cf. *Reg.* v. *Cornwall Quarter Sessions*,
[1956] 1 W.L.R. 906.
[2] See W. A. Robson: *Justice and Administrative Law*, (3rd ed.) 297 *et seq.*
[3] *Cooper* v. *Wandsworth Board of Works* (1863), 14 C.B.N.S. 180.
[4] [1927] 1 Ch. 427.

"administrative" it is clear, as Tomlin, J., said in *Hutton* v. *Attorney-General*,[1] that the test is whether Parliament intended that the exercise of the power should be preceded by a notice and hearing.

G. Investigations

In pursuance of its general supervision of public order, health and safety, the Administration has to make investigations. This it often does by formal official inquiry. Typical are inquiries into railway, air and factory accidents.[2] In the past these have given little cause for complaint. Either lawyers sitting with assessors, or experts have conducted the inquiries. Full opportunity to attend, to be represented, to present evidence, and to cross-examine has been given. The inspector has been empowered to summon evidence. One criticism has been that there was no obligation to publish reports. Nationalisation has brought new problems for these inquiries. They have always been under the close supervision of the Minister, who appointed the inspector, to whom the report was made, and who in his discretion would decide whether to publish. This ministerial control has in the past been unobjectionable because the Minister has been a third party making an impartial investigation into circumstances which might lead to criminal proceedings against another, or to a civil action between two other parties. Now that these inquiries may affect nationalised industries for which the Minister is also ultimately responsible, the Minister can no longer be a disinterested third party. So far, particularly in civil aviation, the Government has turned down suggestions that the procedures at these inquiries should be remodelled in view of this changed relationship between the Minister and the investigation.[3]

The latest administrative venture into the investigational field is perhaps the most interesting. By an Act of 1948[4] a Monopolies and Restrictive Practices Commission was set up

---

[1] At 439. Cf. *R.* v. *Archbishop of Canterbury*, [1944] K.B. 282.
[2] E.g. the Civil Aviation (Investigation of Accidents) Regulations, 1951, S.I., 1951, No. 1653; Factories Act, 1937, Sect. 68.
[3] H.C. 470 of 1949, paras. 2099-180.
[4] Monopolies and Restrictive Practices (Inquiry and Control) Act, 1948; as amended by the Monopolies and Restrictive Practices Commission Act, 1953.

to investigate and report on such of the alleged monopolistic conditions set out in the Act as the Board of Trade referred to it. Its reference might be merely to report on the facts or also to advise whether the facts found showed conditions against the public interest. In so advising it might recommend action, but that action was only to be taken after the matter had been laid before Parliament. The Commission consisted of twenty-five members appointed by the Board of Trade. It might fix its own procedures subject to an obligation to hear those substantially interested unless it was not reasonably necessary or practicable. It could *subpoena* evidence and could take evidence on oath. Although it had minute powers compared with the United States Federal Trades Commission which has power to investigate and adjudicate upon unfair trade practices and to take enforcement measures against their perpetrators it was possible that it might herald the increasing use of the commission as an administrative device.

But the actual development has been strikingly different. The Restrictive Trade Practices Act, 1956, established a Restrictive Practices Court consisting of three puisne judges of the High Court nominated by the Lord Chancellor, one judge of the Court of Session nominated by the Lord President of that Court and one judge of the Supreme Court of Northern Ireland nominated by the Lord Chief Justice of Northern Ireland. In addition there are not more than ten other members, qualified by virtue of their knowledge of or experience in industry, commerce or public affairs, appointed for not less than three years by Her Majesty on the recommendation of the Lord Chancellor who may dismiss for inability, misbehaviour or the incompatibility of a member's employment or interest. A great number of restrictive trade agreements must be registered with the Registrar of the Court and the Court may declare any restrictions to be contrary to the public interest and therefore void. These registrable agreements and arrangements are removed from the purview of the Monopolies Commission (as the older body is now called) which is reduced in size to ten members and is concerned primarily with "single-firm" monopolies and export agreements. Clearly, no attempt can be made to assess the value of this experiment until the new Court has been functioning for some time.

H. General Observations[1]

The account of the various types of administrative tribunal in the preceding sections has been largely uncritical. It is often suggested that there is a needless variety in the constitution and procedures of administrative tribunals, and that a uniform code similar to the American Administrative Procedure Act, 1946, is called for in Britain. It is suggested that no such uniformity is practicable, but some observations will now be made on the principles which should govern Parliament in setting up administrative tribunals.

Adjudications of law and fact in which no question of policy arises should not be carried out by Ministers themselves, or by civil servants in the Minister's name. Many powers to decide matters of law are vested in Ministers: national assistance and national insurance are examples.

The personnel (including clerks) of tribunals deciding issues of law or fact or applying standards should be independent of the Minister with whose department their functions are connected. Preferably, the Lord Chancellor should appoint and dismiss them. They should enjoy that security of tenure and adequacy of remuneration essential to the proper discharge of their duties. Where matters of law may arise, one member of the tribunal ought to be a lawyer: even for factual determinations a legally qualified chairman is better able to rule on procedure and evidence. Where expert knowledge is required to guide the exercise of a discretion or the application of standards, there ought to be technical representation on the tribunal. The personnel of the various national assistance and national insurance tribunals are not sufficiently independent, although the balance between legal and lay members seems satisfactory: it is desirable that the chairman, at least, should be appointed on a permanent basis and be removable only for cause. The Lands Tribunal is an excellent example of the right blend of legal and technical experts in the determination of mixed issues of law, fact and standards.[2] Although

---

[1] See the Report of the National Insurance Advisory Committee under the National Insurance Act, 1946, Sect. 77, on the draft Determination of Claims and Questions Regulations; W. A. Robson: *Justice and Administrative Law* (3rd ed.), Ch. 8; Jackson, "Tribunals and Inquiries," in 33 *Public Administration* (1955) 115; and *Rule of Law* (A study by Inns of Court Conservative and Unionist Society).

[2] In order that the Lands Tribunal shall function satisfactorily, it should not (as

there is much to be said for local lay knowledge on rent tribunals it may be that this should be supported by both expert and legal representation.

The adjudicative processes of housing and town-planning legislation call for separate consideration. If Parliament intends that the only purpose of the public local inquiries shall be to give to the persons affected the opportunity to air their grievances so that the inspector may acquaint the Minister with the state of local feeling before the Minister makes a decision, there is no objection to the inquiry being held by a civil servant in the department: the only necessary qualification is an ability to make an accurate and analytical report. The controversial issues here are whether all matters of fact should not be decided by something akin to judicial process (in which case the considerations of the preceding paragraph are relevant) and whether some of the decisions now made by the Minister on the ground that they are matters of "policy" should not be regarded as the exercise of discretions of a technical nature which could be entrusted to named experts. Under the present arrangements, whether the inquiry is merely a means of "letting off steam," or the investigation of problems of civil engineering, or even whether matters of law are in issue, an objector is allowed only to state his case before one and the same type of official—an inspector in the department who is usually a qualified civil engineer or architect but whose legal equipment is usually limited to the possession of some notes for guidance in the conduct of inquiries drafted a hundred years ago and not revised since that time. The objector has no way of knowing what findings of fact and law are made, or indeed who made them: it is impossible therefore to attempt to make any estimate of the quality of the work of these inspectors.

Those exercising licensing jurisdiction often have to determine facts and law and also to reach decisions which are governed by expert considerations. Transport licensing is of this type, and the arrangements made for the original adjudications are generally satisfactory.

Whether the granting of a licence to carry on a particular

has happened in some instances) assign the hearing of cases containing issues both of law and valuation to a valuer without legal qualifications sitting alone.

trade or profession should ever be entrusted to a local authority is doubtful.[1]

There seems no good reason why the same tribunals should not handle law-fact adjudications arising under different statutes dealing with similar problems. This would enable more full-time appointments to be made, and seems preferable to the present arrangements whereby the same personnel masquerade under different titles.[2] Where the volume of work is heavy, the cases numerous, and the litigants often poor, the tribunals should have local jurisdiction. The administrative tribunals are not in general over-centralised, but even where there is insufficient business to justify a series of tribunals it will usually be best for the tribunal to go on circuit.[3]

A right of appeal may be of considerable psychological importance: it reassures litigants and imbues tribunals with a greater sense of responsibility. Although there are, then, good reasons why those aggrieved by administrative decisions should be able to take the case to a higher tribunal it will be remembered that the ordinary courts can quash all jurisdictional excesses.[4] The main questions are whether there should be an appeal on matters of law, fact, and discretion, and whether the appeal should lie to the courts or to another administrative tribunal.

It is suggested that there should only be a right of appeal on matters of fact where the tribunal is not unanimous or where it gives leave. Normally, there should be such confidence in the factual decisions of a properly constituted tribunal that the expense of a re-hearing can be avoided.[5]

The difficulties inherent in a provision for a right of appeal on points of "law" are not always appreciated by those advocating it. Disputes will usually centre about some statutory expression of variable meaning: is X an "employee,"

---

[1] Cf. the increasing tendency to give to local authorities powers not of licensing but of registration coupled with powers of inspection, e.g. common lodging-houses under Public Health Act, 1936, Sects. 235–48.

[2] The same three persons often sit on the same day and in the same room as the Military Service (Hardship) Tribunal, the Industrial Injuries Local Appeal Tribunal and the National Insurance Local Appeal Tribunal.

[3] E.g. the Lands Tribunal.

[4] See p. 209 *et seq.* for the wide judicial interpretation of "jurisdictional excess."

[5] Cf. *Fulham B.C.* v. *Santilli*, [1933] 2 K.B. 357 at 367; and *Stepney B.C.* v. *Joffe*, [1949] 1 K.B. 599.

is Blackacre an "industrial hereditament"? One American authority has said:[1]

> Matters of law grow downward into roots of fact, and matters of fact reach upward, without a break, into matters of law. The knife of policy alone effects an artificial cleavage where the court chooses to draw the line. . . .

Law is too imprecise a term; so, in the two hundred or so reported decisions on the meaning of a right of appeal on "law" from the Income Tax Commissioners, the courts "have been completely untrammelled by their decisions upon the identical issue in other branches of the Law."[2] The term is also ambiguous in not marking the extent to which insufficiency of evidence is a ground of appeal. How can the adequacy of the evidence be estimated, unless the tribunal of first instance keeps a full record, and when is the expense of that justified? Parliament has not faced up to these problems: perhaps it should identify and give a right of appeal in respect of those statutory definitions which it intends not to be finally interpreted by the tribunal.

The body trying appeals on issues of law should be at least as independent of the Minister as the tribunal with original jurisdiction, and its personnel should be legally qualified. If appeals are likely to be numerous, or the amount in issue small, probably an administrative tribunal is preferable. Subject to those considerations, whether the body is an administrative tribunal or whether the cases are assigned to a particular judge of the High Court seems unimportant,[3] but the building up of a consistent body of case law is hampered if appeals lie to the High Court, and no arrangements are made for one judge to try all of them. Where an administrative appellate tribunal is desirable, there may be an advantage in setting up one tribunal to hear appeals from various administrative tribunals.

It is difficult to say whether appeals from discretions should be permitted. Even when none is permitted, the considerations set out in the preceding paragraphs are material in ascertaining

---

[1] J. Dickinson: *Administrative Justice and the Supremacy of the Law*, 55.

[2] A. Farnsworth: *Income Tax Case Law*, 44. And see p. 228 below.

[3] Why should the appeal from a decision excluding a solicitor or a barrister from the legal aid scheme lie to the High Court under the Legal Aid and Advice Act, 1949, and that of a practitioner under the National Health Service lie to the Minister?

whether to give an appeal from the factual and legal elements of the decisions. It is not easy to justify the present practice on appeals from the exercise of discretions. If the licensing of drivers and conductors of passenger vehicles is a matter for an expert tribunal, why should the exercise of discretion by that body be reviewable by courts of summary jurisdiction? Indeed, there seem to be no cases where the ordinary courts are competent to review the way in which discretionary technical decisions have been made. Ministerial review of discretion is appropriate where the Minister has a political responsibility to maintain uniformity or to prevent the thwarting of governmental policy: his control of town-planning development applications and of transport licensing is presumably justified for this reason. In other cases where discretion ought to be reviewable the task is best performed by a superior administrative tribunal.

That need for cheapness and speed which in part has led to the setting up of administrative tribunals makes the use of ordinary court procedures and rules of evidence impossible. It is suggested that certain minimum safeguards should be insisted on, but beyond that tribunals should have discretion in framing their procedures, which should none the less be published in the interests of those practising before them.

Parties must have notice of the hearing adequate both in time and detail to enable them to prepare their case with full knowledge of the case which they have to meet. In deciding whether there should be an oral hearing it is material to consider whether those reasons which make oral evidence necessary in ordinary actions are cogent in administrative hearings. In some administrative hearings the demeanour of the witnesses may be unimportant and the evidence may be readily obtainable by affidavit. It is thought none the less that there is more public confidence in tribunals before which there is a right to appear in person, and, that even in those instances where it is decided to proceed normally by written evidence, a party should have the right to insist on a hearing. Most tribunals (the Rent tribunals are important exceptions) afford these elementary safeguards. The practice of holding informal adjudications is unobjectionable, for the settle-ment procedures and pre-hearing procedures are the "lifeblood of the administrative process";[1] what must be demanded is that any party dissatisfied with an informal inquiry can have his "day in court." Public confidence in tribunals is increased if they sit in public. Only where a public hearing would be prejudicial to a party should the hearing be in private. Administrative tribunals are on the whole satisfactory in this respect. The main exceptions to the general principle that the public is admitted to administrative tribunals are the National Assistance and National Insurance local tribunals, where the claimant would be embarrassed if his private affairs were discussed in public. There seems no such justification for denying the public access to the hearings of the Military Service (Hardship) committees.[2]

Generally all parties should be entitled to legal representation in order that their case may be presented fully. The objections to this are two: that it favours the wealthy; and that the presence of lawyers on one side may so confuse the other litigant that he is constrained to secure legal representation also. One exception should be made to the suggested general rule: where one party is the Administration, then the Administration should be legally represented only if the private litigant had first decided to have legal representation. These objections would then have little substance.[3] The National Insurance and National Assistance local tribunals and the Military Service (Hardship) tribunals forbid legal representation.

Parties ought to be able to invoke the assistance of the tribunal in procuring evidence. All types of tribunal should therefore have compulsory powers to *subpoena* persons and documents and to administer oaths. National Insurance, National Assistance and Rent tribunals, for example, have not this power. Perhaps also the powers of tribunals should be strengthened by giving them the right to commit for contempt if their orders are disobeyed. It is not the practice to confer this power; indeed, almost all enforcement powers (except those of the Marketing Board tribunals and Transport tribunal) are vested in the ordinary courts.

The whittling down of the *audi alteram partem* rule—the

---

[1] W. Gellhorn: *Federal Administrative Proceedings*, 45.
[2] National Service Act, 1948, Sch. 3.
[3] It is, however, to be regretted that the Legal Aid and Advice Act, 1949, does not extend to administrative tribunals.

Rent tribunals are an example—is indefensible. Because of the vagueness of the scope of this implied rule of natural justice an express right to cross-examine, and to rebut the evidence of the opposing party should be (but only occasionally is[1]) conferred.

Unless a tribunal is required to keep a proper record of its hearings, appeals and judicial review cannot be effective. Very few tribunals (the National Insurance (Industrial Injuries) tribunal is one) are required to keep records.

Most controversial is the question of the extent to which these tribunals shall be bound by rules of evidence. Some of the rules of evidence have the purpose of shielding, for social reasons, certain privileged communications made in confidential relationships, and those ought to apply to administrative tribunals no less than to ordinary courts. Many rules have been framed on the assumption that juries cannot assess the trustworthiness of evidence. Administrative tribunals differ from jury trials in their promptness, inexpensiveness, expertness, and continuity of service. These differences are so material that administrative tribunals ought to hear all relevant evidence except privileged communications. In particular they ought not to be restrained by the hearsay and best evidence rules. Parliament has usually gone too far in that it has generally given tribunals complete freedom to admit and reject such evidence as they choose.

Courts take judicial notice of (i.e. accept without proof) matters which are within the everyday experience of juries. As one commentator has said[2]—

> The very *raison d'être* of an administrative agency may be, and often is, its ability to accumulate knowledge by devoting special attention to a given area. To conduct a hearing, and to base the process of proof, upon the assumption that the agency, like a jury chosen *ad hoc* for the trial, is wholly ignorant of the subject-matter before it, is to dissipate valuable skills, to prolong and make expensive the hearing process whose purpose is expedition and reasonable cost, and sometimes even to reach a result which the agency knows not to be the best possible one.

In short, judicial notice should be extended to official notice of information acquired in the ordinary course of the business of the tribunal. There must, however, be one safeguard: the

---

[1] E.g. Pensions Appeal Tribunal.   [2] W. Gellhorn op. cit. 87.

tribunal must write these facts into the record, and if they are contained in files or reports these should be accessible to parties and subject to cross-examination and rebuttal. The dividing line between the use of such knowledge as a substitute for evidence and the use of the expert knowledge and experience of the tribunal in evaluating and drawing conclusions from the evidence in the record is fine, and there can be no restrictions on the latter process. This matter is not dealt with in statutes setting up tribunals, and the absence of records makes it impossible to comment on the practices of the various tribunals.

Unless reasons for decisions are given, an appeal is impossible. It is not surprising, therefore, that all administrative tribunals from which there is an appeal are required to give reasons. On the other hand, tribunals from which there is no appeal, such as the Rent and National Assistance tribunals, are not compelled to give reasons. All tribunals should give reasons, except to the extent that the process of applying a standard, e.g. of reasonableness, cannot be expressed in writing.[1]

The need for publication of cases establishing new principles is as great as the need to publish leading cases in the ordinary courts. The usual practice is for the appropriate Ministry to publish short summaries of leading decisions; this is done in town planning, national insurance and transport licensing, for example. If it were practicable, commercial publication would be preferable. Failing that, it is thought that the Administration should publish in a series full reports of those decisions which an independent committee of lawyers expert in the topic thinks ought to be published. Publication could be confined to cases decided in appellate tribunals.

All these and many other matters fell to be considered by the strong Committee on Administrative Tribunals and Enquiries set up by the Government in 1955 under the chairmanship of Sir Oliver Franks. Its terms of reference were "To consider and make recommendations on (a) The constitution and working of tribunals other than the ordinary courts of law, constituted under any Act of Parliament by a Minister of the Crown or

---

[1] Thus whereas a rent tribunal which has fixed a "reasonable rent" with reference to other houses which it has seen could not be expected to explain this process at length, it ought to explain why, for example, it has refused to give a tenant security of tenure.

for the purposes of a Minister's functions; (b) the working of such administrative procedures as include the holding of an inquiry or hearing by or on behalf of a Minister on an appeal or as the result of objections or representations, and in particular the procedure for the compulsory purchase of land." The Committee has published six volumes of memoranda from Government Departments and more than twenty days of oral evidence. Its Report is expected in 1957.

CHAPTER V

THE CONTROL OF THE ADMINISTRATIVE AND JUDICIAL POWERS OF THE ADMINISTRATION

Parliamentary Control

A. The Administrative Bodies Subject to Parliamentary Control

It is convenient to divide administrative bodies into three categories when considering parliamentary control. First, there are administrative tribunals, usually appointed by a Minister, determining matters of law or fact, applying standards and exercising discretions within limits defined with more or less certainty by statutes. Secondly there are the Ministers themselves, who make both decisions of policy and decisions of fact and law. Thirdly may be grouped those civil servants who in the course of their departmental duties exercise summary functions, or hold public local inquiries so that the Minister may be informed by them of local feeling on a matter before he decides on his course of action.

Rules of parliamentary procedure provide that a Minister may only be questioned on, and will only take responsibility for, the actions of those who are under his administrative control,[1] and that criticism of actions taken by these persons must be formulated as criticism of the Minister and not of them. These rules would extend to the second, and, presumably, the third of the categories. For example, an allegation of bias on the part of an inspector holding an inquiry under the Town and Country Planning Act, 1947, could be the subject of a question addressed to the Minister of Housing and Local Government. Those in the first category seem to be so independent as not to be subject to ministerial control in the day-to-day performance of their duties (although the Minister may dismiss them); it would seem to follow that the Minister will not be responsible to the House for the way in which they perform these duties.

It is a further rule that reflections must not, save on substantive motions, be cast in parliamentary debate on the

[1] See below, pp. 287–8.

conduct of judges. This includes county court judges and justices of the peace,[1] but it has never been decided whether it extends also to the personnel of administrative tribunals. On principle, the protection should extend to those in the first category, members of the tribunals set up under the National Insurance Act, for example, but probably not to those in the third category.

In the general field of administration, parliamentary criticism, is, of course, free and frequent. While the House of Lords plays its part in this function of Parliament, it is in the House of Commons that the criticism and defence of the Administration are primarily voiced. An analysis has been made by Sir Gilbert Campion (as he then was) of the division of House of Commons time for the period 1906–1937/8, excluding the war years.[2] The figures given here are the average over the whole of this period, but the variation between different sessions is small. First, Government time absorbed 43 per cent of the total; 39 per cent was taken in the discussion of Public Bills and 4 per cent in Government motions and subordinate legislation. Secondly, Opposition time amounted to 31 per cent, of which the greater part was taken in debates on Supply and the remainder on motions and on the Address in reply to the King's Speech. Thirdly, private members' time took 14 per cent; most of this was taken in debates on Bills. Fourthly, the remaining 12 per cent fell in the main to debates on the Budget and the Finance Bill. These figures may be taken as broadly accurate for the period since 1945, except that part of private members' time has been transferred to Government time.

The three fields in which the House of Commons operates, according to Sir Gilbert Campion's analysis, are, first, the formulation and control of policy and the control of administration; secondly, the control of finance; and thirdly, legislation. We are not here concerned with the last.

B. The Extent and Means of Control

1. THE FORMULATION AND CONTROL OF POLICY
AND THE CONTROL OF ADMINISTRATION

The function of the House of Commons to formulate and control policy is exercised, in Sir Gilbert's view, during five different

---

[1] T. Erskine May: *Parliamentary Practice* (15th Edn.), 437–8.
[2] H.C. 189–1 of 1946, *Appendix to Report*.

forms of proceedings. These are the Address in reply to the Queen's Speech, the supply debates, adjournment motions, substantive motions, and question time. The average number of days spent in each session from 1906 to 1937/8, excluding the war years, on these five occasions taken together was 58·5. No great changes in the time spent during this period appear; thus the supply debates for the 1906–13 period averaged 30·5 days and for the 1929–38 period 31·2 days. Adjournment motions increased from 3·4 days to 7·7 days for the same periods. The totals show an increase from 56·9 to 61·1. Question time is not, of course, included in these figures. The average number of days per session was 145·4 so that the amount of time allotted to "control and formulation of policy" was 40 per cent of the whole.[1] To say that the House of Commons formulates and controls policy, and controls administration when debating and questioning on these occasions seems inaccurate. The principles of policy are conceived and formulated by the organs of the political party in power. These principles are applied and the details of policy determined by the Cabinet as the concrete problems arise. The House of Commons considers Government policy, criticises and approves; but at no time does it formulate policy. The idea is so contrary to parliamentary practice, so unworkable in fact and so incompatible with the duties of Her Majesty's Opposition that one suspects the word "formulation" is being used in some particular undefined meaning. Nor does the House "control" policy; here there may be a real danger that the word is being used in a sense slightly other than is usual. The House does clearly act in relation to policy in three ways: it approves, it rejects and it influences. The power of the House to reject Government policy can scarcely be called a controlling power; to control means at least, to restrain and at most, to govern; it is a positive not a negative action; to control policy means to direct a policy towards a certain end, not merely to reject it. If the House controlled policy then the effect of rejecting the Government's policy should be to substitute another, that of the majority. But when the House defeats the Government on a matter of policy, ordinarily it is dissolved and a new House reassembles after the general election.

[1] Ibid. para. 13.

The new House will then consider the new Government's proposals and will approve them. We are concerned here with the nature of the relationship between Parliament and an established Government, and are contending that in such a case Parliament does not in any sense directly control the policy of the Government. We are not concerned with the undoubted power of Parliament to cause a Government to resign by rejecting its proposed policy. A master has power not only to dismiss his servant but also to order him to do certain work in a certain manner. Parliament has the former but not the latter power. Occasionally, as a result of what is said by various Members in the House, the Government modifies its policy; this is closer to control by the House. Policy being determined by the party and the Cabinet, differences within the party are normally settled outside the House and a Government will very seldom debate a policy which it knows is likely to be opposed by a large number of its own supporters. The course of debates does, however, sometimes cause the Government to change its policy but, if so, it is because a major cleavage in its own party becomes clear for the first time during the debate, or because the Government considers that the opposition in Parliament really reflects a very strong opposition in the country and that many votes will be lost if the policy is persisted in. In 1946, opposition in the House and in the country to the introduction of bread rationing was strong but the Government believed that the course was unavoidable and would be justified; it therefore insisted, no doubt hoping that any support it might lose in the country by the action would be regained when the justification became evident. The Hoare-Laval agreement on Abyssinia is a notorious example of the electorate expressing itself clearly through the Press and through Members and of the Government yielding to the pressure; but such occasions are very rare. It remains true that this influence on the Government in the House is in the great majority of cases insufficient to move the Government, which in every major issue expects a certain small number of its supporters to disapprove. The power of the Government Whips over wavering Members is a far greater influence than the speeches of a few individuals. The idea that the House of Commons controls policy is based on the fiction that Parliament controls the Executive and that every Member considers each proposal on its merits, votes according to his own evaluation, and is free from any discipline of party.

The only sense in which the House of Commons controls the administration of the country is that, by Questions, direct representations by Members to Ministers and motions on the adjournment, it checks injustices and reveals particular anomalies or shortcomings in the application of Government policy. But any general control is absent. Mr. Lloyd George, giving evidence before a Select Committee in 1931, pointed out that the House has no real effective and continuous control over the actions of the Executive; that certain subjects such as unemployment, the Estimates and so on are debated in a general way from time to time but that the House has no machinery for examining these questions in close detail; that there is nothing comparable to the finance, surveyors', police, and health committees of local government. He suggested that similar committees should be set up in Parliament with power to obtain all the information available to the Ministers and with authority to examine Ministers and civil servants; such a procedure would, as he admitted, involve the examination of questions of policy.[1] Sir Winston Churchill was of a similar opinion; of the unemployment debates he said: "Every debate has been detached from every other, has been discursive and disconnected, and has just come to a useless futile conclusion," whereas if the matter was debated properly "descending from the general to the particular and taking the conclusions and opinions at each stage and the agreements at each stage," the opinion of the country would be properly guided.[2] The difficulty about such proposals is fundamental and recurring. They tend to place the function of government and administration in the hands of a body too large and too diverse in opinion to exercise it effectively. The function of the House of Commons cannot be to govern or administer; having examined and approved policy, it must not, if government is to be efficient, impede the Executive in the carrying out of that policy. The right to criticise policy

[1] H.C. 161 of 1931, paras. 356–62, 403, 431–4.
[2] Ibid. paras. 1520–6.

and administration must not be confused with the right to direct or control the way in which the policy is translated into action. Nor does the House now exercise this latter function. Mr. Lloyd George was very definite: "It has not got control. I am speaking now after forty years of experience: Parliament has really no control over the Executive; it is pure fiction."[1] Of the House of Commons, Lord Eustace Percy has said: "I think its control over executive action is got by retaining or throwing out the Government. I do not think there is any good in suggesting that the House of Commons has control of executive action of a Government which it wants to keep in power."[2]

2. THE CONTROL OF FINANCE

The divergence between the theory and practice of Commons control over finance is notorious. The control of taxation is limited to the debates on the Budget resolutions and the Finance Bill. The average number of days taken is fifteen, about 10 per cent of the session.[3] Basic changes are very rarely made as a result of the debates and since the effect of the resolutions is felt so directly by the electorate itself, it is to the reactions of that body rather than to the reactions of Parliament that the Government pays particular attention. At the same time, the secrecy which necessarily surrounds the Budget proposals makes consultation with those to be affected impossible, and the representatives of those interests after Budget day may persuade the Government to modify the proposals. So, in December, 1947, the advertising tax was replaced by other arrangements. There is no proceeding in the House for the examination of expenditure by the Government; the way in which public money is being spent is often discussed when policy or administration is under review but the House itself is too large a body to deal effectively with the strictly financial aspects of Government spending. The Select Committee on Estimates and the Public Accounts Committee cover much of the ground. Working under the Public Accounts Committee the Comptroller and Auditor-General and his staff are continuously auditing the accounts of Government departments to ensure regularity and accuracy and to check

---

[1] Ibid. para. 450. [2] Ibid. para. 2040.
[3] H.C. 189–1 of 1946, *Appendix to Report* para. 13.

improper and wasteful expenditure. Although the action of
the Public Accounts Committee is inevitably delayed—in
1946 it was examining the 1944/5 expenditure—it is "a real
factor in putting the fear of Parliament into Whitehall."[1]
The Estimates Committee is appointed "to examine such of
the Estimates . . . as may seem fit . . . and to report what,
if any, economies consistent with the policy implied in those
Estimates may be effected therein." Opinions differ considerably whether the Committee functions satisfactorily. Sir
Malcolm Ramsay, Comptroller and Auditor-General in 1931,
thought it had little value.[2] The main grounds of criticism
are, first, that expenditure is determined primarily by policy
which the Committee may not examine; secondly, that the
Committee has insufficient time in which to do its work; and
thirdly, that it has no expert staff but only a Treasury official.
The 1931 Select Committee on Procedure recommended that
the Committee be enlarged and provided with an adequate
technical staff.[3] Sir John Wardlaw-Milne who was Chairman
of the Select Committee on National Expenditure (the successor
to the Estimates Committee during the 1939–45 period when
there were no Estimates) ascribed the failure of the Estimates
Committee to their reluctance to work through sub-committees.[4]
On the other hand, the Government in 1946 considered the
Committee able to meet the modern requirements of Parliament effectively, although the implication is that sub-
committees should be used.[5] In the late Mr. L. S. Amery's
opinion the Committee does as much as can be done in this
matter by the House of Commons.[6]

Under the present system the main purpose of the Public
Accounts Committee is to see that the money has been spent
as laid down by Parliament and that of the Estimates Committee
to ascertain whether the proposed expenditure is economical.
Sir Gilbert Campion suggested the amalgamation of these
two committees into one Public Expenditure Committee with
six investigating sub-committees; four of these would examine

[1] Ibid. para. 3227 (Mr. H. Morrison).
[2] H.C. 161 of 1931, paras. 363–8 (16).
[3] H.C. 129 of 1932, para. 10.
[4] H.C. 189–1 of 1946, para. 4325 (3).
[5] Ibid. para. 3180 (2).
[6] *Thoughts on the Constitution*, 53. Since 1945 the functioning of the Estimates
Committee seems to have improved considerably.

the Accounts and Estimates of groups of departments while one would be reserved for major inquiries and one for special short-term inquiries into current complaints.[1] The Select Committee on Procedure of 1946 accepted this principle of one committee[2] but the Government rejected it.[3] Sir Gilbert Campion's main argument was that under the present arrangement, in 1946, for example, the Public Accounts Committee was considering the 1944/5 expenditure, the Estimates Committee the 1946/7 Estimates, while in between lies the financial year 1945/6 which is nobody's concern. The single committee would work on a three-year period and be able to check expenditure as it occurred; by requiring immediate explanations from Ministers and civil servants, any waste would be detected and stopped at an early stage. The gap in fact is not so wide as would appear, for the Estimates Committee inevitably investigates what has previously happened and the Public Accounts Committee extends its inquiries to what is happening at the moment. The present Comptroller and Auditor-General stated: "When the Public Accounts Committee considers a report of mine on something that arises out of the past, they almost invariably inquire concerning the present."[4] Further, it is normal procedure for a department immediately after a contract is placed or payment is made to pass the papers to the Exchequer and Audit Department where an officer makes a selective examination which may be followed by an investigation.[5] This overlapping of the two committees is used as an alternative argument for the setting up of one committee. The claim that the House of Commons has a right and a duty to investigate current expenditure, to cross-examine Ministers and officials on the spending or proposed spending of particular sums of money in particular ways, raises once again the fundamental question of the functions of the House and its relation to the Government. Sir Gilbert Upcott was decided in his opinion: "If a Parliamentary Committee were attempting to examine current expenditure

[1] H.C. 189–1 of 1946, *Appendix to Report*, para. 22.
[2] Ibid. para. 43.
[3] 435 H.C. Deb. 5s., cols. 29–32, 443 cols. 1559–60; H.C. 189–1 of 1946, para. 3180 (2) (3).
[4] H.C. 189–1 of 1946, para. 4120 (Sir Gilbert Upcott).
[5] Ibid. para. 187 (1).

in any very literal sense it would be attempting itself to administer which would be in fact quite impossible."[1] A member of
the 1946 Select Committee on Procedure suggested to him
that it would be of very great advantage to the control of
public expenditure if some machinery could be devised to
draw the attention of a Parliamentary Committee to particular
expenditure immediately it occurred. He replied: "I feel
very dubious whether that would be so. I feel it is much more
effective that Departments should be given a clear opportunity
to give their explanations. I feel the procedure you are
suggesting would impose upon a Parliamentary Committee
something very near to the duty of administering the matter
itself."[2] For the Government, the Lord President of the Council
said: "I would not admit that the House itself should share
in the current executive administration. The business of the
House is to act as a check and a watchdog on the current
executive functions. . . . It is the business of the Government
to spend the money."[3] In its memorandum the Government
objected to Sir Gilbert Campion's proposal in these terms:
"A system which subjected every item of departmental
expenditure over a three-year period to the close and searching
scrutiny of a small body of Members would place a very
heavy burden on senior officers and inevitably hamper hte
efficiency of executive action by imposing delays and cramping
initiative."[4]

If the House of Commons has a right, as it undoubtedly has,
to require the Government to explain its proposals and account
for its actions, the Government also has a right to demand
that it be not hampered in the actual administration. If the
view prevails that the function of the House of Commons is
to control the Executive, then the House should constantly
examine every governmental action and continuously be
asking the Government, "Why have you spent this money,
which we have admittedly voted to you for that general
purpose, in this particular way?" This is equivalent to
government by Parliament through the agency of the Cabinet.
What happens in fact is that the Government explains and
defends its policy, acts on that policy and is questioned,

[1] Ibid. para. 4191.
[2] Ibid. para. 4228.
[3] Ibid. para. 3226 (Mr. H. Morrison).
[4] Ibid. para. 3180 (3).

criticised and defended on its action. This is the only way in which government can be effective, and these are the functions the House of Commons is fitted to exercise. As Sir Malcolm Ramsay said in 1931: "If expenditure . . . is to be reviewed in detail by a committee or committees of the House a revolutionary change must be made in procedure and indeed in the constitution."[1]

Judicial Control

A. Historical Summary

The law regarding the judicial review of administrative acts is derived from the common law relating to the supervision by the High Court of inferior jurisdictions such as courts of magistrates. It is unnecessary to treat separately review of the various categories of administrative acts discussed in the preceding chapter. Subject to the exceptions hereinafter outlined the principles are common to them all.

It is impossible to understand these principles without some knowledge of the historical growth of review.[2] Inferior jurisdictions could be checked whenever they acted in excess or in default of jurisdiction. So too administrative acts will be declared illegal by the courts if there is no jurisdiction to carry them out. Properly defined, jurisdiction is the marking off of the area of power: something ascertainable at the outset of a process, the conditions on which the right of a body to act depends. "Those conditions may be founded either on the character and constitution of the tribunal, or upon the nature of the subject-matter of the inquiry, or upon certain proceedings which have been made essential preliminaries to the inquiry. . . ."[3] Review used to be effected by two writs, the writ of certiorari and the writ of error. Besides excess of jurisdiction, the writs lay for fraud and for error of law. Errors of law were those discoverable by perusal of the written record of the tribunal, without having recourse to other evidence. Although the writ of certiorari was probably developed by analogy from the writ of error[4] the writ of error but not of

[1] H.C. 161 of 1931, paras. 363–8 (22).
[2] See D. M. Gordon: "Certiorari and the Revival of Error in Fact" in 42 *Law Quarterly Review* (1926), 521.
[3] *The Colonial Bank of Australasia* v. *Willan* (1874), L.R. 5 P.C. 417, at 443.
[4] Cf. S. A. de Smith: "The Prerogative Writs" in 11 *Cambridge Law Journal* (1951) 40.

certiorari lay also for error in fact. Error in fact does not concern the findings of fact; indeed it is a complaint of a miscarriage outside the adjudication. The most common cases of error in fact were procedural errors and bias on the part of a member of the tribunal. When it is remembered also that the convictions by magistrates formerly had to record *in extenso* every procedural step taken from the beginning, it is clear that the control of the High Court over the magistrates' courts was effective. But from 1848 onwards only a short statutory form of conviction was required in courts of summary jurisdiction.[1] The effect of the abolition in 1852 of the writ of error was to take away control of error in fact;[2] the significance of this was not realised. The effect of these two changes (mitigated of course by the fact that appeals lay from courts of summary jurisdiction to quarter sessions) was that the courts could quash only for excess of jurisdiction, for the comparatively rare fraud, and for error on the face of the record.

Next, these controls were extended by the courts to the licensing justices and then to the various new administrative jurisdictions. It will be recalled that very few of these are required to keep detailed records. In consequence the ability of the High Court to supervise them rests substantially on its interpretation of "excess of jurisdiction." Here logic and expediency part company, and it is precisely because of this that this short historical outline has been given. It is useless to estimate the extent of judicial review by ascertaining the scope of excess of jurisdiction in the decisions of the first half of the nineteenth century. Nor indeed must one assume that the extent of review is the same for all types of inferior tribunals. The plain fact is that the High Court wanted to exercise as much control over these administrative bodies as possible, and has greatly extended the concept of jurisdiction for this purpose. On the other hand, for example, since the courts are averse from meddling with military affairs, they have consistently narrowed and have recently narrowed even more their control (although using precisely the same methods) of courts martial.[3]

---

[1] Summary Jurisdiction Act, 1848.

[2] Common Law Procedure Act, 1852, Sect. 148; Supreme Court of Judicature Act, 1873.

[3] *R.* v. *Secretary of State for War, ex parte Martyn*, [1949] 1 All E.R. 242; *R.* v. *O/C Depot Battalion, R.A.S.C. Colchester, ex parte Elliott*, [1949] 1 All E.R. 373. It is

This extension has been in several directions. Because the courts never admit that there is an extension, purport to be reviewing only for want of jurisdiction, and stress that they cannot sit as a court of appeal on questions of law from these administrative decisions, it is extremely difficult to fix the present limits of judicial review. This task will be attempted later, but for the moment it will suffice to indicate the directions of these extensions. The courts will review any act done in bad faith. They will search for what they consider to be the purpose of legislation and will quash acts carried out for other purposes. They will deny their right to challenge statutory interpretations made by lower tribunals, and yet will discover (and how else than by statutory interpretation?) the considerations which can be regarded in exercising the subordinate power and quash if other considerations have been or must be presumed to have been taken into account. They will sometimes interfere if procedural requirements have not been complied with during the adjudication or if there is not even a scintilla of evidence to support the fact-finding. They will enforce the performance of certain duties.

Much of this comes very close to saying that a tribunal only has jurisdiction to decide a case correctly. It would almost deny a distinction between a decision outside the jurisdiction and a wrong decision within the jurisdiction. It leads to dilemmas which the courts have tried to ignore. For example, if a magistrate commits a procedural error before finding a person not guilty, if that error deprives him of jurisdiction, it would seem to follow that if the accused were re-tried for the same offence, he could not plead *autrefois acquit* because the trial was a nullity.[1] How, too, can the courts reconcile the decision of the House of Lords that bias makes a hearing voidable only,[2] with a view that it deprives the court of jurisdiction? The extent of review is half-way between that of *ultra vires* and appeal. The difference between review and

curious that American jurists assert that judicial control of administrative agencies there which extends to a review of facts to check that there was substantial evidence, as well as to review of law, also stems from the early nineteenth-century English cases. See B. Schwartz: *Law and the Executive in Britain*, 157 *et seq.*

[1] *R. v. Middlesex Quarter Sessions (Chairman)*, [1952] 2 Q.B. 758.
[2] *Dimes* v. *Grand Junction Canal* (1851), 3 H.L.C. 759.

appeal is still material: care must be taken not to cite cases on appeal as authorities for the extent of review.[1] So, on appeal the adequacy of evidence may be investigated and there is an unrestricted right to construe statutes.

B. Scope of Review—Excess of Jurisdiction[2]

I. EXCESS OF POWER

The most straightforward case for review of all administrative acts is where the administrative body exercises a power not given to it by the statute on which it relies. Where the Minister of Transport was authorised to hear appeals from applications to Traffic Commissioners for licences, but was not entitled to deal with revocations of licences, and on an appeal purported to direct the future revocation of a licence, the court quashed his decision on the ground of *ultra vires*.[3] Similar to this would be an act by an improperly constituted tribunal.[4] If, despite a statutory requirement that the chairman of the tribunal must be a barrister, a lay chairman acted, the court could quash for excess of jurisdiction.

2. JURISDICTIONAL FACTS

The courts can intervene if some fact which is a condition precedent to the exercise of the administrative power is non-existent. Although the Home Secretary need follow no procedures in deporting an alien, the courts will intervene if a deportation order affects someone not an alien.[5] This raises a very complex problem: When is there a "jurisdictional fact"? How are the courts to decide whether it is for the tribunal to determine whether a state of affairs exists, or whether that state must exist before the tribunal has jurisdiction to act at all? If there is the erroneous finding of a fact which the tribunal was competent to try, then only a court exercising the functions of a court of appeal, not a supervisory jurisdiction merely, could interfere.

[1] A case the effect of which is frequently misrepresented for this reason is *Minister of National Revenue* v. *Wrights' Canadian Ropes, Ltd.*, [1947] A.C. 109.
[2] See S. A. de Smith, "Wrongs and Remedies in Administrative Law," in 15 *Modern Law Review* (1952), 189.
[3] *R.* v. *Minister of Transport, ex parte Upminster Services, Ltd.*, [1934] 1 K.B. 277.
[4] *R.* v. *Nat Bell Liquors, Ltd.*, [1922] 2 A.C. 128, at 156.
[5] *R.* v. *Secretary of State for Home Affairs, ex parte Venicoff*, [1920] 3 K.B. 72.

The classic judgment is that of Lord Esher, M.R., in *Reg.* v. *Commissioners for Special Purposes of the Income Tax*[1]—

> When an inferior court or tribunal or body, which has to exercise the power of deciding facts, is first established by Act of Parliament, the legislature has to consider what powers it will give that tribunal or body. It may in effect say that, if a certain state of facts exists and is shown to such tribunal or body before it proceeds to do certain things, it shall have jurisdiction to do such things, but not otherwise. There it is not for them conclusively to decide whether that state of facts exists, and, if they exercise the jurisdiction without its existence, what they do may be questioned, and it will be held that they have acted without jurisdiction. But there is another state of things which may exist. The legislature may entrust the tribunal or body with a jurisdiction which includes the jurisdiction to determine whether the preliminary state of affairs exists as well as the jurisdiction, on finding that it does exist, to proceed further or do something more. . . . In the second of the two cases I have mentioned it is an erroneous application of the formula to say that the tribunal cannot give themselves jurisdiction by wrongly deciding certain facts to exist, because the legislature gave them jurisdiction to determine all the facts, including the existence of the preliminary facts on which the further exercise of their jurisdiction depends. . . .

This dictum has been consistently followed in the large number of cases where the problem of jurisdictional fact has since arisen. The courts have had to answer, for example, the following questions: could the Minister of Health, empowered to acquire compulsorily land other than land forming part of "any park, garden or pleasure ground," himself determine whether land was a "park"?[2] Is the decision of a Reinstatement Tribunal that a claimant is an "employee" final?[3] Can an applicant for superannuation ask the court to quash the refusal of the local authority to grant his superannuation on the ground that it wrongly held that he was not an employee?[4] Who determines whether a person is eligible for registration as an "architect,"[5] or whether a house is "fit for human habitation"?[6]

---

[1] (1888), 21 Q.B.D. 313, at 319.
[2] *White and Collins* v. *Minister of Health*, [1939] 2 K.B. 838.
[3] *R.* v. *Ludlow, ex parte Barnsley Corporation*, [1947] K.B. 634.
[4] *Wilkinson* v. *Barking Corporation*, [1948] 1 K.B. 721.
[5] *R.* v. *Architects Registration Tribunal, ex parte Jagger*, [1945] 2 All E.R. 131.
[6] *Hall* v. *Manchester Corporation* (1915), 84 L.J. Ch. 732.

Despite the seeming clarity and certainty of Lord Esher's test, in practice Parliament has so conspicuously failed to give the courts assistance that they are bound to make a creative choice, and it would hardly be surprising if they declared a fact "jurisdictional" when they had already decided that they would like to interfere with the administrative tribunal.

Particularly where there is no appeal from the administrative tribunal the courts go a long way in declaring facts jurisdictional. The Landlord and Tenant (Rent Control) Act, 1949, authorises tribunals to determine the rental equivalent of premiums paid by tenants where "it appears to the Tribunal that . . . any premium has been paid."[1] Yet the courts have quashed such a determination where they have reached the independent conclusion that a premium had not been paid.[2]

The extent of the power of the court is essentially a matter of statutory interpretation. Nowhere is this better illustrated than by cases under the Housing Acts, where the courts are empowered to quash orders affecting property which are outside the powers of the local authority. Orders can be made only for "houses": the courts have said in effect that it is their function to determine the legal meaning of "houses,"[3] although the finding of the facts to which the interpreted definition is to be applied is solely within the jurisdiction of the administrative body.[4]

The tribunal should itself first decide whether on the facts it has jurisdiction;[5] if the statute makes the tribunal's jurisdiction depend on the facts being present, the reviewing court may then determine those facts. This the reviewing court will normally do on the basis of documentary and affidavit evidence. The court may also inquire into conflicts of oral testimony.[6]

---

[1] Sch. 1, para. 1.

[2] *R.* v. *Fulham, Hammersmith, and Kensington Rent Tribunal, ex parte Philippe,* [1950] 2 All E.R. 211.

[3] *In re Butler (Wingfield Mews) No. 2 Clearance Order, 1936,* [1939] 1 K.B. 570; *Birch* v. *Wigan Corporation,* [1953] 1 Q.B. 136.

[4] *In re Bainbridge. South Shields (D'Arcy Street) Compulsory Purchase Order, 1937,* [1939] 1 K.B. 500.

[5] *R.* v. *Fulham, etc. Rent Tribunal, ex parte Zerek,* [1951] 2 K.B. 1.

[6] *R.* v. *City of London Rent Tribunal, ex parte Honig,* [1951] 1 K.B. 641; cf. O. 55B, r. 72 and *White and Collins* v. *Minister of Health,* [1939] 2 K.B. 838 at 859 (*per* Luxmoore, L.J.) *Dicta* of Devlin, J., in *Zerek's* case at 11–13, which might suggest that such disputes of fact cannot be inquired into, do not appear to be borne out by the cases there cited. The court may, however, decline to inquire into disputed

When the statute is construed as empowering the tribunal to decide the facts subject to the statutory terms being properly applied, it will not then be open for the court to review the facts; it will merely decide whether the tribunal has arrived at the correct meaning of the statutory terms used in the Act.[1] There is a third type of jurisdictional fact case: in some cases the courts decide that a particular question is primarily one for the tribunal but that, if there is no evidence on which the tribunal can base its decision, that decision is an excess of jurisdiction.[2]

3. PROCEDURAL DEFECTS

If matters which determine whether a tribunal can enter upon the inquiry are jurisdictional, but those which arise from a miscarriage in the course of the inquiry are not, then it would follow that procedural defects occurring before the hearing will deprive the tribunal of jurisdiction.

The courts have for over a hundred years at least quashed adjudications which have been preceded by breach of such statutory requirements. Some writers deny that these procedural errors should go to jurisdiction, and purport to find authorities in support.[3] The explanation is that the courts will only quash if the statutory requirement is mandatory and not merely directory in terms,[4] so that it can be construed as a condition precedent to jurisdiction.[5] The courts have usually regarded a statutory requirement for notice of hearing[6] and a fortiori a breach of the rule of natural justice about

facts when prohibition is sought, and require the applicant to proceed before the tribunal; he will still be able to challenge the tribunal's decision by certiorari: Reg. v. Tottenham and District Rent Tribunal, [1957] 1 Q.B. 103.

[1] Hall v. Manchester Corporation (1915), 84 L.J. Ch. 732; Estate and Trust Agencies (1927) Ltd. v. Singapore Improvement Trust, [1937] A.C. 898.

[2] R. v. Wisbech Licensing JJ., [1937] 2 K.B. 706 (although the justices had to decide whether there were any "special requirements" rendering it desirable to alter the district's licensing hours, their decision would have been quashed if based on no evidence). Reg. v. Board of Control, [1956] 2 Q.B. 109 (habeas corpus granted because there was no evidence on which the judicial body making the detention order (from whom there was no appeal) could have found that the person so detained was "found neglected" within the meaning of the relevant Act); cf. Richardson v. L.C.C., [1957] 1 W.L.R. 751, C.A.

[3] E.g. D. M. Gordon, 47 Law Quarterly Review (1931) 386, 557, at 566–7.

[4] See above, Ch. III, p. 107.

[5] Dixon v. Wells (1890), 25 Q.B.D. 249; McIntosh v. Simpkins, [1901] 1 Q.B. 487; Alderson v. Palliser, [1901] 2 K.B. 833.

[6] Capel v. Child (1832), 2 Cr. & J. 558.

notice[1] as imposing a condition precedent. The decision of
a rent tribunal has been recently quashed when the local
authority made an unauthorised reference of the issue to the
tribunal.[2]

Where the procedural defect occurs during the hearing,
this would seem to be error not going to the jurisdiction, and
remediable only by way of appeal. To hold otherwise would be
to assert that, although a tribunal had jurisdiction at the outset,
a subsequent procedural mistake relates back to the start and
makes the whole proceeding an excess of jurisdiction. Nevertheless, the courts have quashed administrative acts because
of such procedural defects. It is a fundamental rule of law
that want of jurisdiction cannot be cured by acquiescence or
express waiver; the courts have, however, been driven into
the illogical position of holding that defects which on one
occasion are jurisdictional, can on another be waived.[3]
Indeed, it has recently been held that an appellant from the
decision of an inferior tribunal has thereby waived his right to
have that decision quashed on review.[4]

It may be confidently stated that the courts now will
consistently quash determinations which break the rules of
natural justice.[5] Having lost sight of the old concept of error
in fact, they have to search for some other justification for this
intervention. Uneasily aware that this is something other
than want of jurisdiction, they fight shy of the words "excess
of jurisdiction" and take refuge in vague expressions like "a
denial of justice."[6] Or, with a superficial show of logic, they
say that a hearing with incorrect procedure is equivalent to
"declining jurisdiction" or "no decision"[7] or "refusing to
hear."[8]

Breaches of natural justice apart, the courts do not hold

[1] *Spackman* v. *Plumstead Board of Works* (1885), 10 App. Cas. 229, at 240 (*per*
Earl of Selborne).
[2] *R.* v. *Paddington and St. Marylebone Rent Tribunal, ex parte Bell London and Provincial Properties, Ltd.*, [1949] 1 K.B. 666.
[3] *Park Gate Iron Co.* v. *Coates* (1870), L.R. 5 C.P. 634.
[4] *R.* v. *Pereira, ex parte Khotoo Bawasab*, [1949] W.N. 96.
[5] E.g. *Reg.* v. *Fraser* (1893), 9 T.L.R. 613; *R.* v. *Caernarvon Licensing Justices*,
[1948] W.N. 505; *General Medical Council* v. *Spackman*, [1943] A.C. 627.
[6] *R.* v. *Wandsworth Justices, ex parte Read*, [1942] 1 K.B. 281, at 283 (*per* Viscount
Caldecote).
[7] *Spackman* v. *Plumstead Board of Works* (1885), 10 App. Cas. 229, at 240.
[8] *R.* v. *Caernarvon Justices* (1833), 4 B. & Ad. 86, at 88.

that the breach of rules of procedure always goes to jurisdiction. The courts have sometimes confessed their inability to formulate any test that will decide when disregard of procedure amounts to excess of jurisdiction.[1] This inability is usually cloaked under precedents or vague distinctions between "nullity" and "mere irregularity." In short, supervising jurisdictions from which there is no appeal, and confronted by serious procedural breaches which they wish to check, the courts have disguised the fact that they are changing the law so that they now quash for serious procedural error, but suggest in their judgments that they are still merely preventing excesses of jurisdiction. Whether the procedural breach renders the proceedings a nullity or merely makes them irregular must obviously depend largely on whether the courts wish to intervene.

There is a class of case where the courts, although not acting in an appellate capacity, may quash procedural errors without extending the concept of jurisdiction. The Housing Acts, the Town and Country Planning Acts, and many others empower the court to quash a ministerial order if it is not within the powers of the Act or if "the interests of the applicant have been substantially prejudiced by any requirement of this Act not having been complied with." The courts have so far shirked the task of defining "powers" and "requirements," but it may at least be said that it enables them to quash if procedural steps in the making of the order are not carried out.[2] Therefore, since the New Towns Act requires the Minister to "consider" the report of the inspector, the House of Lords stated that the order could be challenged if the Minister did not consider it.[3] This decision also illustrates the important point that the courts may intervene for non-observance of statutory prescriptions even though the administrative body is not "judicial" in the sense that it need not observe the rules of natural justice.

---

[1] *Martin* v. *Mackonochie* (1879), 4 Q.B.D. 697, at 786.

[2] *Re Bowman, South Shields (Thames Street) Clearance Order, 1931*, [1932] 2 K.B. 621; cf. *Frost* v. *Minister of Health*, [1935] 1 K.B. 286; *Re L.C.C. (Riley Street, Chelsea No. 1. Order, 1938)*, [1945] 2 All E.R. 484; *Smith* v. *East Elloe R.D.C.*, [1955] 1 W.L.R., 380 affirmed [1956] A.C. 736, H.L. In *Darlassis* v. *Minister of Education* (1954), 52 L.G.R. at 319, Barry, J., thought that failure by the Minister to act judicially was an excess of power not a mere breach of a requirement; cf. *Steele* v. *Minister of Housing and Local Government* (1956), 6 P. & C.R. 586.

[3] *Franklin* v. *Minister of Town and Country Planning*, [1948] A.C. 87, at 103.

4. ERROR OF LAW ON THE FACE

Where upon the face of the record it appears that the determination of the inferior tribunal is wrong in law, certiorari will be granted.[1] The leading case of *R. v. Northumberland Compensation Appeal Tribunal, ex parte Shaw* decided that this rule extends to bodies which are not courts of record.[2] A record will always include the document in which the determination is recorded.[3] Denning, L.J., has stated that it also includes the document which initiates the proceedings and the pleadings, if any.[4] The court may order an incomplete record to be completed. If there is no statutory requirement to state reasons in the record, then affidavit evidence setting out those reasons is not admissible.[5] On the other hand, if the record discloses more than is required, an error thereby revealed will afford a ground for quashing.[6] There may be an error of law on the face of the record either because the facts, being fully stated on the record, are plainly inconsistent in law with the decision reached,[7] or because a wrong proposition of law[8] has been

---

[1] *R. v. Nat Bell Liquors, Ltd.*, [1922] 2 A.C. 128 at 160 (*per* Lord Sumner); *R. v. Minister of Health*, [1939] 1 K.B. 232 at 246 (*per* Greer, L.J.).

[2] [1952] 1 Q.B. 338.

[3] Cf. the view of Stable, J., in *Woollett* v. *Minister of Agriculture*, [1954] 2 All E.R. 776 at 785 (reversed on other grounds, [1955] 1 Q.B. 103), that a tribunal's report required by an Act had to be "in the nature of a considered judgment which would expound not merely the result at which the tribunal arrived but also the process by which that conclusion was reached."

[4] *Shaw's* case (above) at 352. *Sed quaere*, at least when the determination of the tribunal is required to be laid down in a particular statutory form; *R. v. Nat Bell Liquors, Ltd.*, [1922] 2 A.C. 128 at 155–6 (*per* Lord Sumner). If an extract from a report is included in the record, then the whole report can be looked at: *R. v. Medical Appeal Tribunal, ex parte Gilmore*, [1957] 2 W.L.R. 498 at 502.

[5] Affidavit evidence is, however, freely admitted to support an application for certiorari based on excess of jurisdiction, breach of the rules of natural justice, and fraud. Denning, L.J., at 353 in *Shaw's* case, stated that the parties could agree that a question of law which was not stated in the record could be argued and settled as if it were so stated; *sed quaere*. And see *ex parte Gilmore* (note 4 above) at 503.

[6] *Per* Lord Sumner in *R. v. Nat Bell Liquors Ltd.* (128) at 155. But when a statute prescribes a short form of conviction and also requires written depositions to be taken, it is not possible to quash for error of law on the ground that insufficient evidence is set out in the depositions. Nevertheless, an error of the law of evidence may constitute an error of law for the present rule.

[7] Cf. *R. v. Birmingham Compensation Appeal Tribunal*, [1952] 2 All E.R. 100; *R. v. Westminster Compensation Appeal Tribunal*, [1953] 1 All E.R. 687; *R. v. Paddington Rent Tribunal*, [1955] 3 All E.R. 391; and the analogous cases on arbitration cited in *Taylor* v. *Barnett*, [1953] 1 W.L.R. 562; *Clark* v. *Carters, Ltd.*, [1944] K.B. 566.

[8] *Champsey Bhara & Co.* v. *Jivraj Balloo Spinning and Weaving Co.*, [1923] A.C. 480. In *Shaw's* case the record did not in the opinion of Denning and Morris, L.JJ. (*contra* Singleton, L.J.) disclose the material facts to which the recorded

relied on in the record. It has been held that a decision expressed by statute to be "final" may be quashed for error on the face.[1]

5. ABUSE OF DISCRETION

The courts have for a long time claimed the right to interfere with the exercise of an administrative discretion. They used to veil their justification for quashing the purported exercise of a discretion in sweeping but vague and ambiguous terms. Characteristic is this dictum of Lord Halsbury[2]—

> . . . when it is said that something is to be done within the discretion of the authorities . . . that something is to be done according to the rules of reason and justice, not according to private opinion . . . according to law and not humour. It is to be, not arbitrary, vague, fanciful, but legal and regular.

The courts will intervene if powers are used for an improper purpose or if they are exercised without taking into account all relevant considerations (and no others).

(a) Improper Purpose

The House of Lords has recognised this as a separate ground for control. In *Leeds Corporation* v. *Ryder*[3] Lord Loreburn said that administrative tribunals must "endeavour to carry out the spirit and purpose of the statute." In the *Arlidge* case Lord Moulton said that an administrative body must avail "itself of its wide powers solely for the purpose of carrying into effect in the best way the provisions of the Act."[4]

It must be understood that this rule of improper purpose gives the lie to any suggestion that English law knows two types

legal proposition applied, but it was held that the concession by the tribunal at the trial that there was a speaking order with an error apparent on the face prevented the tribunal from raising the point on appeal. Although it remains the law that certiorari will not lie merely because a tribunal has misinterpreted a statute, it is thought that, with the revival of error on the face, many such cases where certiorari has been refused on that ground might now be treated as "error on the face." In *R.* v. *Appeal Tribunal, ex parte The Champion Paper & Fibre Co.*, [1956] R.P.C. 323 (the only full report) the issue of how long a patent right should be extended was held to be a question of degree, i.e. of fact, not of error of law on the face of the record.

[1] *R.* v. *Medical Appeal Tribunal, ex parte Gilmore,* [1957] 2 W.L.R. 498.
[2] *Sharp* v. *Wakefield,* [1891] A.C. 173, at 179.
[3] [1907] A.C. 420, at 423.
[4] [1915] A.C. 120, at 147; cf. *Short* v. *Poole Corporation,* [1926] Ch. 66, at 91.

of discretion, qualified and uncontrolled or absolute discretions. This rule is essentially an implied maxim of statutory interpretation—that even though a discretion is expressed in unqualified terms the statute must be taken to read that the discretion must be exercised for the purposes contemplated by the statute, and what these purposes are it is for the court to ascertain.

Ministers, impatient of judicial control, have persuaded Parliament with increasing frequency to vest in them subjective discretions, by using such expressions as "If the Minister is satisfied." *Liversidge* v. *Anderson*,[1] and *Carltona Ltd.* v. *Commissioners of Works*[2] decide that such expressions may prevent the courts from deciding whether the Minister had reasonable grounds for his belief or from reviewing his act because he took into account the wrong considerations. Yet the courts in both cases said that they would quash if the power were not exercised in good faith.[3] By this, they mean that he must, in the words of Sir Alfred Denning,[4] have "the state of mind of an administrator who will . . . after due consideration come to an honest decision as to whether to exercise the power or not, for the purpose authorised by Parliament." Even though unable to evaluate the reasons for a decision, the courts will investigate the honesty and the motives of the actor in order to ascertain whether the act was being performed for the purposes sanctioned by the statute. An illustration was given by the Court of Appeal, when considering a case under the Town and Country Planning Act, 1944: it was there said that if the Minister made a designation order when very little war damage had occurred, that would be bad faith which would invalidate the order.[5] Improper purpose then is wider than bad faith in the sense of dishonesty or corrupt motives. As Lord Sumner said in *Roberts* v. *Hopwood*,[6] even though the Administration act *bona fide* the courts can quash if the discretion is exercised

---

[1] [1942] A.C. 206; but see *Nakkuda Ali* v. *M. F. de S. Jayaratne*, [1951] A.C. 66.
[2] [1943] 2 All E.R. 560.
[3] Cf. *Demetriades* v. *Glasgow Corporation*, [1951] 1 All E.R. 457. In the *Franklin* case, where the courts were again considering a statute conferring a subjective discretion, it was held that a statutory requirement to "consider" imposed the necessity of a "genuine" consideration: *per* Lord Thankerton at 103.
[4] Denning: *Freedom under the Law*, 122.
[5] *Robinson* v. *Minister of Town and Country Planning*, [1947] K.B. 702, at 724 (*per* Somervell, L.J.).
[6] [1925] A.C. 578, at 610.

"for objects which are beyond their powers." Obviously, "improper purpose" is an increasingly important ground of control now that subjective powers are being conferred so extensively on administrative bodies.

In the leading case, *Westminster Corporation* v. *L.N.W. Ry*,[1] underground conveniences were constructed so that the subway leading to them could be used to cross beneath a busy highway. Dismissing the contention that the real object was to make a subway and not the authorised purpose of erecting lavatories with the result that the work was illegal, the court said[2]—

> It is not enough to show that the corporation contemplated that the public might use the subway as a means of crossing the street. . . . In order to make out a case of bad faith it must be shown that the corporation constructed this subway as a means of crossing the street under the colour and pretence of providing public conveniences which were not really wanted at that particular place.

Where a local Act provides that the local authority must approve plans providing for means of entrance for cars to houses from the highway, if the purpose of that Act is to ensure that these communications are properly constructed, the court will interfere if the local authority rejects a plan in order to further its town-planning scheme.[3]

The purpose of the body is a question of fact, and obviously one difficult of proof.[4] If the effect which it was sought to achieve is sanctioned by the law the courts cannot quash merely because members of the body have been actuated by extraneous motives.[5]

---

[1] [1905] A.C. 426; cf. *Sydney Municipal Council* v. *Campbell*, [1925] A.C. 338.

[2] At 432 (*per* Lord Macnaghten).

[3] *Marshall* v. *Blackpool Corporation*, [1933] 2 K.B. 334; cf. *R.* v. *Minister of Health, ex parte Davis*, [1929] 1 K.B. 619, at 624.

[4] *Marquess of Clanricarde* v. *Congested Districts Board for Ireland* (1915), 79 J.P. 481.

[5] *R.* v. *Brighton Corporation, ex parte Shoosmith* (1907), 96 L.T. 762; cf. *Robins (E.) and Sons, Ltd.* v. *Minister of Health*, [1939] 1 K.B. 520, at 537; and *Earl Fitzwilliam's Wentworth Estates Co.* v. *Minister of Housing and Local Government*, [1952] A.C. 362; *Arthur Yates & Co. Ltd.* v. *Vegetable Seeds Committee* (1945), 72 C.L.R. 37 (and see Keir & Lawson, *Cases in Constitutional Law*, 4th Edn., 299). *Contra* if no attempt would have been made to perform the administrative act but for the one dominant unlawful motive in the minds of members; *Sydney Municipal Council* v. *Campbell*, [1925] A.C. 338; *Yates* v. *Vegetable Seeds Committee*, above; and *Thompson* v. *Randwick Corporation* (1950), 81 C.L.R. 87.

(b) Extraneous Considerations

It is not enough that the administrative body has acted for a proper purpose. In the words of Lord Greene[1]—

> The court is entitled to investigate the action of the local authority with a view to seeing whether they have taken into account matters which they ought not to take into account, or, conversely have . . . neglected to take into account matters which they ought to take into account.

It is now a settled principle of English law, recognised by the House of Lords,[2] that the courts will quash administrative acts if those performing them have either acted on extraneous considerations or ignored material considerations. The courts deny that they can interfere with the way in which discretion is exercised,[3] or that they are acting as a court of appeal.[4] They are ensuring only that the discretion is exercised properly,[5] or "according to law"[6] or that the Administration "is not declining jurisdiction."[7]

The difference between a review for excess of jurisdiction and one of the substance of a decision is here very slight. It must be remembered that statutes very seldom list the factors which are to be taken into account. Although the courts frequently say that erroneous interpretation of a statute is not an excess of jurisdiction,[8] they will always interpret the statute to find what are the relevant considerations implied by it and quash only if these are not taken into account. Further, the effect of delimiting the field of considerations may be to cut down the range of discretion to such an extent that only one decision is open to the authority; then the courts may say that discretion is "exhausted" and order the authority to carry out its duty.[9] It has been held that a licensing body may properly exercise its discretion although it announces a general rule within the

---

[1] *Associated Provincial Picture Theatres Ltd.* v. *Wednesbury Corporation*, [1948] 1 K.B. 223, at 233–4.

[2] *Roberts* v. *Hopwood*, [1925] A.C. 578, at 600 (*per* Lord Atkinson); cf. *Pilling* v. *Abergele U.D.C.*, [1950] 1 K.B. 636.

[3] *Smith* v. *Chorley R.D.C.* [1897] 1 Q.B. 678, at 680 (*per* Lopes, L.J.); *Fraser (D. R.) & Co., Ltd.* v. *Minister of National Revenue*, [1949] A.C. 24, at 36.

[4] *Ex parte Tebbitt Bros.* (1917), 116 L.T. 85.

[5] *Roberts* v. *Hopwood*, [1925] A.C. 578, at 600 (*per* Lord Atkinson).

[6] *Reg.* v. *Bowman*, [1898] 1 Q.B. 663, at 666 (*per* Wills, J.).

[7] *R.* v. *Board of Education*, [1910] 2 K.B. 165, at 179 (*per* Farwell, L.J.).

[8] *R.* v. *Minister of Health*, [1939] 1 K.B. 232, at 246.

[9] *R.* v. *Kingston Justices, ex parte Davey* (1902), 86 L.T. 589.

policy of the Act by which it will be guided in deciding particular cases.[1]

Nor will the courts necessarily be deterred from defining the limits of the relevant factors even if the body is entitled to act "as it thinks fit." In *Roberts* v. *Hopwood*[2] the House of Lords held that, although a local authority was empowered to pay its employees such wages as it "may think fit," if it were guided by "eccentric principles of socialistic philanthropy" the act would be *ultra vires*. Well might Bankes, L.J., say that "it is often difficult to draw the line between those cases where the tribunal or authority has heard and determined erroneously upon grounds which it was entitled to take into consideration and those cases where it has heard and determined upon grounds outside and beyond its jurisdiction."[3] Similarly, it has been held that because local authorities owe a fiduciary duty (analogous to that of trustees) to ratepayers in relation to the application of rate funds a general power to run an omnibus undertaking did not entitle them, on philanthropic grounds, to provide free travel for certain classes of old persons.[4]

The legislative tendency to vest Ministers with a subjective discretion has previously been mentioned.[5] The courts say in effect that it is then the legislative intention that the official can take into account any matters which he thinks fit. It follows therefore that the present head of judicial review is inapplicable to those discretions. Whether subjective discretions are conferred must always be a matter of statutory interpretation, but the judicial tendency seems to be to confine them to discretions vested in Ministers of the Crown.[6]

(c) Unreasonableness

When the courts have suggested that they will quash "unreasonable" decisions, they have usually shown that they

---

[1] *R.* v. *Torquay Licensing Justices, ex parte Brockman*, [1951] 2 K.B. 784. A tribunal must not impose conditions on a licensee for the sake of consistency, but must decide each case on its merits: *R.* v. *Flintshire C.C. County Licensing (Stage Plays) Committee*, [1957] 1 Q.B. 350.

[2] See above, p. 222, note 2, at 594. *A fortiori*, if a local authority is authorised to charge "reasonable" rents for its own houses, the court may decide whether the rents charged are reasonable; *Smith* v. *Cardiff Corporation (No.* 2), [1955] Ch. 159.

[3] *R.* v. *Port of London Authority, ex parte Kynoch, Ltd.*, [1919] 1 K.B. 176, at 183.

[4] *Prescott* v. *Birmingham Corporation*, [1955] Ch. 210; but see now Public Service Vehicles (Travel Concessions) Act, 1955.   [5] See above, p. 220.

[6] See *Nakkuda Ali* v. *M. F. de S. Jayaratne*, [1951] A.C. 66.

were quashing because extraneous factors had been considered.[1] Lord Greene has, however, said that unreasonableness may be a head separate from "extraneous considerations."[2] He held that even though the authority are not proved to have taken into account any wrong considerations "it may still be possible to say that . . . they have nevertheless come to a conclusion so unreasonable that no reasonable authority could ever have come to it."[3]

6. INSUFFICIENT EVIDENCE

The United States courts will review administrative findings which are not supported by substantial evidence, that is, by "such relevant evidence as a reasonable mind might accept as adequate to support a conclusion."[4] It has been said that the difference between this and the English "rule that the court cannot substitute its own conclusion for that of the administrative agency chosen by Parliament . . . is, however, of less significance since an English court can fall back on the 'no evidence' rule, i.e. that as a matter of law an inference from the facts does not logically accord with and follow from them, as the late Lord du Parcq once put it."[5] But Lord du Parcq was dealing with income-tax litigation where statute expressly gives a right of appeal on points of "law."[6] It is a well-recognised rule that a right of appeal includes the right to appeal from findings not supported by the evidence. But English law has here always maintained the distinction between "excess of jurisdiction" and "appeal on a point of law" and there is no decided case in England to the effect that a right to quash for excess of jurisdiction extends to circumstances where the decision is against the weight of the evidence.

The courts have justified this by falling back on the orthodox view of jurisdiction that a jurisdictional error must prevent the tribunal from starting the hearing, and cannot be something

---

[1] E.g. *Roberts* v. *Hopwood*, p. 223 above.
[2] *Associated Provincial Picture Theatres Ltd.* v. *Wednesbury Corporation*, [1948] 1 K.B. 223, at 234; *Marquess of Clanricarde* v. *Congested Districts Board for Ireland* (1915), 79 J.P. 481, H.L.
[3] Cf. Lord Reid in *Smith* v. *East Elloe Rural District Council*, [1956] A.C. 736 at 762.
[4] *Consolidated Edison Co.* v. *N.L.R.B.* (1938), 305 U.S. 197, at 229.
[5] E. C. S. Wade in Foreword to B. Schwartz: *American Administrative Law*, vi.
[6] *Bean* v. *Doncaster Amalgamated Collieries, Ltd.*, [1944] 2 All E.R. 279, at 284.

arising during it.[1] Of course, they could have departed from this logical position and said that a court had no jurisdiction to reach a decision unsupported by evidence.

The balance of authority is in favour of the view that a decision arrived at on no evidence at all may not be quashed merely on that account.[2] Even so, "no evidence" may be a ground for quashing a decision for other reasons. It might show bad faith or unreasonableness,[3] it might constitute an error of law on the face of the record,[4] it might bring the decision within the rule of "jurisdictional fact."[5] There is a fourth rather subtle point. To fail to hear evidence is to decline jurisdiction if the refusal is based on a misconception of the province of the tribunal's investigation; on the other hand, if the refusal does not amount to a refusal to deal with the subject-matter but is a mere ruling that the evidence would not prove the subject-matter, there is no failure to determine.[6]

7. STATUTORY CURTAILMENT OF JUDICIAL REVIEW

Sometimes statutes purport to cut down the right of judicial review of administrative decisions, just as they limit the judicial control of delegated legislation. The tendency of the courts to extend "jurisdictional facts" is one manifestation of the general attitude of the courts that statutes are to be presumed not to take away the jurisdiction of the ordinary courts.

The courts have held that a provision that a ministerial decision "shall be final and not subject to appeal to any court"

---

[1] *R.* v. *Nat Bell Liquors, Ltd.*, [1922] 2 A.C. 128.

[2] *Reg.* v. *Shropshire Justices* (1866), 14 L.T. 598; *dicta* in *R.* v. *Nat Bell Liquors Ltd.* (note 1 above); *R.* v. *Minister of Health*, [1939] 1 K.B. 232; *R.* v. *Paddington and St. Marylebone Rent Tribunal, ex parte Kendal Hotels, Ltd.*, [1947] 1 All E.R. 448 at 450. *Contra, R.* v. *Salford Assessment Committee* (1948), 41 R & I.T. 200; *R.* v. *Flintshire C.C. County Licensing (Stage Plays) Committee*, [1957] 1 Q.B. 350 (Parker, L.J., held that mandamus would lie to a licensing authority where there was no evidence to support the particular way in which it exercised its discretion).

[3] *Re Bowman, South Shields (Thames Street) Clearance Order, 1931*, [1932] 2 K.B. 621, at 632; cf. *Re Falmouth Clearance Order, 1936*, [1937] 3 All E.R. 308; *Re L.C.C. (Riley Street, Chelsea No. 1 Order, 1938)*, [1945] 2 All E.R. 484.

[4] See above, p. 218.

[5] *R.* v. *Wisbech Licensing Justices*, [1937] 1 K.B. 706, and above p. 212.

[6] *Reg.* v. *Marsham*, [1892] 1 Q.B. 371; *R.* v. *West Riding of Yorkshire Justices, ex parte Broadbent*, [1910] 2 K.B. 192; D. M. Gordon, 31 *Can. B.R.* (1953) 1158. Sometimes, too, the failure to admit evidence may be a ground for quashing as a procedural defect; thus in *General Medical Council* v. *Spackman*, [1943] A.C. 627, the House of Lords granted certiorari because the G.M.C., by refusing to allow a medical practitioner to bring evidence rebutting a finding of adultery made in divorce proceedings, failed to make a "due inquiry" within the Act.

does not exclude judicial review.[1] Beyond that, there is a
surprising absence of recent judicial interpretation of the legislative attempts to cut down review of administrative adjudications.[2] Is it correct, for example, that Sect. 15 (2) of the National
Service Act, 1948, prevents control by the courts, when it lays
down that "no determination of the Minister, of a Military
Service (Hardship) Committee, of the umpire or of any
deputy umpire made for the purposes of the last three foregoing sections shall be called in question in any court of law"?[3]
Many old English decisions held that statutory attempts to take
away certiorari did not prevent the courts from awarding it
for jurisdictional defects[4].

Canadian courts have gone to remarkable lengths in
preventing exclusion of judicial review. Firstly, they endeavour
to nullify the statutory restriction by saying that the administrative body can only bring it into play if it is acting within its
jurisdiction.[5] A typical Canadian decision is *R. ex rel. Davies*
v. *McDougall Construction Co. Ltd.*[6] A statute provided that
the Workmen's Compensation Board had "exclusive jurisdiction to . . . determine all matters and questions arising
under this Act, and the action or decision of the Board there-
on shall be final and conclusive and shall not be open to
question or review in any Court." The court held that it could
review to determine whether the "matter" was within the
jurisdiction of the Board. Further, a Privy Council decision,
Colonial Bank of Australasia v. *Willan*,[7] lays down that the courts
can quash "upon the ground of a manifest defect of jurisdiction in the tribunal that made it, or of manifest fraud in

---

[1] *R.* v. *Minister of Transport, ex parte H.C. Motor Works, Ltd.*, [1927] 2 K.B. 401;
Taylor v. *National Assistance Board*, [1957] 2 W.L.R. 189 at 193 (*per* Denning, L.J.);
R. v. *Medical Appeal Tribunal, ex parte Gilmore*, [1957] 2 W.L.R. 498. But a provision that a decision "shall not be called in question in any court of law" excludes
review: *R.* v. *Foreign Compensation Commission, ex parte Oak & Timber Co., Ltd.*,
17 April, 1956 (see Vol. 8, p. 244, Evidence, Committee on Administrative
Tribunals and Enquiries).

[2] But see *Smith* v. *East Elloe Rural District Council*, [1956] 2 W.L.R. 888, p. 119
above.

[3] *Pace* R. S. W. Pollard: *Administrative Tribunals at Work*, 17.

[4] E.g. *R.* v. *St. Albans Justices* (1853), 22 L.J. M.C. 142; for others, see S. A de.
Smith, "Statutory Restriction of Judicial Review," in 18 M.L.R. (1955), 575.

[5] Cf. the reasoning of Greer, L.J., in *Minister of Health* v. *The King* (*On the
prosecution of Yaffé*), [1930] 2 K.B. 98 at 157; [1931] A.C. 494 that a provision that
an order shall have effect as if enacted in the Act can only operate if an order is
duly made.

[6] [1930] 1 D.L.R. 621.   [7] (1874), L.R. 5 P.C. 417, at 442.

the party procuring it." This judgment, as interpreted by subsequent Canadian decisions, means that the courts can intervene even though the statute excludes review "upon any ground whatsoever" if there is an excess of jurisdiction.[1] Perhaps the English courts would exercise the more restricted control laid down by Dixon, J., in Australia: that an exclusionary clause will protect a tribunal's decision from review provided "that its decision is a *bona fide* attempt to exercise its powers, that it relates to the subject-matter of the legislation, and that it is reasonably capable of reference to the power given to the body."[2]

It is suggested that the word "determination" in the National Service Act indicates that it is only the substance of the administrative adjudication that cannot be reviewed, and that the section does not interfere with judicial review for excess of jurisdiction.

8. STATUTORY EXTENSION OF JUDICIAL REVIEW

There is no inherent right of appeal from administrative determinations.[3] Many statutes do confer a statutory right of appeal from various administrative bodies; sometimes a statutory right of certiorari is given.[4] It is always a matter of statutory interpretation how far a statutory right of appeal has extended those limits of ordinary judicial review outlined in this chapter.

The common-form provision of the housing and town planning legislation whereby judicial review is allowed if (*inter alia*) the interests of the appellant have been substantially prejudiced by non-compliance with statutory requirements has been previously mentioned.[5] This is an extension only in that it removes any doubt whether a defect of procedure during the adjudicative process can be an excess of jurisdiction; it cuts down review by allowing challenge only within a six weeks' period from the date of the confirmation of the order, by prohibiting any challenge to the order before or after that period,[6]

---

[1] See 30 *Canadian Bar Review* (1952), Sunderland at 69; Laskin at 986.
[2] *R.* v. *Hickman* (1945), 70 C.L.R. at 615; and see R. Anderson, "Parliament and Court," in 1 *University of Queensland L.J.* (1950) 39.
[3] *Racecourse Betting Control Board* v. *Secretary for Air*, [1944] Ch. 114.
[4] E.g. an order of a borough council for payment out of the borough funds may be so challenged: Local Government Act, 1933, Sect. 187.
[5] See above, p. 217.
[6] *Woollett* v. *Minister of Agriculture and Fisheries*, [1955] 1 Q.B. 103.

and by confining to those "substantially prejudiced" the right to complain that requirements have not been complied with.[1]

Frequently a right of appeal or the right to have a case stated to the High Court on "points of law" is given.[2] There is, for example, that right of appeal from the Pensions Appeal Tribunal[3] and from the Transport Tribunal.[4] A person dissatisfied with the decision of the Minister in a dispute between a local authority and its employee about superannuation may require the Minister to state a case to the High Court.[5] The right of appeal on points of law is of course a common provision within the hierarchy of the ordinary courts and it might be thought that its meaning has been determined with certainty. But can it be assumed that a statute which gives a right of appeal on points of law from an expert administrative tribunal gives precisely the same scope of appeal as a statute giving a right of appeal on matters of law from a judge sitting with a jury? The jury is assumed not to know the law, the administrators are; the jury is untrained, the administrators may well be specialists; the jury cannot be expected to make policy decisions, often the administrators are expressly appointed for that purpose. The House of Lords has impliedly recognised this point in the field where there have been by far the most appeals on law from administrative tribunals, income tax, in that it has never relied on decisions relating to appeals from the ordinary courts in determining the extent of the appeal from the Income Tax Commissioners.[6]

It is suggested, therefore, that no useful end is attained by an exhaustive analysis of the judicial decisions on the extent of a right of appeal on points of law from other ordinary courts. The division between law and fact in jury trials is not

---

[1] In *Smith* v. *East Elloe Rural District Council*, [1956] A.C. 736 (see above, p. 119) the House of Lords held that the effect of the rather similar provision contained in the Acquisition of Land (Authorisation Procedure) Act, 1946, was to prevent review after six weeks (and, *obiter* by two judges, even during the six weeks) even though bad faith were proved.

[2] There is no right to demand a case stated: *Walsall* v. *L.N.W. Ry.* (1878), 4 App. Cas. 30, except under statutory authority, e.g. from courts of summary jurisdiction, e.g. *Pilling* v. *Abergele U.D.C.*, [1950] 1 K.B. 636.

[3] Pensions Appeal Tribunals Act, 1943, Sect. 6 (2).

[4] Railways Act, 1921, Sect. 26; Transport Act, 1947, Sch. 10, para. 5. See also Nurses Act, 1943, Sects. 5 and 8; Police Pensions Act, 1948, Sect. 5; National Assistance Act, 1948, Sect. 38.

[5] Local Government Superanuation Act, 1937, Sect. 35.

[6] See above, p. 194.

itself analytical, but practical; how else could "probable cause" for prosecution or whether an instrument is under seal be matters of law? So, too, logical analysis of the terms "law" and "fact" is of little use in determining the extent of appeal given by various administrative statutes.[1]

The difficulty is most acute when statutes include words of variable meaning, for example "producer" or "employee." If a statute gives a right of appeal on law and a party wishes to challenge the administrative holding that he is a "producer," is that an appealable point of law? It is submitted that this is a matter of interpretation of the particular statute. Has the legislature intended that the determination of this by the lower tribunal shall be final? Among the factors to be considered are the comparative qualifications of administrator and judge to decide this point; if the issue is a technical one within the administrator's field of competence then perhaps no appeal is intended; if it is merely the interpretation of a non-technical word in common use then the judges may often be presumed to be empowered to decide on appeal. It may be relevant whether the issue of law is a fundamental principle or the relatively minor application of an established rule. As a guide to judicial behaviour, it is impossible to discount the judicial tendency to increase the scope of review the less confidence there is in the particular tribunal.

Where a "right of appeal" is given the courts will interpret this as a right to a rehearing (and not an appeal on law only) in the same way as an appeal from the High Court is treated by the Court of Appeal.[2]

C. Methods of Review

The complexities of the subject of judicial review of administrative action are not exhausted merely by a consideration of the extent of review. There is no one comprehensive proceeding for reviewing these acts. The remedies, for no practical

---

[1] And see *Edwards* v. *Barstow*, [1956] A.C. 14; *British Launderers' Research Association* v. *Borough of Hendon Rating Authority*, [1949] 1 K.B. 462; *Driscoll* v. *Church Commissioners for England*, [1957] 1 Q.B. 330 (*per* Denning, L.J.); *Wootton* v. *Central Land Board*, [1957] 1 W.L.R. 424.

[2] *Allender* v. *Council of the Royal College of Veterinary Surgeons*, [1951] 2 All E.R. 859. For a list of statutes giving such a right of appeal, and the applicable procedural rules, see O. 59, r. 38. There is the same right to a rehearing if the appeal lies to the justices; *Stepney B.C.* v. *Joffe*, [1949] 1 K.B. 599. See also *Reg.* v. *Minister of Housing and Local Government*, [1955] 1 W.L.R. 29.

reason, are plural; some of them cannot be used if another remedy is available; the lines between them are imprecise and shifting; the judges employ vague concepts (which they do not define) in marking the boundaries of each remedy; the student will scan the law reports in vain for any sound reasons to justify these complexities, or indeed any explicit judicial recognition of their existence.

I. PROHIBITION AND CERTIORARI

Superior courts have long controlled any excesses of jurisdiction on the part of inferior courts by orders (formerly writs) of prohibition and certiorari. Prohibition restrains the tribunal from proceeding further in excess of jurisdiction, whereas certiorari quashes any order made by the lower court without jurisdiction. When the courts were called upon to supervise the various new administrative jurisdictions, as they had been furnished with no new special controlling devices, they naturally turned to prohibition and certiorari which they had been accustomed to use in the control of quarter sessions and other inferior tribunals.

Sometimes the two orders overlap: in one action the applicant may seek to quash an order and to prevent some further excess; for prohibition will lie so long as there remains "something to which prohibition can apply, some act which the respondents if not prohibited may do in excess of their jurisdiction, including any act, not merely ministerial, which may be done by them in carrying out any quasi-judicial order which they have wrongly made."[1]

Both orders are available for excesses of administrative jurisdiction;[2] in addition, certiorari lies for error on the face of

---

[1] *Estate and Trust Agencies (1927), Ltd.* v. *Singapore Improvement Trust*, [1937] A.C. 898, at 917-8 (*per* Lord Maugham); cf. *R.* v. *Chancellor of St. Edmundsbury and Ipswich Diocese, ex parte White*, [1948] 1 K.B. 195, at 215 (*per* Wrottesley, L.J.); Devlin, J., said in *R.* v. *Fulham, Hammersmith, and Kensington Rent Tribunal, ex parte Zerek*, [1951] 2 K.B. 1, at 11 that prohibition and certiorari are available only for *plain* excesses of jurisdiction; *sed quaere:* no such limitation on mandamus and declaratory judgments is known.

[2] It is sometimes said that certiorari will not lie for abuse of discretion (above, pp. 219-24); e.g. de Smith, 15 *M.L.R.* (1952), 200. Although there is some historical justification for this view, there seem to be too many decisions to the contrary for this view to be now supportable; e.g. *R.* v. *Registrar of Pontypridd County Court*, [1948] 1 All E.R. 218; *Reg.* v. *Agricultural Land Tribunal*, [1953] 1 All E.R. 1182; *Reg.* v. *Fulham Rent Tribunal*, [1953] 2 All E.R. 4 (omitted from [1953] 2 Q.B. 147); *Seereelall Jhuggroo* v. *Central Arbitration and Control Board*, [1953] A.C. 151.

the record, and to quash decisions obtained by fraud.[1] Certiorari must normally be sought within six months after the
date of the proceedings.[2] Both orders are discretionary.[3]

The courts have readily held that these orders can lie to
administrative tribunals deciding issues of law and fact
between parties. They have, however, usually said that only
"judicial" acts can be supervised by them. At the same time
they have wished to control as many forms of administrative
action as possible.[4] The result is a strained and still imprecise
interpretation of "judicial."

The classic definition of the scope of these orders is that of
Atkin, L.J., in R. v. *Electricity Commissioners*,[5] when he said that
they lie "wherever any body of persons having legal authority
to determine questions affecting the rights of subjects, and
having the duty to act judicially, act in excess of their legal
authority." This definition has been consistently followed by
the courts, but has not yet been considered by the House of
Lords. There can now be no doubt that these orders lie to
tribunals which have to exercise a discretion as well as to
decide matters of law and fact. Administrative bodies exercising
liquor licensing functions are subject to the orders:[6] Lord
Goddard, C.J., recently described a suggestion to the contrary
as "without foundation."[7]

When the definition of Atkin, L.J., is examined closely, it is
seen that it does not materially assist in the clarification of the
scope of the orders because he does not define who has a "duty
to act judicially." The courts have usually applied the definition without facing this difficulty; the result is that they have
great discretion in deciding whether or not they will supervise a
particular administrative activity. In one of the few cases
where the definition was analysed[8] the Court of Appeal

---

[1] R. v. *Leicester Recorder*, [1947] K.B. 726.
[2] O. 59 r. 4(2).
[3] R. v. *Minister of Health*, [1936] 2 K.B. 29; *Ex parte Fry*, [1954] 1 W.L.R. 730.
They may be granted even though some other remedy is available; *Reg.* v. *Wimble-
don Justices*, [1953] 1 Q.B. 380.
[4] *Reg.* v. *Local Government Board* (1882), 10 Q.B. 309, at 321 (*per* Brett, L.J.); cf.
R. v. *Boycott, ex parte Keasley*, [1939] 2 K.B. 651.
[5] [1924] 1 K.B. 171, at 205.
[6] R. v. *Johnson*, [1905] 2 K.B. 59; R. v. *Woodhouse*, [1906] 2 K.B. 501, reversed
on other grounds *sub nom. Leeds Corporation* v. *Ryder*, [1907] A.C. 420.
[7] R. v. *Caernarvon Licensing Justices*, [1948] W.N. 505, at 506.
[8] R. v. *L.C.C., ex parte The Entertainments Protection Association*, [1931] 2 K.B. 215.

granted certiorari to quash the *ultra vires* grant of a licence
for the Sunday opening of a cinema. Slesser, L.J., held that
the obligation of the local authority to consider an application
for a licence was tantamount to "a duty to act judicially" even
though the statute did not expressly provide that opponents
were entitled to a hearing. This decision has been criticised
on three counts.[1] It is said that when Atkin, L.J., used the
word "subjects" he meant individuals, not the public, whereas
this case concerned matters of public, not of private, interest.
There is nothing in the judgment to suggest that he did intend
to limit "subjects" in the way suggested. It is enough if
the rights are merely those shared by all citizens.[2] It is
further objected that no "right" but only the privilege to
apply for the grant of a right was here affected. Though
logically supportable, this argument would lead to the
ridiculous result that certiorari would lie on the revocation
but not on the refusal to grant a licence. It has been further
suggested that the decision conflicts with the decision of the
House of Lords that licensing is an "administrative" act.[3] This
argument rests on the false premise that "judicial" and "administrative" have constant meanings; in this very case the House
of Lords expressly left open the question whether certiorari
would lie, although they had declared the act "administrative"
in the sense that a wide discretion was vested in the licensing
body.

The task of interpreting the phrase "having the duty to
act judicially" is made harder because the courts have often
assumed that the orders would lie when, and only when, the
rules of natural justice are presumed to apply to the particular
administrative determination. However, the orders may lie
even though the courts hold that a particular administrative
body need not observe the *audi alteram partem* rule.[4]

Some dicta indicate that "judicial" is here used in contrast

---

[1] D. M. Gordon, 10 *Canadian Bar Review* (1932), 198.

[2] *R. v. Minister of Health, ex parte Villiers*, [1936] 2 K.B. 29. *R. v. Thames Magistrates' Court, ex parte Greenbaum* (1957), 55 L.G.R. 129, C.A., held that a citizen
particularly aggrieved by a licensing decision was entitled to certiorari *ex debito
justitiae*, even though not a party; the grant to other inconvenienced citizens was
discretionary.

[3] *Boulter* v. *Kent Justices*, [1897] A.C. 556.

[4] *R. v. Brighton and Area Rent Tribunal, ex parte Marine Parade Estates (1936),
Ltd.*, [1950] 2 K.B. 410; *Hanily* v. *Minister of Local Government and Planning*, [1952]
2 Q.B. 444; cf. *R. v. Minister of Health, ex parte Dore*, [1927] 1 K.B. 763.

to "ministerial,"[1] and that certiorari and prohibition lie whenever there is "a pronouncement, finding, or order binding upon the parties concerned and imposing a legal obligation or liability, or otherwise affecting property or legal rights of individuals."[2] It is suggested that they do not lie in all cases of discretionary administrative action affecting the rights of citizens. They will lie if a body "has to consider proposals and objections and consider evidence" but not if "an administrative body in arriving at its decision at no stage has before it any form of *lis* and throughout has to consider the question from the point of view of policy and expediency."[3]

2. MANDAMUS

The order of mandamus is available to command any person, court or other body to carry out a public duty imposed upon them either by statute or common law. In contrast to prohibition and certiorari, it lies also in respect of non-judicial acts. It does not lie against the Crown, nor against a servant of the Crown if the duty is one which he has to perform only in the capacity of agent for the Crown.[4] If, on the other hand, the duty is imposed on the servant himself, then subjects to whom it is owed may enforce it by an order of mandamus.[5]

Mandamus lies to enforce a duty; it is usually said that it lies in respect of ministerial but not discretionary acts. The clearest case of its exercise is where a tribunal refuses to carry out its duty.[6] The courts often have to decide whether a

---

[1] *R.* v. *Woodhouse*, [1906] 2 K.B. 501, at 535 (*per* Fletcher Moulton, L.J.).

[2] D. M. Gordon: "Administrative Tribunals and the Courts" in 49 *Law Quarterly Review* (1933) 102.

[3] *Reg.* v. *Manchester Legal Aid Committee*, [1952] 2 Q.B. 413. Certiorari lies to: the former Board of Education required to decide the rates of teachers' pay, *Board of Education* v. *Rice*, [1911] A.C. 179; surgeon certifying disablement, *R.* v. *Postmaster-General*, [1928] 1 K.B. 291; school medical officer certifying that a child was backward, *R.* v. *Boycott*, [1939] 2 K.B. 651; a local authority granting cinema licences, *R.* v. *L.C.C.*, [1931] 2 K.B. 215; a legal aid committee, *R.* v. *Manchester Legal Aid Committee, supra*; a local authority hearing town planning applications, *R.* v. *Hendon R.D.C.*, [1933] 2 K.B. 696. Certiorari does not lie to: a textile controller revoking a dealer's licence, *Nakkuda Ali* v. *Jayaratne*, [1951] A.C. 66; police commissioner revoking a cab driver's licence, *R.* v. *Metropolitan Police Commissioner*, [1953] 1 W.L.R. 1150 (but see Gordon, "The Cab Driver's Licence Case," in 70 *L.Q.R.* (1954), 203); chief fire officer exercising disciplinary authority over a fireman, *Ex parte Fry*, [1954] 1 W.L.R. 730; bodies merely having power to report to some other deciding body, *Reg.* v. *Statutory Visitors Caterham*, [1953] 2 All E.R. 766.

[4] *Reg.* v. *Lords Commissioners of the Treasury* (1872), 7 Q.B. 387.

[5] *Reg.* v. *Commissioners for Special Purposes of the Income Tax* (1888), 21 Q.B. 313.

[6] *R.* v. *L.C.C., ex parte Corrie*, [1918] 1 K.B. 68.

particular statute imposes a duty or a discretion, and it seems that where they want to interfere, they tend to give statutes a mandatory effect. Moreover, the courts employ mandamus to compel the exercise of a discretion one way or the other, for there is a duty to exercise the discretion.[1]

If these were the limits of the scope of mandamus, it would be of limited importance as a method of reviewing administrative action, because only rarely does the Administration refuse to act at all. It is the glosses on the supposed principle that it does not lie for discretionary acts that make it a valuable remedy. It has been shown above that the courts have regarded as excesses of jurisdiction acts carried out for improper purposes or acts based on wrong considerations.[2] The courts have granted mandamus in those circumstances, holding that where a discretion is abused it is not exercised at all, and therefore that mandamus is required to enforce the carrying out of the duty of the body to exercise its discretion according to law.[3] Often in the same proceedings certiorari will lie to quash the order already made, and mandamus will be granted to enforce the proper performance of the discretionary act. Sometimes mandamus may control a discretion even more closely. The court may exclude so many considerations as being wrong ones that the administrative body is left without a choice, and must act in a particular way; in such a case the court will order it to act in that manner.[4]

Mandamus is certainly wider in scope than certiorari in that it is not limited to "judicial"[5] bodies. On the other hand, its scope is narrower in that it does not lie for errors on the face of the record which do not constitute an "abuse of discretion."[6] Mandamus seems to lie for the same "excesses of jurisdiction" as certiorari.[7]

[1] R. v. Bishop of Lichfield (1734), 7 Mod. 217.
[2] See above, p. 219, et seq.
[3] Reg. v. Adamson (1875), 1 Q.B.D. 201; Reg. v. Bowman, [1898] 1 Q.B. 663; R. v. Housing Tribunal, [1920] 3 K.B. 334.
[4] R. v. Kingston Justices, ex parte Davey (1902), 86 L.T. 589.
[5] See above, p. 231.
[6] See above, p. 219.
[7] Contra S. A. de Smith, 15 Mod. L.R. (1952) at 205–6. First, he denies that mandamus lies "to a body that has wrongfully assumed and then exercised jurisdiction over a matter outside its competence"; but the only case cited, Reg. v. Nicholson, [1899] 2 Q.B. 455, cannot be regarded as a conclusive authority—one of the two reasons for the Divisional Court's decision supports his view, but the Court of Appeal confirmed the decision on quite different grounds. Secondly, he denies

A most difficult problem is the nature of the interest which a successful applicant for mandamus must possess. Professor Wade[1] states that he must show "that the duty is owed to himself and not merely to the public at large." It is suggested that the authorities on which this proposition is based do not fully support it. Moreover, it would mean that the rule is the same as for the plaintiff in an action for breach of statutory duty. Confusion seems to have been caused by a dictum of Lord Esher[2] that "mandamus would not lie against the Crown . . . the Secretary of State only is duly responsible to the Crown and has no legal duty imposed upon him towards the subject." Lord Esher was contrasting "subject" not with the "public" but with the Crown. Indeed, in an earlier case[3] he had said that "where officials [have] a public duty to perform, and [have] refused to perform it, mandamus will lie on the application of a person interested to compel them to do so." No case seems to have been decided solely on the basis that the applicant for mandamus must prove that a duty is owed to him."[4] On the other hand, several cases have held that it is sufficient if the applicant proves that he has some special interest in the subject-matter.[5] The judges consider whether the interest of the applicant in the performance of the public duty is one which merits judicial support, weighing in the scales the general interest in the preservation of public rights and liberties and the need to prevent unnecessary litigious interference with the Administration.

The applicant for mandamus must show that his request for performance of the duty has been refused. The making

that mandamus will issue where a hearing is vitiated by the interest of its members. Certainly, *Reg.* v. *Kent JJ.* (1880), 44 J.P. 298, so decided, but it was contradicted by *Reg.* v. *L.C.C.*, [1892] 1 Q.B. 190, the principle of which seems to have been accepted in later cases, e.g. *R.* v. *Brighton Corporation* (1916), 80 J.P. 219, and *R.* v. *Prestwich Corporation* (1945), 109 J.P. 57.

[1] "The Courts and the Administrative Process" in 63 *Law Quarterly Review* (1947) 164, at 170.

[2] *Reg.* v. *Secretary of State for War*, [1891] 2 Q.B. 326, at 339.

[3] *Reg.* v. *Commissioners for Special Purposes of the Income Tax* (1888), 21 Q.B. 313 at 317.

[4] This was one of the two grounds of decision in *Reg.* v. *Lewisham Union*, [1897] 1 Q.B. 498. An unreported dictum of Channell, J., cited with approval (*obiter*) by Avory, J., in *R.* v. *Manchester Corporation*, [1911] 1 K.B. 560, also indicates that the applicant must prove that the duty is owed to him.

[5] *Reg.* v. *Cotham*, [1898] 1 Q.B. 802; *Reg.* v. *Leicester Guardians*, [1899] 2 Q.B. 632; *R.* v. *Manchester Corporation*, [1911] 1 K.B. 560; *Reg.* v. *Belfast Corporation*, [1954] N.I. 122.

of the order is always in the discretion of the court. Except
that they will not issue it where there is some other equally
convenient and effectual remedy (even extra-judicial[1]) the
courts have not articulated the factors which they consider.
Perhaps the relevant factors include those emphasised in
United States decisions:[2] would its issue be futile? Would it
embarrass the Administration in the carrying out of its essential
tasks? Is supervision by the court of the execution of the order
impracticable? Or is the enforcing of the duty otherwise
contrary to the public interest?

3. DECLARATORY JUDGMENT

Coercion is not always necessary to ensure that the law is
obeyed. Litigants will often be content to ascertain their
legal rights and duties safe in the knowledge that, once the
law is determined, it will be observed. This is particularly
true of public bodies, which could not withstand the public
criticism which would follow upon disregard of their legal
obligations. It is for this reason that cases stated, arbitrations
and what is dealt with now, declaratory actions, are so freely
resorted to. Order 25, r. 5 provides—

> No action or proceeding shall be open to objection, on the
> ground that a merely declaratory judgment or order is sought
> thereby, and the court may make binding declarations of right
> whether any consequential relief is or could be claimed, or not.

Declaratory judgments could be obtained against the
Crown[3] before the Crown Proceedings Act, which has now
confirmed their availability against the Crown and its officers.[4]
Barnard v. *National Dock Labour Board*[5], which held that a
declaration could be granted although the fact that six months
had expired and the inability to obtain discovery of documents
in certiorari proceedings would have prevented that order from
lying, has no doubt made practitioners more aware of the
scope of this remedy. It lies for any excess of jurisdiction and

---

[1] *Pasmore* v. *Oswaldtwistle U.D.C.*, [1898] A.C. 387. For a collection of cases,
see G. E. Robinson: *Public Authorities and Legal Liability*, Ch. VI. The Crown Proceedings Act, 1947, Sect. 40 (5), provides that the fact that some other remedy has
been created by that Act does not limit the discretion of the court to make an order
of mandamus where it might have done so before the Act.
[2] W. Gellhorn and C. Byse: *Administrative Law*, 407 *et seq.*
[3] *Dyson* v. *Attorney-General*, [1911] 1 K.B. 410; [1912] 1 Ch. 158.
[4] Sect. 23 (2) (*b*).   [5] [1953] 2 Q.B. 18.

perhaps for error of law on the face of the record.[1] The High Court may not in such an action rehear an issue of law and fact which it was within the power of the tribunal to decide. Whether an error of law which is not on the face of the record can be reviewed is uncertain.[2] Unlike mandamus, it may be given against the Crown; it does not share with certiorari and prohibition any limitation to "judicial acts;" it can range freely over all administrative action whether legislative, judicial or administrative; facts as well as law can be investigated.[3]

If the administrative body is exercising some summary power, which affects the citizen who wishes to question its legality, although he may not use the prerogative orders he can raise the matter in a declaratory action; e.g., can the local authority raise the rents of municipal houses?[4] can it dismiss a teacher?[5] can it lay gaspipes in a private street without the permission of the adjoining landowner?[6] Declaratory judgments have often been sought by local authorities to decide, for example, whether they can run a laundry[7] or a printing press[8], or need buy land for an open space if its owner has been refused planning permission because it has been scheduled as an open space[9] Disputes between public bodies are also conveniently resolved by this method.[10] Sometimes, also, a trader might be threatened with some criminal penalty if he carries on business without a licence. Instead of doing the act and running the risk of criminal proceedings he may seek a ruling in advance on the legality of his proposed activity.[11]

The grant of the remedy is in the discretion of the court. The House of Lords has laid down that it will not ordinarily be granted so as to deprive an administrative body of a juris-

---

[1] *Barnard's* case, above; *Healey v. Minister of Health*, [1995] 1 Q.B. 221. *Barnard's* case was approved by the House of Lords in *Vine v. National Dock Labour Board*, [1957] 1 W.L.R. 106 (workman entitled to both declaration and damages for interference with status, although the interference was a nullity).
[2] Cf. *Lee v. The Showmen's Guild of Great Britain*, [1952] 2 Q.B. 329 at 346.
[3] *Ruislip-Northwood U.D.C. v. Lee* (1931), 145 L.T. 208.
[4] *Belcher v. Reading Corporation*, [1950] Ch. 380.
[5] *Hanson v. Radcliffe U.D.C.*, [1922] 2 Ch. 490.
[6] *Davies v. Ripon Corporation*, [1928] Ch. 884.
[7] *Attorney-General v. Fulham Corporation*, [1921] 1 Ch. 440.
[8] *Attorney-General v. Smethwick Corporation*, [1932] 1 Ch. 562.
[9] *Epsom and Ewell Corporation v. Streatham Property Investment Trust, Ltd.*, [1949] Ch. 38.
[10] *Manchester Corporation v. Audenshaw U.D.C. and Denton U.D.C.*, [1928] 1 Ch. 127.
[11] *Gingell, Son and Foskett, Ltd. v. Stepney B.C.*, [1908] 1 K.B. 115.

diction expressly vested in it.[1] Uthwatt, J., has said that it will not ordinarily be granted where "any substantive relief, based on the meaning attached to the provision construed, must be sought in another jurisdiction."[2] Although a matter is within some inferior jurisdiction, the High Court will intervene by declaratory judgment if for some reason it has in the particular case powers which at the time are not enjoyed by the inferior tribunal. For example, in one case[3] the Crown was in temporary possession of a reclaimed foreshore and expressed a willingness to pay a sum of money in lieu of rates on the basis of the rateable value of the foreshore. The ordinary rating procedures were not immediately available against the owners of the foreshore because they were not then in beneficial occupation: the court determined the rateable value on a declaratory judgment. Of course the court will decide in a declaratory action the extent of the jurisdiction of an inferior tribunal.

Other factors considered by the courts in exercising their discretion are whether there is an alternative remedy and whether the order, if made, will be effective. An interesting illustration of the exercise of the discretion is provided by *Dyson* v. *Attorney-General*.[4] The applicant sought a declaration that notices issued by the Commissioners of Inland Revenue relating to income-tax and threatening him with penalties for non-compliance were invalid. Although it would have been open to Dyson to set up this invalidity if he had been prosecuted, the High Court granted a declaratory judgment against the Crown. They were influenced by the fact that large numbers of people were affected and that criminal proceedings were threatened. It must not be assumed that a person may as of right forestall a civil action against him by getting a declaration in advance that his opponent has no good cause of action against him.[5] That certiorari is available will not deter the court from making a declaratory order.[6]

[1] *Barraclough* v. *Brown*, [1897] A.C. 615.
[2] *Attorney-General* v. *Dean and Chapter of Ripon Cathedral*, [1945] Ch. 239, at 249.
[3] *Barwick* v. *S.E. & Chatham Ry. Cos.*, [1921] 1 K.B. 187; cf. *Sivyer* v. *Amies*, [1940] 3 All E.R. 285.
[4] [1911] 1 K.B. 410.
[5] *Guaranty Trust Co. of New York* v. *Hannay and Co.*, [1915] 2 K.B. 536.
[6] *Cooper* v. *Wilson*, [1937] 2 K.B. 309; *Taylor* v. *National Assistance Board*, [1956] P. 470; [1957] 2 W.L.R. 189.

Merely hypothetical issues cannot be raised by declaratory action.[1] Nor can extra-legal claims such as that of the claim of a civil servant to his pay be determined in declaratory actions.[2]

The general rule is that declaratory actions can only be brought by individuals if they join the Attorney-General as a party. If the Attorney-General does not consent to the use of his name by the private relator, there is no appeal from that refusal.[3] A private plaintiff need not join the Attorney-General if some private right of his own is also interfered with, or if he suffers damage peculiar to himself from the interference with the public right.[4]

One defect restricts the usefulness of the declaratory judgment: as with the prerogative orders it is available in the High Court only, not in the county court.[5]

4. INJUNCTION

In the United States actions for declaratory judgments are usually combined with actions for injunctions in a single proceeding. Their common characteristic is their equitable origin, but it is stated that in the United States "the injunction as a means of reviewing administrative action is gradually moving away from its historical foundations in equity and is becoming a general-utility remedy for use whenever no other form of review proceeding is clearly indicated."[6]

English law, too, recognises a link between the declaration and injunction. They are commonly treated together in the textbooks, and actions for injunctions must be brought in the name of the Attorney-General at the relation of the private plaintiff subject to the same two exceptions as declaratory actions.[7] But the injunction is comparatively unimportant as a method of reviewing administrative action in England,

---

[1] *Re Barnato decd.*, [1949] Ch. 258.
[2] *Nixon* v. *Attorney-General*, [1930] 1 Ch. 566; [1931] A.C. 184.
[3] *L.C.C.* v. *Attorney-General*, [1902] A.C. 165.
[4] *L.P.T.B.* v. *Moscrop*, [1942] A.C. 332, at 345 (*per* Lord Maugham).
[5] *De Vries* v. *Smallridge*, [1928] 1 K.B. 482.
[6] K. C. Davis: "Forms of Proceedings for Judicial Review of Administrative Action" in 44 *Illinois Law Review* (1949) 565, at 576.
[7] *Boyce* v. *Paddington Corporation*, [1903] 1 Ch. 109; [1906] A.C. 1. It seems that even the Attorney-General must prove not merely the defendant's violation of a statute but also his infringement of a *public right*: *Attorney-General* v. *Bastow*, [1957] 1 Q.B. 514.

and is not regularly combined with a declaratory action for that purpose.

The explanation may lie in the fact that injunctions have never been available against the Crown. Although they are available against Government departments in parts of the Commonwealth,[1] they were probably not available at common law against servants of the Crown in England. In any case the Crown Proceedings Act, 1947, provides in effect that no injunctions can be granted against the Crown or any of its servants.[2] This serious flaw in the remedies for administrative action is probably due to the characteristic unwillingness of the British Executive to be subject to judicial control if some issue of policy might conceivably arise. The Treasury Solicitor has said that this immunity is essential because the Crown might otherwise be prevented by an injunction from overriding the law in an emergency.[3] This seems to take no account of the prerogative rights of the Crown in an emergency, untouched by the Act, and of the discretionary[4] nature of injunctive relief.

An injunction, therefore, is only available against those administrative bodies which do not share the privileges of the Crown. It is much used to prevent *ultra vires* action by local authorities. Its value is enhanced because it may be mandatory in the sense of ordering something positive to be done.[5] As in the case of the prerogative orders, disregard of the order of the court may be followed by imprisonment for contempt of court.

5. HABEAS CORPUS

The legality of any restriction of movement imposed on an individual can be challenged by the writ of habeas corpus. By it an alien may challenge the validity of a deportation order,[6] or illegal military detention may be prevented.[7] The

---

[1] E.g. Australia: *Attorney-General* v. *Williams*, [1913] S.R. (N.S.W.) 295.
[2] Sect. 21 (1).
[3] Sir Thomas Barnes: "The Crown Proceedings Act, 1947" in 26 *Canadian Bar Review* (1948) 387, at 395 (writing in an unofficial capacity).
[4] When the Attorney-General seeks to enforce a public right, the court ought not ordinarily to refuse him an injunction on the ground that another equally effective remedy is open to him: *Attorney-General* v. *Bastow*, [1957] 1 Q.B. 514.
[5] Local authorities also use the procedure themselves, particularly to secure observance of byelaws: *Attorney-General* v. *Sharp*, [1931] 1 Ch. 121.
[6] *Eshugbayi Eleko* v. *Government of Nigeria*, [1931] A.C. 662.
[7] *R.* v. *Governor of Wormwood Scrubbs Prison, ex parte Boydell*, [1948] 2 K.B. 193. It would also be an appropriate method of reviewing a quarantine order.

Executive has no right of appeal from a decision on the merits to set him free, whereas if his application is refused he may apply to any other division of the High Court and possibly to any other judge of the same division to have the case heard afresh. Proceedings for habeas corpus take precedence over all other court business.

6. ACTIONS FOR DAMAGES

Judicial review of administrative action may often be effected by instituting a suit for damages. A suit for false imprisonment will raise the validity of detention by the Administration;[1] the legality of the exercise of summary powers can often be settled by suing for trespass, nuisance or negligence.[2] Similarly, public authorities are subject to the ordinary remedies available for the protection of property held on charitable trusts, and in proceedings brought by the Attorney-General to protect it, the courts may decide whether the property has been dealt with in an unlawful manner.[3]

7. STATUTORY APPEALS

This subject has been covered in the analysis of the scope of judicial review.[4]

8. DISOBEDIENCE

A person who disputes the legality of administrative action may disobey an administrative order and plead that illegality in subsequent criminal or civil proceedings against him.

Other Control

The influence of public opinion on the way in which administrative powers are used is considerable, and is similar in kind to that exercised over the legislative powers.[5] Public opinion becomes effective when it is the expression of organised groups. Sometimes these groups are formed by individuals having a common interest. Other groups are formed on the initiative of the Administration specifically to advise departments.[6] There

---

[1] *Liversidge* v. *Anderson*, [1942] A.C. 206.
[2] Cf. *Abbott* v. *Sullivan*, [1952] 1 Q.B. 189 at 201–3.
[3] *Attorney-General* v. *Wilson* (1840), Cr. & Ph. 1.
[4] Although certiorari would lie against magistrates for a procedural error (refusing cross-examination) the point could still be raised as "wrong in law" under the Magistrates' Courts Act, 1952, Sect. 87 (1): *Rigby* v. *Woodward*, [1957] 1 W.L.R. 250.
[5] See above, p. 121.   [6] See above, p. 133.

follow here only descriptions of some of the bodies which exist to form a link between the Administration and industry.[1]

In the first place are those national bodies which are presided over by a Minister. These include the National Production Advisory Council on Industry, the National Joint Advisory Council, the National Consultative Council for the Building and Civil Engineering Industries, the Engineering Advisory Council, the Engineering Industry Advisory Panel, and the Heavy Electrical Plant Committee. Secondly, those presided over by a Government officer include the Economic Planning Board, the Building and Civil Engineering Joint Committee, the Building Industry Production Sub-Committee, the Advisory Committee of Specialists and Sub-Contractors, the Advisory Committee on Contractor's Plant, the Horticultural Liaison Group, and the Hill Farming Advisory Committee. Thirdly, those under other chairmanship include the Fuel Efficiency Committee, the National Youth Employment Council, the National Advisory Council on the Employment of the Disabled, the Building Apprenticeship and Training Council, the National Brick Advisory Council, the Committee of the Salt Glazed Pipe Industry, the Gauge and Tool Advisory Council, the Machine Tools Advisory Council, the National Advisory Council for the Motor Manufacturing Industry, and the Shipbuilding Advisory Committee.

This is a formidable and no doubt incomplete list. The bodies are composed, in most cases, of representatives from both sides of the industries, technicians and members of Government departments. In addition to these national bodies there are others at a local or regional level. These include the Regional Boards for Industry, Local Employment Committees, Regional Joint Committees for Building and Civil Engineering, and Area Brick Committees.

These various bodies were not set up by statute and their functions are determined by their terms of reference. They give advice and make representations to the Administration. They are in no sense directly controlling bodies but their recommendations have considerable influence on the plans and actions of the Administration. Their existence does not in any way lessen the importance of the consultation which

[1] See *Government and Industry* (H.M.S.O. 1948).

takes place between the Administration and such bodies as the Federation of British Industries, the Executive Council of the Trades Union Congress, the local authorities' associations and the very many organisations of a political, professional, industrial, and cultural character. All these bodies perform the function of informing and urging action on the Administration and together exercise the control of public opinion. The extent to which the Administration heeds the innumerable voices urging various and conflicting courses of action is for the Administration to decide.

CHAPTER VI

SUITS AGAINST THE ADMINISTRATION

DICEY argued that one of the great merits of the British constitution was that Rule of Law which (*inter alia*) allowed actions to be brought in the ordinary courts against the officer responsible in the same manner as against other citizens.[1] He contrasted this with French law, by which, he suggested, officials were exempted from the application of the ordinary law of the land. What he did not stress, however, were the immunities from suit enjoyed by the Crown.

The feudal principle was that just as no lord could be sued in the court which he held to try the cases of his tenants, so the King, at the apex of the feudal pyramid, and not subject to the jurisdiction of any higher court, was not suable. One could, from the reign of Edward I onwards, maintain a cause of action against the King by petition of right, but there was no remedy if the King refused to consider the petition. A petition of right was not available for torts, other than those within the province of a real action.[2] The principle, traceable to Bracton,[3] though it rests on an insecure historical foundation,[4] that the King can do no wrong, accounts for this exception. In addition, the King had many other substantive and procedural privileges. These privileges, originally personal to the King, survived the establishment of the constitutional monarchy, and afterwards applied to the Crown as the personification of the State as well as to the King in person. Nor was the Crown vicariously liable for the torts of its servants.[5]

With the great increase of administrative functions and the creation of a large number of new administrative bodies in the nineteenth century it became most important to define the boundaries of the "Crown." Two decisions of the House of Lords in the eighteen-sixties effectively arrested any tendency

---

[1] A. V. Dicey: *Law and the Constitution* (9th Edn.) 195.
[2] A petition of right would lie, for example, in respect of an interference with an easement: *Clifton's* case, Y.B. 22 Ed. III. 12.
[3] Bracton, f. 107a.
[4] L. E. Ehrlich: *Proceedings against the Crown (1216–1377)*, 42.
[5] *Viscount Canterbury* v. *Attorney-General* (1842), 1 Ph. 306.

to clothe all of these bodies with royal privileges, although they furnished no sharp definition of the "Crown."[1] Only those which were organs of the general government of the country were to have Crown immunities; that a body had public functions was not enough. Thereafter administrative bodies were of two types, those nestling under the umbrella of the Crown and virtually free from legal liability, and the remainder, subject to common law.

The increasing interference by the State with the citizen in this century has underlined the unsatisfactory state of the law. The courts sought to alleviate by legal ,fiction the most obvious injustice: that the Crown could not be sued for the torts of its servants. An action was brought against a Crown servant as nominal defendant, on the understanding that the Crown would satisfy any judgment against him. A Royal Commission submitted a draft bill of reform in 1927,[2] but the bill did not become law. When, in 1946, the House of Lords refused to uphold the fiction of the nominated defendant[3] reform could no longer be delayed. The Crown Proceedings Act, 1947, subjected the Crown, with serious reservations, to private law. Other public authorities remained subject to private law to the same extent, substantially, as the private citizen.

In the nineteenth century many European countries, with France in the van, largely deprived administrative bodies of these immunities, and imposed on all of them, whether central or local organs of administration, a uniform body of public law administered by administrative courts. It was contended that all administrative bodies should be subject to the same law, which was to be a separate system of law from that controlling private persons. That law must recognise that the need to perform public services is paramount. So, if the Administration wishes, on grounds of public policy, to alter the terms of a contract, it may do so on payment of the appropriate compensation to the contractor. Further, individuals who suffer loss greater than their fellows at the hands of the administrative machine would recover damages whether or not there had been an administrative fault; for example, the

[1] *Mersey Docks and Harbour Board Trustees* v. *Cameron* (1864), 11 H.L.C. 443; *Mersey Docks and Harbour Board Trustees* v. *Gibbs* (1866), L.R. 1 H.L. 93.
[2] Cmd. 2842.
[3] *Adams* v. *Naylor*, [1946] A.C. 543; *Royster* v. *Cavey*, [1947] K.B. 204.

tenant of a house, flooded while the fire brigade is extinguishing a fire next door, may recover his loss from the Administration. Risk, not fault, is the new basis of administrative liability in France. It is also argued there that special courts, whose members have experience of administrative processes as well as legal training, are required in order that these new principles may be developed and applied.

What lessons do these innovations provide for English law in the future? It is difficult to reject the case for a uniform law governing all administrative bodies. Further, as will be seen in this chapter, English law has been compelled to acknowledge, however grudgingly, that some deviations from private law are unavoidable in the case of public authorities. English judges are plainly desirous of evolving fair principles of administrative liability, but are circumscribed by their adherence to private-law concepts. It may well be that Parliament should give the courts freedom of movement by enacting a new code governing suits against the Administration. That is not to concede that the adjudication of these suits need be removed from the ordinary courts.

There is, then, no separate English law of administrative liability. An account must be given, however, of those rules which particularly affect administrative bodies. An examination of the tortious liability of public authorities will be followed by an account of the special rules affecting the liability of the Crown in tort. Then contractual and quasi-contractual liability and other substantive and procedural limitations on the liability of public authorities will be successively discussed.

Tort
A. Public Authorities[1]

In general the ordinary principles of tort govern administrative bodies. Many problems arise from the fact that most of these bodies are created, and have powers and duties conferred and imposed on them, by statutes.

I. VICARIOUS LIABILITY

They are vicariously liable for the torts of their servants acting in the course of their employment. The doubt whether

[1] The rules discussed in this section A apply to the Crown, subject, where applicable, to the principles of Crown liability in tort outlined in B below.

a corporation is liable for the torts of its servants committed in the course of some activity which is *ultra vires* the corporation is of particular importance for administrative bodies.[1] Further difficulty is caused by the rule that a master is vicariously liable only for the torts of those over whom he has control. Many public officers, although appointed and dismissible by some administrative body, have duties cast on them directly by statute or common law; that body cannot be sued for torts which they commit in the course of those duties.[2] Thus, the municipal corporation, the watch committee of which has appointed a policeman, is not liable for any unlawful arrest made by him.[3] The determining factor is not the status of the official, but the nature of the particular duty during the execution of which he commits the tort.[4]

2. STATUTORY DUTIES AND POWERS

(a) Statutory Authority as a Defence

Administrative bodies can often effectively discharge their functions only if their interference with private rights is legalised. The courts have laid down that if the statutory direction is imperative there is no liability in tort, but that a mere permissive authorisation will not afford a defence to an action in tort.[5] That distinction is deceptively simple; it is suggested that the problem is always one of interpreting the particular statute. The question is: "Did the statute under which the authority acted authorise the particular interference with the plaintiff in such emphatic terms that it clearly intended to take away his common law right to sue?" It is incorrect to state that only a duty, and not a power, to act can exempt from liability, for a statute may provide that, if a power is exercised, the

---

[1] *Poulton* v. *London & S.W. Ry.* (1867), L.R. 2 Q.B. 534; *Campbell* v. *Paddington Corporation*, [1911] 1 K.B. 869.

[2] *Stanbury* v. *Exeter Corporation*, [1905] 2 K.B. 838; the Local Fuel Overseer is another officer appointed by the local authority but not controlled by it: Coal Distribution Order, 1943, S.I. 1943, No. 1138, Part V. Cf. *Harrison* v. *National Coal Board*, [1951] A.C. 639; *National Coal Board* v. *England*, [1954] A.C. 403.

[3] *Fisher* v. *Oldham Corporation*, [1930] 2 K.B. 364.

[4] This distinction has never been expressly drawn in an English decision, but it is recognised in South Africa and Australia: e.g. *Union Government* v. *Thorne*, 1930 A.D. 47; *Field* v. *Nott* (1939), 62 C.L.R. 660; it cannot be assumed, therefore, that a local authority is never liable for the torts of its policemen. See also *Baume* v. *Commonwealth* (1906), 4 C.L.R. 97; G. Sawer, 5 *Res Judicatae* (1953), 14.

[5] *Metropolitan Asylums District Board* v. *Hill* (1881), 6 App. Cas. 193.

immunity arises.[1] Of course, if the authorised act is performed negligently, the public body will be liable except in
the unlikely event of its being able to prove an authorisation
wide enough to exempt it from liability for negligence.[2]

Where the statute gives no clear indication, the courts must
consider whether the injury complained of is an inevitable
result of performing the authorised act,[3] and must consider
whether the public importance of the act is such that it must
be presumed to override the private interests affected.[4] A
statute often makes special provision for compensating those
damnified by acts which it authorises;[5] clearly such a provision may be material, if not decisive, in ascertaining whether
Parliament intended to take away a common-law right of
action.[6] A further important consideration is the nature of
the power. Powers to execute some particular work or carry
on some particular undertaking, such as building a reservoir
or a generating station, "are, in the absence of clear provision
to the contrary in the Act, limited to the doing of the particular
things authorised without infringement of the rights of others,
except in so far as any such infringement may be a demonstrably
necessary consequence of doing what is authorised to be done."[7]
On the other hand, powers to execute a variety of specified
works (which will usually involve interference with private
rights) at the discretion of some public body (such as catchment
boards), in the furtherance of the general functions of that
body can rarely be subject to the implied limitation that
private rights are not to be infringed, where that would prevent
the body from doing the very work which it was established
by statute to do.

(b) Action for Breach of Statutory Duty

The distinction between duties and powers assumes great
importance in the event of a failure to act. If the statute

---

[1] *Hammersmith etc. Ry. Co.* v. *Brand* (1869), L.R. 4 H.L. 171.
[2] *Geddis* v. *Bann Reservoirs Proprietors* (1878), 3 App. Cas. 430.
[3] *Manchester Corporation* v. *Farnworth*, [1930] A.C. 171.
[4] W. Friedmann: "Statutory Powers and Legal Duties of Local Authorities"
in 8 *Modern Law Review* (1945) 31, at 36.
[5] E.g. Public Health Act, 1936, Sect. 278.
[6] *Marriage* v. *East Norfolk Rivers Catchment Board*, [1950] 1 K.B. 284, at 305–6
(*per* Jenkins, L.J.).
[7] Ibid. 307.

confers a discretion whether to act or not, then nobody may complain of the non-exercise of power. On the other hand, "it cannot be doubted that, where a statute provides for the performance by certain persons of a particular duty, and some-one belonging to a class of persons for whose benefit and protec-tion the statute imposes the duty is injured by failure to perform it, prima facie, and, if there be nothing to the contrary, an action by the person so injured will lie against the person who has so failed to perform the duty."[1] This is not a claim for negligence but is a separate remedy given by the common law to make effective, for the benefit of an injured plaintiff, his right to performance by the defendant of the defendant's duty.[2] If the plaintiff has been the victim of mischief which the Act was designed to prevent,[3] and if he can further show that the Act, viewed in the circumstances in which it was made and to which it relates, was intended to impose in addition to a public duty a duty enforceable by an aggrieved individual, he may bring a civil action for breach of statutory duty.[4]

The courts have frequently complained that Parliament has made the ascertainment of this statutory intention difficult,[5] and they have developed certain principles to guide them in this task. If the statute prescribes no remedy for breach of the duty which it creates, the courts will readily assume that a civil action accrues to a person damnified by the breach.[6] When a penalty or other specific remedy is provided, the general rule is that no action for breach of statutory duty lies.[7] "Whether the general rule is to prevail, or an exception to the

---

[1] *Groves* v. *Wimborne*, [1898] 2 Q.B. 402, at 415–6 (*per* Vaughan Williams, L.J.).

[2] *L.P.T.B.* v. *Upson*, [1949] A.C. 155, at 168 (*per* Lord Wright).

[3] *Gorris* v. *Scott* (1874), L.R. 9 Ex. 125.

[4] *Phillips* v. *Britannia Hygienic Laundry Co.*, [1923] 2 K.B. 832, at 842 (*per* Atkin, L.J.).

[5] E.g. *Cutler* v. *Wandsworth Stadium, Ltd.*, [1949] A.C. 398, at 410 (*per* Lord du Parcq).

[6] Despite the unqualified terms in which this principle is expressed in the *Cutler* case by Lord Simonds (at 407) and Lord Normand (at 413) it seems that, even though no express remedy is given by the Act, the availability of another remedy, e.g. mandamus, may be a ground for rejecting a claim for breach of statutory duty where only a public duty appears to be imposed: *Glossop* v. *Heston and Isleworth Local Board* (1879), 12 Ch. D. 102, at 116 (*per* James, L.J.); *Phillips* v. *Britannia Hygienic Laundry*, [1923] 2 K.B. 832, at 838 (*per* Bankes, L.J.).

[7] *Atkinson* v. *Newcastle Waterworks Co.* (1877), 2 Ex. D. 441. If the Court finds that the prescribed remedy is inadequate it may grant an injunction to restrain the breach: *Attorney-General* v. *Sharp*, [1931] 1 Ch. 121; *Stevens* v. *Chown*, [1901] 1 Ch. 894.; and see above p. 240.

general rule is to be admitted, must depend on the scope and language of the Act which creates the obligation and on considerations of policy and convenience."[1] Moreover, the draftsmen of statutes passed after these principles were enunciated in the nineteenth century are to be presumed to have had in mind this principle of construction.[2] Exceptions to this general rule have been common where statutes have imposed duties on employers for the benefit of workmen, but they have been less common in the case of statutes imposing duties (and penalties for the breach of them) on public authorities.[3]

(c) Misfeasance and Nonfeasance

The courts have frequently been called upon to decide whether undertakers executing works are under a duty to use care in the maintenance of the works. A conflict of precedents appears to have been resolved satisfactorily by *Fisher* v. *Ruislip-Northwood U.D.C. and Middlesex C.C.*[4] In that case a motorist was able to recover in negligence from the defendants, who had not lit in the hours of darkness an air-raid shelter, which they had erected on a highway under statutory power, and with which the motorist had collided. Where the legislature authorises the creation and maintenance of a work which would be dangerous unless precautions be taken, there is a duty at common law to take care unless the legislature has, on the true construction of the statute, manifested an intention that the relationship created between the undertaker and the public should not import a duty to take care. In effect, the common law duty exists independently of the statutory power or duty conferred or imposed. It is because common law duties are mainly duties of forbearance a breach of which may be committed only by misfeasance that the statement that public authorities are liable for misfeasance but not for nonfeasance[5] is (actions for breach of statutory duty apart)

[1] *Pasmore* v. *Oswaldtwistle U.D.C.*, [1898] A.C. 387, at 397–8 (*per* Lord Macnaghten).
[2] *Cutler* v. *Wandsworth Stadium, Ltd.*, [1949] A.C. 398, at 411 (*per* Lord du Parcq).
[3] *Dawson and Co.* v. *Bingley U.D.C.*, [1911] 2 K.B. 149, and the other cases discussed in G. E. Robinson: *Public Authorities and Legal Liability*, Ch. 4.
[4] [1945] K.B. 584; cf. *Darling* v. *Attorney-General*, [1950] 2 All E.R. 793.
[5] For the problem of liability for nonfeasance in nuisance and *Rylands* v. *Fletcher*, see *Pride of Derby and Derbyshire Angling Association* v. *British Celanese, Ltd.*,

an approximation to the truth. The statement is particularly appropriate to highway authorities. By reason of a long-standing anomaly, highway authorities, including the Crown,[1] are not liable for their failure to carry out their common law or statutory duties to repair highways,[2] an immunity which is narrowly construed.[3]

An important case which illustrates the liability at common law of public bodies entrusted with powers is *East Suffolk Rivers Catchment Board* v. *Kent*.[4] The defendants were empowered but not bound to take anti-flood measures. They took steps to drain off flooded land; had they done it with due care the land would have been flooded for a shorter period. Because the land would have been flooded for an even longer period had they not acted at all, they were held not liable in negligence. The duty to take care and breach of the duty had been proved, but not damage, i.e. increased damage caused by the defendants' conduct.

(d) Mandamus

A person aggrieved by the failure of a public body to carry out its duty may also apply for an order of mandamus commanding the public body to carry out its duty. This remedy is discretionary and it is not granted where the court believes that some other equally convenient remedy is available.[5]

B. The Crown

I. VICARIOUS LIABILITY

Sect. 2 (1) of the Crown Proceedings Act, 1947, makes the Crown suable in tort by enacting that "the Crown shall be subject to all those liabilities in tort to which, if it were a private person of full age and capacity, it would be subject in respect of torts committed by its servants or agents." This liability is,

[1953] Ch. 149, and *Smeaton* v. *Ilford Corporation*, [1954] Ch. 40; cf. G. Sawer, 18 *Modern Law Review* (1955), 541.

[1] Crown Proceedings Act, 1947, Sect. 40 (2) (*e*); the Minister of Transport, an agent of the Crown, is a highway authority under the Trunk Roads Acts, 1936–46.

[2] *Russell* v. *Men of Devon* (1788), 2 T.R. 667; Sir William Holdsworth: *History of English Law*, Vol. X, 319.

[3] E.g. *Skilton* v. *Epsom and Ewell U.D.C.*, [1937] 1 K.B. 112.

[4] [1941] A.C. 74.

[5] See above, p. 236.

however, subject to many special provisions which must now be examined.

Subsect. (6) enacts—

> No proceedings shall lie against the Crown by virtue of this section in respect of any act, neglect or default of any officer of the Crown,[1] unless that officer has been directly or indirectly appointed by the Crown and was at the material time paid in respect of his duties as an officer of the Crown wholly out of the Consolidated Fund of the United Kingdom, moneys provided by Parliament, the Road Fund, or any other Fund certified by the Treasury for the purposes of this subsection, or was at the material time holding an office in respect of which the Treasury certify that the holder thereof would normally be so paid.

The effect of this subsection is that the Crown will be vicariously liable only for the torts of those persons who are servants of the Crown at common law and who are also appointed directly or indirectly by the Crown and paid out of the Consolidated or other specified funds.

The rules for defining at common law "a servant of the Crown" are even now lacking in precision. The courts, when called on to decide whether any public bodies set up by statute in the last hundred years are agents of the Crown, have found the statutes themselves singularly unhelpful, and have refused to lay down definite criteria. The Court of Appeal has decided in *Tamlin* v. *Hannaford*[2] that the Transport Commission is not the agent of the Crown, and, therefore, it may be assumed that none of the nationalised industries is an agent of the Crown. On the other hand, the House of Lords has held that the Central Land Board is a Crown agent.[3] It may be said that there are several criteria which from time to time the judges have thought relevant. These include: Is the body performing tasks formerly carried on by private enterprise?[4] To what extent is it subject to ministerial control, for example, has it independent discretionary powers,[5] must it consult a Minister

---

[1] Sect. 38 (2) provides that " 'officer', in relation to the Crown, includes any servant of His Majesty, and accordingly (but without prejudice to the generality of the foregoing provision) includes a Minister of the Crown."

[2] [1950] 1 K.B. 8.

[3] *Glasgow Corporation* v. *Central Land Board*, [1956] S.L.T. 41; for the expressions used by their Lordships, see below, p. 307.

[4] *Mersey Docks and Harbour Board Trustees* v. *Gibbs* (1866), L.R. 1 H.L. 93, at 107 (*per* Blackburn, J.).

[5] *Metropolitan Meat Industry Board* v. *Sheedy*, [1927] A.C. 899, at 905 (*per* Viscount Haldane).

before it acts, can a Minister give it directions? Is its function one which has historically been regarded as governmental?[1] Is it incorporated? Is it subject to Government audit? Is its authority general or local?[2] Is it a mere domestic body?[3] Is execution against its property allowed? The main criterion now seems to be whether the body is performing a function analogous to that performed by Crown servants and under some degree of control by a Minister of the Crown.[4]

If a corporation is a servant of the Crown, then its servants are also servants of the Crown to whom the Crown Proceedings Act will apply. The rule that one servant of the Crown is not liable for the torts of another will normally prevent an alternative action against the corporation from being brought. Lord Atkin has said that incorporated departments can be sued for torts committed by themselves[5] (i.e. when the liability is not vicarious), and this seems unaffected by the Crown Proceedings Act. There will be many circumstances where a plaintiff will have to join both the Attorney-General (in accordance with Sect. 17 (3)) and the corporation as defendants, and ask for a "Bullock" order for costs.[6]

The effect of Sect. 2 (6) is that there are some torts committed by common law servants of the Crown, for which it is not liable. Although the courts have indicated that policemen may be Crown servants,[7] this subsection excludes them, for they are neither appointed nor paid by the Crown. Nor does Sect. 2 (3), which makes the Crown liable for torts committed by officers in the course of functions vested in them as such by the law, affect policemen, because Sect. 2 (3) applies only to officers within Sect. 2 (6). Sect. 2 (6) does not affect torts within Sect. 3 which deals with infringements of patents and copyright. It also prevents the Crown from being liable for the torts of borrowed servants; on the other hand the Crown is subject to the common law rules about liability for the torts of independent contractors even though it does not pay and

---

[1] *Lane* v. *Cotton* (1701), 1 Raymond 646.
[2] *Dunbar* v. *Guardians of Ardee Union* (1897), 2 Ir. Rep. 76.
[3] *Rowell* v. *Pratt*, [1936] 2 K.B. 226.
[4] *Bank voor Handel en Scheepvaart N.V.* v. *Administrator of Hungarian Property*, [1954] A.C. 584.
[5] *Mackenzie-Kennedy* v. *Air Council*, [1927] 2 K.B. 517, at 532–3.
[6] *Bullock* v. *London General Omnibus Co.*, [1907] 1 K.B. 264.
[7] *Fisher* v. *Oldham Corporation*, [1930] 2 K.B. 364.

appoint them.[1] Since the subsection applies only to "an act, neglect or default of an officer of the Crown" it would seem not to extend to Sect. 2 (1) (b) and (c) where the liability is that of the Crown itself not arising out of vicarious liability for the act of an officer. Sect. 1, to which Sect. 2 (6) does not apply, makes the Crown liable whenever a petition of right could previously have been filed. Suits within its scope include those for nuisance or detinue,[2] or those which could formerly have been brought against the Minister of Transport.[3] The proviso to Sect. 2 (1) excludes the Crown from vicarious liability if no action would lie against the servant himself. This may have been inserted, unnecessarily,[4] to prevent the Crown from being liable where the servant would have the defence of Act of State. It makes the Crown not liable if one of its servants tortiously injures a spouse, although an action would lie against masters (other than the Crown) of servants who commit torts against their spouses.[5]

2. NON-VICARIOUS LIABILITY

The Crown Proceedings Act does not impose on the Crown merely a vicarious liability in tort. There are circumstances where liability is not vicarious but where it arises out of a direct duty of the master owed to the third person, with the servant the instrument of its performance; this is recognised in the Act by paragraphs (b) and (c) of Sect. 2 (1) which make the Crown liable for breach of the duties of an employer to an employee and for breach of the duties attaching at common law to the ownership, occupation, possession, or control of property. These paragraphs do not cover all cases of direct duty owed by a master; for instance, they do not include the duty of a hospital authority to provide an efficient system of drug administration, which was a basis of liability of the defendants in *Collins* v. *Hertfordshire C.C.*[6]

The Crown is liable for breach of statutory duty only where

---

[1] Sects. 38 (2), 40 (2) (d).
[2] *Bucknall* v. *R.* (1930), 46 T.L.R. 449; Sir William Holdsworth: *History of English Law*, Vol. IX, 41.
[3] The Ministry of Transport Act, 1919, Sect. 26 (1).
[4] The Crown is liable only for "torts" of servants. An act of a servant for which Act of State is a defence would not be a "tort."
[5] *Broom* v. *Morgan*, [1953] 1 Q.B. 597.
[6] [1947] 1 K.B. 598; *Cassidy* v. *Ministry of Health*, [1951] 2 K.B. 343.

the statutory duty is "binding also upon persons other than the Crown and its officers."[1] This unnecessarily restrictive provision seems to have been inserted on the mistaken assumption that Ministers upon whom statutes have imposed general duties, e.g. the duty of the Minister of Education to provide educational facilities, would otherwise be answerable in the courts as well as in Parliament for failure to perform those duties.[2]

3. EXCEPTIONS

The United Kingdom accepts no liability for judicial errors, even where persons may have been imprisoned for crimes of which they were later proved innocent.[3] Nor is it liable for torts committed by any person while executing judicial process.[4]

The Crown is liable for the negligent transmission or loss of registered postal packets to the extent of their market but not replacement value, but not exceeding the maximum amounts laid down in Post Office Regulations.[5] For the negligent transmission or loss of other postal packets, or for anything done or omitted to be done in relation to telephonic communications, neither the Crown nor its employees is liable.[6]

A member of the armed forces who is the victim of a tort by the Crown or by another member of the armed forces in circumstances which would be attributable to service for purposes of pensions may not sue for personal injuries, nor may his personal representatives claim in respect of his death.[7] Joint tortfeasors with the Crown or a member of the armed forces in such circumstances will be unable to recover contribution from the Crown.

Contract

England has no separate law of administrative contract.[8] The

---

[1] Sect. 2 (2).
[2] Sir Thomas Barnes: "The Crown Proceedings Act, 1947" in 26 *Canadian Bar Review* (1948) 387, at 391; see above, pp. 248–50.
[3] Sect. 2 (5).   [4] Sect. 2 (5).
[5] Nor is there liability in contract: *Triefus & Co., Ltd.* v. *Post Office*, [1957] 3 W L.R. 1.
[6] Sect. 9 (1).
[7] Sect. 10. The section also applies when members of the armed forces are performing civil defence training and duties; Civil Defence (Armed Forces) Act, 1954, Sect. 1 (3). The exemption from liability still applies even if an award of a pension is refused; *Adams* v. *The War Office*, [1955] 3 All E.R. 245.
[8] None of the English standard works on contract refers to administrative or governmental contracts. But see J. D. B. Mitchell: *The Contracts of Public Authorities*.

liability of the Administration on its contracts is recognised.
The provision that a citizen could sue the Crown on its con-
tracts only by petition of right after obtaining the fiat of the
Attorney-General has been abolished by Sect. 1 of the Crown
Proceedings Act, which states—

> Where any person has a claim against the Crown after the
> commencement of this Act, and, if this Act had not been passed,
> the claim might have been enforced, subject to the grant of His
> Majesty's fiat, by petition of right or might have been enforced
> by a proceeding provided by any statutory provision repealed
> by this Act, then, subject to the provisions of this Act, the claim
> may be enforced as of right, and without the fiat of his Majesty,
> by proceedings taken against the Crown for that purpose in
> accordance with the provisions of this Act.

The statutory provisions referred to are those which provided
that certain departments might "sue and be sued."[1] Before
the Act, incorporated departments not expressly made suable
could be sued even on contracts made as an agent for the
Crown, if that were the intention of the incorporating statute.[2]
It is probable that they can still be sued,[3] for the schedule of
statutes repealed does not include them.

The law of governmental contracts makes the usual assumption of English law that the ordinary principles of private law
should apply to administrative bodies. None the less, the
special circumstances attending these contracts make some
variations from these principles inevitable. Administrative
bodies other than the Crown and some of its instrumentalities
are statutory corporations; they are, therefore, subject to the
principle of *ultra vires* and the rules controlling the form of
contracts entered into by corporate bodies. Parliamentary
control of expenditure introduces considerations irrelevant
in private contracts. The importance of preventing corruption
in the public service is acknowledged by special provisions
about tenders and disclosure of interest. A further characteristic of administrative contracts, and the one which French

---

[1] E.g. Minister of Supply; see *Minister of Supply* v. *British Thomson-Houston
Co. Ltd.*, [1943] K.B. 478, and Sch. 2 of the Act.

[2] *Graham* v. *Commissioners of Public Works and Buildings*, [1901] 2 K.B. 781;
International Ry. Co. v. *Niagara Parks Commission*, [1941] A.C. 328.

[3] Glanville Williams: *Crown Proceedings*, 6, denies this on the ground that the
Act applies to proceedings against any "officer of the Crown," an expression which,
he states, "for all parts of the Act" includes a department. His argument is, with
respect, fallacious because the definition sections cited by him do not apply to
Part I, in which Sect. 1 is contained.

administrative law regards as dominant,[1] is the overriding public interest in the completion of contracts for public works and services. This interest is secured by widespread use of standard terms and conditions. Administrative bodies have a monopoly in the supply to the public of various services such as power, water and telephones; for these, special rules are necessary. It has been assumed that the normal employer-employee relationship is not fully applicable to the civil service. All these matters call for separate treatment.

One further point is that contract can be used to accomplish regulatory ends of government. Perhaps the best example is the fair-labour-standards resolution passed by the House of Commons.[2] Government contractors are required to fulfil its obligations,[3] transport operators are granted licences and certain industries, for example, the sugar beet industry, are subsidised only on the condition that they adhere to it.

A. Public Authorities as Corporations

The contracts of most public authorities other than the Crown[4] will be void if they relate to functions which the authority is not authorised by statute to perform. Nor can a public authority by contract disable itself from exercising its powers.[5]

Public authorities have no general exemption from the rule that contracts made by corporations must be under seal, such as is enjoyed by those incorporated under the Companies Act, 1948.[6] Their contracts not made under seal will ordinarily be unenforceable. This is subject to some exceptions. Business convenience dictates that contracts relating to trivial matters of daily occurrence or urgent necessity need not be under

---

[1] G. Jèze: "Théorie du contrat administratif" in 60 *Revue de Droit Public* (1943) 251.

[2] See 427 H.C. Deb. 5s. col. 718.

[3] E.g. Clause 51 of the General Conditions of Government Contracts for Building and Civil Engineering Works—September 1948, Form CCC/Wks/1: "The Contractor shall, in the execution of the contract, observe and fulfil the obligations upon contractors specified in the Fair Wages Resolution passed by the House of Commons on the 14th October, 1946. . . ."

[4] Boroughs are created by Royal Charter, not by statute; for the effect of this see *Attorney-General* v. *Leicester Corporation*, [1943] Ch. 86.

[5] *Birkdale District Electric Supply Co.* v. *Southport Corporation*, [1926] A.C. 355; *William Cory & Son, Ltd.* v. *City of London Corporation*, [1951] 2 All E.R. 85.

[6] Sect. 32.

seal.[1] Corporations engaged in trading may make simple contracts through their agents. Whether public authorities carrying on trading functions are within this exception is undecided.[2] A party to a contract required to be under seal may sue a party who has received the benefit of it;[3] this right of action is available either to the corporation or to parties contracting with it. Moreover, the equitable doctrine of part performance may be invoked where the plaintiff, who has partly performed a contract in such circumstances that it would be inequitable for the court to deny the relief prayed for, seeks specific performance of a contract to which that relief is applicable.[4]

B. Financial Control and Agency

The United States is not liable on a contract made by its agent unless he has express statutory authority to make it or there is an appropriation adequate to its fulfilment.[5] In England, on the other hand, the ordinary principles of agency apply to public officers.[6] They are not required to have express authority in order to bind their principals,[7] and they are not themselves liable on contracts unless they have contracted personally.[8] It is usually stated that the common law principle that an agent who acts without the authority of his principal may be sued for breach of warranty of authority does not apply to Crown servants.[9] In *Dunn* v. *Macdonald*,[10] the only English case which is cited in support of this view, an

---

[1] *Wells* v. *Kingston-upon-Hull Corporation* (1875), L.R. 10 C.P. 402. See also *Wright (R. A.) & Son Ltd.* v. *Romford B.C.*, [1956] 1 W.L.R. 896 which held that the requirement of sealing is not complied with merely because a contract has been made in accordance with standing orders and signed by someone authorised by those standing orders—see Local Government Act, 1933, Sect. 266.

[2] See the case last cited and *Bourne & Hollingsworth* v. *St. Marylebone B.C.* (1908), 24 T.L.R. 322.

[3] *Lawford* v. *Billericay R.C.*, [1903] 1 K.B. 772.

[4] *Crook* v. *Corporation of Seaford* (1871), L.R. 6 Ch. 551.

[5] R.S. § 3732, 12th June, 1906.

[6] *Macbeath* v. *Haldimand* (1786), 1 T.R. 172.

[7] But it seems, from *A.-G. for Ceylon* v. *A. D. Silva*, [1953] A.C. 461, that, where a Crown servant derives his powers from statute, he has no authority other than that actually conferred—the doctrine of ostensible authority does not apply.

[8] *Palmer* v. *Hutchinson* (1881), 6 App. Cas. 619. So loath are the courts to find that a civil servant has contracted personally that there is no reported case of a civil servant, capable in the circumstances of binding the Crown, and not having expressly contracted on his own behalf, being held to have contracted personally.

[9] E.g. Sir Frederick Pollock: *Contracts* (13th ed. 1950), 87 n.

[10] [1897] 1 Q.B. 401, 555.

action for breach of warranty of authority failed against an
official of the Crown who purported to engage another for a
fixed term. The case is of doubtful authority, nevertheless,
both because the warranty (that the official was authorised
to engage staff on those terms) was one of law arising from the
interpretation of the contract, and because it is not clear whether
the plaintiff relied on the misinterpretation—he may have
had notice of the lack of authority of the agent. Although the
decision has been followed in Canada[1] and Ireland,[2] it is
submitted that English courts do not have to accept it as
authority for the proposition that an agent of the Crown can
never be sued for breach of warranty of authority.

The working out of the implications for Government-
citizen relationships of the tenet of constitutional law, first
formulated in 1688, that control of public expenditure lay with
Parliament, was left to the courts. By way of a corrective for the
absence of a rule requiring express authority of an agent, it
would not be surprising if there were some special rule about
appropriations. It is usually stated that Crown contracts are
invalid if Parliament has not made an express appropriation
for the purposes of the contract.[3] This is a misreading of the
authorities, as an Australian decision has recognised.[4] It rests
chiefly on an *obiter dictum* of one judge in *Churchward* v. *Reg.*,[5]
which has been considerably modified by several decisions in
this century in which Viscount Haldane played a prominent
part.[6] It is submitted that the law is as follows: a contract
made by an agent of the Crown acting within the scope of his
ostensible authority is a valid contract by the Crown; in the
absence of a Parliamentary appropriation either expressly or
impliedly referable to the contract, it is unenforceable.

The above rule does not extend to contracts made on behalf
of administrative bodies other than the Crown, although the
ordinary principles of agency also govern their contracts.

---

[1] *O'Connor* v. *Lemieux* (1920), 60 Ont. L.R. 365.
[2] *Kenny* v. *Cosgrave*, [1926] 1 Ir. R. 517.
[3] Halsbury: *Laws of England*, Vol. VI, 488.
[4] *New South Wales* v. *Bardolph* (1934), 52 C.L.R. 455.
[5] (1865), 1 Q.B. 173, at 209 (*per* Shee, J.).
[6] *Commercial Cable Co.* v. *Government of Newfoundland*, [1916] 2 A.C. 610; *Mackay*
v. *Attorney-General for British Columbia*, [1922] 1 A.C. 457; *Auckland Harbour Board*
v. *R.*, [1924] A.C. 318; *Attorney-General* v. *Great Southern and Western Ry. Co. of
Ireland*, [1925] A.C. 754; *Commonwealth of Australia* v. *Kidman*, [1926] A.L.R. 1
(P.C.).

Financial control may be exercised sometimes through the law of *ultra vires*. Contracts by a local authority to pay wages greatly exceeding the prevailing local wage rates have been held unreasonable and *ultra vires*.[1] Central audit and the power to withhold Exchequer grants for inefficiency are other substitutes for the rule in *Churchward* v. *Reg.*[2] in the case of public authorities other than the Crown.

C. The Prevention of Corruption

Local authorities are required by the Local Government Act, 1933,[3] "in the case of contracts for the supply of goods or materials or for the execution of works" to frame standing orders providing for the publication of notice of their intention to contract and for tenders to be invited. On the other hand, neither the Crown nor the nationalised corporations are under any comparable legal obligation. The purchasing departments of the Crown have lists of approved contractors, the composition and mode of framing of which are treated as confidential. Private tender seems more common than public tender.[4]

Stringent provisions regarding disclosure of interests apply to the members of local authorities. A member who, or whose spouse, is an employee, member of a company, or partner of a person with a direct or indirect pecuniary interest in a contract or other matter must disclose that interest, and is prohibited from taking part in the discussion and from voting.[5] Failure to comply is a criminal offence. Officers of local authorities are subject to a similar disability.[6]

Rather surprisingly, the officers of the Crown are under no legal duty to disclose their interest in proposed contracts.[7] Of

---

[1] *Roberts* v. *Hopwood*, [1925] A.C. 578; cf. *Prescott* v. *Birmingham Corporation*, [1955] Ch. 210.   [2] (1865) 1 Q.B. 173.   [3] Sect. 266.

[4] H. A. Fox: "British Government Contract Requirements" in 2 *Comparative Law Services* (*U.S. Dept. of Commerce*) (1939) 507.

[5] Local Government Act, 1933, Sect. 76. The holder of shares, the par value of which does not exceed £500, or the holder of shares not exceeding one hundredth of the total capital, may, after disclosure of that interest, discuss and vote: Local Government (Miscellaneous Provisions) Act, 1953, Sect. 15.

[6] Local Government Act, 1933, Sect. 123; cf. the regulations applicable to the various nationalised industries, e.g. Electricity (Central Authority and Area Boards) Regulations, 1947, S.R.O. 1947, No. 1750, regs. 2 and 3.

[7] Members of the Atomic Energy Authority are, however, required to disclose their interest in proposed contracts; Atomic Energy Authority Act, 1954, Sch. 1, para. 5.

course, the bribe or offer of a bribe to any public officer or the acceptance by him of such a bribe is a misdemeanour.

D. Standard Terms and Conditions

The paramount interest of the State in the proper completion of the work which is the subject-matter of the contract is secured in France by the special principles of *contrat administratif* built up by the *Conseil d'Etat*. If a contractor is in default, the State may recover damages for delay, and complete the contract at the expense of the contractor or determine it. The State may make unilateral modifications of the contract subject to the right of the contractor to the same profit, and has full powers of supervision and direction during the execution of the contract. Whenever the public interest demands it the State may rescind the contract on payment of compensation. English law has no similar principles of governmental contract. The same practical result is achieved, because Government departments only contract on the basis of certain fixed standard terms and conditions.

These acknowledge the overriding rights of the State as a contractor. The Ministry of Works standard building contract may be used by way of example.[1] Clause 7 empowers the Government supervising officer to give directions how the work is to be carried out, and gives him the right of uncontrolled supervision. Clause 8 enables the Government to have the necessary work done at the expense of a contractor who disobeys these directions. Clause 9 authorises modifications by the supervisor subject to adjustments of the contract price. Clauses 44 and 45 enable the Government to determine the contract at any time on written notice.

Whereas the contractor with the Government in France is bound by a separate law of administrative contract, his English counterpart must purchase the appropriate Standard Conditions from His Majesty's Stationery Office to discover the extra-legal rules which will bind him. This tendency towards a new quasi-administrative law—income-tax concessions, War Damage practice notes, and the Motor Insurance Bureau are other examples—must be carefully watched.[2]

[1] Form CCC/Wks/1 September, 1948; cf. the usual provision in contracts made by local authorities that goods and materials supplied shall be in accordance with specifications of the British Standards Institution.

[2] See above, p. 43.

E. The Administration as the Supplier of Services to the Public

Whatever the nature of the arrangements made to supply to the public such essentials as gas, water, electricity, telephone services, and transport, the interest of the Administration in the services is always recognised. If private enterprise supplies the service, then the State regulates the charges and conditions under which it is administered. The present British practice is for the State itself (e.g. telephones) or public corporations (e.g. gas, electricity, coal, broadcasting, air and some land transport) or local authorities (e.g. water) to supply these services direct to the consumer.

Characteristic of the legal arrangements made are the provisions of the Gas Act, 1948, Sect. 56 of which provides that gas shall be supplied on the conditions set out in a schedule to the Act. This imposes a duty to supply gas, and lays down detailed rules about (*inter alia*) the laying of pipes, the recovery of charges, the right to cut off supply in case of default, liability for escape of gas and rights of entry and inspection.[1]

It is important to decide whether the relationships between the supplier and consumer are contractual. If they are not the ability of a consumer to recover damages for breach may depend on his proving that an action in tort for breach of statutory duty was given by the statute.[2] If there is a contract, its performance may be compellable by specific performance or sometimes by injunction, but probably not by mandamus. In the absence of a contract, the only available method of compelling performance is mandamus.

In *Read* v. *Croydon Corporation*[3] Stable, J., held that there was no contractual relationship between the defendants as suppliers of water and the plaintiff consumer "although rights and obligations may be created thereunder similar to, or identical with, rights which may be created by contract." He

---

[1] And see The Rights of Entry (Gas and Electricity Boards) Act, 1954.

[2] Pp. 248–51 of this chapter. No action lay against the Petroleum Board for failure to supply petrol to retailer: *Eric Gnapp, Ltd.* v. *Petroleum Board*, [1949] 1 All E.R. 980. This is consistent with previous decisions that no duty is owed by public utilities to individual consumers, e.g. *Clegg Parkinson* v. *Earby Gas Co.*, [1896] 1 Q.B. 592. Sometimes, a separate action under the rule in *Donoghue* v. *Stevenson* may lie, e.g. *Barnes* v. *Irwell Valley Water Board*, [1939] 1 K.B. 21.

[3] [1938] 4 All E.R. 631, at 648.

was able to cite many dicta[1] in support but there are perhaps just as many to the effect that the relationship is contractual.[2] Although it cannot be regarded as finally settled whether there is a contract between statutory undertaker and consumer, it is submitted that the relationship is contractual:[3] the contract is made when the undertaker, satisfied that the consumer is entitled to the service, commences to supply him; whether or not there is a formal agreement does not affect the juridical nature of the relation, for there is an offer and acceptance. The element of compulsion in these arrangements will not prevent the formation of a contract, nor will the co-existence of a right of action in tort. It has long been recognised that carriers, innkeepers and others professing public callings, though under a duty to exercise their calling at the behest of the public and capable of being sued in tort, may still be sued in contract. So dominated by the notion of status is English law that the slightest degree of consent is sufficient for a contract. The compulsory statutory terms are merely part of a contract, and not inconsistent with its existence any more than are the statutory provisions about leases in the Law of Property Act, 1925, the Landlord and Tenant Act, 1927, and the Leasehold Property (Repairs) Act, 1938, inconsistent with the leases in which they are incorporated.

F. Public Authorities and Their Employees

The employees of public authorities other than the Crown are normally in contractual relationship with their employers and have the usual remedies in the event of a breach of contract. Their employers usually have the same freedom of contract as other employers. To this there are a few exceptions. Some local government officers may only be appointed and dismissed with the consent of a Minister.[4] Many officers are by law

---

[1] E.g. *Clegg Parkinson* case, at 595 (*per* Wright, J.); *Milnes* v. *Mayor of Huddersfield* (1886), 11 App. Cas. 511, at 523 (*per* Earl of Selborne).

[2] *Edmundson* v. *Mayor of Longton* (1902), 19 T.L.R. 15, at 16 (*per* Lord Alverstone, C.J.); *Countess of Rothes* v. *Kirkcaldy & Dysart Waterworks Commissioners* (1882), 7 App. Cas. 694, at 707 (*per* Lord Watson); *Barnes* v. *Irwell Valley Water Board*, [1939] 1 K.B. 21, at 44 (*per* Slesser, L.J.); *Griffiths* v. *Smith*, [1941] A.C. 170, at 208 (*per* Lord Porter). See also *Postmaster-General* v. *Wadsworth*, [1939] 4 All E.R. 1.

[3] See the symposium on Compulsory Contracts in 43 *Columbia Law Review* (1943).

[4] E.g. medical officers of health, sanitary inspectors; the Home Secretary must approve the appointment by the Watch Committee of a chief constable.

required to be appointed "during the pleasure of the council,"[1] but the local authority may still agree not to dismiss without reasonable notice.[2] The members of the boards of the various nationalised corporations are appointed for fixed terms on conditions determined by the Minister and approved by the Treasury.[3]

A civil servant is ordinarily dismissible at pleasure. Some writers say that there can be no contractual relation between the Crown and its servants.[4] This is too wide, and seems to derive from an unjustified assumption that the principle that members of the armed forces never have a contract with the Crown applies to civil servants. That rule depends on the fact that the sovereign has prerogative control of the armed forces.[5] It is submitted that Lord Hobhouse stated the law regarding civil servants accurately[6]—

> Unless in special cases where it is otherwise provided, servants of the Crown hold their office during the pleasure of the Crown; not by virtue of any special prerogative of the Crown, but as such are the terms of their engagement.

It is generally said that a statute, but not an express term in a contract, may alter the rule that a civil servant is dismissible at pleasure. *Dunn* v. *Reg.*[7] is not, as is usually assumed, a binding authority for this denial of the effectiveness of an express contract, because the appointing officer acted outside the scope of his authority, but *obiter dicta* of the Court of Appeal[8] and a decision of a court of first instance[9] suggest that a person employed for a fixed period subject to dismissal for misconduct can be dismissed at will. Subsequent dicta have been conflicting. Both Lord Atkin[10] and Denning, J.,[11] have held that a civil servant is employed on a contract of service containing an

---

[1] E.g. the treasurer, surveyor and general staff of a county council; the town clerk, treasurer, surveyor, and general staff of a borough; the clerk, treasurer, surveyor, and general staff of a district council.

[2] Local Government Act, 1933, Sect. 121.

[3] E.g. Electricity (Central Authority and Area Boards) Regulations, 1947, S.R.O. 1947 No. 1750. See below, pp. 277–9.

[4] E.g. Ridges: *Constitutional Law* (8th ed. G. A. Forrest) 198 n.

[5] *Dickson* v. *Combermere* (1863), 3 F. & F. 527; *China Navigation Co.* v. *Attorney-General*, [1932] 2 K.B. 197, at 215 (*per* Scrutton, L.J.).

[6] *Shenton* v. *Smith*, [1895] A.C. 229, at 234–5.

[7] [1896] 1 Q.B. 116; cf. Glanville Williams, op. cit. 64.

[8] *Hales* v. *R.* (1918), 34 T.L.R. 589.

[9] *Denning* v. *Secretary of State for India in Council* (1920), 37 T.L.R. 138.

[10] *Reilly* v. *R.*, [1934] A.C. 176, at 179.

[11] *Robertson* v. *Minister of Pensions*, [1949] 1 K.B. 227, at 231.

implied term that he is dismissible at pleasure, but that the Crown is bound by its express promises in a contract of service. Tucker, L.J., has, on the other hand, said that such a provision is "a clog on the right of the Crown to dismiss at any time."[1]

It would be consistent with the authorities to declare the law as follows: that there is an implied term in the contract of civil servants that the Crown may dismiss them at will, that the implied term may be expressly or impliedly excluded, that a provision for dismissal for cause will exclude it, but that employment for a fixed term will not in itself be inconsistent with the implied term.[2] Of course it is the Crown practice not to contract that a servant may be dismissed for cause.

It is further commonly stated that a civil servant may not sue for arrears of pay. True, a member of the armed forces may not,[3] but the authorities respecting civil servants are scanty. The case relied on is *Lucas* v. *Lucas and High Commissioner for India*,[4] where, following a Scottish decision,[5] it was held that the pay of a civil servant could not be attached because it was not an enforceable debt in the hands of the Crown.[6] Because the decision can be supported on the different ground that the rule of court controlling garnishee proceedings did not bind the Crown, because it was assumed that the military precedents could be relied on, and because the numerous English and Commonwealth decisions to the contrary[7] were not cited, it is suggested that the *Lucas* case is an untrustworthy precedent, and that civil servants may be able to recover arrears of their pay.

National Councils manned by representatives of employees and employers work out the terms of employment of employees of public authorities, including civil servants. Nevertheless it

---

[1] *Rodwell* v. *Thomas*, [1944] K.B. 596, at 602.
[2] See Lord Goddard to same effect in *Terrell* v. *Secretary of State for the Colonies*, [1953] 2 Q.B. 482 at 499. But he is of the opinion that in the ordinary case an established civil servant is a public officer appointed by, but not in contract with, the Crown; *Inland Revenue Commissioners* v. *Hambrook*, [1956] 2 Q.B.641 at 654; [1956] 3 All E.R. 338.
No changes are made by the Crown Proceedings Act, 1947. See Sect. 1.
[3] *Leaman* v. *R.*, [1920] 3 K.B. 663; and see Army Act, 1955, Sect. 144.
[4] [1943] P. 68.
[5] *Mulvenna* v. *Admiralty*, [1926] S.C. 842.
[6] See D. W. Logan: "A Civil Servant and his Pay," in 61 *Law Quarterly Review* (1945) 240.
[7] E.g. *Bushe* v. *Reg.*, *The Times* Newspaper, 29th May, 1869; *Sutton* v. *Attorney-General* (1923), 39 T.L.R. 294; *Carey* v. *Commonwealth* (1921), 30 C.L.R. 132.

has been held that those settled terms do not form part of the contract of employment of a civil servant.[1] There are no restrictions on employees of public authorities joining trade unions,[2] and the negotiating machinery for them is substantially similar to that for other employees.[3]

Superannuation schemes affect most employees of public authorities. The Superannuation Acts, 1843 to 1949, providing for civil-service pensions prevent a claimant from suing for them.[4] The Local Government Superannuation Acts, 1937–53 provide that disputes between local authorities and employees on pensions are to be settled by the Minister of Housing and Local Government, a system which has been judicially criticised.[5]

In France and many other countries on the Continent relations between the Administration and its employees are treated not as contractual but as regulatory. Matters of discipline and promotion are handled by administrative bodies. An official aggrieved by their decision may have it nullified for excess or abuse of power by the *Conseil d'Etat*. He may also recover salary or pension by proceedings before the *Conseil d'Etat*. Supporters of the British system sometimes aver that a similar administrative system enures for the benefit of civil servants. It is said that Treasury regulations ensure that no one is dismissed or has his promotion retarded without full consideration of his case by the head of the department or some other responsible officer. The great distinction between the French and English methods is that the English one affords no legal protection. The procedure cannot be challenged in the courts; if he is dismissed without being given an opportunity of being heard, he has no legal redress. If Treasury regulations are disregarded, the courts cannot consider his grievance.[6]

---

[1] *Rodwell* v. *Thomas*, [1944] K.B. 596.

[2] The Trade Disputes and Trade Unions Act, 1946, rescinded the rule that civil service unions could not be affiliated to the T.U.C.

[3] For a full account of the National Councils (often called Whitleyism) and other methods of negotiation, see Sir Cecil Oakes and W. L. Dacey: *An Outline of Local Government Law and Finance in England and Wales* (9th ed. 1950) ch. 18; and see e.g. Electricity Act, 1947, Sect. 53.

[4] *Nixon* v. *Attorney-General*, [1931] A.C. 184.

[5] *Wilkinson* v. *Barking Corporation*, [1948] 1 K.B. 721, at 728 (*per* Scott, L.J.). The Minister may, and on the direction of the High Court, must, state a case to it on a point of law.

[6] The police organisation makes a better comparison with the French system. The Police Regulations, 1952, S.I. 1952 No. 1704, and the Police (Discipline) Regulations, 1952, S.I. 1952 No. 1705 (as amended) which have legal effect, make

G. Freedom of Executive Action

In one case only has the court indicated that the Crown can plead executive necessity by way of defence to an action for breach of contract.[1] The observation by the judge in the court of first instance was *obiter*,[2] and Denning, J.,[3] has since concluded that the doctrine of executive necessity can apply only "where there is an implied term to that effect or that is the true meaning of the contract." This latter dictum seems satisfactory.

Quasi-Contract

Public authorities other than the Crown are subject to quasi-contractual liabilities in the same manner as private citizens. The effect of Sect. 1 of the Crown Proceedings Act is that the Crown may be sued in quasi-contract only when, before the Act, a petition of right would have lain for an action in quasi-contract. It is generally agreed that a petition of right was available whenever the recovery of money or property in the hands of the Crown was sought. If the view of the Court of Appeal that petition of right would lie only in those specific cases[4] is sound, then, in the remaining cases of quasi-contract the Crown is still not liable. However, it seems better to accept the view of Viscount Dunedin[5] that petition of right was available whenever "in consequence of what has been legally done any resulting obligation emerges" in which case there are now no restrictions on suing the Crown in quasi-contract.

Special Rules[6]
A. Substantive Limitations on Liability of the Crown[7]

I. STATUTES BINDING THE CROWN

General words in a statute do not as a rule of construction bind

detailed rules about dismissal, promotions, etc., and any excess of power or a serious infringement of prescribed procedure may be quashed by the courts: see *Cooper* v. *Wilson*, [1937] 2 K.B. 309.

[1] *Rederiaktiebolaget Amphitrite* v. *R.*, [1921] 3 K.B. 500; cf. *Birkdale District Electric Supply Co.* v. *Southport Corporation*, [1926] A.C. 355.

[2] But see Mitchell, op. cit. Ch. 2.

[3] *Robertson* v. *Minister of Pensions*, [1949] 1 K.B. 227.

[4] *Anglo-Saxon Petroleum Co.* v. *Damant*, [1947] K.B. 794.

[5] *Attorney-General* v. *De Keyser's Royal Hotel, Ltd.*, [1920] A.C. 508, at 530.

[6] The special rules applicable to public bodies relating to limitation of actions formerly contained in the Limitation Act, 1939, have been repealed. The Law Reform (Limitation of Actions, etc.) Act, 1954, generally assimilates the law applicable to proceedings against the Crown and other public bodies to that applicable in other cases.

[7] This section, together with sections B and C is applicable to all actions against the Crown, whether in tort or otherwise.

the Crown to its prejudice unless by express provision or by necessary implication.[1] The Crown Proceedings Act provides[2] that "except as therein otherwise expressly provided, nothing in this Act shall . . . (*f*) affect any rules of evidence or any presumption relating to the extent to which the Crown is bound by any Act of Parliament." It is expressly provided by the Crown Proceedings Act that the Maritime Conventions Act, 1911, Part II of the Law Reform (Married Women and Tortfeasors) Act, 1935, and the Law Reform (Contributory Negligence) Act, 1945, shall bind the Crown. Other acts creating or affecting tortious liability, e.g. the Fatal Accidents Acts, will bind the Crown only if Sect. 2 (1) of the Crown Proceedings Act, subjecting the Crown to the liabilities in tort of the private person "subject to the provisions of this Act," can be construed as an "express" provision within Sect. 40 (2) (*f*).

2. ESTOPPEL

Estoppel by deed does not bind the Crown,[3] at least when the Crown is deceived in its grant.[4] Estoppels by record and estoppels by conduct bind the Crown.[5]

B. Remedies Against the Crown

At common law mandamus did not lie to the Crown[6] nor to its servants acting as such,[7] a rule unaltered by the Crown Proceedings Act.[8] Although other members of the British Commonwealth grant injunctions against Government departments[9] it was doubtful whether they would be granted in England at common law.[10] The Crown Proceedings Act pro-

[1] *Madras Electric Supply Corporation* v. *Boarland*, [1955] A.C. 667; cf. *Province of Bombay* v. *Municipal Corporation of the City of Bombay*, [1947] A.C. 58; *Bank voor Handel en Scheepvaart N.V.* v. *Administrator of Hungarian Property*, [1954] A.C. 584.

[2] Sect. 40 (2).

[3] *Attorney-General to the Prince of Wales* v. *Collom*, [1916] 2 K.B. 193, at 204 (*per* Atkin, J.).

[4] F. E. Farrer: "A Prerogative Fallacy: 'That the King is not bound by Estoppel' " in 49 *Law Quarterly Review* (1933) 511.

[5] *Robertson* v. *Minister of Pensions*, [1949] K.B. 227, at 231 (*per* Denning, J.); see also *Minister of Agriculture and Fisheries* v. *Matthews*, [1950] 1 K.B. 148 and *In re 56 Denton Road Twickenham*, [1953] Ch. 51.

[6] *Reg.* v. *Powell* (1841), 1 Q.B. 352.

[7] *Reg.* v. *Lords Commissioners of the Treasury* (1872), 7 Q.B. 387.

[8] Sects. 38 (2), 21 (2).

[9] E.g. Australia: *Randwick Municipal Council* v. *Nott* (1940), 14 L.G.R. 222.

[10] *Rankin* v. *Huskisson* (1830), 4 Sim. 1813; *contra*, Robertson: *Civil Proceedings By and Against the Crown*, 21.

vides that only a declaratory judgment in lieu of an injunction may now be granted against the Crown or its officers as representing the Crown.[1]

C. Procedural Limitations in Suits Against the Crown

1. DISCOVERY OF DOCUMENTS

The Crown is empowered, whether or not it is a party to the litigation, to refuse to produce documents if to do so would be contrary to the public interest. Thus, for example, departmental files are never produced. This principle, on which *Duncan* v. *Cammell Laird & Co. Ltd.* is the leading case,[2] is confirmed by the Crown Proceedings Act.[3] The head of the appropriate department is the sole arbiter of the public interest here, and the courts must always accept his ruling. This power has frequently been used in an arbitrary manner to the prejudice of private litigants in circumstances which have evoked judicial criticism.[4] It has recently been confirmed that public authorities other than the Crown do not possess this privilege.[5]

2. TRIAL AT BAR AND VENUE

The Crown has the right in any case in which it is interested to demand a trial at bar before a Divisional Court of the Queen's Bench Division. It also has the choice of venue. The justification for these rights, which the Crown Proceedings Act preserves,[6] is said to be "the administrative difficulties which Government departments would experience if they had to make their records available elsewhere than in London."[7]

---

[1] Sect. 21 (1), (2). *Harper* v. *Home Secretary*, [1955] Ch. 238; *Merricks* v. *Heathcote-Amory*, [1955] Ch. 567; (though injunctions would lie against officers in their personal capacity). In *Underhill* v. *Ministry of Food*, [1950] 1 All E.R. 591, it was held that this section did not authorise the grant of a declaratory judgment in lieu of an interlocutory injunction. *Sed quaere* whether there is not still a right to grant an interlocutory declaration independently of this section?

[2] [1942] A.C. 624.

[3] Sect. 28.

[4] E.g. *Ellis* v. *Home Office* [1953] 2 Q.B.135; *Broome* v. *Broome*, [1955] P. 190; cf. *Glasgow Corporation* v. *Central Land Board*, [1956] S.L.T. 41 (in Scotland the courts have a discretion to admit the document even though the Crown is unwilling to produce). For present Crown practice, see the Lord Chancellor's statement, 197 H.L. Deb. 741–8, 6th June, 1956.

[5] *Blackpool Corporation* v. *Locker*, [1948] 1 K.B. 349, at 380 (*per* Scott, L.J.).

[6] Sects. 19 and 40 (2) (*g*).

[7] Bickford Smith: *Crown Proceedings Act, 1947,* 41.

3. ENFORCEMENT OF JUDGMENTS

Judgments against the Crown cannot be enforced either by execution or attachment.[1] Breach of the duty to pay judgment debts expressly imposed by the Act on departments is prevented by Sect. 2 (2) from being the subject of a civil action.

[1] Sect. 25 (4).

CHAPTER VII

PUBLIC CORPORATIONS

Historical Introduction

THE institution of the public corporation as a method of administration is not new. The appointment of *ad hoc* bodies is often the most obvious method of dealing with a particular problem which has arisen. While examples of such bodies can be found from early times, the present development may be said to date from the first half of the nineteenth century and, in particular, from 1834, when the Poor Law Commissioners were established.[1]

The Mersey Docks and Harbour Board which was set up in 1857[2] as a result of rivalry between Liverpool and Birkenhead may be taken as an example of the earlier type of public corporation. The Act provides for a Board of twenty-eight unpaid members of whom twenty-four are elected by payers of dock rates for four-year terms, six retiring each year; the remaining four are appointed by the Minister of Transport. In 1908 the Port of London Authority was created[3] consisting of seventeen members elected by payers of dues, wharfingers and owners of river craft, one member elected by wharfingers alone and ten members appointed by the Admiralty (1), the Minister of Transport (2), the L.C.C. (4), the City Corporation (2) and Trinity House (1). All members serve for a term of three years; all retire together but may be re-elected or re-appointed. The chairman and vice-chairman (who are appointed by the Authority, not necessarily from its own members) and the chairman of committees may be paid but payment is normally made only to the chairman of the Authority.

A common characteristic of these two bodies is the large proportion of elected members. Since both are local bodies and represent a limited group of interested persons, such an arrangement is workable. Where a corporation is to have

[1] Poor Law (Amendment) Act, 1834.
[2] Mersey Docks and Harbour Board Act, 1857.
[3] Port of London Act, 1908, Sect. 1, Sch. 1; see now Port of London (Consolidation) Act, 1920, Sect. 6, Sch. 2.

national powers, this method of appointment is more difficult. The Forestry Commission, as first established in 1919,[1] had ten members appointed by the Crown, one of whom was an M.P., while three others had paid, full-time appointments. The term of office was five years and re-appointment was usual.

The Electricity (Supply) Act, 1926, established the Central Electricity Board.[2] This body of a chairman and seven members was appointed by the Minister of Transport for terms of five to ten years. The Minister was advised by the Act when making appointments to consult representative bodies in the fields of local government, electricity, commerce, industry, transport, agriculture, and labour. Members of the House of Commons were not eligible. All members were paid but only the chairman was full-time.

The method of direct appointment by the Government was discarded when the London Passenger Transport Board was set up in 1933.[3] The seven members were appointed by a group of six appointing trustees. These trustees were the chairman of the L.C.C., a representative of the London and Home Counties Traffic Advisory Committee, the chairman of the Committee of London Clearing Bankers, the president of The Law Society, the president of the Institute of Chartered Accountants and, for subsequent appointments, a member of the Board itself. Appointment to the Board was for not less than three nor more than seven years. The chairman and vice-chairman were full-time members on large salaries; the part-time members were also paid. Members were to have experience and capacity in transport, industrial, commercial, or financial matters or in the conduct of public affairs and two members were required to have not less than six years experience in London local government. Members of the House of Commons were ineligible. For present purposes, the chief interest in this body is the method of appointment. The method was widely criticised both because the trustees might be ignorant of the problems and might change frequently and because the Minister of Transport, and therefore Parliament, had no control.

[1] Forestry Act, 1919, Sect. 1, as amended by Forestry Act, 1927, Sect. 1; for present constitution see Forestry Acts, 1945, Sect. 1 and Forestry Act, 1951, Sects. 1, 18.　　[2] Sect. 1.
[3] London Passenger Transport Act, 1933, Sect. 1, Sch. 1.

Many other corporations were established during the period before 1940. The British Broadcasting Corporation in 1926,[1] the Racecourse Betting Control Board in 1928,[2] the Coal Mines Re-organisation Commission in 1930,[3] the Wheat Commission in 1932,[4] and the British Overseas Airways Corporation in 1939[5] are further examples. Many of these have, with those outlined above, been the subject of detailed study.[6] What has been said is intended to do no more than indicate the nature of the problems of appointment, structure and responsibility which formed the background to the same problems which were encountered in the period following 1945.

Analysis

The analysis which follows deals only with some of the more important public corporations created since 1945.[7] These are divisible into three groups.

The first group consists of the National Coal Board,[8] the Central Electricity Authority[9] and Area Electricity Boards, the Gas Council and Area Gas Boards, the British Transport Commission[10] and the London Transport Executive, and the Air corporations. The common characteristic of these corporations is that they control industrial or commercial undertakings which supply commodities or facilities, on payment, to the general public. They are managerial-economic bodies. The Coal Board is charged with the duties of working and

[1] Royal Charter, Licence and Agreement (Cmd. 2756); for documents at present in force see Cmd. 8579, 8605.
[2] Racecourse Betting Act, 1928, Sect. 2.
[3] Coal Mines Act, 1930, Sect. 11.
[4] Wheat Act, 1932, Sch. 1.
[5] British Overseas Airways Act, 1939, Sect. 1, Sch. 1.
[6] See, in particular, W. A. Robson (ed.): *Public Enterprise*; T. H. O'Brien: *British Experiments in Public Ownership and Control*; H. S. Morrison: *Socialisation and Transport*; L. Gordon: *The Public Corporation in Great Britain*; Sir Arthur Street: *The Public Corporation in British Experience* and *British Government since 1918* (Chap. 5); R. E. Cushman: *The Independent Regulatory Commissions* (Chaps. VIII, IX).
[7] For general surveys see W. Friedmann: "The New Public Corporations and the Law" in 10 *Modern Law Review* (1947), 233, 377; W. A. Robson: "The Public Corporation in Britain To-day" in 63 *Harvard Law Review* (1950), 1321, and (ed.) *Problems of Nationalised Industry*; D. N. Chester: "Organisation of the Nationalised Industries" in 21 *Political Quarterly* (1950), 122, and *The Nationalised Industries; A Statutory Analysis* (2nd Ed.).
[8] Referred to hereafter as the Coal Board.
[9] Originally known as the British Electricity Authority; the name was changed by Electricity Reorganisation (Scotland) Act, 1954, Sect. 15, Sch. 1 Pt. II. It is referred to hereafter as the Electricity Authority.
[10] Referred to hereafter as the Transport Commission.

getting the coal in Great Britain, securing the efficient development of the coal-mining industry and making supplies of coal
available.[1]

The Electricity Authority is required to develop and maintain an efficient, co-ordinated and economical system of electricity supply for all parts of England and Wales and for that
purpose to generate and acquire supplies of electricity which
it then transmits for distribution to the twelve Area Boards
over which it exercises a general control.[2] The Gas Council
is required to advise the Minister of Power on questions
affecting the industry, to promote and assist the efficient
exercise and performance by the twelve Area Gas Boards of
their functions and to settle research programmes.[3] The Area
Gas Boards are required to develop and maintain an efficient,
co-ordinated and economical system of gas supply in their
areas.[4] The Transport Commission is under a general duty to
provide railway services for Great Britain, to provide or
secure the provision of an adequate and properly co-ordinated
system of passenger transport in London, and to provide, to
such extent as may appear to the Commission to be expedient,
other transport services, facilities for traffic on inland waterways and certain port facilities.[5] The Air corporations have
power to provide air transport service and to carry out all
other forms of aerial work in any part of the world.[6]

[1] Coal Industry Nationalisation Act, 1946 Sect. 1 (1).
[2] Electricity Act, 1947 (referred to hereafter as E.A.), Sect. 1 (1) (2). Under
this Act there were established fourteen Area Boards, the other two being the South
East Scotland Board and the South West Scotland Board. These two were
merged in the South of Scotland Board which, like the North of Scotland Board,
is independent of the Electricity Authority—see Electricity Reorganisation
(Scotland) Act, 1954. In this chapter, consideration is limited to England and
Wales. For the Report of a Committee (Chairman: Sir Edwin Herbert) appointed
"to inquire into the organisation and efficiency of the electricity supply industry
in England and Wales in the light of its working under the Electricity Act, 1947,
and to make recommendations," see Cmd. 9672 (1956).
[3] Gas Act, 1948 (referred to hereafter as G.A.), Sects. 2 (1), 3.
[4] G.A., Sect. 1 (1).
[5] This wording is based on the provisions of the Transport Act, 1953, which
amended the Transport Act, 1947, and introduced a measure of denationalisation
of the road haulage and road passenger services. See Transport Act, 1947 (referred
to hereafter as T.A.), Sect. 3 (1) as redrafted by Transport Act, 1953, Sect. 25 (1).
See also Transport Act, 1953, Sects. 1–6, 18, and Transport (Disposal of Road
Haulage Property) Act, 1956.
[6] Air Corporations Act, 1949 (referred to hereafter as A.C.A.), Sects. 1 (1),
3 (1). This Act replaces the similar provisions of Civil Aviation Act, 1946, and
Airways Corporations Act, 1949. The corporations are the British Overseas Airways Corporation and the British European Airways Corporation.

The second group of corporations consists of Regional Hospital Boards and New Town Development Corporations. The fourteen Regional Hospital Boards form part of the national health service scheme and, through Hospital Management Committees, manage and control the hospitals within their regions.[1] The function of a New Town Development Corporation is to secure the laying out and development of a new town.[2] These are managerial-social bodies. Their purpose is to administer organisations which supply services necessary to the social and physical health of the community.

The third group consists of the Agricultural Land Commission and the Central Land Board. The Agricultural Land Commission is charged with the principal functions of managing and farming land which is vested in the Minister, or for which he is responsible, and advising and assisting him generally.[3] The functions of the Central Land Board conferred by the Town and Country Planning Act, 1947,[4] have been much reduced by the abolition of development charges[5] but the Board was preserved to play an important financial part under the Act of 1954.[6] The status of these two corporations in relation to the Ministries under which they work is very similar. They can be broadly classified as regulatory-social bodies.[7]

---

[1] National Health Service Act, 1946 (referred to hereafter as N.H.S.A.), Sects. 11, 12. The Boards are referred to hereafter as the Hospital Boards.

[2] New Towns Act, 1946 (referred to hereafter as N.T.A.), Sect. 2 (1) (2). The corporations are referred to hereafter as New Town Corporations.

[3] Agriculture Act, 1947 (referred to hereafter as A.A.), Sect. 68 (1). The Commission is referred to hereafter as the Land Commission.

[4] Referred to hereafter as T.C.P.A.

[5] Town and Country Planning Act, 1953, Sect. 1.

[6] Town and Country Planning Act, 1954. Under Sect. 63 of this Act, an Order in Council may provide for the winding up and dissolution of the Central Land Board and the transfer to the Minister of Housing and Local Government of any outstanding functions.

[7] Sir Arthur Street classified quasi-Government bodies as regulatory (non-industrial), regulatory (industrial) and managerial. As he says, it is unsafe to generalise about such bodies: "Like flowers in Spring, they have grown as variously and profusely and with as little regard for conventional patterns. They are even less susceptible of orderly classification . . . a new species often suggests a new genus" (*British Government since 1918*, 160). Cushman has two major divisions: departmental (which are regulatory), and non-departmental (which may be regulatory, operating or service). He writes: "My friend Professor Laski examined this classification and remarked without enthusiasm that it was probably as good as any, but that, of course, logical classification of these agencies is impossible because of the hit-or-miss way in which they have been set up and the lack of any logical consistency in their organisation or functions." (*The Independent Regulatory*

This list of corporations is by no means exhaustive, even when limited to those created since 1945, nor is the classification precise. Among those omitted are the Independent Television Authority, the Atomic Energy Authority, and the Iron and Steel Board.[1]

A. Constitution

Each of these corporations consists of a governing body.[2] Each has a chairman and members, the number being limited, except for the Hospital Boards, by the constituent Acts.[3] No statutory limit is laid down for the fourteen Hospital Boards but the average number of members appointed is about thirty.[4] The other bodies have a membership of fifteen or less. The members of the Electricity Authority must include four of the chairmen of the Area Boards (appointed in rotation).[5] The Gas Council is composed of a chairman, a deputy chairman, and the chairmen of the twelve Area Boards.[6] Some of the members of the corporations are part-time only.[7]

The chairmen and members are appointed by the appropriate Minister,[8] who has an almost complete discretion in this matter. He is required, in the case of the fuel and power and transport corporations,[9] to appoint persons appearing to him to be qualified as having had experience of and having shown

Commissions, 508–9). Those set up since 1945, being part of a deliberate policy, do show more coherence.

With those here called regulatory-social may be compared the regulatory-economic marketing boards, development councils, and the Monopolies and Restrictive Practices Commission.

[1] See Television Act, 1954; Atomic Energy Authority Act, 1954; Iron and Steel Act, 1953.

[2] See W. A. Robson: "The Governing Board of the Public Corporation" in 21 *Political Quarterly* (1950), 135.

[3] The provisions relating to constitution are set out in C.I.N.A., Sect. 2 (as amended by Coal Industry Act, 1949, Sect. 1) and S.R. & O. 1946 No. 1094; E.A., Sect. 3 and S.R. & O. 1947 No. 1750; G.A., Sect. 5 and S.I. 1948 Nos. 2233, 2465; T.A. Sect. 1, Sch. 1, 2; A.C.A. Sect. 2, Sch. 1; N.H.S.A., Sch. 3 and S.R. & O. 1947 No. 1298; N.T.A., Sch 2; A.A., Sect. 68, Sch. 9; T.C.P.A., Sect. 2 and S.R. & O. 1947 No. 2294.

[4] See S.R. & O. 1946 No. 2158 and 1947 No. 1297.

[5] E.A., Sects. 3 (2) (*a*) (*b*); sub-para. (*c*) is repealed by Electricity Reorganisation (Scotland) Act, 1954, Sect. 15, Sch. 2, Pt. I.

[6] G.A., Sect. 5 (4).

[7] See e.g. Coal Industry Act, 1949, Sect. 1 (3); T.A., Sect. 1 (2).

[8] See below, p. 279 note 2.

[9] Fuel and power corporations means the Coal Board and the Electricity Authority, Gas Council and their Area Boards. Transport corporations means the Transport Commission and the London Transport Executive. For names, salaries, allowances and tenure, see Cmd. 9660 (1956).

capacity in industrial, commercial or financial matters, applied science and the administration or organisation of workers.[1] For the Land Commission the words are similar.[2] One or more members of the New Town corporations must have local knowledge.[3] No qualifications are prescribed for the Air corporations, the Central Land Board, or the Hospital Boards except that at least two members of the latter must be experienced in mental health services. Before appointing to the New Towns corporations or the Hospital Boards the Minister must consult local authorities;[4] for the latter he must also consult professional bodies;[5] before appointing to the London Transport Executive or the Area Electricity Boards, he must consult the Transport Commission and the Electricity Authority, respectively.[6]

Membership of the House of Commons is expressly made a disqualification for appointment to all the corporations, except the New Town corporations and the Hospital Boards.[7] No person who has a financial or other interest likely to affect prejudicially the discharge of his functions may be appointed to the Transport Commission or its Executive.[8]

The Minister has very wide powers of dismissal. Two general provisions apply to the fuel and power, New Town and Air corporations and to the Central Land Board. These empower the Minister to dismiss a member who is absent from board meetings, without the Minister's permission, for three or six months (this also applies to members of Hospital Boards) or who is, in the Minister's opinion, unable, unfit or incapable of performing his duties. There are various other provisions such as, in the case of the fuel and power corporations, engaging in another trade or business, or holding certain other appointments; for New Town and Air corporations and the Central Land Board, becoming bankrupt or making a composition with creditors. For Hospital Boards the power to dismiss is detailed

---

[1] The phraseology varies slightly. At least two members of the possible fifteen members of the Transport Commission must be appointed after consultation with the Secretary of State for Scotland (Transport Act, 1953, Sect. 25 (2) (a)).
[2] A.A., Sect. 68 (6).
[3] N.T.A., Sch. 2, para. 1.
[4] Ibid.; N.H.S.A., Sch. 3, Pt. I.
[5] As in last note.
[6] T.A., Sch. 2, para. 1; E.A., Sect. 3 (3) (a).
[7] For express provision to this effect see N.H.S.A., Sch. 3, Pt. IV, para. 4.
[8] T.A., Sect. 1 (5).

at some length.[1] Members of the fuel and power corporations are required to disclose their interests in similar undertakings and the Minister may require their disposal.[2]

The ordinary tenure of office is, for the fuel and power corporations, required by the Acts not to exceed five years;[3] for the Hospital Boards, a fixed period of three years after initial appointments of one, two and three years to ensure that all do not retire together;[4] for the other corporations, to be "in accordance with the terms of appointment."[5] All members are eligible for reappointment.

B. Area Boards and the London Transport Executive

The statutes relating to electricity, gas and transport establish corporations which are subordinate to the principal bodies. Thus, for distributive and other functions, England and Wales is divided into twelve electricity areas.[6] Each area is managed by an Area Board which, while it has many functions of its own, is subject to the directions and general control of the Electricity Authority.[7] Similarly, there are twelve Area Gas Boards.[8] The Gas Council, however, does not enjoy the same powers as the Electricity Authority, there being far more devolution in the gas industry. This is reflected in the membership of the Gas Council which, as already noted, consists of the chairmen of the Area Boards under a chairman and a deputy-chairman.

Under the Transport Act, 1947, there were set up six Executives to exercise, as agents for the Transport Commission, functions delegated to them by the Commission relating to railways, docks and inland waterways, road haulage, London Transport, hotels and road passenger transport respectively.[9] Of these only the London Transport Executive remains, the

---

[1] S.R. & O. 1947 No. 1298.

[2] S.R. & O. 1946 No. 1094, Reg. 3; 1947 No. 1750, Reg. 2 (1) (a); S.I. 1948 No. 2233, Reg. 2 (1) (a).

[3] In the case of the four chairmen of Area Boards who are members of the B.E.A., appointment to the B.E.A. is for a term not exceeding three years.

[4] S.R. & O. 1947 Nos. 1297, 1298.

[5] To introduce uniformity for New Town corporations, new members are to serve for an initial period of not less than two years; the composition of the corporations is reviewed annually (549 H.C. Deb. 5s. 992–3; February 28th, 1956).

[6] E.A., Sch. 1 and above p. 274, note 2.

[7] Ibid., Sect. 6 (1).   [8] G.A., Sch. 1.

[9] T.A., Sect. 5 and S.I. 1949 No. 1130.

functions of the others either having been discontinued or being exercised by the Commission.[1]

The Coal Industry Nationalisation Act, 1946, makes no provision for devolution of function or authority. Such devolution exists but the various Divisions and Areas are not corporations.

C. Ministerial Powers

The appropriate Minister[2] has power to give to the Coal Board, Electricity Authority, Gas Council, Area Gas Boards, Transport Commission, and the Air corporations, directions of a general character as to the exercise and performance by the corporations of their functions, in relation to matters appearing to the Minister to affect the national interest. He is required to consult with the corporation concerned before giving any directions.[3] In relation to Hospital Boards, the Land Commission, and the Central Land Board, the power is to give directions of a general character, or directions simply.[4] The power over New Town corporations is more specific. Thus proposals for development or for acquisition of land are subject to Ministerial approval; in addition, the Minister may give directions to these corporations restricting or controlling the exercise of their statutory powers.[5] Similarly, the Minister may limit the powers of the Air corporations to such extent as he thinks desirable in the public interest, by making the exercise of any power depend on his general or specific authority.[6] The Coal Board, Transport Commission, Electricity Authority, and Area Gas Boards are required to act on lines settled from time to time and approved by the Minister when

[1] For the abolition of the five Executives see S.I. 1952 No. 1726 and 1953 No. 1291. The administration of the railways was re-organised (see Transport Act, 1953, Sects. 16, 17 and S.I. 1954 No. 1579) but no new corporate bodies were created. The Transport Act, 1953, Sect. 25 (3) confers on the Minister the power to provide that there shall be no Executives.
[2] The Minister of Power for coal, electricity and gas corporations; the Minister of Transport and Civil Aviation for the transport and Air Corporations; the Minister of Health for Hospital Boards; the Minister of Housing and Local Government for the Central Land Board and New Town corporations; the Minister of Agriculture, Fisheries and Food, for the Land Commission.
[3] C.I.N.A., Sect. 3 (1); E.A., Sect. 5 (1); G.A., Sect. 7 (1); T.A., Sect. 4 (1); A.C.A., Sect. 5.
[4] N.H.S.A., Sect. 12 (1); A.A., Sect. 68 (7); T.C.P.A., Sect. 3 (1).
[5] N.T.A., Sects. 2 (3), 3 (1), 4, 5.
[6] A.C.A., Sect. 3 (5).

they are framing programmes of reorganisation or development involving substantial outlay on capital account; before approving such proposals of Area Gas Boards, the Minister must consult the Gas Council.[1] The Minister has similar powers over the functions of these corporations and Area Electricity Boards relating to training, education and research; here, however, the Area Gas Boards are under close control by the Gas Council.[2]

There is a general obligation on the corporations, with the exception of the London Transport Executive and the Hospital Boards,[3] to furnish the Minister with information which he requires, to submit returns and accounts to him, and to provide him with facilities for verification of the information, "in such manner and at such times as he may require."[4] The Electricity Authority is further required to answer similarly for its Area Boards[5] which, and this applies also to the Area Gas Boards, are obliged to supply such information to their parent bodies.[6]

In times of war, whether actual or imminent, or of great national emergency, the Minister may by order take over the Air corporations, wholly or in part.[7]

D. Annual Reports

Each corporation, with the exception of the Hospital Boards, the London Transport Executive, and the Area Electricity Boards, is required, after the end of the financial year, to report to the appropriate Minister on the exercise and performance of its functions and on its policy and programmes. The Minister must lay the report before Parliament. The Area Electricity Boards report to the Electricity Authority

---

[1] C.I.N.A., Sect. 3 (2); T.A., Sect. 4 (2); E.A., Sect. 5 (2); G.A., Sect. 1 (5).
[2] C.I.N.A., Sect. 3 (3); T.A., Sect. 4 (3); E.A., Sects. 5 (3), 6 (2); G.A., Sect. 4 (1) (2).
[3] Neither is a true exception; the Transport Commission is under the obligation; the Hospital Boards act on behalf of the Minister.
[4] C.I.N.A., Sect. 3 (4); T.A., Sect. 4 (6); E.A., Sects. 5 (5), 6 (4). For the gas corporations, the provision is to furnish the information, etc., to the Minister "in such manner and at such times as he may *reasonably* require;" see G.A., Sect. 7 (3). The New Town and Air corporations are required to permit authorised persons to inspect books, etc., and to afford such explanation as those persons or the Minister may *reasonably* require; see N.T.A., Sect. 13 (7); A.C.A., Sect. 23 (6) (7).
[5] E.A., Sect. 5 (6).
[6] E.A., Sect. 6 (4); G.A., Sect. 2 (4).
[7] A.C.A., Sect. 26 (1).

which incorporates these reports with its own.[1] When the Minister presents the Electricity and Gas reports he must report also on his own functions save where, in his opinion, this would be contrary to national security.[2]

The reports laid before Parliament must contain any Ministerial "directions" given in the course of the year, unless the Minister has notified to the corporation his opinion that it is against the national interest to do so. This provision applies to the Coal Board, the Air corporations and the Land Commission.[3] For the Transport Commission, Electricity Authority, Gas Council, and Area Gas Boards and the Central Land Board there is a similar provision but the word "security" replaces "interest."[4]

Various other reports have to be made; those relating to finance and those made by consumers', consultative, and advisory Councils are discussed below.[5]

E. Financial

The fuel, power, and transport undertakings, which supply commodities and facilities on payment to the public, are required to be self-supporting. They are therefore fixed with a general statutory duty so to exercise and perform their functions as to secure that their revenue is sufficient to meet outgoings properly chargeable to revenue account, taking one year with another.[6] For this purpose the revenues of the Electricity Authority and its Area Boards are combined while those of the Gas Council and each Area Gas Board are kept separate; the London Transport Executive and the Transport Commission form one undertaking. The Minister may make limited advances to the Coal Board on account of capital expenditure.[7]

The Hospital Boards, Land Commission, Central Land Board and New Town corporations, not being money-making concerns,

---

[1] C.I.N.A., Sect. 54 (1); E.A., Sect. 8 (1) (2) (5); G.A., Sect. 10 (1) (5); T.A., Sect. 4 (7); A.C.A., Sect. 23 (1) (2); N.T.A., Sect. 13 (6); A.A., Sect. 70 (1) (6); T.C.P.A., Sect. 2 (7). The Reports of the Electricity Authority and each of the Area Boards are in practice published separately; see, for example, H.C. 234–48 of 1953–4.
[2] E.A., Sect. 8 (5); G.A., Sect. 10 (5). For electricity, see, for example, H.C. 249 of 1953–4.
[3] C.I.N.A., Sect. 54 (2); A.C.A., Sect. 23 (3); A.A., Sect. 70 (2).
[4] T.A., Sect. 4 (7); E.A., Sect. 8 (2); G.A., Sect. 10 (2); T.C.P.A., Sect. 3 (2).
[5] Pp. 279–80, 302–6.
[6] C.I.N.A., Sect. 1 (4) (c); E.A., Sect. 36; G.A., Sect. 41; T.A., Sect. 3 (4).
[7] C.I.N.A., Sect. 26 as amended by Coal Industry Act, 1956, Sect. 1.

are in a different category. The approved expenses of the first three are met by the appropriate Minister.[1] To enable a New Town corporation to defray expenditure properly chargeable to capital account, the Minister may make advances which are repayable; for other purposes, the Minister may make grants.[2]

The Air corporations occupy a mid-way position between these two groups. They provide services on payment but they require subsidies. They are therefore placed under a statutory duty to exercise their powers so as to secure that the services are developed to the best advantage and are provided at reasonable charges. The Minister may, however, make grants.[3]

The fuel, power, transport, and Air corporations may borrow temporarily and various limits are prescribed.[4] The Electricity Authority, Gas Council, Transport Commission and the Air corporations may issue stock.[5] But Sect. 42 of the Finance Act, 1956, provided that any sum which these corporations had power to borrow by the issue of stock might instead be raised by the taking of an advance from the appropriate Minister; advances under this section should not together exceed £700m. and no such advance should be made after the end of March, 1958. While in force, this procedure is intended to replace and not merely to supplement the power of the corporations to issue stock. The Treasury may issue Government stock on behalf of the Coal Board.[6] These powers are subject to Ministerial and Treasury control.

All corporations, with the exception of the Central Land Board, are required to keep proper accounts, which are examined by auditors appointed by the Ministers. The statement of accounts and the auditor's report are laid before Parliament by the Ministers. In the case of New Towns corporations, Hospital Boards and the Land Commission the

---

[1] N.H.S.A., Sect. 54 (1); A.A., Sect. 105 (1); T.C.P.A., Sect. 3 (5).

[2] N.T.A., Sect. 12 (1) (2) as amended by N.T.A., 1955, Sect. 1.

[3] A.C.A., Sects. 3 (1), 13–17.

[4] C.I.N.A., Sect. 27 as amended by Coal Industry Act, 1951, Sect. 1 (4); E.A., Sect. 39 and G. A., Sect. 42 as amended by Gas and Electricity (Borrowing Powers) Act, 1954, Sect. 1; T.A., Sect. 88 (1) as amended by T.A., 1953, Sect. 26 (1) and Transport (Borrowing Powers) Act, 1955, Sect. 1 (for London Transport Executive, see T. A., Sect. 5 (8)); A.C.A., Sects. 8 (1), 12 as amended by A.C.A., 1953, Sect. 1.

[5] E.A., Sects. 39 (2), 40; G.A., Sects. 42 (2), 43; T.A., Sects. 88 (2), 89 as amended by T.A., 1953, Sect. 26 (1), Sch. 5, Pt. I and Transport (Borrowing Powers) Act, 1955, Sect. 1; A.C.A., Sects. 8 (2), 9, 12.

[6] C.I.N.A., Sects. 32, 33.

accounts are also reported on by the Comptroller and Auditor-General.[1]

There are provisions requiring the establishment of reserve funds and dealing with the disposal of surplus revenues.[2] The fuel, power, transport and Air corporations are required to build up reserve funds which may only be used for the purposes of the particular corporations. The Ministerial power o giving directions extends to these funds and may be used to give specific instructions; a similar provision applies to the power of the Electricity Authority to give directions to its Area Boards. Any surplus revenues of the Coal Board and electricity corporations are subject to like control; an Air corporation must apply any such surplus as the Minister, with the approval of the Treasury and after consultation with the Chairman, may direct.

F. Commentary on these Provisions

The division of these public corporations into groups, although used above merely for the convenience of exposition, raises a question of importance.

Those in the first group are under the least control by the appropriate Ministers while those in the last group are under the greatest control. The industrial and commercial corporations in the first group are to a large extent independent and financially autonomous.[3] They have been deliberately made free of close departmental control. Their relations with their employees and with the general public, the quality of the commodities and facilities they supply and the charges they make are all the responsibilities of the corporations. To this there are two exceptions. First, the Transport Commission must have its charges scheme approved by the Transport Tribunal which, following a judicial procedure, hears the cases for and against its

---

[1] C.I.N.A., Sect. 31; E.A., Sect. 46; G.A., Sect. 50; T.A., Sect. 94; A.C.A., Sect. 22; N.H.S.A., Sect. 55; N.T.A., Sect. 13; A.A., Sect. 70 (5). In the last statute there is no provision requiring the accounts to be examined by auditors appointed by the Minister.

[2] C.I.N.A., Sects. 29, 30; E.A., Sects. 43, 44; G.A., Sect. 47; T.A., Sect. 92; A.C.A., Sects. 18, 19

[3] For a classification of these corporations according to their financial relationship to Ministers, see the memorandum by the Clerk to the Select Committee on Estimates (Mr. H. R. M. Farmer) presented to the Select Committee on Nationalised Industries (H.C. 235 of 1952–3, Minutes of Evidence, p. 1).

proposals.[1] Secondly, the reliance of the Air corporations on subsidies diminishes their independence.[2] The salaries and allowances of the members of the corporations in this first group are determined by the Minister, with the approval of the Treasury, but are paid out of the revenues of the corporations; the Transport Commission pays the members of the London Transport Executive.[3] One provision which is common to all these corporations, with the exception of the Transport Commission and its Executive, confers general powers. Thus it is provided that the Coal Board "shall have power to do any thing and to enter into any transaction . . . which in their opinion is calculated to facilitate the proper discharge of their duties [as prescribed] or the carrying on by them of any such activities as aforesaid, or is incidental or conducive thereto."[4] The words for the other corporations are similar.[5] The powers of the Transport Commission are set out in considerable detail, as are the activities in which that corporation may not engage.[6]

The corporations in the second and third groups have less freedom of action. While it is true that the requirement that the Minister shall consult certain bodies before appointing the members of Hospital Boards and New Town corporations may suggest a certain independence, there are provisions which more closely limit the powers of these corporations. First, all these corporations are financially dependent on the Exchequer; this is not wholly so for the New Town corporations. Secondly, the fact that the Land Commission and Central Land Board are subject to Ministerial directions of a general character, that Hospital Boards are subject to "directions" simply and that the powers of the New Town corporations may be restricted by directions implies a greater Ministerial control than that exercised over the fuel, power and transport corporations. Thirdly, Hospital Boards and New Town corporations are required to submit many of their proposed actions

---

[1] T.A., Sects. 76–81 as amended by T.A., 1953, Sects. 20–24. In practice, Ministers have recently shown themselves more prepared to control transport charges than the charges of other public corporations.

[2] Both are now self-supporting.

[3] C.I.N.A., Sect. 2 (6); E.A., Sect. 3 (6); G.A., Sect. 5 (6); T.A., Sch. 2, para. 2 (5); A.C.A., Sch. 1, para. 9.   [4] C.I.N.A., Sect. 1 (3).

[5] E.A., Sect. 2 (5); G.A., Sects. 1 (4), 2 (5); A.C.A., Sect. 3 (2).

[6] T.A., Sect. 2 as affected by T.A., 1953, Sects. 1, 18.

for Ministerial approval. Fourthly, neither Hospital Boards nor the Central Land Board have been granted any general powers. Fifthly, Hospital Boards and the Central Land Board exercise their functions "on behalf of the Crown."[1] Sixthly, the salaries and allowances of the members of the Land Commission and Central Land Board are paid by the Minister with the approval of the Treasury.[2] The salaries of members of New Town corporations, however, are determined by the Minister with the approval of the Treasury and are paid by the corporations, while members of Hospital Boards only receive payment for loss of remunerative time, or, exceptionally, for expenses and subsistence.[3]

This distinction between the corporations in the first group on the one hand and those in the second and third groups on the other becomes important when the question has to be decided whether any corporation is to be regarded as a Crown servant.[4]

It will have been noted that the method of appointment of the members of the corporations is uniform. All are appointed by the Minister. The devices of election (wholly or in part) or of appointing trustees have not been used; nor are the members representative of any other organisations. Leaders of trade unions and of employers' federations have in fact been appointed to the corporations but they have been appointed as individuals, not as representatives. Nor are consumers represented. It has been suggested that probably for some time to come most of the corporations in the first group will be composed of such elements as (a) a person with previous experience of the industry under commercial ownership—usually a high executive, (b) an ex-trade-union officer of standing, (c) a former civil servant of exceptional ability, (d) a leading financial expert or accountant, (e) an engineer or scientist—"with an occasional retired general or air marshal thrown in."[5] Different considerations obviously

---

[1] N.H.S.A., Sects. 12 (1), 13 (1); T.C.P.A., Sect. 3 (3).

[2] A.A., Sch. 9, para. 23; T.C.P.A., Sect. 2 (4).

[3] N.T.A., Sch. 2, para. 7; N.H.S.A., Sch. 3, Pt. IV, para. 2 (c), as amended by N.H.S. (Amendment) Act, 1949, and S.R. & O. 1947 No. 1330, S.I. 1949 No. 2340.

[4] See below, pp. 306-9.

[5] W. A. Robson: "The Governing Board of the Public Corporation" in 21 *Political Quarterly* (1950), at 139-40.

apply to the Land Commission, Central Land Board and the Hospital Boards and, to a lesser extent, to New Town corporations.

The three groups of subordinate corporations (Electricity and Gas Area Boards and the London Transport Executive) are dissimilar in status. In relation to their parent bodies, the Area Gas Boards are in the strongest position. They are, indeed, not truly subordinate. The chief functions under the Gas Act, 1948, are performed by the Area Boards with the Gas Council as an advisory body; the chief functions under the Electricity Act, 1947, are divided between the Electricity Authority and the Area Boards and the overriding responsibility rests on the former. The Transport Commission is responsible for all functions but delegates responsibility to the London Transport Executive. The constitution of the Gas Council sharply contrasts with that of the Electricity Authority or the Transport Commission and reflects the predominant position of the Area Gas Boards. Further, before appointing the members of the Area Gas Boards, the Minister is not required to consult the Gas Council. Ministerial directions are given to Area Gas Boards themselves; there is only a limited power to give directions to Area Electricity Boards and no such power in the case of Executives. Each Area Gas Board is required to balance its own accounts, whereas the Electricity Authority and the Transport Commission are required to produce one account for the whole of their undertakings. Finally, returns, accounts and annual reports are made direct to the Minister by Area Gas Boards, and not to the parent authority.[1]

The position of the London Transport Executive is peculiar because it is constituted as an agent of the Transport Commission. There does not seem to be any special reason why the agency concept should have been introduced. The policy-making and co-ordinating functions of the Transport Commission could have been provided for by other means. Once the delegating scheme has been made and approved, very considerable powers pass to the Executive which becomes both administratively and legally responsible.

The ministerial powers to issue directions to the corporations

---

[1] The relationship between the consultative councils and the gas and electricity authorities also reflects the comparative independence of the Area Gas Boards.

constitute the formal connection between the appropriate Minister and the members.[1] They also form the basis of responsibility to Parliament. The requirement that directions should not be contained in the annual reports if the Minister is of opinion that to do so would be contrary to the national interest, has been criticised.[2] The word "interest" which appeared in the Coal Industry Nationalisation Act, 1946, the Civil Aviation Act, 1946, and the Agriculture Act, 1947, was replaced by the word "security" in the Acts of 1947 and 1948 which constituted the Transport Commission, Central Land Board and the electricity and gas corporations. However, the Air Corporations Act, 1949, which replaced the Civil Aviation Act, 1946, continued to speak of "interest." The number of formal directions made by Ministers has been small.

Parliamentary Control

The nature and extent of parliamentary control over public corporations can best be examined in relation to three types of procedure: debates, questions, and proceedings in committees.

A. Debates

There are principally seven occasions on which debates may arise. First, there may be an amendment to the Address in reply to the Queen's Speech. Motions of this kind being general in character are likely to relate to the whole policy of nationalisation. Thus on 2nd November, 1948, in the House of Commons an amendment was moved which regretted that, "notwithstanding the grave international situation and the continuing gap in our overseas trade, Your Majesty's Government should obstinately persist in a policy of nationalisation which has already imposed heavy burdens on consumers and taxpayers alike and is impeding the enterprise and initiative which is (sic) essential to our recovery." A long debate followed.[3] Secondly, the Opposition may use one of their days in Committee of Supply. On a motion to reduce the vote for

[1] See H. S. Morrison: "Public Control of the Socialised Industries" in 28 Public Administration (1950), 3–6 and 176–7.
[2] W. Friedmann: "The New Public Corporations and the Law" in 10 Modern Law Review (1947), at 248–9, 392.
[3] 457 H.C. Deb. 5s., cols. 683–810, 862–988.

the Ministry of Civil Aviation, the position of the Air corporations has been fully discussed.[1] Thirdly, there may be
motions on the adjournment. On one of these the power of the
Transport Commission to prepare road passenger area schemes
was discussed:[2] on another, New Town corporations were the
subject.[3] Fourthly, debates often take place when the annual
reports of the corporations are laid before Parliament.[4] Fifthly,
a corporation may be obliged to introduce a Private Bill and the
Second Reading debate may go beyond the immediate purposes of the Bill.[5] Sixthly, there will be a limited opportunity
to discuss any particular aspect of a corporation's power and
duties where a Minister is required to lay before Parliament a
statutory instrument relating to a corporation. Lastly, there
may be motions on other occasions as, for example, on a vote of
censure or when the Lord President of the Council, on 25th
October, 1950, moved a general motion on the public accountability of the socialised industries.[6]

B. Questions

On most of the occasions outlined above, what is debated is
either the general policy of nationalisation or the general policy
of a particular corporation. A debate on any subject is necessarily limited, in the main, to generalities; exceptionally,
debates on the adjournment may be, and debates on motions
to annul or approve statutory instruments will be, particular.
In matters of ordinary departmental administration, letters
to the Minister or questions in Parliament are the normal ways
in which details are criticised. The Minister is the responsible
authority. Where the actions of a public corporation enjoying
a considerable degree of statutory independence of the
appropriate Minister are complained of, a difficulty arises.
Ministers will not accept responsibility for actions which are
not within their power to control. The powers of Ministers in
relation to the fuel and power, transport and air corporations

---

[1] 462 H.C. Deb. 5s., cols. 195–326.

[2] 470 H.C. Deb. 5s., cols. 2299–308.

[3] 468 H.C. Deb. 5s., cols. 1651–60.

[4] See, for example, 469, H.C. Deb. 5s., cols. 1415–530 (Coal Board) and 470
H.C. Deb. 5s., cols. 1343–456 (Transport Commission).

[5] 461 H.C. Deb. 5s., cols. 1765–823 (Transport Commission). See the Speaker's
ruling at col. 1765.

[6] 478 H.C. Deb. 5s., cols. 2803–927.

are, as shown above, limited. They have not, in the phrase which is often used, power to control the "day-to-day" administration of these corporations.

Before a question can be put on the Order Paper in the House of Commons, it has to pass the Clerks at the Table who work under the Speaker. The Clerks may reject a question if it is directed to a Minister who is not the responsible authority, or because a Minister has previously refused, on this ground, to answer a similar question. No Minister can, in any case, be compelled to answer any question.[1] Questions on day-to-day administration of the public corporations governing nationalised industries have, therefore, been refused by the Clerks. The Speaker indicated that in the last resort only a Minister could say whether the question was one which fell within his responsibility.[2] This whole matter was discussed on several occasions in the House of Commons[3] and finally the Speaker made a proposal, which was accepted, in these words—

> I propose to leave the Rule which excludes Questions on matters outside Ministerial responsibility, unchanged. But I am prepared, if it is generally approved, to exercise my discretion to direct the acceptance of Questions asking for a statement to be made on matters about which information has been previously refused, provided that, in my opinion, the matters are of sufficient public importance to justify this concession.

The test of "public importance" is left wholly to the Speaker's discretion. The Speaker concluded—

> I should like to add that, of course, it by no means follows that Ministers will be bound to answer any Questions which I have allowed as being of "public importance"; that is their affair.[4]

It is clear that, as the Speaker has said, "The Rules relating to Questions are much stricter than the Rules about Debates."[5] The Lord President of the Council has said "The eligibility of the question depends upon the nature of the statute and the powers which the Minister has got." He went on to indicate the sphere of Ministerial responsibility—

[1] T. Erskine May: *Parliamentary Practice* (15th Edn.), 340–1.
[2] 446 H.C. Deb. 5s., cols. 1816–7.
[3] 445 H.C. Deb. 5s., cols. 565–71; 446 cols. 1814–20; 447 cols. 987–8; 448 cols. 391–456; 449 cols. 169–72, 1630–4; 451 cols. 642–5, 1635–43.
[4] 451 H.C. Deb. 5s., col. 1636 (7th June, 1948).
[5] 449 H.C. Deb. 5s., col. 172; and see col. 1631.

It includes, for example, the appointment, salaries and conditions of service of board members; programmes of research
and development; programmes of education and training;
borrowing by the boards, which, I think, includes capital expenditure; the form of accounts and audits; annual reports;
pensions schemes; compensation for displacement; and various
matters concerned with consumer councils.[1]

In addition, apart from their inclusion in annual reports, the
Minister is responsible to Parliament for directions which he
gives to the corporations.[2]

C. Committees

The Committee of Public Accounts (of the House of Commons) is appointed each Session "for the examination of the
accounts showing the appropriation of the sums granted by
Parliament to meet the public expenditure, and of such other
accounts, laid before Parliament as the Committee may think
fit."[3] The fuel and power and transport corporations fall
within the second part of this order of reference. The Air
corporations certainly fall within the second and will fall within
the first part also for years in which they receive subsidies. The
other corporations are all centrally financed and so fall within
the first part. From the 1946–7 session to that of 1951–2, the
Committee in fact examined the accounts of the Air corporations in each of four sessions, of one or other New Town
corporation in each of four sessions, and of the Coal Board and
the Transport Commission each on one occasion. One or
more of the members of the corporation, the accounts of which
are under examination, gives evidence to the Committee, the
Accounting Officer of the Department concerned is present and
sometimes the auditors of the corporation are called. The
Comptroller and Auditor General is also present.[4] The
control of the Committee and of the Comptroller and Auditor
General over the accounts of the fuel and power, transport and

[1] 478 H.C. Deb. 5s., col. 2801. For effect of Questions on day-to-day administration see cols. 2904–5 (Mr. Oliver Lyttelton).
[2] The Select Committee on Nationalised Industries reported in the session of
1951–2 that no major extension of the machinery for questions to Ministers was
desirable (H.C. 332 of 1951–2).
[3] See above, pp. 205–9.
[4] See the memorandum by the Clerk to the Select Committee on Estimates
(Mr. H. R. M. Farmer) presented to the Select Committee on Nationalised
Industries (H.C. 235 of 1952–3, Minutes of Evidence, pp. 1–2).

(if unsubsidised) Air corporations is less than it is over those of the other corporations and those of Government Departments, because there is no power to examine their accounts in detail in the corporations. Control is limited to the accounts as presented and laid before Parliament.[1] Thus on one occasion before the Committee the chairman of the Transport Commission questioned whether he was obliged to produce the accounts of the Road Haulage Executive.[2]

The Select Committee on Estimates (of the House of Commons)[3] has no power to examine the estimates of the fuel and power, transport and (unsubsidised) Air corporations because their estimates are not presented to the House.[4] The Committee has power to examine the estimates of the other corporations.

The other Committee which has powers over public corporations is the Select Committee on Nationalised Industries (of the House of Commons). In 1951 a Select Committee was appointed to consider the methods by which the House was informed of the affairs of the nationalised industries and to report what changes, having regard to the provisions laid down by Parliament in the relevant statutes, might be desirable. The first Report of this Committee related to Parliamentary Questions and has been referred to above.[5] The second Report considered the possibilities of setting up a Committee of the House of Commons or of both Houses and recommended that a Committee of the House of Commons should be established with an officer of the status of the Comptroller and Auditor General.[6] The Committee[7] which eventually emerged in 1955 on a Government motion was weaker in staff and more restricted in scope. By its terms of reference, the Committee was excluded from the consideration of matters which (a) had been decided by or clearly engaged the responsibility of any Ministers; (b) concerned wages and conditions of employment and other

---

[1] H.C. 235 of 1952–3, Minutes of Evidence Q. 81–3 (Sir Frank N. Tribe).
[2] Ibid., Q. 34–6 (Mr. H. R. M. Farmer).
[3] See above, pp. 205–9.
[4] H.C. 235 of 1952–3, Minutes of Evidence, p. 2, and Q. 25–6 (Mr. H. R. M. Farmer).
[5] H.C. 332 of 1951–2 (See above, p. 290, note 2).
[6] H.C. 235 of 1952–3; for the debate on this Report, see 523 H.C. Deb. 5s., cols. 833–962 (8th February, 1954).
[7] This Committee and its successor are also Select Committees.

questions normally decided by collective bargaining arrangements; (c) fell to be considered through formal machinery, established by the relevant statutes; or (d) were matters of day-to-day administration. The Committee obtained information from the Departments in order to discover what was excluded under paragraph (a) and what were the statutory powers of Ministers. The Committee reported at the end of 1955 that the only matters on which it would wish to or could usefully obtain further information fell under one or other of the excluded matters in paragraphs (a) to (d) and so the Order of Reference left insufficient scope.[1] The Government therefore reconsidered the question and, at the end of 1956, a motion was accepted by the House of Commons (after the defeat of an Opposition amendment) for the setting up of a Select Committee with these terms of reference: to examine the Reports and Accounts of the Nationalised Industries established by Statute whose controlling Boards are appointed by Ministers of the Crown and whose annual receipts are not wholly or mainly derived from moneys provided by Parliament or advanced from the Exchequer. The Lord Privy Seal said: "We have come to the conclusion . . . that it is wiser to try not to debar the Committee from discussing certain questions by a series of specific prohibitions . . . but simply to trust to the good sense and good will of the Committee itself;"[2] the Committee would not have an officer of the status of the Comptroller and Auditor General but would have the advice and assistance of the Senior Treasury officers in charge of the Treasury Divisions concerned with the industries.

D. Conclusion

It is generally admitted that the proper relationship between Parliament and the public corporations has not yet been established. The difficulty is inherent in the nature of the corporations. Those administering industrial and commercial undertakings have been granted, by their constituent statutes, a large degree of freedom from ministerial and departmental control. This is generally regarded as desirable, but a corporation which is to some extent independent of the Minister

[1] H.C. 120 of 1955–6 (Special Report from the Select Committee on Nationalised Industries).
[2] 561 H.C. Deb. 5s., col. 595 (November 29th, 1956) (Mr. R. A. Butler).

is to that extent not responsible to Parliament. The Minister is the link. On his power depends parliamentary control. Yet in practice his actual power is greater than his statutory power. His influence and his power to give directions are more important than the directions themselves; indeed the fact that he has the power is often sufficient by itself. Over this indirect influence, however, Parliament has little control. The Minister may indicate to a corporation what he thinks desirable and this informal and indirect method prevents Parliament from exercising an influence which is co-extensive with that of the Minister.[1] Mr. George Strauss, M.P., who, as Minister of Supply, had powers of giving directions to the Iron and Steel Corporation similar to those exercisable by Ministers in relation to the fuel and power and transport corporations, has said: "Every week on one morning I spent an hour or two with the Chairman and the Deputy Chairman of the Corporation considering every single problem, not only of national interest but on every conceivable detail concerning that Corporation. There was not a single problem with which I was not concerned."[2]

All this is far less important in the case of such bodies as the Land Commission and Central Land Board. These bodies are, in any case, very much under the control of the Minister; they are little more than institutionalised parts of a greater administrative machine. Few Questions are asked concerning their activities[3] and none seems to have been refused by the Clerks of the House of Commons. The position of the New Town corporations and Hospital Boards is half-way, in the matter of independence, between those corporations just mentioned and those administering nationalised industries. They have many statutory duties to perform but they cannot be financially

[1] See Ernest Davies: "Ministerial Control and Parliamentary Responsibility of Nationalised Industries" in 21 *Political Quarterly* (1950), 150; H. S. Morrison "Public Control of the Socialised Industries" in 28 *Public Administration* (1950), 4. This indirect ministerial influence has generally been criticised as being contrary to the spirit and intention of the constituent Acts (see the article by Ernest Davies quoted above). In *Tamlin* v. *Hannaford*, [1950] 1 K.B. 18 at 23–4, Denning, L.J., however, said that the power to give directions was inserted lest the corporations should not prove amenable to the Ministers' suggestions as to the policy they should adopt.

[2] H.C. 120 of 1955–6 (Minutes of Evidence taken before Select Committee on Nationalised Industries) p. 36.

[3] For examples, see, for Central Land Board, 458 H.C. Deb. 5s., cols. 190–1; 463 col. *29*; for the Land Commission, 458 cols. 863–4; 460 cols. 566–7.

independent. It is not clear how much responsibility Ministers
are prepared to assume. The Minister of Housing and Local
Government has said, in the course of a debate, that for him to
inquire whether the number of cars used by a New Town
corporation was really necessary or not would be in complete
conflict with the spirit of the Act.[1] Questions concerning
hospitals seem always to be answered by the Minister of Health.

Whatever modifications are made in parliamentary procedure, it seems unlikely that the control of public corporations
can ever adequately be exercised wholly by a national
representative assembly. The difficulty in finding the appropriate formula for the Select Committee on Nationalised
Industries seems to confirm this. Moreover the dangers of too
close control by Parliament over the fuel, power, transport, and
air corporations (in particular) are real. "Autonomy and
responsibility to Parliament quarrel,"[2] and too much responsibility probably means less efficiency.[3] Other methods of
control must be created.[4]

Judicial Control
A. Liability of Public Corporations

The constituent Acts do not, with one exception, expressly
provide that the corporations shall be liable. The exception is
to be found in the National Health Service Act, 1946, which
provides that a Hospital Board "shall, notwithstanding that it is
exercising functions on behalf of the Minister . . . be entitled
to enforce any rights acquired, and shall be liable in respect of
any liabilities incurred (including liabilities in tort), in the
exercise of those functions, in all respects as if the Board . . .
were acting as a principal, and all proceedings for the enforcement of such rights or liabilities, shall be brought by or against
the Board . . . in its own name."[5] The other corporations are
liable because, in the absence of statutory provisions to the
contrary, they are in the same position as other legal persons.[6]

---

[1] 468 H.C. Deb. 5s., col. 1658.
[2] Sir Geoffrey Heyworth (H.C. 235 of 1952–3, Q. 754; see next note).
[3] For warnings against increased Parliamentary control, see evidence of Mr.
Herbert Morrison, Lord Reith and Sir Geoffrey Heyworth before Select Committee on Nationalised Industries (H.C. 235 of 1952–3).
[4] For a discussion of some of the supplementary controls see 478 H.C. Deb. 5s.
cols. 2803–927, especially cols. 2813–22.   [5] Sect. 13.
[6] Formerly many of the corporations had a special period of 3 years for limitation of actions (C.I.N.A., Sect. 49; E.A., Sect. 12; G.A., Sect. 14; T.A., Sect. 11;

The Transport Act, 1947, provides in Sect. 5 (9) that, as respects matters for the time being falling within the scope of a scheme whereby the powers of the Transport Commission are delegated to an Executive, any rights, powers and liabilities of the Commission shall be treated as those of the Executive which shall, to the exclusion of the Commission, be treated as the employer of any officers or servants of the Commission who are under the control of the Executive. Legal proceedings are to be brought against the Executive, to the exclusion of the Commission, although any judgment or order requiring the Executive to pay a sum of money is, if the Executive fails to pay within fourteen days, enforceable against the Commission. If the Executive makes a contract which is outside the scope of its scheme, it is presumably not liable for breach under this provision. The question then arises whether the Commission can be sued. The Act further provides in Sect. 5 (10) that in addition to the powers exercisable by the Executive by virtue of any such delegation, the Executive shall, except so far as the Commission may otherwise direct, have power, at the request of the Commission to do, as agent for the Commission, anything which the Commission has power to do. This provision presumably puts the other contracting party on inquiry whether such a request has been made. Since the provisions of Sect. 5 (9) do not apply, the Commission and not the Executive must be sued in an action brought under Sect. 5 (10). Where it is doubtful whether the Executive or the Commission should be sued, the suit will have to be brought in the alternative.

B. Statutory Duties and Powers

All the corporations, except the Hospital Boards and Central Land Board, have general duties, functions or objects.[1] These are couched in the imperative. So also are the provisions which require the fuel, power, and transport corporations to balance their budgets.[2] To these general duties clauses are linked those which give general powers.

The powers of the Transport Commission are detailed; so are the duties and powers of the Central Land Board. The

N.T.A., Sect. 17; A.C.A., 1953, Sect. 3). But these provisions were repealed by Law Reform (Limitation of Actions) Act, 1954, and the corporations are no longer specially protected.

[1] See above, pp. 273-5. [2] See above, p. 281.

Hospital Boards are in a different position because their duties and powers are derived from the Minister of Health. He has the overriding duty of providing hospital and specialist services.[1] But he is required to set up Hospital Boards to act on his behalf and they are then under a duty to administer the services in accordance with his regulations and directions.[2]

I. ENFORCEMENT OF STATUTORY DUTIES

(a) Mandamus

The nature and scope of the order of mandamus have already been described.[3] Its particular application to public corporations needs further examination.

There are two types of duties cast on the public corporations by their constituent Acts. The first is owed to the Minister, and covers the duty to obey directions, to furnish the Minister with information, to make returns, accounts and annual reports. A Minister is not debarred by the nature of his office from applying for a mandamus[4] although, in view of the other methods of persuasion open to him, it is unlikely that he would be obliged to resort to this course of action. The possibility of a powerful corporation, such as the Coal Board, the Electricity Authority or the Transport Commission, refusing to comply with a particular Ministerial direction is not, however, fantastic. The Minister would appear to have the necessary interest, there does not appear to be an alternative legal remedy and the duty is a public duty. The courts have indicated that the statutory right to inspect and take copies of particular documents is one which, in proper circumstances, is enforceable by mandamus.[5] In the National Health Service Act, 1946,[6] there is the following provision—

> (1) Where the Minister is of opinion, on complaint or otherwise, that any Regional Hospital Board . . . have failed to carry out any functions conferred or imposed on them by or under this Act, or have in carrying out those functions failed to comply with any regulations or directions relating thereto, he

---

[1] N.H.S.A., Sect. 3.   [2] Ibid. Sects. 11, 12; S.I. 1948 No. 60.
[3] This section should be read in conjunction with pp. 233–6.
[4] For example of statutory mandamus on default of other authority see Education Act, 1944, Sect. 99 (1) and compare N.H.S.A., Sect. 57 (3).
[5] R. v. Southwold Corporation ex parte Wrightson (1907), 97 L.T. 431.
[6] Sect. 57.

may after such inquiry as he may think fit make an order declaring
them to be in default.

(2) . . . the members of the [*Regional Hospital Board*] body shall
forthwith vacate their office and the order shall provide for the
appointment, in accordance with the provisions of this Act, of new
members of the body . . .

A fuel or power or transport corporation might refuse to
carry out a direction on the ground that it was particular and
not general and therefore not within the powers of the Minister.
It seems unlikely that the courts would accept jurisdiction to
determine this question. The difficulty is that the Acts use
words such as "power", "duty," "may" and "shall" which at
first sight seem to create legal relationships between Ministers
and the corporations, but which are probably meant as an
attempted definition of political relationships. Consider the
problems involved in determining any legal relationship
between the Lord President of the Council and the Atomic
Energy Authority in these provisions: "(2) The Lord President
of the Council shall have power to give the Authority such
directions as he may think fit and the Authority shall comply
with any directions so given. (3) The said directions may be
general or particular in character, but no such direction shall
be given except after consultation with the Authority, and the
Lord President of the Council shall not regard it as his duty to
intervene in detail in the conduct by the Authority of their
affairs unless in his opinion overriding national interests so
require."[1] It would not be surprising if the Courts refused
to regard these words as creating legally enforceable rights and
duties.

The second type of duty is one which is owed to the general
public and is contained in the general duties, functions or
objects clause. It requires the corporation to provide a proper
and efficient service. Thus the Area Electricity Boards are
required to "plan and carry out an efficient and economical
distribution . . . to persons in their area who require" the
supplies.[2] Is a mandamus available to an ordinary user or to
one who wishes to enjoy the benefit of the facility?

In the first place, it must be remembered that the issuance of
the order is discretionary. Secondly, the fact that the statutory

[1] Atomic Energy Authority Act, 1954, Sect. 3.
[2] E.A., Sect.1 (2).

provision uses the imperative "shall" and not the permissive "may" does not mean that the courts will necessarily regard the obligation as mandatory.[1] Thirdly, it is arguable that the interest of an actual or potential user of the service is insufficient for the purpose of obtaining the order. The nature of the applicant's interest is closely connected with the nature of the corporation's duty. In *R. v. City of London Assessment Committee*[2] the rating authority was refused a mandamus to direct the assessment committee to make certain entries in valuation lists and it was said that an ordinary rate-payer certainly could not have succeeded. The applicant must show, it is said, that he has a legal right to the performance of a legal duty. That the statutes impose a duty is clear; the duty is owed, it might be thought, to the public; if the applicant can show that as a member of the public he has a particular interest in the performance of the duty (because he, more than other members, is suffering by the neglect) then he would seem to have a legal right. Fourthly, there may be an alternative remedy. In the case of the Hospital Boards, the section quoted above seems to provide such a remedy. The party affected may complain to the Minister. But the existence of consumer, consultative, and advisory councils and committees,[3] would not, it is suggested, provide such an alternative. The order of mandamus is issued where there is no other means of obtaining justice. In 1899, Darling, J., said: "I think that justice there means justice as it is meted out to persons in these courts as between party and party . . . I think that justice there means *remedium iuris*." He therefore held that the order could issue although there was a statutory provision which empowered another authority to take action to remedy the defect.[4] It is true that this principle does not seem to have been accepted in *Pasmore* v. *Oswaldtwistle U.D.C.*[5] where the right of complaint to the Local Government Board on the failure of a local authority was held to exclude the issuance of mandamus. There, however, the right of complaint was to a body which was empowered to order the duty to be performed, and, in default, to appoint a person to perform the duty. A consumers' body has no such power; it

[1] See above, p. 107.   [2] [1907] 2 K.B. 764.
[3] See below, pp. 309–15.
[4] *R. v. Leicester Guardians*, [1899] 2 Q.B. 632, at 638.
[5] [1898] A.C. 387.

may only make representations to another body which can take action; and the powers are limited. It may therefore be doubted whether recourse to the consumers' body would be considered an alternative remedy. It is difficult, in any event, to see how such recourse could be held to be equally convenient, beneficial and effectual. Fifthly, a corporation may be regarded as a Crown servant; even so, the duty would seem to be imposed on the corporation itself and therefore the issue of mandamus would not be debarred on this ground. Sixthly, Area Boards are expressly obliged, in certain circumstances, to supply electricity and gas when requested to do so.[1]

A case can therefore be made out for the issuing of a mandamus to enforce the duties imposed on the corporations by the statutes. But whether it will issue is doubtful, especially in the case of those owed to the public, and the attitude of the courts will be decisive. While they may be anxious to enable an individual to require a public corporation to carry out its duties, they may be reluctant to allow the administration of these vital services to be impeded by a multitude of complaints.

Finally, the Transport Act, 1947, Sect. 3[2] which sets out the "General duty of the Commission" provides in sub-sect. (5): "Nothing in this section shall be construed as imposing on the Commission, either directly or indirectly, any form of duty or liability enforceable by proceedings before any court or tribunal to which they would not otherwise be subject." At first sight this might seem to prevent any action to enforce any duty imposed by the section. But the effect of the words "form of" is not clear. If non-enforceability of any duty or liability whatsoever under the section is the intention, then these two words are superfluous. It is therefore arguable that mandamus is not excluded and that the sub-section is designed to ensure that no new forms of duty or liability are created by this section. Nevertheless, any other objections to the availability of mandamus would still have to be overcome.

(b) Actions for Damages

This has already been discussed above.[3] It may be that the

---

[1] Electric Lighting (Clauses) Act, 1899, Sch. para. 27 (as incorporated and amended by E.A., Sect. 57 (2), Sch. 4, Pt. III; G.A. Sch. 3, para. 8.

[2] Sect. 3 (1) (2) (3) has been redrafted by Transport Act, 1953, Sect. 25 (1) (see above, p. 274) but Sect. 3 (5) is not affected. [3] See p. 241.

courts will hold that the powers of the Ministers and the various consumers' bodies show that the intention of Parliament was to exclude individual right of action for breach of statutory duty.[1]

The substitution of a political for a legal remedy may, however, be thought insufficient. The problem is an example of the difficulty of extending private law remedies to public law obligations. Dealing with a similar question, Tucker, L.J., said in 1949—

> With the growth of statutory corporations to which monopolies are given by the statutes creating them, it may become of supreme importance to decide, on the construction of the relevant statute, to what extent, if any, a refusal by a statutory body to do business with a particular trader may afford that trader a right of action.[2]

Sect. 3 (5) of the Transport Act, 1947, quoted above, is also relevant to the action for damages.

2. EXCESS AND ABUSE OF POWERS

The powers of the new public corporations are derived solely from statutes and statutory instruments. They have no general common law powers; they are similar in this respect to county, urban and rural district councils, not to boroughs. The constituent Acts, except those relating to Hospital Boards, the Central Land Board and the Land Commission, provide that the statutory powers given relate only to their capacity as statutory corporations and nothing in the empowering sections is to be construed as authorising the disregard by the corporations of any enactment or rule of law.[3] The corporations are therefore subject to the doctrine of *ultra vires* in its full force. Any action may be challenged and the corporation must be able to point to its statutory power. The Acts contain both general and specific empowering provisions; there is little value in trying to guess the interpretation that will be placed by the courts on any particular specific provision. What is important, however, is to try to assess the effect of the general provisions and the

---

[1] For earlier example of similar problem, see *Johnston* v. *Consumers' of Gas Co. Toronto*, [1898] A.C. 447.

[2] *Eric Gnapp Ltd.* v. *Petroleum Board*, [1949] 1 All E.R. 980, at 985.

[3] C.I.N.A., Sect. 49 (4); E.A., Sect. 2 (9); G.A., Sects. 1 (9), 2 (6); T.A., Sect. 2 (8); A.C.A., Sect. 7 (2); N.T.A., Sect. 2 (4). This provision also preserves the effect, if there were any doubt, of cases like *Metropolitan Asylums District Board* v. *Hill* (1881), 6 App. Cas. 193.

extent to which the courts are likely to admit the validity of any challenge.

The importance of these sections is seen when the general *powers* provisions are examined. The fuel and power corporations and the Land Commission are all empowered, with slight terminological differences, "to do anything or to enter into any transaction which in their opinion is calculated to facilitate the proper discharge of their duties or is incidental or conducive thereto."[1] The New Town corporations are given certain powers and are then empowered "generally to do anything necessary or expedient for the purposes of the new town or for purposes incidental thereto."[2] The provision for the Air corporations follows that of the majority except that, as for New Town corporations, the words "in their opinion" do not appear.[3] As already noted,[4] the Acts constituting the Transport Commission, Hospital Boards, and Central Land Board have no general powers sections.

Before discussing the general question of *ultra vires*, there are two sets of provisions which require special attention. First, the Air Corporations Act, 1949, empowers the Minister by order to limit the powers of the Air corporations to such extent as he thinks desirable in the public interest, by providing that any power specified shall not be exercisable except in accordance with a general or special authority given by him. This order is to be laid before Parliament and is subject to annulment.[5] Similarly, the Minister may give directions to any New Town corporation, restricting the exercise by them of any of their powers or requiring them to exercise those powers in a specified manner. Before giving any such direction the Minister must consult with the chairman or deputy-chairman "unless he is satisfied that on account of urgency, such consultation is impracticable." These directions are not required to be laid before Parliament, but the Act provides that any transaction between any person and any corporation acting in purported exercise of their powers shall not be void by reason only that it was carried

---

[1] C.I.N.A., Sect. 1 (3); E.A., Sect. 2 (5); G.A., Sects. 1 (4), 2 (5); A.A., Sect. 68 (4).
[2] N.T.A., Sect. 2 (2).
[3] A.C.A., Sect. 3 (2).
[4] See above, p. 284.
[5] Sect. 3 (5).

out in contravention of such directions unless that person had actual notice of the directions.[1] The effect of these provisions seems to be that if a person contracts with an Air corporation which is acting without the general or special authority of the Minister as required by an order, then that contract is void whether or not the order has at that time been issued by H.M. Stationery Office or laid before Parliament (Sect. 3 (2) of the Statutory Instruments Act, 1946, only protects persons prosecuted for an offence) ;[2] but if the contract is with a New Town corporation it is valid unless the person actually knew of the ministerial direction. Secondly, the Minister may by an order relating to an Air corporation define the powers conferred so far as he thinks it desirable so to do for the purpose of securing that the public are properly informed as to the general nature and scope of the activities in which the corporation may engage; but nothing in any such order is to prejudice the generality of the powers conferred. The order is to be laid before Parliament and is subject to annulment.[3] Suppose that a Minister in such an order defines as a power of the corporation a power to take certain action and that an individual affected wishes to claim that such action is *ultra vires* the Act. Can he succeed? On the one hand it may be argued that the Minister has by a validly-made statutory instrument declared that the corporation is to have the necessary power and that this is legislation amending the Act; on the other hand, the Minister's powers are to "define" the statutory powers and not to add to or detract from them. The fact that the definition is subjected to a procedure usually reserved for legislative matter does not necessarily give it the character of legislation. *A fortiori*, it would be idle for an individual to claim that an action of the corporation was *ultra vires* on the ground that it was implicitly excluded by the Minister's definition although admittedly within the general statutory powers. This would seem to render superfluous the "without prejudice" provision quoted above. If on the other hand this provision is held to be neither superfluous nor merely declaratory, it is arguable that the Minister's order can extend the powers of the corporation and is therefore legislative.

[1] N.T.A., Sect. 2 (3).

[2] See above, p. 109: *aliter*, if *Johnson* v. *Sargant and Sons*, [1918] 1 K.B. 101, is strictly followed; see above, p. 108.   [3] A.C.A., Sect. 3 (3).

Certain actions are expressly put beyond the powers of the corporations by the constituent Acts. Thus the Electricity Authority is forbidden to manufacture electrical plant or fittings for export[1] and Area Boards are similary forbidden, whether for export or otherwise:[2] Area Boards may not sell, hire or supply electrical plant.[3] These provisions are clearly designed to effect a division between the administrative functions of the central and area authorities. To a lesser extent, this policy is adopted in the Gas Act, 1948—lesser, because of the greater powers of the Area Gas Boards and the correspondingly smaller powers of the Gas Council.[4] The provision that the Electricity Authority may not manufacture plant or fittings for export is a policy decision on the national level. Into this category also fall the provisions which forbid the Transport Commission to compete with taxi-cab owners, companies dealing in the sale of road vehicles and garage proprietors.[5] Similarly, the Air corporations may not, save by an order subject to parliamentary annulment, manufacture air-frames or aero-engines or airscrews.[6] In such cases the application of the doctrine of *ultra vires* presents no problems save in the interpretation of the statutory words. The application is more difficult in the case of the general powers provisions.

As noted above,[7] the general power conferred on most corporations is "to do any thing or to enter into any transaction which in their opinion is calculated to facilitate the proper discharge of their duties or is incidental or conducive thereto." The practical problem may be encountered if the corporations decide to engage in undertakings for the purpose of raising money towards their general expenses; indirectly such undertakings would, no doubt, facilitate the discharge of their duties. Some restrictions must, however, be placed on this phrase. Air corporations convey their passengers by coach between the air terminal and the airport. If they carried, for payment, those living near the airport to and from the air terminal to fill coaches that would otherwise be partly empty, would this be *ultra vires*? If not, would stopping *en route* to pick up casual travellers be so? Airports have restaurants; could

---

[1] E.A., Sect. 2 (3).
[3] Ibid.
[5] T.A., Sect. 2 (1) proviso, (2) (4) (d).
[7] See above, p. 301.

[2] E.A., Sect. 2 (3) (4).
[4] See above, p. 286.
[6] A.C.A., Sect. 3 (3).

they have night-clubs to amuse air travellers delayed through no fault of their own? Such devices might ease the financial burden and so facilitate the discharge of the duty on the Air corporations "to secure that the services provided by the corporation are provided at reasonable charges." The problem is similar to that which faces local authorities in their endeavours to raise revenue. The provisions conferring general powers on the New Town and the Air corporations are similar to those quoted at the beginning of this paragraph, but do not contain the words "in their opinion."[1] In such cases, how far will the courts in practice feel themselves entitled to interfere? Will they calculate to decide whether the action taken facilitated the discharge of functions? Will they set up their standards of what is calculated to facilitate? Or will they be content if it is shown that the corporation calculated that the action would facilitate? Perhaps the courts are likely to follow the principles laid down by Lord Greene in *Associated Provincial Picture Houses, Ltd.* v. *Wednesbury Corporation.*[2] That is to say, if the words "in their opinion" do occur the courts will not upset the decision of the corporation on the ground that it was unreasonable but will upset it if they feel that the decision was so unreasonable that no reasonable body of men could have arrived at it, or if bad faith or corruption is proved. Where, on the other hand, the words do not occur, the position is more doubtful. It is unlikely that the courts will regard their powers as *more* limited in such a case. Will they regard them as *less* limited? The general tendency of the courts to-day is not to interfere with decisions which administrative authorities have by statute been empowered to take, but the strength of this tendency is unknown. If the words "in their opinion" are clothed with significance by the courts, a distinction may have to be drawn between actions which are calculated to facilitate and those which are "incidental or conducive," for the statutory phraseology in the example quoted at the beginning of this paragraph is ambiguous; it is not clear whether the words "in their opinion" are meant to apply also to the last five words in that quotation.

In the Gas Act, 1948, the words "proper discharge" are

---

[1] N.T.A., Sect. 2 (2).
[2] [1948] 1 K.B. 223.

replaced by "exercise or performance."[1] It seems likely that "proper" merely means in good faith and not corruptly, and therefore gives to the courts no power which they do not already exercise.

When powers are given in wide terms, the courts may be called on to declare that the purpose of a particular exercise is not authorised by the statutory provision. This form of judicial control has already been discussed. In *Earl Fitzwilliam's Wentworth Estates Co.* v. *Minister of Town and Country Planning*,[2] it was contended that a compulsory purchase order made by the Central Land Board and confirmed by the Minister was invalid on this ground. The ultimate purpose of the power to make such an order was to be "connected with the performance of their functions" under the Town and Country Planning Act, 1947.[3] One of the principal functions of the Central Land Board was to collect development charges under this Act and this power was given, at least in part, to facilitate this collection. In the Court of Appeal, Somervell and Singleton, L.JJ., held that one of the purposes of making the order was the performance of this function and that therefore the order was valid. Denning, L.J., dissented, holding that the Central Land Board had also another purpose which was dominant: the enforcing of sales at existing use value. This, he said, was an improper purpose since Parliament had not given the power to make compulsory purchase orders to enable the Central Land Board to enforce this policy. The prescribing of this policy and its enforcement by the threat of compulsory purchase was, in effect, legislation without parliamentary authority. This dissenting judgment shows how general powers may be restricted in effect by their dependence on the statutory functions of the corporations. The majority judgments, on the other hand, show the difficulties which face a party who seeks to have an order invalidated on the ground of improper purpose.[4] These difficulties

[1] G.A., Sect. 2 (5).
[2] [1951] 1 K.B. 203 (Birkett, J.); affirmed, [1951] 2 K.B. 284 (C.A.) and [1952] A.C. 362 (H.L.); and see *Travis* v. *Minister of Local Government and Planning* [1951] 2 K.B. 956; *Hanily* v. *Minister of Local Government and Planning*, [1952] 2 Q.B. 444.
[3] Sect. 43 (1).
[4] On appeal, the House of Lords unanimously confirmed the opinion of the majority judgments, *sub nom.*, *Earl Fitzwilliam's Wentworth Estates Co.* v. *Minister of Housing and Local Government*, [1952] A.C. 362.

are greatly increased when no reasons are given by the authority for its actions.

C. Public Corporations as Crown Servants

The difficulty of deciding whether a public corporation is a servant of the Crown has already been indicated and it has been suggested that the degree of control exercised by the Government over the corporations should be the determining test.[1]

Dr. Glanville Williams has suggested that none of the new public corporations should be regarded as a Crown servant and that the division of the corporations into industrial and commercial on the one hand and "social service" corporations on the other is not a valuable distinction for this purpose.[2] It is, however, clear that functionally the Coal Board, for example, is less controlled by the Government than the Land Commission and that the corporations do fall into separate groups. The following propositions can be advanced.

First, the fuel and power, transport and Air corporations are not so dependent on the Crown as to have the status of Crown servants. All these corporations have considerable statutory powers; they administer large and self-contained undertakings; they have considerable financial responsibility and are, with the exception of the Air corporations, required by statute to be self-supporting; the power of the appropriate Minister to give general directions is only exercisable when the national interest is involved. The Transport Commission has been held not to be a Crown servant or agent.[3] Secondly, the Central Land Board and the Land Commission may be contrasted with these bodies. These two corporations are, it is suggested Crown servants. They perform functions which are part of a larger scheme for which a Minister is responsible and their powers are limited. Financially they are utterly dependent on the Ministers and on Parliament. The ministerial power to issue general directions is not restricted to matters affecting the national interest. In *Tamlin* v. *Hannaford*,[4] Denning, L.J., clearly thought that the Central Land Board, exercising its functions "on behalf of the Minister," was a Crown servant,[5] and in *Earl Fitzwilliam's Wentworth*

---

[1] See above, pp. 252–3.   [2] *Crown Proceedings*, 21–8, 30–7.
[3] *Tamlin* v. *Hannaford*, [1950] 1 K.B. 18.   [4] See last note.   [5] At 25.

Estates Co. v. *Minister of Town and Country Planning,* Birkett, J.,
said that it might "from most points of view," be regarded as a
new Government department.[1] In *Glasgow Corporation* v.
Central Land Board, Viscount Simonds said that the Board
"represented the Crown"; Lord Normand said that the Board
was the Crown; Lord Radcliffe said that the Board was "an
agency of the Crown"; and Lord Keith said that the Board
was "at least a servant of the Crown." In this case these
opinions related to the powers of the Board to claim Crown
privilege to withhold the publication of documents.[2] Thirdly
Hospital Boards seem to have been created Crown servants.
These bodies also act on behalf of the Minister, performing
functions primarily entrusted to him. Financially, they are
dependent and much controversy has followed from economies
which the Minister has required; their functions are part of
the national health service for which the Minister is undoubtedly
responsible.[3] The power of the Minister to control by regulations and discretions is unlimited. Finally, the position of
New Town corporations is very difficult to determine. Sir
Ernest Gowers, writing as chairman of Harlow Development
Corporation, has protested forcibly against the considerable
control on matters of detail and discretion which is exercised
by the Minister.[4] The construction of new towns is, however,
an undertaking distinct from other functions relating to town
and country planning, although clearly closely connected with
them. New Town corporations derive nearly all their financial
support from the Minister and no major decisions can be taken
without his approval. Whether this control is sufficient to make
them so dependent on the Minister as to be classified as Crown
servants can only be decided by the courts.

The problems which follow if a corporation is held to be a

---

[1] [1951] 1 K.B. 203, at 211. And see Denning, L.J., in Court of Appeal where
he refers to the Central Land Board as "a government department," [1951] 2
K.B. 284 at 311, 314.

[2] [1956] S.L.T. 41 at 42, 44, 46, 47.

[3] Hospital Boards have been made liable (N.H.S.A., Sect. 13 (1)). But it is
arguable that if they are Crown servants, actions should, under the Crown
Proceedings Act, 1947, be brought against the Crown and that this Sect. 13 (1) is
thus amended or repealed. The Ministry, however, clearly does not take this
view: see memorandum of Ministry of Health of 15th September, 1949 (208 *Law
Times* 209).

[4] See Harlow Development Corporation *Third Annual Report* (H.C. 7 of 1950–1)
p. 103.

servant of the Crown have been exhaustively discussed else-where.[1] One point only needs to be taken here and is exem-plified by reference to the Central Land Board. The Board came into existence before the Crown Proceedings Act, 1947, became operative on 1st January, 1948.[2] Assuming that it is a Crown servant, it is not clear whether it could have been sued in tort before 1948. It has no funds of its own and Crown funds could not be touched. One authority suggests that in such a case, no action would have lain at all.[3] Another authority sug-gests that an action could have been brought if the tort had been committed by the corporation itself.[4] A Crown servant can have no servants, since its inferior "employees" are equally Crown servants; no question of the vicarious liability of such a corporation can therefore arise.

If the Board could have been sued, then the Crown can now be sued for torts committed by the Board or by the other Crown servants working under the Board. To this there is a possible objection based on Sect. 2 (6) of the Crown Proceedings Act, 1947, which provides that the Crown shall not be liable for any officer of the Crown unless that officer has been appointed, directly or indirectly, by the Crown and is paid out of moneys provided by Parliament. The Board (as distinct from its members) is not paid. If therefore the Board *itself* commits a tort, is the Crown liable? It cannot be argued that the Board is a servant of the Crown but not an officer of the Crown because the Crown Proceedings Act provides that "officer" includes "servant."[5] The Crown is, however, made liable for torts committed by its servants *or agents*.[6] It may therefore be possible to evade the difficulty by calling the Board an agent of the Crown for this purpose.

If, on the other hand, the Board could not have been sued before the Crown Proceedings Act, then it seems that the Crown is not liable for its torts in view of the proviso to Sect. 2 (1) which reads: "Provided that no proceedings shall lie against the Crown by virtue of paragraph (*a*) of this subsection

---

[1] See Glanville Williams, op. cit.
[2] The operative date for sections of T.C.P.A. relating to Central Land Board was 6th August, 1947.
[3] *Roper* v. *Public Works Commissioners*, [1915] 1 K.B. 45.
[4] Atkin, L.J., in *Mackenzie-Kennedy* v. *Air Council*, [1927] 2 K.B. 517 at 532-3.
[5] Crown Proceedings Act, 1947, Sect. 38 (2).
[6] Ibid. Sect. 2 (1) (*a*).

in respect of any act or omission of a servant or agent of the Crown unless the act or omission would apart from the provisions of this Act have given rise to a cause of action in tort against that servant or agent or his estate." This provision does not affect the liability of the Crown for the torts of those Crown servants who work under the direction of the Board. They would have been liable before 1948 and are "officers" within the meaning of Sect. 2 (6).

Other Control

The nationalisation of coal, electricity, gas and transport, the establishment of Hospital Boards and New Towns and the activities of the Land Commission and the Central Land Board have resulted in a considerable amount of discussion in the Press, on public platforms, in pamphlets, articles, and books. The merits and demerits of these bodies have been argued on political and economic grounds. The effect of these disputations has no doubt been considerable, although there has been a tendency to avoid fundamental changes at least until the corporations have had an opportunity to overcome their initial difficulties. In addition, the Acts which established the nationalised industries sought to create bodies which would give to the consumer an opportunity to state particular grievances and criticisms. These bodies must now be explained and their value appraised.

A. Consumers' Bodies

(i) *Gas and Electricity.* For each Gas and Electricity Area Board there is a consultative council, composed of from twenty to thirty members appointed by the Minister.[1] Not less than half nor more than three-fifths (electricity) or three-quarters (gas) are appointed from a panel of persons nominated by local authority associations from members of local authorities. The remainder are appointed to represent commerce, industry, labour, agriculture (electricity only), and the general interests of consumers and other persons or organisations interested in the development of the commodity in the area. The chairman is, *ex officio*, a member of the Area Board. The Minister may dismiss a member of any council who is absent from meetings

[1] G.A., Sect. 9 and S.I. 1949 No. 787; E.A., Sect. 7 and S.I. 1948 No. 898.

for six consecutive months or is unfit or incapable. There must be no gap between meetings of more than three months. The term of appointment is for a period not exceeding five years but members are eligible for reappointment. The duties of these councils are as follows: First, to consider any matter affecting the service (including the variation of tariffs and the provision of new or improved facilities) which is the subject of a representation made by a consumer or which they think ought to be considered and to notify their conclusions to the Area Board where action appears necessary. Secondly, to consider and report to the Board on a matter referred to them by the Board. Thirdly, to make representations to the Board on the Board's general plans and arrangements (which must be communicated to them). In addition, each council is required to submit to the Minister a scheme for appointment by the council of committees or individuals to be local representatives within the area.

The relationship of these two groups of councils to other bodies differs. An electricity consultative council may, after the Area Board has considered any conclusions, reports or representations, make its own representations to the Electricity Authority. The Electricity Authority, after consultation with the Area Board and the consultative council, may, if it appears that a defect is disclosed in the Area Board's general plans and arrangements, give directions to the Area Board. Further, the consultative council may make representations to the Minister on any matter arising out of its representations to the Authority and the Minister may notify the Authority of any defect which appears to him to have been disclosed in the Area Board's general plans and arrangements; the Authority then gives directions to the Area Board. A gas consultative council has quicker access to the Minister. This results from the fact that an Area Gas Board enjoys, in relation to the Gas Council, greater independence and power than does an Area Electricity Board. A gas consultative council may make representations to the Minister, after the Area Board has considered the matter, without reference to the Gas Council. Then, if it appears to the Minister, after consultation with the Gas Council, that there may be a defect in the Area Board's general plans and arrangements, the Minister refers the representations for inquiry and report to a person appointed by him after consultation with the Lord Chancellor and, after considering the report, may give directions to the Area Board, sending a copy to the Gas Council. Electricity consultative councils may, and gas consultative councils must, make annual reports to their Area Boards which incorporate them in their own annual reports.

(ii) *Coal.* Two central bodies have been established, as required by the Acts. These are the Domestic Coal Consumers' Council and the Industrial Coal Consumers' Council.[1] Members are appointed by the Minister to represent the Coal Board; the number is left to the Minister's discretion and at present the Domestic Council has a chairman and twenty-four members while the Industrial Council has a chairman and twenty members. The Minister may dismiss a member of any council who is shown to be ineligible or is absent from more than four consecutive meetings or is unfit or incapable. The councils must meet not less than once every three months. The members of the Industrial Council are appointed to represent consumers, sellers and suppliers of coal, coke and manufactured fuel for industrial purposes or other purposes involving supply in bulk. The members of the Domestic Council are appointed to represent the same groups where the fuel is used for domestic purposes and other purposes not covered by the Industrial Council. The duties of these councils are similar to those of the gas and electricity councils. The councils report to the Minister, not to the Coal Board. The Minister has power to appoint regional councils either on the recommendation of the councils or otherwise. The chairmen of the councils are not *ex officio* members of the Coal Board. The councils are required to make annual reports to the Minister, who lays them before Parliament.

(iii) *Transport.* The Transport Act, 1947,[2] provides for the establishment of a Central Transport Consultative Committee and for area transport users' consultative committees. Whether or not there are users' committees covering parts of Scotland and Wales, there must be set up one users' committee for each of those countries. Both central and users' committees are appointed by the Minister and consist of an independent

[1] C.I.N.A., Sect. 4 and S.R. & O. 1946 No. 2129.   [2] Sect. 6.

chairman, representatives of agricultural, commercial, industrial, shipping and labour interests, and of local authorities, and members appointed from among persons nominated by the Transport Commission, including at least one member of the Commission in the case of the Central Committee. The Minister may appoint not more than two additional members. The Committees are required to meet not less frequently than twice a year. Minutes, recommendations and conclusions are sent to the Minister and the Commission in the case of the Central Committee and to the Central Committee and the Commission in the case of the area committees.[1] The duties of these committees are similar to those of the consultative committees already discussed.

The Act of 1947 also set up the Transport Tribunal.[2] This Tribunal takes over the functions of the Railway Rates Tribunal and many of those of the Railway and Canal Commission. The Transport Tribunal has a chairman of legal experience, one member experienced in commercial affairs and one member experienced in transport business. The Tribunal can hear complaints that reasonable facilities are not provided and that undue preference has been given; complaints can be made by local authorities and associations of traders. Charges schemes for the Commission's services have to be confirmed by the Tribunal and may be altered on application or reviewed. Objections may be made to the Tribunal by any representative (including a local authority) of any class of persons using the services or facilities to which the scheme relates.

(iv) *Air*. An Air Transport Advisory Council consisting of a chairman and four members has been established.[3] The chairman, who is required to be a barrister, advocate or solicitor of not less than seven years standing, is appointed by the Lord Chancellor. The members are appointed by the Minister of Transport and Civil Aviation and two are required to be experienced in transport services. No member or employee of the Air corporations may be a member of the Council.

---

[1] Minutes, recommendations and conclusions of the area committees for Wales and for Scotland are required to be sent to the Minister also (Transport Act, 1953, Sect. 29).

[2] T.A. Pt. V as amended by Transport Act, 1953, Sects. 20–24.

[3] Civil Aviation Act, 1949, Sect. 12 (replacing Civil Aviation Act, 1946, Sect. 36) and S.R. & O. 1947 No. 1224.

The chairman and any member may be dismissed by the Lord Chancellor and Minister respectively if his other duties or interests conflict with his membership, if he considers representations in which he has a special interest, if he becomes bankrupt or makes a composition with creditors, if he absents himself from meetings, if he is incapacitated by illness, or if he is otherwise unable or unfit to perform his duties.

The duty of the Council is to consider any representation from any person with respect to the facilities provided or charges made by the corporations. The Council may refuse to consider a representation which, in their opinion, is frivolous or vexatious, or has already been sufficiently considered or relates to an international agreement to which His Majesty's Government is a party. The Minister may refer to the Council questions relating to facilities or charges or any matter which relates to improvement in the services. The Council reports on any representation or question to the Minister with recommendations. They may appoint assessors to advise them. No member may consider any representation or question in which he has any special interest which may tend to interfere with his impartial examination. Both the Minister and the corporations are required to provide the Council with necessary information. The Council makes an annual report to the Minister who lays it before Parliament together with a statement of any action taken by him.

The Council may sit in public or in private and may, if it chooses, give an oral hearing. Its conclusions are not to be made known except in its report to the Minister.

B. Commentary on these Provisions

Bodies of the kind described can perform one of two functions. They can act in an advisory capacity to the appropriate Minister or corporation or they can act as exponents of consumers' needs and demands, as watchdogs and critics. It is difficult for them efficiently to perform both functions. The reports of the Electricity consultative councils seem to show this divergence of function.[1] Some stress the need for the "closest liaison" between the council and the Area Board

---

[1] For first annual reports (with those of Area Boards) see H.C. 337–50 of 1948–9.

and attempt to justify to the consumer the actions of the
Board.[1] Others indicate that they consider their function is
to safeguard the interests of the consumer.[2] The Industrial
and Domestic Coal Consumers' Councils are clearly ill-
constituted to deal with a large variety of small complaints,
and while the former seems to have some influence as an
expression of the opinion of several important and powerful
organisations, the Domestic Council seems to serve no useful
function.[3] Its reports verge on the naïve and platitudinous.
The Central Transport Consultative Committee seems to be
designed as an advisory body. The area committees are only
slowly being set up and their value cannot as yet be assessed.

The Transport Tribunal is by far the strongest independent
body which has been set up alongside an administering
authority. It acts sometimes as an advisory committee; the
confirmation of a charges scheme after hearing objections is, in
reality, the final stage of a legislative process; it decides
disputes on rates and charges, examines the reasonableness of
facilities and investigates claims of undue preference. The
Tribunal (with its predecessors) has gained great and valuable
experience and authority and provides an excellent example
of the usefulness and limitations of a judicial body attempting
to hold the balance between a monopoly and the ordinary
user. Its jurisdiction will extend to more forms of public
transport as the Act of 1947 is further applied.

The Air Transport Advisory Council seems, perhaps inevitably, to be fulfilling its advisory function far more efficiently
than its functions as a hearing body for complaints. It is
designed as an administrative tribunal but there does not seem
to be any compelling reason why this should be so. Like the
Industrial and Domestic Coal Consumers' Councils, it has
heard very few complaints. In the first eighteen months of its
existence, the Air Transport Advisory Council received only
twenty-three representations from the public. On the other
hand, it seems to have performed a useful function in considering applications from charter companies for permission

---

[1] See, for example, report of the South-western Council, H.C. 340 of 1948–9.
[2] See, for example, report of South-eastern Council, H.C. 338 of 1948–9.
[3] For annual reports see H.C. 189 of 1947–8, H.C. 219 of 1948–9, H.C. 106 of
1950.

to operate scheduled services as associates of the Air corporations.[1]

In short, these various bodies have not succeeded in providing a forum for complaints by consumers. Those which are single central bodies are not constituted to perform this function. Even the electricity and gas councils, operating on a regional basis, with more localised subordinate committees or individuals, have failed to evolve a simple and well-known procedure. At present, the gas, electricity, coal, and transport councils and committees are interesting as an administrative device and as a constitutional development, but of little practical value as organs of consumer representation.

[1] For Annual Reports see H.C. 155 of 1948-9 and H.C. 40 of 1950.

INDEX